War and Reason

War and Reason

Domestic and International Imperatives

Bruce Bueno de Mesquita
and
David Lalman

Yale University Press

New Haven and London

Published with the assistance of the A. Whitney Griswold Publication Fund.

Set in Times Roman type by DEKR Corporation, Woburn, Massachusetts.
Printed in the United States of America by Vail-Ballou Press, Binghamton, New York.

Library of Congress Cataloging-in-Publication Data
Bueno de Mesquita, Bruce, 1946–
War and reason : domestic and international imperatives / Bruce Bueno de Mesquita and David Lalman.
p.   cm.
Includes bibliographical references and index.
ISBN 0-300-05202-2 (cloth)
        0-300-05922-1 (pbk.)
1. International relations.   2. Balance of power.   3. War (International law)
I. Lalman, David.   II. Title.
JX1391.B83   1992
327.1'1—dc20   91-41847 CIP

A catalogue record for this book is available from the British Library.

The paper in this book meets the guidelines for permanence and durability of the Committee on Production Guidelines for Book Longevity of the Council on Library Resources.

10 9 8 7 6 5 4 3 2

With affection, appreciation,

and admiration for our teachers

and our friends

A. F. K. Organski

and

William H. Riker

Contents

Figures

Tables

Preface

International relations research has been dominated by a state-centric, realist view of foreign policy. Nations are widely believed to pursue the maximization of power or security because to do otherwise is to diminish their chances of survival. The realist and neorealist perspectives have encouraged a natural focus on war and its avoidance. We set out to address questions of just that nature: what causes war, and how can it be avoided? Yet this book has grown in directions we did not anticipate. We have written about foreign policy choices and their implications for a wide variety of events, including, but not limited to, war and peace. The book is neither primarily about war nor illustrative of a rational-choice approach to realism. It is a general assessment of foreign policy choices, using a game-theoretic approach coupled with statistical and case-history analysis and embedded primarily within a perspective that takes very seriously the consequences of domestic political choices on foreign policy actions.

We propose two competing theories of international interactions. In one, the realpolitik/unconstrained international interaction game, we assume that immediate foreign policy objectives are determined by the structure of the international context in which nations relate to one another. In the other, the domestic/constrained international interaction game, national leaders choose courses of action to maximize their view of the national welfare or at least the interests of supportive constituents, given that domestic political processes have first determined the goals or objectives to be pursued. We deduce the necessary and sufficient conditions for several classes of events: negotiation, maintenance of the status quo, acquiescence of one rival to another without resort to violence, capitulation by one adversary to the other following an initial use of force, and war. We address these outcomes under conditions of full information and limited information.

The theory leads us to examine four norms of action that are widely believed to encourage cooperation in an otherwise anarchic world. We find that two of the norms generally foster peace, although we also assess their robustness in the face of uncertainty. We find considerable theoretical encouragement and empirical support for the notion that cooperation is a common response to disputes, despite the absence of mechanisms for enforcing promises in international affairs.

We propose solutions to several empirical puzzles about the behavior of democracies toward one another and toward nondemocratic states. We also examine several features of war, including stakes, expected costs, and their impact on system transformation. This volume, then, addresses questions of cooperation and conflict; full information and incomplete information; deductive logic and empirical evidence. Although we begin as agnostics with regard to the domestic and realist versions of the theory, the evidence adduced here strongly supports the domestic variant of the game we propose and just as strongly contradicts the realpolitik version. Whether our theory of foreign policy is credible remains for the reader to judge. We have endeavored to make judgment feasible by proffering the formal logic and the empirical evaluations that seem germane to the assessment of our theory: we deduce and test more than twenty-five propositions about international affairs.

In developing this book we have incurred a great many intellectual debts. Foremost is our debt to James Morrow of the Hoover Institution, who has been a constant source of intellectual stimulation. Jim has been tireless in his willingness to teach, prod, cajole, criticize, and inspire us. He has saved us from countless errors in our theorizing and has tried to save us from others.

Others who have helped us with discussions, criticisms, and helpful hints are Christopher Achen, Byeonggil Ahn, Jeffrey Banks, Randall Calvert, George Downs, James Fearon, Yi Feng, Kurt Taylor Gaubatz, Robert Jackman, Chae-Han Kim, Woosang Kim, Jacek Kugler, Alan Lamborn, Susanne Lohmann, T. Clifton Morgan, John Oneal, Joe Oppenheimer, Kenneth Organski, Robert Pahre, James Ray, Diana Richards, Valerie Schwebach, Randolph Siverson, Piotr Swistak, Tyll Van Geel, Barry Weingast, and Samuel Wu. The students in Political Science 376/576 at the University of Rochester in the winter of 1991, including Luke Bellocchi, David Hayes, Roger James, Stacey Knobler, Kirke Lawton, Fiona McGillivray, Arthur Mitchell, Jeffrey Newman, Alexander Powell, Joseph Tonon, and Alastair Smith, provided helpful suggestions and criticisms of the manuscript. Passages from *The Secret History of the Mongols* are reprinted here with Paul Kahn's gracious permission. We also appreciate the generosity with which data were made available to us by Charles Gochman, Zeev Maoz, J. David Singer, and other participants in the Correlates of War Project.

This book began under the editorial guidance of Marian Neal Ash, who has been a source of delight and inspiration during our long association with Yale University Press. She is missed. John S. Covell has proved to be a most worthy replacement. We are grateful for his wonderful patience. Mary Pasti was invaluable in the final stages of editing the manuscript.

Much of what is good and nothing that is wrong in this book is due to those whom we acknowledge.

Some of the financial support for this project was graciously provided by a grant from the United States Institute of Peace. The opinions, findings, and conclusions or recommendations expressed in this book are those of the authors and do not necessarily reflect the views of the United States Institute of Peace. Additional support was generously provided by the Hoover Institution, which also provided a congenial base from which to undertake this research. General intellectual stimulation was our frequent companion at the institution, where one of us is a permanent fixture and the other spent a year as a National Fellow. No less stimulating were our colleagues in the Departments of Political Science at the University of Rochester and the University of Maryland, respectively.

Finally, we want to thank Arlene, Erin, Ethan, and Gwen Bueno de Mesquita and Christine DeGregorio for tolerating us during the long haul from conceptualization to completion of this project. In the end, all research is flawed, and we have no doubt that this is true of this undertaking. The fault lies, as always, with the other guy.

May 1991

Part I

A Theory of Foreign Policy

sen the best course of action, given their constrained opportunities,
enhance the welfare of the people?

Goya's captions suggest a tension between the rational calculation
costs and benefits and the blind emotions and passions that lead to
tragic acts of war. This tension is not new for students of war.
crates, Herodotus, and Thucydides were fascinated by it more than
o millennia ago every bit as much as we of the nuclear age. And
eir answers were no less varied than ours.

Socrates, speaking of the division between the body and the soul,
plains the origins of war by noting that "the body . . . by filling us
full of loves, and lusts, and fears, and fancies, and idols, and every
rt of folly, prevents our ever having, as people say, so much as a
ought. For whence comes [sic] wars, and fightings, and factions?
r wars are occasioned by the love of money, and money has to be
quired for the sake and in the service of the body" (Plato 1937, 449–
). For Socrates, war was less the consequence of rational calcula-
ons of benefits and costs than the product of emotion and lust.
lthough such a perspective could be compatible with the reasoned
ursuit of goals, Socrates seems to have believed that war resulted
om personal passions untempered by thoughtful objectives.

Miltiades, on the eve of the battle of Marathon, weighed the general
nterest of the citizens of Athens before engaging the Medes. Herodo-
us reports Miltiades' exhortation to his fellow generals:

> Never, since the Athenians were a people, were they in such danger as
> they are in at this moment. If they bow the knee to these Medes, they are
> to be given up to Hippias, and you know what they then will have to suffer.
> But if Athens comes victorious out of this contest, she has it in her to
> become the first city of Greece. Your vote is to decide whether we are to
> join battle or not. If we do not bring on a battle presently, some factious
> intrigue will disunite the Athenians, and the city will be betrayed to the
> Medes. But if we fight, before there is anything rotten in the state of Athens,
> I believe that, provided the Gods will give fair play and no favour, we are
> able to get the best of it in the engagement. (Herodotus 1954, book vi,
> sec. 109)

Certainly these are nobler motivations for war than simple avarice.
Here we also see the essence of a reasoned approach to the fundamental choice between war and peace. Miltiades' calculation of the
interests at stake brings him to the conclusion that the Athenians
should risk defeat at the hands of the much larger Persian army. If the

Chapter 1

Reason and War

At the age of sixty-four, the great Spanish artist
Lucientes began his series of etchings entitled *Dis*
The horrors of the Peninsular War and, indeed, of a
depicted in scenes, some witnessed personally by Go
of by word of mouth, that leave no doubt that wa
inventions. The second of these etchings is caption
sin ella": "With reason or without it." This is the e
of warfare.

Is war the product of blind passion or of reasoned
razón o sin ella" shows a horridly realistic vision of
to support a belief in blind passion. Soldiers fire poin
ants armed with daggers and sticks. Blood runs from
face of a dagger-wielding man who lunges at a soldi
that must seem an eternity, the soldier will surely kill
utter a silent plea at the image, frozen in time, before
stay the hands of soldier and peasant, to preserve a
reason where fury and passion reign.

Goya's later etchings from the Peninsular War stand
trast to the realism of his earlier images of men and wo
one another furiously, bestially, pitilessly. In the seven
Goya depicts a demonic figure writing in a book resting
clawed feet protruding from beneath. Captioned "Cont
eral"—"Against the general welfare"—could this be t
"Con razón o sin ella?" Does war arise from considerat
to the general welfare? These are the issues that motiva
Is war fought with reason or without, and if with reason,
contrary to the general interest?

What might reason or the general welfare mean for fo
For us, questions of reason address the method of condu
affairs. The reasoning process about choices of action by
the connection between their actions and their objectiv
welfare concerns the connection between the goals of t
and the objectives and actions of those statesmen. H

Athenians "do not bring on a battle presently . . . the city will be
betrayed to the Medes," whereas by fighting, the Athenians have some
chance of winning ("provided the Gods will give fair play and no
favour").

That Thucydides believed in the existence of universal truths about
war is evident from his well-known statement "It will be enough for
me, however, if these words of mine are judged useful by those who
want to understand clearly the events which happened in the past and
which (human nature being what it is) will, at some time or other and
in much the same ways, be repeated in the future. My work is not a
piece of writing designed to meet the taste of an immediate public, but
was done to last forever" (Thucydides 1954, book 1, para. 22). If
universal principles exist, as Thucydides suggests, what guides them?
We return to Goya's caption "Contra el bien general." What defines
the general welfare in all states, and is that general welfare the objective behind policies of war and peace?

Can we today imagine that war is an instrument for advancing the
national welfare? Can war still be viewed as a rational, calculated
action, rather than as a mistaken or accidental consequence of policy?
Can all wars be understood within a single theoretical framework, or
are the antecedents of cataclysmic wars so different from those of
lesser disputes that fundamentally different theories are required for
each type of conflict? Can war be fought with reason and for the
general welfare?

Nothing in history has made the rationality of war a more urgent
issue than the flight of the Enola Gay on August 6, 1945. When its
bomb-bay doors opened and its cargo of one atomic bomb fell over
Hiroshima, the world was compelled to ask whether future wars would
be guided by rationality or irrationality. This same question was prom-
inently discussed after the battle of Ypres in 1915, when German
commanders exposed the world to the horrors of chemical warfare for
the first time in modern history.[1] And it was raised when the cannon
was introduced into warfare, when gunpowder was introduced, and
even when the horse cavalry charge was introduced. So long as people
invent ever-greater means of their own destruction, it will be prudent

1. We say modern history because some evidence indicates that the ancient Romans
used poisonous projectiles in their wars. Of course, poison-tipped arrows were
well known in Africa, the Americas, and elsewhere. Even biological warfare has
a rather old pedigree. Lord Jeffrey Amherst is known, for instance, to have ordered
the distribution of blankets infected with smallpox among enemy American Indian
tribes in 1763 (McNeill 1976, 222).

1.1: Con razón o sin ella, by Francisco Goya. Courtesy of the Fogg Art Museum, Harvard University, Cambridge, Mass. Gift of Philip Hofer.

to question the rationality of their actions, whether the actions involve calamitous violence or appeasement and acquiescence.

The rationality of war has been approached from a variety of perspectives. Philosophical, historical, statistical, and mathematical methods have been brought to bear on this crucial issue. For the past several years, mathematical and empirical approaches have been joined together to investigate the implications for war and peace embedded in the axioms of self-interested, expected-utility-maximizing behavior. This study follows that practice of using formal modeling techniques combined with empirical assessments. We explain why we chose this methodology in the final section of this chapter, but to start with, we focus on some of the substantive questions of concern to us.

First, we try to improve upon the basic formulation of the conditions for war and other foreign policy choices suggested in our own earlier studies (Bueno de Mesquita 1981, 1985; Bueno de Mesquita and Lalman 1986; Lalman 1988). In doing so, we propose a game-theoretic framework for understanding not only war and peace but also a wide variety of interactions between nations, whether friendly or hostile, cooperative or conflictual. Our aim is to build better theory and to

1.2: Contra el bien general, by Francisco Goya. Courtesy of the Fogg Art Museum, Harvard University, Cambridge, Mass. Gift of Philip Hofer.

build it not from whole cloth but cumulatively from the research that has preceded this investigation. Second, we investigate the consistency between the theory of international interactions set out here and the record of international relations during the past two centuries or more. Third, we examine how well our game-theoretic analysis fares in comparison with several important alternative lines of argument. And fourth, we conclude with some speculations about the practical policy implications of the theory.

The book is organized into four sections. Part I includes chapters on the substantive, theoretical, and epistemological underpinnings of our approach, the structure and rules of our international interaction game, and the identification of the full-information conditions required for each outcome of the game to be an equilibrium outcome. In this chapter we begin to draw distinctions between two fundamental views of international affairs: a realist view and a domestic view. In chapters 2 and 3 we explore these as competing variants of the international interaction game. The variant that we refer to as the realpolitik/unconstrained interaction game treats foreign policy demands as emanating from a realist or neorealist perspective on international affairs in which the choice of demands is a function of the structure of the international situation unconstrained by domestic objectives. In this perspective, structural features of the system influence the magnitude of demands that foreign policy leaders dare to make. The second variant, which for want of a better term we call the domestic/constrained interaction game, takes seriously the notion that foreign policy choices emanate from domestic political considerations.[2] In this perspective, foreign policy elites act as agents for the goals of their domestic population. Part I concludes with an assessment of the empirical support for each of these different points of view.

In part II we explore the implications of the theory with respect to questions of values and norms of action. It includes a chapter that identifies possible strategies for promoting international cooperation and for avoiding violence, as well as theoretical and empirical assessments of the efficacy of several widely discussed norms of action. These are evaluated under the assumption that information is perfect and are then reevaluated under the assumption that information is imperfect. In the next chapter we undertake a close analysis of the role of domestic opposition to the use of force as a means of promoting peace or encouraging violence. We also evaluate hypotheses concerned with the observation that democracies do not appear to wage wars with one another, although they do wage wars against nondemocratic states. The international interaction game suggests some new propositions that may elucidate the debate regarding the behavior of democracies toward one another. We develop these propositions by opening the black box of domestic politics, which is typically sealed tightly shut in studies of international relations. The importance of domestic politics is highlighted, then, in part II, as well as being a center of concern in the domestic variant of the game developed in part I.

2. For stylistic purposes we sometimes refer to the realpolitik/unconstrained game as just the realist perspective or the realpolitik perspective. Although constraints operate in this version of the game as in any game, we mean by *unconstrained* that the choice of demands is not influenced by the domestic political agenda. We also refer to the domestic/constrained variant as just the domestic perspective. The specific constraint referred to in this label concerns the impact that the domestic political agenda has on the selection of foreign policy objectives. We believe our use of these terms is consistent with the most commonly associated interpretations of these concepts in the foreign policy and international relations literature, but we do not insist on this claim. The only meanings we uphold for these terms are specified in our definitions.

In part III, we evaluate the consequences of the theory for the realist focus on power and security as forces that drive foreign policy choices. Here we directly compare our theory to balance-of-power and power preponderance perspectives. We deduce several propositions complementary to the theory of power transition or hegemonic stability, some that are consistent with balance-of-power and power preponderance arguments and some that are incompatible with either. Most of the propositions deduced from the international interaction game are subjected to empirical tests to assess their merits compared to those of alternative points of view. In another chapter in part III, we develop a detailed case history of the Seven Weeks' War, fought in 1866 between Prussia and Austria, with the intention of showing how the game can help enrich our understanding of the strategic details of specific events. Through broad-based empirical tests and detailed case analysis we hope to foster confidence not only in the external validity, or generality, of the international interaction game but also in its internal validity, or rich contextual potential.

Although we set out with no preconceived notions about the relative merits of the realpolitik and domestic interpretations of the game we propose, the logic and evidence developed in this book provide a foundation for the claim that a perspective that is attentive to the domestic origins of foreign policy demands gives a richer and empirically more reliable representation of foreign affairs than a realist emphasis. The results from parts I, II, and III have strong positive and normative implications. We explore the advantages and disadvantages of leaving diplomacy to the diplomats—as some realists would have us do—or encouraging an attentiveness to the politics of domestic interest groups and bureaucracies as vehicles for shaping foreign policy objectives.

Finally, in part IV we try to assess the ramifications of our theory for foreign policy strategies in times and relations of calm and stress. Here we not only summarize and highlight key elements of our study but also explore the possible value such research may have for dealing with problems in the emerging world order. We identify questions for future research implied by this undertaking and conclude with a hope for richer theory and more reliable evidence as the two critical prongs to future research.

The first appendix is a detailed accounting of the measurement and coding procedures used for the empirical components of this study. We urge those readers concerned with the statistical evidence to examine this appendix before going on to chapters 3–7. The second appendix contains technical proofs of two propositions in chapter 5.

It is not essential, however, for understanding the arguments or political implications of those propositions.

The remainder of this chapter concerns three matters: (1) the origin of foreign policy goals as understood from an unconstrained, realist or neorealist perspective and from a constrained, domestic point of view; (2) the implications of these alternative outlooks for the concept of a unitary actor and for the assumption of rationality; and (3) the reasons for using a formal modeling approach coupled with empirical tests, rather than a more historically oriented method of analysis.

WAR'S REASON: REALISM AND DOMESTIC POLITICS

We begin our investigation with an acknowledgment that international affairs can be distinguished from other aspects of politics. Most politics is constrained by recognized rules and procedures. Voting, for instance, takes place according to some explicit method, whether it be the secret ballot, a show of hands, or a voice vote. The summation of votes to select winners and losers likewise follows prescribed rules. Much is known about the implications for candidates competing in a plurality voting system or a proportional representation system. The properties of various rules for aggregating votes, including, for instance, the Borda count method, the March Hare system, run-off election systems, plurality systems, approval voting methods, and so forth, have been carefully explored because the rules of each system are specific and explicit (Riker 1982; Ordeshook 1986). Amendment procedures in legislatures are governed by clear rules of order that constrain the sequence of events and even the unfolding of debate. Constitutions and lesser laws bring some degree of order to national and subnational politics that facilitates explanation and prediction. Equilibria can be and often are induced by structure, agenda, and other mandated items (Kramer 1972; Davis, DeGroot, and Hinich, 1974; Shepsle and Weingast 1981, 1987; Riker 1986).

Few such rules or structures exist in international affairs. It is true that there is an extensive code of international law intended to govern a variety of interactions ranging from the most minor commercial intercourse to the rules of war and to the very structure of the global and interplanetary environment. Yet, unlike laws and rules within states and many other organizations, the arrangements and structures that exist between nations are not easily enforced.

Borders, for instance, induce considerable structure in the relations among nations, making some prone to conflict with each other and others virtually certain to live in peace or at least in ignorance or indifference to each other's wants (Starr and Most 1976, 1978; Siverson and Starr 1990). But no credible international mechanism exists to fix borders or to arbitrate disputes when a powerful party to the dispute wishes to enforce an alternative resolution. For instance, in spite of the condemnation of virtually every nation in the world, Iraq violated the border of Kuwait in 1990; Germany violated the borders of Poland, Belgium, and too many others between 1939 and 1945; the Soviet Union swallowed Latvia, Lithuania, and Estonia in much the same way that the United States and the earlier American colonies swallowed the territory of the Indian nations, and on and on into the remotest antiquity.

The fundamental difficulty in studying international conflict is that sound theory must rely on mechanisms that are internal to the states choosing the path of war or peace. Existing structures, such as the distribution of power, borders, or international law, cannot by themselves impose outcomes. As Henry Kissinger has observed, "In a society of Sovereign states, an agreement will be maintained only if *all* partners consider it in their interest. They must have a sense of participation in the result. The art of diplomacy is not to outsmart the other side but to convince it either of common interests or of penalties if an impasse continues" (1982, 214). In the absence of external enforcement mechanisms, agreements must be self-enforcing.

To be sure, the loose structural factors of international politics—polarity, balance of power, long cycles, borders, regimes—may constrain individual choices, but they do not determine behavior. We hope in the following chapters to demonstrate that this contention is correct, and in trying to do so, we develop a theory of international relations that provides insights into the existence of equilibria in international politics and that relates those equilibria in part to domestic political factors. We hope to show the conditions under which disputes are resolved peacefully and those under which violence and war are anticipated. We try to show when the status quo is expected to prevail and when change is likely to take place. We will show that love of the status quo is not a guarantee of the peace, just as a desire for change need not be a threat to that peace. We will demonstrate that even the widespread adoption of norms to prevent violence is no guarantee of cooperation and that cooperation is the most likely outcome of international interactions, even among purely self-interested actors, in a world that precludes binding commitments.

We begin our inquiry by assuming that national governments are the central agents of policy implementation in international affairs. They, as the metaphorical embodiment of the general welfare, are the natural unit of analysis even for a theory, such as ours, that is grounded in the axioms of individual rationality. We assume that national government exists so that citizens can freely pursue their interests without fear of their neighbors. However disparate the objectives of those who reside in different countries, the purpose of national government is one and the same: to secure citizens against foreign incursion. Yet how national leaders go about advancing those interests—we recall Goya's question "Contra el bien general?"—is much contested.

Two perspectives are at the core of debate in the study of international affairs. From one viewpoint, foreign policy goals grow out of the political leadership's interest in advancing the welfare of the state within the international community, unencumbered by considerations of domestic affairs. The other outlook indicates that foreign policy goals grow out of the give and take of domestic politics, with all its prospects for generating problems of coherence in the aggregation of individual preferences. Lacking any a priori reason to accept one or the other position, we began this study as agnostics with regard to the debate between these two different perspectives.

In the realist perspective, the very structure of nations and the incentives and punishments that confront decision makers fosters a commonality of interests among all leaders charged with responsibility for choices that affect the prospects of war. Realist theorists insist that foreign policy leaders—professional diplomats, if you will—select policy goals by examining the external constraints and opportunities that confront their nation. In the realist or neorealist view, all nations share a common interest in enhancing their power or security, and therefore, all nations are always in a state of competition and potential conflict.

Where do the goals or preferences of leaders come from? For the (neo)realist theorist the answer is that foreign policy goals are selected *within* the foreign policy context, with little or no regard for how this or that goal might advance one or another decision maker's domestic political agenda. Goals are selected to advance power or security considerations and are constrained by the structural characteristics of the system.

We have in mind by the realpolitik/unconstrained version of our international interaction game something similar to Kenneth Waltz's third image. As Waltz observes, "Because any state may at any time use force, all states must constantly be ready either to counter force with force or to pay the cost of weakness. *The requirements of state action are, in this view, imposed by the circumstances in which all states exist*" (1959, 160, emphasis added), or, more succinctly, "Everyone's policy depends upon everyone else's" (226). According to this (neo)realist viewpoint, foreign policy leaders live in a rarefied world of high politics that is responsive to external pulls and tugs but is relatively inattentive to and unconstrained by the low politics of domestic affairs (Kaplan 1957; Morgenthau 1973; Waltz 1979; Posen 1984).[3] This select attention is the essential feature of the realpolitik variant of the game we propose.

A realist outlook requires that the articulation of foreign policy goals arises from the need to protect the state. "Covenants, without the sword, are but words, and of no strength to secure a man at all" (Hobbes 1962, 129). The quest for national security takes precedence over all lesser domestic considerations. For the realist, the specific policies a state pursues are structurally constrained by the nation's endowments of power, geography, alignments, and the like. The leader, then, is the conventional unitary actor selecting policy objectives with the constraints of the international environment firmly in mind and implementing strategies to maximize those chosen objectives. To be sure, domestic political pressures, especially in the form of costs for utilizing force, may constrain actions, and leaders may be punished after the fact for policies that clearly have failed (Denzau, Riker, and Shepsle 1985; Bueno de Mesquita, Siverson, and Woller 1991), but it is fundamentally the leader's understanding of international circumstances that dictates the selection of the state's tactical and strategic actions.

The second perspective is at the heart of arguments favoring a bureaucratic politics or interest group point of view (Allison 1971; Posen 1984; Bueno de Mesquita, Newman, and Rabushka 1985; Putnam 1988). Domestic constituencies—whether in a democratic or in an authoritarian society—express preferences. Some political participants may seek to maximize the external security of the nation by accommodating the demands of rivals, whereas others may desire to expand military capabilities to maximize jobs in local defense industries. Some may promote protectionist trade barriers or a free trade regime, or they may promote pacifist policies that guarantee no use of force, or policies that expand the size of the defense budget for defensive purposes (but that also may be interpreted by rivals as reflecting aggressive intentions). Each constituency is interested in influencing

3. We present the (neo)realist view as a paradigmatic ideal type within which numerous contending theories currently exist. All such theories share a common core of ideas that derogate domestic politics as a central concern of international affairs by emphasizing external structural circumstances and a common power- or security-enhancing goal as determinants of state actions.

the policies pursued by the national leadership. The leadership, in turn, is dependent on those constituencies for its continuation in office and so wishes to meet their desires to the greatest extent possible. This dependency is at the heart of the domestic/constrained variant of the game we propose. As Charles Beard has claimed, "However conceived in an image of the world, foreign policy is a phase of domestic policy, an inescapable phase" (Waltz 1959, 80).[4]

At the same time, leaders must be conscious of the costs they will bear if their responsiveness to domestic pressures leads to foreign policy disasters. They confront the additional serious problem that the foreign policy goals of competing domestic groups may themselves be incompatible and irreconcilable. Those who subscribe to a domestic point of view note that the internal political processes may be dominated by bureaucratic infighting, interest group competition, and a narrow pursuit of localized interests, even at the expense of secure or stable foreign relations. Worst of all, the domestic political process may be characterized by Condorcet's paradox: the fact that individual preferences are well ordered is not sufficient under majority rule procedures to guarantee that collective choices will be coherent.

When cyclical social preferences exist—and they are more and more likely as the number of relevant choosers increases or the number of dimensions to the issues at hand increases—they may make nonsensical any notion of the pursuit of "the national interest" (Niemi and Weisberg 1968; Krasner 1978; Bueno de Mesquita 1981). Yet this does not mean that goals are not chosen and pursued. Indeed, it does not even mean that the relevant foreign policy elites know that a social intransitivity exists. The structure of the domestic political process in which goals surface may mask the existence of cycles. Discussions between leaders and their advisers and constituents, for instance, may pit alternatives against one another, eliminating seemingly inferior options until only one choice still looks viable.

The domestic fabric of decision making may induce a choice that is inferior in two senses. The selection process may eliminate an alternative that is strongly, even unanimously preferred over the option finally chosen, thereby implying that the actual decision is inferior

4. As with the realpolitik version of our theory, this version is a generic ideal type. Numerous specific theories are consistent with the core concept of the domestic/unconstrained model. Each discounts international structural considerations to some extent as explanations of foreign policy behavior, emphasizing instead domestic processes, whether they are electoral, bureaucratic, interest group oriented, elite machinations in a smoke-filled room, or whatever. This is, for instance, the heart of Waltz's (1959) second image.

from a domestic political standpoint. Furthermore, the selection process may lead to the elimination of an alternative that is preferred by
domestic groups attentive to the foreign policy environment, thereby
implying that the actual decision is inferior from a foreign policy
standpoint. The domestic groups may even unanimously prefer an
eliminated option over a chosen policy exactly because that choice
makes the most sense in the strictly foreign policy context. In that
case, the unanimously preferred but unchosen alternative may be
equivalent (or identical) to the goal that would have been pursued if
such decisions were left up to the key foreign policy elite, as in the
realist view. Thus, even if domestic constituencies, like realist foreign
policy elites, give priority to alternative goals as a function of international circumstances, still the structure of domestic politics may
induce an outcome that is inferior from a foreign policy perspective
(Ostrom and Job 1986; Russett 1989; James and Oneal 1991; Morrow
1991b; Gaubatz 1991a, 1991b).

The impact of domestic politics on foreign policy choices can be
profound even if the domestic structure does not lead to cyclical
preferences. For instance, weighting alternatives from most preferred
to least preferred by each interested party (as in the Borda count
method) can yield different results than does a run-off system, which
in turn can yield an entirely different policy choice than would arise
if a plurality system were used. These differences in policy choices
can arise even though preferences are held constant across rules of
aggregation and even though there is a Condorcet winner (Riker 1982).
As we have emphasized, the political structure of decision making can
sometimes determine policy choices or at least severely constrain the
set of feasible outcomes. The domestic political process can—though
it need not—turn aside a goal that would have been selected in a realist
context.

A fundamental objective of our investigation, therefore, is to as-
certain how the empirical record matches deductions derived from the
realist and domestic perspectives. We will explore how these two
points of view alter predictions, given that options on foreign policy
actions are the same in both perspectives but the demands or proposals
brought forward are different.

REALISM VERSUS DOMESTIC POLITICS

The selection of foreign policy goals and the role of senior foreign
policy elites varies greatly depending on whether foreign policy
choices are conceptualized from a realist perspective or a domestic

politics point of view. We have seen some hints of how these different views of foreign policy can lead to quite different expectations regarding the objectives a nation pursues in the foreign policy context. Now we will explore the implications that these alternative views have for the unitary actor assumption and for the assumption of rationality.

We view power, policy, and place as the foundation stones of international politics. Through each, national leaders establish the agendas that promote international peace or war, prosperity or privation, glory or dishonor. No one of these stones is sufficient to build a polity secured against foreign invasion or a citizenry content with its lot in the world. What good does it do a state to have a preponderance of power if its citizens cannot agree upon the use to which that power should be put (Organski and Kugler 1980; Lamborn 1990)? What good does it do a state to be remote from its enemies if that very remoteness also limits its ability to pursue the citizens' interest in commerce and communication? What good does it do a state to accept the policies of its rivals, removing thereby any conflict of interest, if its citizens do not themselves generally share in the desire to promote those very policies? Security devolves from the ability to pursue objectives without undue fear of foreign reprisals (Morrow 1991a; Lalman and Newman 1991). It is the freedom to choose a course of action restrained only by domestic considerations of what is desirable, right, and proper. We build our theory around this notion of the state as an agent pursuing the security and interests of its citizens, the principals for whom it exists and acts. We emphasize, however, that different societies may seek entirely different policies and goals and that it is the quest for those goals that is one driving force behind international interactions.

In our view, the basic interactions of international affairs occur within dyads or pairs of nations (Zinnes 1968). We assume that each nation's foreign policy is the outcome of a complex process of give and take, perhaps among elites from competing countries or among competing elites (and masses) within a society such that the nation's policies can be represented as a coherent reflection of some process of domestic preference aggregation. We assume that each nation's chief executive—whether a monarch, a dictator, or a freely elected representative of the people—acts as if his or her welfare and the preferences of those whose support is needed to retain power were the same. Indeed, the record of leaders who have experienced war suggests that such an assumption is well warranted. During the past two centuries, the leaders of nations defeated in wars they began have had significantly foreshortened tenures in office, whereas those who have initiated victorious wars substantially extend their average time in power or the stability of their regime (Bueno de Mesquita, Siverson, and Woller 1991). In decisions that carry the risk of war, national leaders have strong personal incentives to link their own actions to the welfare of their supporters.

A problem arises, however, in theorizing about this linkage between the actions of leaders toward other states and the welfare of constituents within their own state. As we have seen, one view of the world— the realist view—suggests that leaders select policies vis-à-vis putative rivals to maximize the welfare of their own state (and presumably themselves) in the foreign policy context. The other view constrains such leaders to take fully into account the domestic costs and benefits associated with alternative foreign policy goals.

The realist view makes a fairly strong assumption of a unitary actor. The leader is the person who decides what goals to choose and what strategy to implement in pursuit of those goals. The goals (perhaps in terms of power or security) are determined by assessing the constraints of the international environment and thereby determining what is the most that can be gained on net given those constraints. Strategic actions are then chosen by the key leader—the unitary actor—to arrive at the best possible expected outcome.

In the alternative view the unitary actor assumption is somewhat weaker. Here there is a domestic political process that leads to the selection of foreign policy goals. That process may be more or less attentive to foreign policy constraints and, indeed, may select inferior policies, as noted earlier. The key foreign policy leader, the unitary actor, undoubtedly plays a role in shaping foreign policy objectives but is not the only source of influence. In this view the unitary actor is an agent charged with implementing actions in pursuit of whatever objectives result from the domestic political process. Like the realist unitary actor, the domestic unitary actor is responsible for selecting the strategic actions required to implement the society's objectives to the best of his or her ability. Unlike the realist unitary actor, the domestic unitary actor is not charged with defining the aims of foreign policy. These aims originate from the domestic political process. We are reminded, for instance, that Woodrow Wilson's internationalist view prevailed over U.S. isolationism in 1917. Yet he was unable to overcome isolationist opposition to U.S. membership in the League of Nations.

Whichever view is taken, we still postulate that in prospectively conflictual circumstances the structure of the situation induces in all leaders a primary interest in maximizing those interests of the state that ensure for themselves the opportunity to survive in a leadership

position and the concomitant opportunity to pursue their more indi-
vidualistic preferences. The actions required to maximize those interests differ depending on whether one focuses only on the foreign policy
environment (as in the realist view) or also on domestic pressures (as
in the constrained, domestic view) in defining the situation.

Either of our unitary actor assumptions—the unitary actor as the
person who determines goals and the actions required to promote the
goals or the person who is given the goals and assigned to carry them
out—is not quite so encompassing as is common in much research on
international affairs. When we construct our model of international
interactions in the next chapter, we assume the existence of domestic
political opposition to some foreign policies even in the realist context
and that such opposition imposes costs on leaders. We treat this
opposition as an important constraint on the foreign policy leadership—as a punishment for selecting "bad" strategies (but not as a
punishment for selecting "bad" goals). This cost term, then, is compatible with either view of how goals are selected. It does not treat
interest groups as a rival source of decision making but rather as
reactors to the choice of actions by the leadership.

We also assume that decision makers are rational in the sense that
they do what they believe is best, given the constraints of the situation.
Naturally, their beliefs may be mistaken and therefore ex post knowledge of outcomes is not an appropriate yardstick for evaluating their
ex ante judgments. Edward Creasy, in the preface to *The Fifteen
Decisive Battles of the World* (1851), makes this quite clear when he
writes, "We thus learn not to judge of the wisdom of measures too
exclusively by the results. We learn to apply the juster standard of
seeing what the circumstances and the probabilities were that surrounded a statesman or a general at the time he decided on his plan."

Our assumption of rationality is not particularly exclusionary. By
assuming rationality, we accept that the actions of national leaders are
motivated by the desire to pursue some valued goal or goals, but we
do not limit the content of such goals or their source. Leaders or the
publics who determine goals may be interested in maximizing wealth,
security, religious zeal, ideological purity, or any of a host of other
objectives that have been thought to be central to foreign affairs at
one time or another. Our theory is not about what goals people hold
but rather about how they behave given their goals. It is about the
instrumental selection of actions to maximize expected utility given
particular aims. Consequently, we are particularly interested in how
goal-seeking behavior is constrained by circumstances that make some
goals or some strategies more likely to succeed than others. Our model

of rationality, then, ultimately joins together the two main intellectual traditions in international relations: the realist viewpoint and the domestic perspective.

Models in which decision makers are assumed to be rational, expected utility maximizers have often been categorized as realist theories. We do not f 'v share that view. Rational actor models can—and usually do—repi esent the bringing together of at least some realist and some nonrealist, liberal, or domestic perspectives. This is true of both variants of the game we propose in the next chapter.

Rational decision makers are motivated by their values and constrained by their power. Preferences over alternative strategies or outcomes are the foundation of all choice models. Such preferences, or the utility attached to them, are in part expressions of the values that decision makers hold.[5] Such values are the core concept of nonrealist theories. But rational actors do not make choices naively on the basis of their preferences. Indeed, in many circumstances to do so would be irrational. Rather, the array of individual values is modified by the realization that some strategies, some courses of action, are more likely to succeed than others and by the recognition that some ends are more attainable than others. In international affairs power is often a prominent determinant of the probability of attaining this or that end. Thus, models of rational behavior take into account the nonrealist's focus on values and the realist's focus on power as constraints on action. These constraints are at the core of instrumental rationality, which is the perspective taken here (Zagare 1990).

To evaluate decision making from either the realpolitik or the domestic point of view, we find it helpful to represent the selection of actions and strategies through a formal model. The remainder of this chapter explains the epistemological bases for our choice of methodology.

WHY MODEL INTERNATIONAL RELATIONS?

Some might wonder why we take the path of abstract model construction before turning to a close examination of history. After all, no theory, regardless of its logical validity, elegance, or intellectual appeal, can substitute for a hard look at the facts. No abstraction is likely ever to be a practical guide to behavior until it has been con-

5. One of the earliest explicit theories of rational decision making was expostulated by Blaise Pascal and was motivated by his desire to promote the value of a belief in God (Hacking 1975).

fronted by reality. And we will most assuredly not allow ourselves to be swept away in theorizing without frequent recourse to the test of history.

We model because we believe that how we look at the facts must be shaped by the logic of our generalizations. We are deeply committed to the notion that the evidence cannot be both the source of hypotheses and the means of their falsification or corroboration. By approaching our analytic task from a modeling perspective we improve the prospect that our propositions follow from a logical, deductive structure and that the empirical assessments are derived independently from the theorizing. But why look with such abstraction and in so arcane a manner as to rely on mathematical constructs in our quest for human understanding? If the deductions do not follow logically, then the formal structure will facilitate discovery of this condition.

Students of international relations have always been interested in constructing models of conflict, although it is only lately that models have been embedded in very precise formalism. Often past models have been motivated by a desire to distill and understand a particular event, such as World War I or the Cuban missile crisis. Sometimes the informal modeling process has been concentrated on providing insights into a few important but very rare events, like hegemonic or power transition wars. Occasionally, as in Robert Jervis's (1976) model of the relation between misperception and conflict behavior, or Robert North's event-interaction model of crises, a goal has been the identification of universal-law-like generalizations.

Since the end of World War II, there has been a proliferation of modeling in the study of international relations. Hans Morgenthau (1973) suggested a model of the balance of power at roughly the same time that Bernard Brodie introduced a general model of deterrence. In counterpoint to their perspectives, Kenneth Organski (1958) suggested the power transition model of cataclysmic great power wars while George Modelski (1987) suggested a model of long cycles. While these realist theories dominated discourse, Karl Deutsch, Ernst Haas, Robert Keohane and Joseph Nye, and others promulgated models of cooperation and integration as an alternative view of international interactions. Many other prominent theorists proposed equally interesting and provocative models of conflict processes.

During roughly the same period, two more formalized models, with their assumptions clearly set out, were also introduced into the literature. We have in mind Lewis Fry Richardson's (1960) arms race model, which assumes a mechanistic stimulus-response pattern of behavior, and Thomas Schelling's (1960) deterrence model, which assumes rational, welfare-maximizing behavior.

It would be unfair to say that one set of models has dominated another set during the past few decades. Rather, there has been a proliferation of approaches with few, if any, earlier constructs being wholly set aside. But it is clear that theoretical modifications and empirical tests of the Richardson and Schelling models have been facilitated by a clearer understanding of what each model assumes about the world. Modifications of the less formalized constructs have been more problematic.

Formalism certainly does not guarantee the construction of useful theory, but it facilitates the avoidance of inconsistencies. Formalism strives for direct, clear, and unambiguous statements. It helps minimize the "that's not what I meant" discussions while revealing for all to see both the strengths and the weaknesses of the argument.

Sometimes there seem to be very good reasons to avoid modeling and to turn directly to empirical evaluations of the "real" world. This perspective holds most appeal to those students of international relations who are deeply concerned about the specific details, texture, and context of a singular incident. We recognize that each event is necessarily singular in the totality of its particulars, and this, presumably, is why the study of international affairs has so emphasized detailed investigations of individual events.

We strive to adopt methods that distinguish the particular from the general and that provide explanations optimizing internal and external validity. For us, theory and conceptualization serve to organize ideas as history while data serve to evaluate generalizations in light of particular observations. One without the other is incomplete and not satisfying.

Models often highlight specific and peculiar circumstances that help the analyst search out particular relations that might otherwise go unnoticed. Our discussion of the Fashoda Crisis in chapter 3 or the *Punktation* of Olmütz in chapter 4, for instance, shows how a model can help in a detailed, particularistic investigation of an individual event, as does our illustrative assessment of the Greek-Turkish crises over Cyprus in chapter 5 and the Sino-Indian War in chapter 6, or our more thorough evaluation of the Seven Weeks' War in chapter 7.[6] The

---

6. *Punktation* is a German term that is not easily translated into English. Weaker than a treaty, it is approximately equivalent to a protocol, memorandum of understanding, or, perhaps, a joint communiqué. It typically represents a statement of intentions, as between sovereigns, without the formal ratification process that characterizes a treaty.

statistical analyses in chapters 3, 4, 5, and 6 similarly highlight the breadth of the generalizations deduced from the international game structure we propose and facilitate comparisons of the realist/unconstrained and the domestic/constrained perspectives.

The art of modeling resides in the ability to sense what is of primary importance, as distinguished from what is of only secondary consequence. It relies on the selection of details for inclusion or exclusion in a simplified representation of reality. The science of modeling depends on the ability to extract testable, falsifiable relationships among variables that follow in a logically coherent fashion, so that the connection between the model's structure and its empirical implications is clear and consistent. These latter functions are best assured of being fulfilled when all of a model's assumptions are explicit.

Whether a model improves our understanding of some feature of the world cannot be determined solely by its internal structure. The usefulness of a model depends upon its ability to elucidate previously not-so-well-understood empirical phenomena, to account for seeming anomalies without creating excessively many new ones. Models without testable empirical referents are not refutable and so may be indistinguishable from metaphysical arguments. Models with such referents provide an inducement to invent the tools of measurement necessary to test their implications, to turn the historian's lens anew on the record of observations.

Today we have only a few tested models of international relations and an only slightly larger collection of testable, but as yet untested, models. Still, even in their very early stage of development, explicit formal models of international relations have contributed in a progressive way to our empirical knowledge. Even though our commitment to the benefits of explicit logic motivates the modeling that characterizes much of this volume, it is our commitment to the importance of empirical assessment that motivates our attention to the historical record, albeit too often our empiricism must be crude and our indicators inadequate. Perhaps our study can be in some small way an inducement to others (and to ourselves) to construct the tools of measurement that are necessary to test comprehensively the implications of our and other theories of international interaction. We cannot emphasize enough how important we believe it is for all social science research to marry careful reasoning with systematic empirical analysis and close scrutiny of specific events.

Of the approaches to model building that one might take—including models of evolutionary processes, cognition, structural imperatives, temporal imperatives—we choose to focus on models of choice processes. We do so, using a game-theoretic perspective, because we believe this approach holds out great promise for explaining hitherto seemingly anomalous behaviors. Other approaches may also hold out as good or greater promise. The give and take of alternative research agendas will, in time, help resolve that issue.

In adopting the method of game-theoretic analysis we recognize an important responsibility. The method is abstract and often difficult for those not experienced with axiomatic models. Yet we fervently wish to communicate, and create an exchange of ideas, with all who are interested in understanding how nations relate to each other. However obscure the method may seem, our message is straightforward: national foreign policies appear to be consistent with the implications of the international interaction game we propose, particularly with its constrained, domestic variant. Such policies appear to comply even with some of the most subtle implications of the theory and to be consistent with even severe tests of our deductions. We are mindful that it is our burden to make all of our results and our analytic logic accessible to every prospective reader. We endeavor to do so without shirking our responsibility to demonstrate the logic of our propositions.

We chose the approach we have taken because we believe it has specific qualities that facilitate an exchange of ideas and because we think it is particularly well suited for addressing fundamental puzzles of international affairs. Many of the most interesting facets of international interactions relate to sudden, seemingly chaotic or catastrophic changes in behavior. An abrupt change between peaceful and violent relations, for instance, or between an anarchic structure and cooperative interaction is puzzling to many perspectives on human interaction. But game theory provides a foundation from which abrupt changes in behavior can be understood even when underlying circumstances change only slightly or smoothly. The emphasis of game theory on equilibrium conditions—the mapping of strategies from which unilateral defection diminishes an actor's welfare—helps clarify threshold conditions required for changes in anticipated outcomes. These threshold conditions often act as trip wires: behavior remains unaltered as the threshold is approached until the threshold is actually crossed. Then behavior may become very different. Much of our analysis is concerned with the identification of substantively significant thresholds and with anticipated changes in those thresholds that result from uncertainty and imperfect information about the circumstances that decision makers find themselves in.

The capacity to account for sudden changes, as well as smooth progressions, adheres to the game-theoretic approach to understanding the roles played by misperception, uncertainty, and learning. Beliefs often—perhaps always—guide behavior. Observations inconsistent with beliefs may begin to encourage revised perceptions about the intentions or objectives of others. Such revised perceptions do not automatically translate into altered behavior. As in real life, games with limited information are constructed to reflect that beliefs are not readily abandoned but rather change after a preponderance of new information makes it too costly to continue to adhere to old views. Game theory provides an explicit model for specifying when enough new information is enough to alter behavior. The assessment of such information conditions is a recurring theme throughout this book.

These abilities of game theory to help identify crucial thresholds of beliefs, capabilities, and values encourage us to pursue this line of reasoning. Game theory provides models of decision making, learning, and choice under conditions of interdependence. These are all central features of international interactions.

The thrust of the remainder of this investigation is to develop a fuller understanding of how expected costs and benefits shape decision making. The strategies available to nations are the means by which they can realize such gains or losses. We turn now in chapter 2 to an elaboration of the game structure that will inform our investigation in the hope that we will be able to answer Goya's questions about war, "Con razón o sin ella?" and "Contra el bien general?"

Chapter 2

The International Interaction Game

The head bone's connected to the
neck bone. The neck bone's connected to the shoulder bone. The
shoulder bone's connected to the
back bone.
—Anonymous, "Dry Bones"

Make but a show of war and you
will have peace.
—Livy, *Discourses on the First
Ten Books of Titus Livius*

One of the central problems in the study of international affairs is how
the sequence of actions taken by states may lead to conflict or to
peacefully resolved differences. To analyze the paths and pitfalls along
the way to resolving disputes and to consider if indeed disputes arise
at all, we describe in this chapter a set of what we believe to be
fundamental interactions between nations. Decision makers assess the
desirability of outcomes according to the various costs and benefits
that the outcomes are anticipated to entail. Decision makers also
choose their strategies with an awareness of how the countervailing
actions available to their antagonists alter the course of international
relations. Such problems fall within the purview of game theory. We
recognize that the conduct of international politics involves a much
broader array of decisions and actions than those we formalize as part
of our model. Certainly, other decisions undertaken by nation-states
are very important parts of international interactions. Much of the
importance of these other forms of international discourse is, however,
in terms of how they effect the potential for war and international
conflict. Whether an action is expected to precipitate armed conflict
with another state is a primary consideration, carrying with it the

essential function of the state—the protection of the populace. "The first duty of the sovereign, that of protecting the society from the violence and invasion of other independent societies, can be performed only by means of military force" (Smith 1937, 653). To disregard the use of force is to discount the importance of the survival of the state (or, in many instances, the survival of a regime). All models that incorporate the decision to use force are dealing with interstate relations at the most basic levels.

The course of events leading to or away from international conflict is always diverse and complex in its details. Thus we would not expect any two historical events to be identical, certainly not in their specifics. No account of an event, no model, no history, is complete in its representation. Learning from an understanding of general phenomena, whether for the historian or for the social scientist, requires a concentration on essential features—in this case, the structure rather than the specifics of interstate interactions. Our model is an attempt to delineate interrelated decisions around international military crises, highlighting the opportunities for peaceful relations, which are juxtaposed against the sometimes great dangers imposed by negotiating in the presence of a potential resort to arms. We incorporate a number of aspects of international disputes, ranging from concern over the military costs if an action precipitates an attack by an antagonist to concerns over domestic political opposition. In addition, once we have explored the nonobvious, unanticipated implications of our model under the assumption that both players are fully informed about the preferences and the intentions of the opponent, we turn to an analysis of the game under the condition of imperfect information.

We begin our analysis from the standpoint of an individual decision maker who makes strategic choices in the name of the state. This viewpoint is recognizable as the conventional unitary actor principle used by many scholars studying interstate relations (Morgenthau 1973; Waltz 1979; Organski and Kugler 1980; Gilpin 1981; Bueno de Mesquita 1981; Morrow 1985; Powell 1987; Zagare 1987; Lalman 1988; and many others). Although there is some controversy over this assumption, particularly when it is applied haphazardly or with little awareness of its implications and limitations, there is less difficulty when the assumption is applied to confrontations where the use of military force is an alternative. In these situations, most, if not all, modern states formally confer on a single individual the choice to invoke force.

Perhaps some of the controversy surrounding the unitary rational actor assumption can be cleared up by keeping in mind what the assumption involves and how we are to interpret the real world in light of the analytic results. So long as decisions to negotiate or to use force are made rationally (or as if instrumental rationality were operative), it does not matter, in the context of our model, whether the decision is made by a single actor or by a group. If decisions are not made rationally, whether the source of the irrationality is the individual's mental processes or some group decision process, so much the worse for our model—and, perhaps, so much the worse for the world. Whether the assumption of a rational unitary actor is useful or trivializes the analysis of international interactions is, ultimately, an empirical question. If this and our other assumptions help make sense of historical patterns of behavior, then they are useful and do not excessively simplify and trivialize what is undoubtedly a very complex process.

What precisely is meant by a unitary actor is rarely spelled out in much detail by researchers who find this assumption convenient. Because we address two alternative views of the unitary actor, it is essential that we be explicit about the meaning of the assumption we make. At the outset of our investigation we are not committed to either a realist/unconstrained or a domestic/constrained interpretation of the unitary actor. As noted earlier, the realist assumption requires that the selection of national foreign policy objectives and the choice of actions to implement the chosen goals are both made as if by a single, rational leader. The domestically constrained interpretation assumes that goals are determined by the domestic political process in each state, tempered by interested constituencies that are attentive to the constraints of the international environment. In this view, the unitary actor assumption implies that actions and strategies, but not goals, are chosen as if by a single, rational leader.

It would be inaccurate to portray any particular researcher as believing that policy choices are made wholly as if domestic politics are irrelevant. Hans Morgenthau—the quintessential realist—acknowledged with regret that domestic politics had crept into the foreign policy process:

> If nations who are sovereign, who are supreme within their territories with no superior above them, want to preserve peace and order in their relations, they must try to persuade, negotiate, and exert pressure upon each other.
>
> The new parliamentary diplomacy is no substitute for these procedures. On the contrary, it tends to aggravate rather than mitigate international conflicts and leaves the prospect for peace dimmed rather than brightened. Three essential qualities of the new diplomacy are responsible for these

unfortunate results: its publicity, its majority votes, and its fragmentation of international issues. (1973, 530–31)

Morgenthau characterizes an ideal world as one in which domestic factors are excluded from foreign policy choices. There are, to be sure, clear variations in the degree to which the domestic context or the international context is believed to shape national foreign policy goals.

Stephen Krasner (1978) describes the contemporary pulls and tugs between what we call the domestic/constrained point of view and the dominant view of realism or neorealism. He agrees that foreign policies emerge as part of a complex interaction by elites within their international and their domestic settings. In the end, however, Krasner, like Kenneth Waltz and other neorealists, assumes that the international domain takes precedence, thereby reasserting a state-centric view of international relations and accepting the stronger unitary actor assumption.

Shifting more toward the domestic politics end of the spectrum, Robert Putnam (1988) envisions international negotiations taking place against the backdrop of domestic affairs. He speculates that foreign policy elites use the real or alleged intransigence of their domestic constituencies as a bargaining chip in international negotiations.

Tilting still further in the direction of conceding a fundamental role to domestic politics in shaping foreign policy, Bruce Bueno de Mesquita, David Newman, and Alvin Rabushka (1985) and Bueno de Mesquita (1990) describe the domestic bargaining setting as central to influencing what foreign policy elites can bring to the international negotiating table. In their view, the domestic process determines each actor's set of demands, and the international process determines ultimate outcomes, whether through a bargaining process or through violence.

Others before us have taken seriously the possibility that some features of international affairs are best explained by looking outward at the international system, whereas other aspects are best understood by looking inward at the organizational, bureaucratic, and interest group politics of the state in question. Waltz (1959, 1979), Graham Allison (1971), Barry Posen (1984), and Alan Lamborn (1990) provide four such examples. Waltz, for instance, addresses foreign policy as arising in part from the ambitions and aspirations of the individual, from the pressures and competing interests within the state, and, finally, from the structure and circumstances of the international system. In his later explorations of international affairs, he seems increasingly to place greatest emphasis on the role of the international system, rather than on man or the state, perhaps because he envisions all states as having a common core goal—the maximization of national security. Conversely, Allison emphasizes the pivotal importance of bureaucratic, organizational factors within states in foreign policy, although he, too, addresses carefully the role of external structures and pressures. Unlike the approach taken here, Allison associates rational action exclusively with the realist, structural perspective, viewing internal, bureaucratic, or organizational politics as driven by heuristics or standard operating procedures. Although we now recognize that such heuristics and standard operating procedures are elements of rational calculations in situations in which information is costly, at the time Allison wrote his seminal work, it was generally believed that rationality required a comprehensive assessment of all possible alternative courses of action.

Still more recently, Posen has investigated military doctrines in the context of two competing theoretical positions, an organizational process point of view and a neorealist, balance-of-power perspective. Although he finds some support for each outlook within his three detailed case studies, he concludes that there is somewhat more reason to rely on a neorealist, balance-of-power perspective than on the domestic-oriented, organizational point of view. Lamborn presents one of the first significant efforts to integrate theories of domestic politics and theories of statecraft into a coherent view of foreign policy. He provides several important steps toward assessing the trade-off between the foreign policy risks faced by decision makers and the domestic political risks associated with their choices.

Here we construct variants of a single theory that take into account the two alternative views of the unitary actor: the unitary actor as the chooser of foreign policy goals and strategies versus the unitary actor as the chooser of strategies alone. Like Waltz, Allison, Posen, and Lamborn before us, we begin without a predisposition toward either alternative. We depart from them in utilizing a more formalized approach to exploring the implications of each perspective. We end up favoring the constrained, domestic perspective as a better portrayal of international affairs—not that we disagree with Morgenthau and other realists when they note the international miseries that can arise in the name of domestic politics. Indeed, our deductions and evidence offer some support for their fears. But we are engaged in a positive process of trying to understand how international politics works, not a normative process. One surely cannot hope to make a better world without first understanding it better as it is.

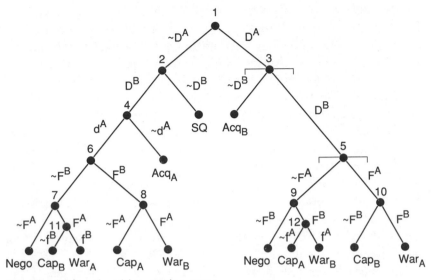

2.1: The international interaction game.

Most common analytic objections to the unitary actor assumption are aimed at the stronger, realist variant. Kenneth Arrow's (1951) general impossibility theorem is often cited as a criticism of this version of the unitary actor assumption. Arrow shows us that even if rational individuals aggregate their preferences according to rules meeting certain conditions of fairness, there can be no guarantee that group decisions will be coherent. This result is very strong in the sense that all the conditions are required in order to obtain it; weakening the conditions allows the possibility of aggregate rationality. Beyond our previously mentioned belief that decisions about the use of force are not group decisions, we would also claim that the decision processes concerning the use of force do not meet the fairness conditions required by Arrow's theorem. That is not to say that the process by which *goals* are chosen does not meet the conditions of the theorem.

Another aspect we should bear in mind when moving back and forth between the abstract world of game theory and the world we perceive through our senses is that some of the results we obtain are disconcerting in spite of assuming rationality. If we assumed that decisions are anything less than rational, these results would be even more disturbing because we cannot hope to escape unpleasant results by somehow improving the rationality of the participants.

Our full game of sequential decisions is depicted in figure 2.1. The purpose of this game is to represent the skeletal features of the conduct of international affairs. The game highlights the consequences of countervailing actions by rivals. The analogues in the world of policymaking are the standard operating procedures of contingency planning and the assessments of scenarios of potential responses by an opponent. Tensions between states in the form of conflicting interests can be resolved through numerous events, ranging from the peaceful acceptance of the status quo to the resolutions of conflicting interests that follow from military contests.

Quite often states allow tensions to go uncontested and hence unresolved by their tacit acceptance of the status quo. This acceptance of the status quo could be for reasons as prosaic as that the differences between the states are negligibly small. But more interesting from a theoretical standpoint are choices to let policies go unchallenged be cause the challenge might have unpleasant, undesired consequences.

The game in figure 2.1 is capable of separating for analysis our concerns regarding the conduct of international affairs. For example, the structure is capable of separating the peace that is due to an insufficient tension between states from the peace that is due to deterrence. "Normal diplomacy" is at once distinguished from extraordinary or crisis diplomacy. The complexity and the danger of international affairs is suggested by the paths that lead to the conflictual subgames below nodes 5 and 6. We refer to these subgames as crisis subgames, the possibility of military conflict being imminent. We wish to emphasize that the larger game captures a great deal of international relations and extends well beyond the field of conflict studies. Interacting nations need not be belligerent antagonists, but including the crisis subgame as part of the overall structure reflects one of the distinguishing aspects of international politics: international affairs are conducted against a background of potential conflict. After perusing the game, we are left with some sympathy and respect for the skills of national leaders and diplomats who must play it. Our investigations deepen our appreciation of the difficulties faced by the players, for the consequences of their actions can, though they do not always, involve very high stakes, and the conduct of international affairs hazards unintended consequences. The crisis subgame beginning at node 5, which focuses directly on conflictual consequences, will be analyzed once we have developed and analyzed the larger game, which addresses the broader conduct of international relations.

The game begins with a "move by nature" that furnishes one state or the other an opportunity to take the initiative in an effort to govern the development of events. This move by nature may be thought of as the circumstances under which the game begins, and it is not dissimilar to the selection of the player to move first in a chess game. The main difference is that the selection mechanism for chess games is presumed fair and does not advantage one player over the other; circumstances, however, may well be biased in favor of one of the states. Such bias and any advantage attributable to having the initiative may be due to geographic considerations, a recently realized technological advantage, or any of a host of other factors.

The state that is favored by circumstances has a choice of two initial moves: to make a demand (D) of the other state or to forgo making a demand (D̃). In the realpolitik variant of the game, the magnitude of any demand that is made is chosen to maximize the actor's expected utility at the end of the game. In the domestic variant, the magnitude of any demand that is made is determined primarily by domestic political factors that are exogenous to the international setting. Given the demands, actions are selected to maximize the actor's expected utility at the end of the game. Demands are accompanied by the threat to use force if they are not complied with, and the demands may be about anything so long as the two players can attach a value to them. We are not concerned here with the specific contents of prospective disputes. We do care that objectives vary in magnitude, and we care about how such variation affects the process by which international interactions evolve.

The actor designated by nature as the first to move is named state A. Moving second, state B has a choice between making a demand and not making a demand of A. An initial sequence in which each player chooses not to make a demand leads to a noncontentious continuation of the status quo. This condition is described by $\tilde{D}^A$, $\tilde{D}^B$, with the actors indicated by the superscript. The sequence D^A, $\tilde{D}^B$ represents an acquiescence by B to A's demand. An acquiescence could also be made by A if A forgoes its option to initiate only to be confronted by a demand from B to which A then yields, $\tilde{D}^A$, D^B, $\tilde{d}^A$. The paths to these outcomes are peaceful. Either the two parties find the status quo mutually agreeable, or the adjustments to the status quo are made before any recourse to arms.

The other paths lead to subgames where strategy choices include the use of force as an option. These are the subgames we refer to as crisis games. Players involved in crisis games must face decisions of whether to carry out their (implicit or explicit) threats to use force. At this juncture, decision makers directly confront the potential for military conflict. In the next chapter we explore the necessary and sufficient conditions to arrive at these crisis games within the overall

structure of the international interaction game under the realpolitik
and the domestic variants.

The crisis subgames arise at nodes 5 and 6 of figure 2.1. Within our
model these nodes are reached by distinct paths. If A makes a demand
and B counters with a demand of its own, D^A, D^B, the countries reach
a military crisis at node 5. If A does not initiate the dispute and hence
allows B the option of initiating, A can then issue a counterdemand,
$\bar{D}^A$, D^B, d^A. A counterdemand can range from a refusal to stand down,
to an insistence that B cease engaging in some behavior or begin
engaging in some other behavior, to an insistence that B transfer some
tangible benefit to A. A counterdemand does not terminate the game
but carries it forward to a crisis: once a demand has been brought
forward, a failure by either nation to acquiesce and satisfy the other
results in what we call a military crisis.

Our notion of a military crisis deserves some discussion at this
point. We have characterized a crisis as beginning at that moment
when states A and B have each tabled demands and neither has conceded to the other. Up until the crisis stage, the use of force in the
dispute has not been imminent. That is, the leaders' strategic choices
have not yet involved military options. They have maneuvered back
and forth, giving and taking, bargaining over the issues that separate
them. A military crisis occurs when the parties are unwilling to accept
the current state of affairs (or the current arrangement of policies) and
have not found a mutually acceptable rearrangement without the threat
of force (Lalman 1988). They may choose to seek a new arrangement
through negotiation ($\bar{F}$), or they may choose to resolve their differences by resorting to the force of arms (F). This notion of a crisis is
different from and yet essentially consistent with the notions used by
several others (Brecher and Wilkenfeld 1989; James 1988; Snyder and
Diesing 1977; Weiner and Kahn 1962; Hermann 1972; Young 1968).
Core interests in terms of the physical security of the state are at risk.
Information on the interests and the intentions of the antagonist are
at a premium, and decision makers are likely to perceive a constraint
in the time needed to gather or confirm the desired information. Our
game structure highlights the importance of information. When we
analyze the game in the next chapter under the condition of perfect
information and then again under the condition of imperfect information, we will elaborate on the information properties of the game. Here
we wish to point out only that when playing the game, or when making
interactive decisions in foreign policy, information and beliefs about
the preferences and opportunities available to the opponent are critical
to the choices made. If the situation evolves to the point of a military

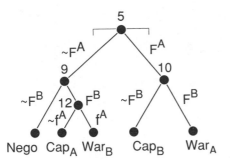

2.2: The crisis subgame.

crisis, it is difficult to turn back. Only one opportunity to avoid the costs of violence remains. If a leader believes that the opponent's preferences have foreclosed the option of negotiating, that leader will have to choose whether to initiate a conflict or to enter one initiated by the opponent.

The crisis subgames at nodes 5 and 6 are mirror images of each other, differing only in which actor has the first move. After making allowances for this difference, our discussion of the subgame starting at node 5 and depicted in figure 2.2 holds for the subgame starting at node 6 as well. The crisis at node 5 is precipitated by B's refusing to grant A's demand. A may choose to negotiate ($\tilde{F}^A$) or to escalate the dispute, driving the situation further down the tree by initiating the use of force (F^A) and ensuring that the outcome will be violent. If A elects not to fight and offers to negotiate and B responds by also negotiating, then the outcome is that negotiation continues—violence has been averted (for the time being).

However, if A chooses to escalate the dispute by using force, B may choose to capitulate to A's first strike, F^A, $\tilde{F}^B$, or B may choose to strike back, F^A, F^B. The full description of the strategy required to arrive at this outcome from the larger game is D^A, D^B, F^A, F^B. Both nations have elected to fight, nation A being the first to resort to arms. The war has been initiated by A. Following David Lalman (1988), we distinguish war from other forms of violence according to strategic choice. Both parties must choose the fight option to arrive at an outcome of war. A decision by B to yield after the initial escalation by A—D^A, D^B, F^A, $\tilde{F}^B$—results in an unreciprocated use of force, what we call a capitulation by B (Cap_B). The Japanese, for example, apparently hoped, by attacking Pearl Harbor, that a crippling blow to the American Pacific Fleet would lead to a U.S. capitulation rather than war (Prange 1981; Russett 1972).

Table 2.1
Outcomes of the Crisis Subgame

Nonviolent	Violent
Status quo	*Capitulation by A*
Acquiescence to A's demand	*Capitulation by B*
Acquiescence to B's demand	*War initiated by A*
Negotiation	*War initiated by B*

Should A forgo its opportunity to initiate, there is still the possibility for armed conflict. A could find itself either capitulating to the use of force by B—D^A, D^B, $\tilde{F}^A$, F^B, $\tilde{f}^A$—or fighting a war initiated by B—D^A, D^B, $\tilde{F}^A$, F^B, f^A. Allowing for this range of outcomes is important not just theoretically but substantively as well. There are many situations where decision makers are concerned about the potential for a preemptive use of force by an antagonist. Their considerations differ significantly from the considerations that prevail when the concern is war. As we will see when we develop the payoff structure of the game, having a capitulation to the use of force as a target of a military intervention entails different benefits and costs than does a war and hence must be explicitly accounted for in the model. Taking the possibility into account is important in the conduct of international affairs even if such events occur only rarely. The anticipation of an attack may provoke a "revolt upon the expectation of evil intended" (Thucydides 1959, 10–12). The fear of having to capitulate may itself precipitate the preemptive use of force, thereby averting the need to capitulate.

Note that each outcome to the crisis game is an empirically observable event for which data are currently available. Nearly all of our theoretical conclusions can be tested against the historical record of international conflict and peace. The model encompasses eight different outcomes. Five of the eight represent outcomes to the crisis subgames; three of the eight avert the crisis. The eight outcomes, with crisis outcomes in italics, are listed in table 2.1.

ASSUMPTIONS

The players select strategies as a function of both the values they attach to alternative outcomes and their beliefs about how their adversary will respond to their strategic decisions. Decision makers are assumed to respond to the circumstances they find themselves in by making the choice they believe maximizes their expected utility from that stage of the game onward. They cannot precommit themselves to one or another course of action, but they can act in anticipation of their opponent's actions. The inability to make precommitments springs from the realization that in international affairs there is no binding authority to enforce agreements between states. It is akin to the common realist assumption that the international system is anarchic. Some theorists believe that this assumption must be relaxed to account for the incidence of cooperation among self-interested actors. We retain the assumption that binding commitments are not possible in both our realpolitik/unconstrained and our domestic/constrained versions of the international interaction game. This condition does not preclude cooperation among self-interested actors in either interpretation of the game. Furthermore, abandoning it seems to us to introduce unrealistic inducements to cooperation and unrealistic impediments to conflict in the study of international affairs.

Nations persist or desist in a course of action—whether it be honoring, ignoring, reinterpreting, or breaking some previous promise or threatening some unpleasant action—because the leadership believes that such action is the best way to pursue the national interest. Where no courts and no police exist to enforce agreements, only beliefs about future consequences of current actions can mediate between short-term current interests and long-term prospects. Therefore, we assume a non-cooperative game, which we solve in accordance with subgame perfection (Selten 1975).

A subgame perfect equilibrium for a game is an equilibrium for every part of the game from that node forward. Subgame perfection requires that decision makers be forward-looking rather than myopic (Brams and Wittman 1981), anticipating the consequences of their actions in selecting from alternative paths. Choices are not made solely in terms of local, short-term benefits but also in terms of the subsequent effects and anticipated reactions of others to the chosen course of action. In the realpolitik variant, the forward-looking aspect of decision making extends to the selection of demands, as well as to the choice of actions. The realpolitik version treats demands as endogenous to the international interaction game. In the domestic variant, demands are presumed to be endogenous to some domestic political process, not spelled out here, which likely varies from state to state and which precedes the actions we investigate. In this variation of the game, then, the magnitude of any demand is taken as given, rather than treated as endogenous to the international interaction.

Here we limit decision makers to looking down the paths of a single confrontation, a single play of the international interaction game, which we call the medium term. We conceptualize short-term maximization as behavior that focuses only on the very next available foreign policy choice—the next move. The medium term is the completion of a sequence of moves that constitutes a single play of the international interaction game. The long term may be thought of as the indefinite repetition of interactions.

Myopic "fire fighting" is a form of limited rationality in which the costs of looking for information even one step ahead of the current situation are assumed to be too high to incur. In the perspective we take toward international affairs, we do not give much attention to fire-fighting behavior. It is hard to imagine such shortsightedness as a significant component of, for instance, crisis management. It can produce disastrous foreseeable and avoidable consequences. Although we do not rule out disaster—a concern with understanding the causes of disaster represents part of our motivation for undertaking this investigation—we do assert that national leaders do not blindly plunge forward without regard to the precipice before them. We recognize in our model that leaders do make mistakes, but we assume that they do not choose knowingly to act contrary to the medium- or longer-term interests of their nation.[1]

Neither do we focus much of our analysis on repeated play. There are three reasons for our primary—but not exclusive—attention to medium-term maximization. First, the so-called folk theorem of game theory informs us that in indefinitely repeated play virtually anything can be supported as a possible equilibrium. If decision makers can look down an indefinitely repeating sequence of choices and if they are fully rational, with no information costs for looking ahead, then there is likely to be a strategic path to just about anywhere. This possibility is not helpful in devising clear conditions of falsifiability unless we could climb into the head of each decision maker or unless we impose strong assumptions about the expected frequency distribution of particular mixed-strategy equilibria. What is more, even if interactions between states are repeated indefinitely, it does not follow that the game is repeated, as we make clear below.

1. One might apply such a myopic view to our game as a means of thinking about evidence that crises lead to panicked decision making. Some psychological research on reactions to stress might support such a view.

Second, Jeffrey Banks and Rangarajan Sundaram (1990) show that repeated games in which rationality is bounded by concerns about information costs revert to the single-stage equilibria of the game. That is, if decision makers are constrained by the costs associated with the complexity of their choices—complexity in terms of the number of stages and number of transition states from one strategy pair to another in the long-term, repeated game—then the Nash equilibria supported in the playing out of a single sequence of the game are the Nash equilibria for the repeated game.[2] Thus, if we assume that repeated play involves such information costs, then behavior that maximizes one's welfare over the medium term is behavior that is expected to maximize welfare over the long term. In international affairs, nations spend considerable sums of labor and money in the quest for information. It is clear that information costs are not inconsequential in the formation of national strategies in structuring relations between states. This observation bolsters our confidence that medium-term maximization—bounded rationality in the context of the playing out of a single sequence of moves—is the appropriate focus of our research. Such a focus properly takes into account the real limitations on information that must be confronted by policymakers.

The third and most important reason for focusing on the medium-term is that the outcomes of such critical international interactions as war or national capitulation change the game between nations. War, for instance, rarely leaves the belligerents with the status quo ante. Indeed, in all likelihood, the purpose of war is to restructure relations between adversaries. War serves to remove uncertainties about capabilities, expectations, and the like, reshaping beliefs and future prospects (Blainey 1973). International interactions change the fundamental circumstances in which national choices are made, so subsequent interactions do not repeat previous ones. Even though the structure of moves remains unaltered, the payoffs characterizing alternative moves are precisely what change as a result of previous experiences in foreign affairs. In the future, decision makers confront a revised set of expected payoffs, thereby diminishing the relevance of the repeated game concept for the international interactions of interest here.

The medium-term orientation of our research does not preclude the prospect that national actions are chosen with an eye toward reputa-

2. A set of strategies constitutes a Nash equilibrium if no player's welfare can be improved by a unilateral change of strategy by that player. We use the concept of equilibrium throughout this work in this sense and not to mean balance or stability, as is sometimes the case among international relations researchers.

tion building. Because our game is sequential and contains many subgames, the actors within our proposed structure have opportunities to build reputations by, for instance, enforcing or backing down from their initial demands. The beliefs and subsequent actions of rivals take such choices into account. Furthermore, the payoff structure we propose explicitly includes cost terms that are linked to reputation. As we explain below, nations that capitulate bear a cost in terms of lost face, just as nations that utilize force bear costs in terms of the magnitude of domestic constraints on forceful behavior. Beliefs about the size of these constraints can create an expectation that a nation is hawkish or dovish.

Our primary focus, then, is on subgame perfect equilibria within a single playing out of the international interaction game. We assume that beliefs about actions further down the international interaction sequence, rather than expectations of indefinitely repeated play or any prospect of making binding commitments, help shape choices of action.

We assume that national leaders prefer certain outcomes at the terminal nodes of the game. Their preferences in strategies are formed in accordance with the costs and benefits associated with each outcome. For example, the outright capitulation to a demand may entail some loss in welfare, and yet a capitulation does avoid additional marginal costs in terms of the spent human and material resources of fighting. Thus the preference rankings at the terminal nodes show the basic predilections of the decision makers with regard to the demands in dispute, together with their expectations of obtaining the various costs and benefits. To continue our example, it is possible that in some circumstances capitulation is preferable to standing firm, because the cost of standing firm outweighs the benefits.

We will return to these assumptions from time to time in the course of our analysis to investigate the ramifications of dropping various conditions in turn. We adopt this method in the hope of gaining a better understanding of the costs and benefits of certain assumptions adopted by us and by other students of international relations. Later we will see that dropping some assumptions simply leads to stronger conclusions, and hence those assumptions are superfluous for certain results. Other conclusions hang critically upon a single assumption. Such dependence is not inherently a bad thing, for it refocuses our attention on the importance of that assumption and on how it could be considered controversial. Our assumptions, like any others, are restrictions on the domain of applicability for our results. A failure of a case to meet a set of assumptions does not falsify the results of the analysis; it makes the results nonapplicable to that case. There still remains a responsibility to go beyond a mere claim that some particular case or set of cases does not meet the assumptions. Some explanation should be given for why such cases do not qualify according to the assumptions.

The range of values associated with the outcomes by national leaders is established according to our assumptions. Seven assumptions establish the set of admissible preference orderings and the play of the game.

ASSUMPTION 1. *The players choose the strategy with the greatest expected utility, given that they are playing subgame perfect strategies.*

ASSUMPTION 2. *The ultimate change in welfare resulting from a war or from negotiation is not known with certainty. Hence, arriving at a war node or at negotiation yields an expected value, assessed according to the subjective probabilities of gaining welfare and the subjective probabilities of losing welfare. We restrict the probabilities in such lotteries: $0 < P < 1.0$. All probabilities are treated as subjective unless stated otherwise.*

ASSUMPTION 3. *In contrast to assumption 2, capitulations result in changes in welfare that are certain rather than probabilistic. The probability that the capitulating state loses is 1.0, as is the probability that the challenging state wins its demand.*

ASSUMPTION 4. *All nations prefer to resolve their differences through negotiation rather than war.*

ASSUMPTION 5. *Measured from the status quo (SQ) are $U^i(\Delta_i)$, the utility one expects to gain by obtaining one's demands, and $U^i(\Delta_j)$, the utility one expects to lose by acceding to the adversary's demands. The value of these terms is restricted such that $U^i(\Delta_j) < U^i(SQ) < U^i(\Delta_i)$.*

ASSUMPTION 6. *Each outcome has a set of potential benefits and/or costs appropriately associated with it. We make restrictions on the various costs such that α, τ, γ, $\phi > 0$; and $\tau > \alpha$.[3] The term $\alpha_i(1 - P^i)$ is the expected cost in lost life and property for nation i associated*

---

3. A mnemonic for the cost terms may help: α is the cost borne by the *a*ttacker for fighting *a*way from home in a war; τ is the cost borne by the *t*arget in a war; γ is the cost borne by a state that *g*ives in after being attacked; and ϕ is the domestic political cost associated with the use of *f*orce.

with fighting away from i's home territory; $\tau_i(1 - P^i)$ is the cost in lost life and property that i expects if it fights at home as the target of an attack; $\gamma_i(1 - P^i)$ is the cost in life, property, and lost face or credibility from absorbing a first strike to which the attacked party gives in; and $\phi_i(P^i)$ is the domestic political cost (apart from life and property) associated with using force rather than diplomacy to try to resolve differences.

ASSUMPTION 7A: THE REALPOLITIK VARIANT. *The magnitude of actor i's demand $[U^i(\Delta_i)]$, if any, is determined by i to maximize i's expected utility within the international context, without regard for the wishes or objectives of domestic political constituencies.*

ASSUMPTION 7B: THE DOMESTIC VARIANT. *The magnitude of actor i's demand $[U^i(\Delta_i)]$, if any, is determined by the domestic political process in nation i. That process is determined by internal political rules, procedures, norms, and considerations and may or may not be attuned to foreign policy considerations.*

Assumption 1 stipulates that we are dealing with national decisions made in a rational (expected-utility-maximizing) and forward-looking manner. As we commented earlier, decisions need not be made by a single decision maker who formulates foreign policy. Regardless of the internal political processes involved, foreign policy decisions carrying with them the threat of force are made according to coherent, well-ordered preferences.

Assumptions 2 and 3 concern the probability of a nation's being ultimately successful in gaining its goals, given alternative combinations of strategic choices by A and B. In our game structure, if either party initiates the use of force, the adversary has the option to defend itself. We assume that a decision not to defend oneself with force in the face of a forceful challenge is a decision to accept defeat (assumption 3). A nation choosing not to fight back forfeits the full demand of the challenging state. The crucial feature of such a capitulation is not the lack of retaliation—some minimal use of force could, in principle, be permissible within this category of event—but rather the full surrender to the adversary's demands and the assurance of defeat. In events other than capitulations, gains and losses are probabilistic, not determinate. Before going into negotiations or wars, the other terminal events in the crisis game structure, real-world decision makers do not know with certainty the payoffs associated with these processes; they can base their decisions only on estimates of how negotiations or wars will ultimately be resolved. We are reminded of an aphorism that was a favorite with Dwight Eisenhower: "Rely on planning, but never trust plans" (Greenstein 1982, 133).

We cast negotiations and wars as risky prospects. The adversaries may win, or they may lose. That is, they may gain their demands (Δ_i) or they may lose and yield to the demands of the adversary (Δ_j). The expected value of the risk is evaluated as the value gained if one's demands are won [$U^i(\Delta_i)$], weighted by the subjective probability of winning (P^i) summed with the value of the opponent's demands [$U^i(\Delta_j)$], which is weighted by the subjective probability of losing ($1 - P^i$). Thus nations A and B evaluate the risky components of outcomes as lotteries. For example, negotiations are thought of as risky events, where one can expect to obtain something between one's own demands and the demands made by the opponent. For A,

$$\text{Nego}_A = P^A[U^A(\Delta_A)] + (1 - P^A)[U^A(\Delta_B)].$$

For B,

$$\text{Nego}_B = P^B[U^B(\Delta_B)] + (1 - P^B)[U^B(\Delta_A)].$$

Our theoretical results do not depend on how the decision makers arrive at the probabilities in these lotteries (soothsayers included). Consistent with their being subjective, the probabilities are allowed to vary across decision makers. Later, when we turn to the empirical testing of the theory, we introduce and operationalize (in appendix 1) a particular conception of how decision makers might estimate probabilities: the probability of succeeding is the relative share of the capabilities the adversaries expect to have available.

In negotiation, as in war, the outcome is expected to be partially dependent on the relative capabilities of the antagonists, together with the contributions of their respective supporters (Bueno de Mesquita and Lalman 1986; Banks 1990). We assume that the anticipated compromise outcome of negotiation is akin to the weighted version of "split the difference" (Rubinstein 1982), so that in negotiation neither participant anticipates satisfying his or her full initial demand. The value of the negotiation lottery is, then, the expected compromise outcome in a negotiation. The anticipated distribution of gains and losses at the end of a negotiation is assumed by each player to equal its expected value for the negotiation. In the case of war, we assume that the same lottery is operative because the main lever in negotiations is the tacit threat of force if the issues are not suitably resolved. In war it is likely, however, that the actual distribution of gains or losses at the end is not equal to the value of the lottery. Rather, the winner is likely to gain all or most of what was demanded, whereas the loser is likely to have to cede all or most of what the victor desires. But the expected value, as distinct from the actual outcome, of the ultimate resolution of the dispute is the same as the expected value of a negotiation, less the transaction costs of the war. In the case of the war lottery, the probability terms serve as probabilities of achieving the desired objective. In the negotiation lottery, the probability terms serve as weights that effect the compromise settlement.

In assumption 6 we assume that the costs of conflict differ between initiators and target nations in terms of expected losses in life and property ($\tau_i > \alpha_i$). Our justification for this assumption is that initiators can have greater control over the venue of fighting. The expected costs to a nation of being engaged in combat on its own territory are greater than the expected costs to that same nation of conducting warfare on someone else's territory. The rationale for this interpretation is that the number of combatants and the amount of material and productive capacity exposed to destruction are more at the discretion of the nation's leaders when fighting is abroad than when fighting is at home. The loss of civilian lives and nonmilitary property is not so easily controlled when the fighting takes place on one's own territory unless one capitulates. Even in the grisly discussions of strategic nuclear war, cost advantages are frequently attributed to initiation because of the hotly debated potential of a first strike to reduce the retaliatory ability of the adversary. Hardened sites and mobile missile systems are designed to remove this advantage. The heat of the debate, in our view, is due to the importance to strategic choice of removing the inequalities in these cost terms.

We further assume that anticipated losses in life and property vary with the military advantage of the contending sides. We assume in particular that one's anticipated losses increase as the relative probability of success of the adversary rises, so that the expected costs are partially a function of the subjective belief one has in the prospects of defeat. We assume that the expected losses in life and property from fighting away from home and as the target are, respectively, $\alpha_i(1 - P^i)$ and $\tau_i(1 - P^i)$, so that weak states facing strong rivals expect larger losses in life and property than larger states do, all else being equal. In keeping with the logic of relating costs to the prospects for success, we assume that the expected cost of capitulating after absorbing a first-strike blow is larger, the greater the power of the rival: $\gamma_i(1 - P^i)$.

We recognize that the assumption that $\tau_i > \alpha_i$ can give rise to some confusion, especially along two dimensions. The first likely source of confusion concerns a comparison between initiators and targets of attack. Our assumption does not state that initiators of aggression suffer or expect to suffer smaller losses in life and property than do their targets. It makes no comparison at all between initiators and targets. That is, we do not assume anything about the expected magnitudes of τ_i compared to α_j. Doing so would require an interpersonal comparison of utilities, which is unacceptable. Rather, the assumption states only that for any given nation i, the losses it expects are larger if it is attacked than if it attacks. The assumption stipulates a condition about a counterfactual, unobservable alternative state of the world. The condition we have assumed stipulates that a first-strike advantage exists.

A second possible source of misunderstanding arises from the observation that in war, defense is generally easier than offense. This may be true, but it is unrelated to the assumption we have made. Such arguments are about the ease of projecting capabilities and not about the costs incurred, given particular capabilities. Still, one might argue that $\alpha_i > \tau_i$ because, for instance, the incentive to fight effectively and efficiently is greater when defending one's home territory than when fighting in some far-off place. Fighting away from home also involves less familiarity with the terrain, the climate, and the like, which also raises the costs of combat. In any case, in assumption 6 we assume the existence of a first-strike advantage in terms of the anticipated costs (not in terms of the probability of success), but we do not assume that the first-strike advantage must be particularly large or small. Indeed, it is entirely possible for the difference in the costs to be close to zero or for it to be very large. Generally, the equilibrium results from our theory do not depend on the size of the first-strike advantage, although several significant results do hinge on its existence. For a further discussion of this issue, we suggest seeing Machiavelli (1950, chap. 12).

An additional word should be said about the parameter γ_i. We have not restricted the magnitude of this term relative to the other cost parameters. The term γ_i reflects the costs of absorbing an unanswered blow. It includes such psychological effects as loss of face and loss of credibility and reputation, as well as such tangible losses as are involved in the destruction of life and property. Although the tangible costs are almost surely smaller in the event of a capitulation than in the event of war, we cannot say that the overall value of γ_i is necessarily larger or smaller once the psychological dimension is factored in. Hence, we do not restrict the magnitude of this term.

Assumption 6 also attributes a direct cost to the decision to initiate the use of force. We view this cost as primarily political in nature. It entails the domestic political opposition to using force to accomplish political goals. The failure to achieve policy goals through negotiation and diplomacy is a failure of the leadership to obtain the goals while avoiding the costs of military conflict. Immanuel Kant addressed this set of costs specifically:

> If . . . the consent of the citizens is required in order to decide whether there should be war or not, nothing is more natural than that those who would have to decide to undergo all deprivations of war will very much hesitate to start such an evil game. For the deprivations are many, such as fighting oneself, paying for the cost of war out of one's own possessions, and repairing the devastation which it costs, and to top all the evils there remains a burden of debts which embitters the peace and can never be paid off on account of approaching new wars. (Kant 1977, 438)

Costs arising from domestic opposition include demonstrations in the streets, electoral defeat, coups d'état, and difficulties in obtaining the funds with which to wage war. For example, congressional resistance to appropriating funds imposed direct political costs on U.S. policymakers associated with the Vietnam War during the late 1960s and early 1970s. Politicians must take such costs into account just as surely as they must be attentive to the expenditure of lives and national wealth. The very need to resort to force suggests a failure of diplomacy, a political failure of the national leadership, and it opens opportunities for opposition factions. Recall that the cases of interest in our analysis, in accord with assumption 4, are those in which both parties prefer negotiation to war—negotiating is Pareto superior to waging war. Settling international disputes at the negotiation table is less costly than settling them on the battlefield, and the failure to do so reflects poorly on the leaders' conduct of foreign affairs. A major interest of our work is to develop a fuller understanding of how domestic political costs shape crisis decision making. With some exceptions (for instance, Brito and Intriligator 1980), domestic political concerns in game-theoretic investigations of international relations have been given short shrift. We exercise what Barry O'Neill calls the modeler's discretion to determine "whether 'national interests' or any other motive are the players' goals" (1989, 6). Our model certainly does not presume "rational decision-makers who are impervious to the need to placate their domestic opponents or, indeed, to any influences other than the strategic requirements of responding to adversaries abroad" (Rosenau 1971, 101)—quite the contrary. We further assume that domestic costs rise with the subjective probability of success in a dispute, so that the domestic cost term is $\phi_i P^i$. The notion here is that the more powerful participant in a dyadic relationship bears a greater burden for finding a peaceful resolution of differences. Domestic populations are assumed to dislike bullying and to punish those who employ violence if their power should have made them persuasive enough to resolve their disputes without it.[4]

Assumption 7a is the fundamental restriction required for the realpolitik variant of the game. It stipulates that domestic choice processes do not influence foreign policy goals or the determination of the national interest. Assumption 7b, in contrast, captures the fundamental quality of the domestic variant of the game. It attributes the selection of foreign policy objectives to the vagaries of domestic affairs, rather than to the preferences of a single foreign policy leader. Assumption 7b allows us to evaluate anticipated actions for any feasible array of demands, whereas assumption 7a significantly restricts that array as a function of the structure of the international situation. Neither assumption implies a specific model of domestic political processes. Rather, assumption 7a says any such process is irrelevant, and assumption 7b says that we can treat as a given the demands that emanate from a domestic process, without necessarily knowing what that process is. Assumption 7a—the realpolitik variant—suggests that there is no reason to work back to an evaluation of domestic processes, for we can predict foreign policy demands just by knowing the structural imperatives of the international context. In contrast, assumption 7b—the domestic variant—suggests that a next step in research is to link a model like the one we propose here to appropriate models of domestic political processes in order to predict the specific demands likely to arise within particular domestic political contexts.

Within our game, nations A and B realize gains and losses according to the strategies available. As we discussed above, except for combinations of strategies that lead to a capitulation, an acquiescence, or the maintenance of the status quo, the gains and losses are cast as probabilistic payoffs. Table 2.2 gives the values associated with the event at each of the terminal nodes in the full game in figure 2.1.

---

4. We recognize that this assumption can be controversial. "Rally round the flag" effects and other phenomena may suggest that decision makers receive a political reward for strong actions, including the use of force. But there are always some who oppose the use of force. We do not assume that such a group is necessarily large or small, but rather that such opponents always exist.

Table 2.2
Outcomes and Expected Utilities for Nation i

SQ	$U^i(SQ)$
Acq_j	$U^i(\Delta_i)$
Acq_i	$U^i(\Delta_j)$
Nego	$P^i[U^i(\Delta_i)] + (1 - P^i)\,[U^i(\Delta_j)]$
Cap_j	$U^i[\Delta_i - \phi_i(P^i)]$
War_i	$P^i(U^i[\Delta_i - \phi_i P^i - \alpha_i(1 - P^i)]) + (1 - P^i)(U^i[\Delta_j - \phi_i P^i - \alpha_i(1 - P^i)])$ ✳
Cap_i	$U^i[\Delta_j - \gamma_i(1 - P^i)]$
War_j	$P^i(U^i[\Delta_i - \phi_i P^i - \tau_i(1 - P^i)]) + (1 - P^i)(U^i[\Delta_j - \phi_i P^i - \tau_i(1 - P^i)])$

Table 2.3
Nation i's Preferences for Outcomes

Outcome	Ordinal restriction on ordering	Possible preference rank
SQ	$>$ Acq_i, Cap_i	7 to 3
Acq_j	$>$ all other outcomes	8
Acq_i	$>$ Cap_i	5 to 2
Nego	$>$ Acq_i, Cap_i, War_i, War_j	7 to 5
Cap_j	$>$ War_i, War_j	7 to 3
War_i	$>$ War_j	5 to 2
Cap_i	—	4 to 1
War_j	—	4 to 1

Note: Eight is the highest ranking, and one is the lowest.

RESTRICTIONS ON PREFERENCES

Our assumptions imply restrictions on the eight outcomes in terms of the order of preferences that leaders are allowed to hold. Displayed in table 2.3 are the rankings for the outcomes for any nation i that can be assigned under the restrictions imposed through our assumptions.

We discuss each of the restrictions in turn and note here that the restrictions themselves are interesting in the context of international relations. These restrictions are operative regardless of the version of the game being analyzed, although in practice some prove more salient in one variant of the game than in another.

In the first row, i finds the status quo superior to an acquiescence to j's demand (Acq_i) and superior to a capitulation to the use of force

(Cap$_i$). By assumption, $U^i(SQ) > U^i(\Delta_j) \rightarrow SQ > Acq_i$; even the smallest demand made by the antagonist j is a change in the status quo detrimental to i. The utility to i of a capitulation to the antagonist (Cap$_i$) is less than the utility of acquiescing to j's demands (Acq$_i$), entailing as it does the additional costs in lost face, life, and property: $U^i(SQ) > U^i(Acq_i) > U^i(Cap_i)$.

A peaceful acquiescence by the opponent (Acq$_j$) to the demands made by i is superior for i to all other outcomes. This outcome is superior to the status quo and to Acq$_i$, for $U^i(\Delta_j) < U^i(SQ) < U^i(\Delta_i)$. Comparing Acq$_j$ to the expectations from negotiating, recall that we have assumed negotiations are evaluated as the expectations from a lottery over the demands made by both parties. Negotiated outcomes are never obtained with certainty, hence we assume that the probability of gaining a demand is never equal to zero or one: $0 < P < 1.0$. We show that as P^i approaches arbitrarily close to 1.0, nation i prefers acquiescence by j to negotiation. Acq$_j$ > Nego:

$$U^i(\Delta_i) > P^i[U^i(\Delta_i)] + (1 - P^i)[U^i(\Delta_j)].$$

For arbitrarily small ϵ and positive utilities for the demands,

$$U^i(\Delta_i) > (1 - \epsilon)[U^i(\Delta_i)] + \epsilon[U^i(\Delta_j)],$$

which means that

$$0 > -\epsilon[U^i(\Delta_i) - U^i(\Delta_j)].$$

Gaining one's demands with certainty when the other party acquiesces is preferable to negotiating and obtaining them with something less than certainty or obtaining something less than the initial demand. The remaining outcomes are inferior to Acq$_j$ and are violent. An acquiescence by j means that i certainly receives all of its demands (Δ_i) without suffering any costs. Acq$_j$ > Cap$_j$:

$$U^i(\Delta_i) > U^i[\Delta_i - \varphi_i P^i].$$

Compared to War$_i$, an acquiescence by j is preferred because the risk of losing the war is removed and the costs of a war that i initiates, $-[\phi_i P^i + \alpha_i(1 - P^i)]$, are avoided. Acq$_j$ > War$_i$:

$$U^i[\Delta_i - \phi_i P^i - \alpha_i(1 - P^i)] > U^i[\Delta_j - \phi_i P^i - \alpha_i(1 - P^i)], \quad U^i(\Delta_i) > U^i(\Delta_j).$$

$$U^i[\Delta_i - \phi_i P^i - \alpha_i(1 - P^i)] > P^i(U^i[\Delta_i - \phi_i P^i - \alpha_i(1 - P^i)])$$
$$+ (1 - P^i)(U^i[\Delta_j - \phi_i P^i - \alpha_i(1 - P^i)]),\ P^i \neq 1.0.$$

$$U^i(\Delta_i) > U^i[\Delta_i - \phi_i P^i - \alpha_i(1 - P^i)],\ 0 > -[\phi_i P^i + \alpha_i(1 - P^i)].$$

$$U^i(\Delta_i) > P^i(U^i[\Delta_i - \phi_i P^i - \alpha_i(1 - P^i)])$$
$$+ (1 - P^i)(U^i[\Delta_j - \phi_i P^i - \alpha_i(1 - P^i)]).$$

Capitulating to an opponent is, of course, inferior to having the opponent yield to one's demands. $Acq_j > Cap_i$:

$$U^i(\Delta_i) > U^i(\Delta_j - \phi_i P^i),\ U^i(\Delta_i) > U^i(\Delta_j),$$

and

$$0 > -\phi_i P^i.$$

Finally, Acq_j is preferred over War_j just as it was over War_i, except in this instance the costs saved are even greater. $Acq_j > War_j$:

$$U^i[\Delta_i - \phi_i P^i - \tau_i(1 - P^i)]$$
$$> U^i[\Delta_j - \phi_i P^i - \tau_i(1 - P^i)],\ U^i(\Delta_i) > U^i(\Delta_j).$$

$$U^i[\Delta_i - \phi_i P^i - \tau_i(1 - P^i)] > P^i(U^i[\Delta_i - \phi_i P^i - \tau_i(1 - P^i)])$$
$$+ (1 - P^i)(U^i[\Delta_j - \phi_i P^i - \tau_i(1 - P^i)]),\ P^i < 1.0.$$

$$U^i(\Delta_i) > U^i[\Delta_i - \phi_i P^i - \tau_i(1 - P^i)],\ 0 > -[\phi_i P^i + \tau_i(1 - P^i)].$$

$$U^i(\Delta_i) > P^i(U^i[\Delta_i - \phi_i P^i - \tau_i(1 - P^i)])$$
$$+ (1 - P^i)(U^i[\Delta_j - \phi_i P^i - \tau_i(1 - P^i)]).$$

Acquiescing is preferable to capitulating ($Acq_i > Cap_i$) because the amount of utility lost from the conceded change in policy is the same in both circumstances, but the costs expected from absorbing a first strike, $\gamma_i(1 - P^i)$, are saved when one acquiesces: $U^i(\Delta_j) > U^i[\Delta_j - \gamma_i(1 - P^i)]$.

Negotiating is preferred to Acq_i, Cap_i, War_i, and War_j. Assumption 4 postulates the preference to resolve differences through negotiation rather than through war ($Nego > War_i, War_j$). We need not have made this assumption; it operates to restrict our attention to the more interesting cases (and it is implied by assumptions 2 and 5). Negotiating is preferred to acquiescing because it affords at least some expectation of gains. It is likewise preferred to capitulating, not to mention the avoidance of the costs incurred as the target of a violent attack.

Cap_j, a capitulation by the opponent, is preferred to either war outcome. Here, all of one's own demands are obtained (no lottery over the demands of the opponent), and war costs are avoided.

Initiating a war (War$_i$) is preferred to having the other state initiate the war (War$_j$). Recalling that $U^i(\Delta_i) > U^i(\Delta_j)$ and that $\tau_i > \alpha_i$, War$_i$ > War$_j$:

$$P^i(U^i[\Delta_i - \phi_i P^i - \alpha_i(1 - P^i)]) > P^i(U^i[\Delta_i - \phi_i P^i - \tau_i(1 - P^i)]),$$

and

$$(1 - P^i)(U^i[\Delta_j - \phi_i P^i - \alpha_i(1 - P^i)])$$
$$> (1 - P^i)(U^i[\Delta_j - \phi_i P^i - \tau_i(1 - P^i)]).$$

Therefore,

$$P^i(U^i[\Delta_i - \phi_i P^i - \alpha_i(1 - P^i)]) + (1 - P^i)(U^i[\Delta_j - \phi_i P^i - \alpha_i(1 - P^i)])$$
$$> P^i(U^i[\Delta_i - \phi_i P^i - \tau_i(1 - P^i)])$$
$$+ (1 - P^i)(U^i[\Delta_j - \phi_i P^i - \tau_i(1 - P^i)]).$$

In other words, the War$_i$ lottery involves lower costs than the War$_j$ lottery, making initiation by i more attractive than initiation by j.

Capitulating to the opponent (Cap$_i$) and fighting a war initiated by the opponent (War$_j$) are not necessarily preferred to any of the outcomes, although we see from the table that a number of other outcomes are preferred to them.

The possible ordinal positions the outcomes can occupy when these restrictions are simultaneously taken into account are described in the last column of table 2.3. Here one is the least preferred position and eight the most preferred. Either player is allowed to hold a preference order admissible under these restrictions. Clearly, in spite of the restrictions we have imposed, a very large number of pairings of preference orders ($52 \times 52 = 2{,}704$) are possible in principle.[5] Although the number of still-admissible pairings makes for a great deal of complexity, as do the strategy choices we have described, the number of pairings also makes for a rich game structure. Within this framework we intend to explore the interactions of nations as they pursue their interests. The framework allows us to go beyond the analysis of conflict to investigate the cooperative, nonconflictual interactions that account for so much of international affairs.

5. All these orderings can arise under any information conditions in the domestic account of the international interaction game. In practice, the endogeneity of demands in the realpolitik version will serve to eliminate many of these orderings under full information conditions.

Table 2.4
Distribution of Outcomes with
Complete Information and Uniformly
Distributed Preferences

Outcome	Frequency	Percentage
SQ	232	8.6
Acq$_B$	824	30.5
Acq$_A$	180	6.7
Nego	1428	52.8
Cap$_B$	0	0
War$_A$	40	1.5
Cap$_A$	0	0
War$_B$	0	0

In this regard it is important to recall that even though the game we propose is noncooperative, the outcomes that can arise in equilibrium can be and often are cooperative. That the game structure is noncooperative does not imply that the decision maker's actions within the game cannot be cooperative. Rather, it merely restates what we have already indicated: decision makers in international relations cannot and do not make binding, strictly enforceable commitments. That states cooperate with one another is quite a natural possibility in this as in other noncooperative games. Indeed, if one assumes that each of the 2,704 admissible combinations of preferences over outcomes is equally likely, that assumption 7b—the domestic variant—is operative and that information is complete, then a negotiated, cooperative settlement of disputes is the maximum likelihood equilibrium outcome in the international interaction game (Rummel 1979, 1981). If one substitutes assumption 7a—the realpolitik variant—then the only possible full information outcomes of the game are negotiation or the status quo. This claim is made more precise and proved in chapter 3. The self-interest of the actors, maximizing their welfare across the play of the game, dictates, in either case, that they try to avoid violent interactions. The distribution of outcomes under the assumption of uniformly distributed preferences, domestically determined goals, and full information is summarized in table 2.4.

Looking at table 2.4, which is based solely on the structure of the game, assumption 7b, and the auxiliary assumptions of full information and uniformly distributed preferences, we can make some interesting observations. A crisis that ends in a capitulation without reciprocated violence must necessarily have involved some misperception of relevant information by at least one key decision maker. The dispute would otherwise have been settled at the precrisis stage. Similarly, if a war is initiated by the state that was not the initiator of the dispute, then some uncertainty about crucial information must have existed, otherwise a different outcome would have arisen. Yet war can be the equilibrium outcome of the game even if everyone preferred to negotiate and even if everyone was fully informed.

International relations are unlikely to occur under circumstances of uniformly distributed preferences. Consequently, table 2.4 is not intended to convey empirical expectations so much as reveal the feasible set of equilibria under full information. In the next chapter, we develop an array of theorems and corollaries regarding the necessary and sufficient conditions for each event of the international interaction game to be a possible equilibrium outcome and explore some perhaps surprising implications of the game under full information.

Chapter 3

Foreign Policy Decisions with Full Information

I know. You know I know. I
know you know I know. We know
Henry knows. And Henry knows
we know it. We're a knowledge-
able family.
—Geoffrey to Eleanor of Aquitaine
The Lion in Winter

In this chapter we pose a number of questions of perennial importance
in the study of international politics and analyze them in the context
of the game of international interactions set out in chapter 2. That the
game structure is elaborate creates an opportunity to address a wide-
ranging set of issues; it also creates more than a little difficulty in
arriving at solutions. In later chapters we address problems that arise
when players do not have perfect information. For now, let us consider
the standpoint of fully informed decision makers who are interacting
with each other. They are both aware of each other's preferences and
of the sequence of actions described by the international interaction
game and their own place in that sequence. In other words, the international interaction game is for them a game of complete and perfect
information.

One of the widely acknowledged benefits of applying the tools of
game theory to various problems in political behavior is its heuristic
value. Game theory often directs our attention to the difficulties, created by the structure of the interactions, that may be encountered in
arriving at certain outcomes. It points to problems of the "you can't
get what you want, no matter how much you may want it" variety.
Even abstractions in the form of full-information games show us that
there are reasons to favor some explanations over others.

Game-theoretic models explicitly represent outcomes as the result of interactive decisions. Players do not choose specific outcomes but rather courses of action. The choice of action in a game—just as in the real world—is based on the courses of action available to the antagonist, taken together with the values the decision makers attach to the outcomes. Thus, playing the game, like reaching decisions, is informed by identifying contingencies, assessing their likelihood, and evaluating their consequences. Game theory reveals the structure of decision making.

In regard to the assumption of perfect information, claims have been made that certain outcomes can occur only when information is imperfect, that the outcomes are somehow a mistake or at least due to imprecise knowledge. The most notable event discussed in this context is war. Perhaps the most succinct statement of this view is offered by John Stoessinger, who says, "On the eve of each war, at least one nation misperceives another's power" (1974, 229).

Stoessinger's confidence in the importance of uncertainty or mis-perception as a fundamental element in all wars is echoed by other prominent theorists. Geoffrey Blainey, for instance, contends that "when nations prepare to fight one another, they have contradictory expectations of the likely duration and outcome of the war" (1973, 246) and that "wars can only occur when two nations decide that they can gain more by fighting than by negotiating" (159). According to Blainey's theory, our assumption 4 from chapter 2 (hereafter 2.A4)—that negotiation is always preferred to war—should guarantee that war can never arise under full-information conditions in the model we set forth, regardless of which version of the game is employed.

In a similar vein, the game-theoretic treatment of the balance of power proposed by Emerson Niou, Peter Ordeshook, and Gregory Rose leads them to conclude that "presently, we can imagine cir-cumstances in which countries are uncertain not merely about the resources of others, but also about what others believe about capa-bilities. . . . Even though we do not consider the strategic imperatives occasioned by this second type of uncertainty, the analysis this volume offers is nevertheless relevant to inferring the consequences of such uncertainty for war. Specifically, a thesis that our analysis supports is that such uncertainty is a necessary condition for war" (1989, 59). Indeed, in the cooperative game they propose, uncertainty is necessary if war is to arise. They do not establish that uncertainty is a universal characteristic of war, however.

After a war has caused great human and material loss, it is only reasonable to look back to the period before the war and identify some agreement between the parties that would have been less costly for both. Seemingly, at least one of the parties must have misunderstood the capabilities or the interests of the opponent. But to say that mis-understandings—or misperceptions—could generate a war is different from saying that misunderstandings are required for war. The distinction here is simply the difference between necessary conditions and sufficient conditions. In this chapter we use a full-information model and arrive at a set of conditions leading to war, thereby contradicting the claims that an outcome of war can occur only if information is incomplete or if fighting is preferred to negotiation. Instead, we show that Blainey, Stoessinger, and others apparently are right that war requires imperfect information if the realpolitik variant of the game is operative in real-world international affairs. If, however, the domestic variant better describes foreign policy decisions in the real world, then war is entirely feasible even under conditions of full information. Later we explore the effect of beliefs and uncertainty on the risk of war. Then we show when mistaken beliefs about a rival increase or decrease the risk of such conflicts under each of the variants of the game.

Although the domestic/constrained version of our game structure permits war under conditions of full information, we do find that some of the events at the terminal nodes are unobtainable for fully informed players even when goals are picked in response to domestic political factors. A war initiated by the player with the second move in the game, *B*, will not occur, nor will either decision maker be forced to capitulate to the use of military force by the other so long as they know how their opponent ranks the outcomes in order of preference. For these events to occur, there must be some degree of miscalculation or misperception according to either version of the international inter-action game.

SOLVING EXTENSIVE FORM GAMES

The solution concept we use in this chapter is that of subgame perfect equilibrium. For a strategy (or complete set of actions at every node of the game) to be an equilibrium, the moves must lead to payoffs that no player could improve on by a unilateral change in behavior. For an equilibrium strategy in a game to be subgame perfect, it must induce an equilibrium in every one of its subgames (Ordeshook 1986). A subgame is formed as a partition of a larger game. A legal subgame begins at one of the nodes of the larger game, includes the subsequent nodes of the game, and is formed without breaking any of the information sets. In the international interaction game of figure 2.1, each node is a complete information set. An example of a subgame, and the game we will use to illustrate the method of solving an extensive form game, is the crisis subgame discussed in chapter 2. In a game of perfect information, the players know at which node they are located when they make a choice. No information sets include more than one node in this game, so the problem of breaking information sets does not arise. We can form subgames of the international interaction game at any node by simply including the rest of the game from that point onward. In subsequent chapters, in contrast, we alter the international interaction game so that information sets can include more than one node. In those cases, we introduce uncertainty into the decision-making problem. There we must take care that these information sets remain intact.

Our first set of results is obtained under the conditions that each player is fully aware of the structure and the payoffs in the game and aware that the other has this knowledge—it is common knowledge. The technique for solving such extensive form games is straightforward. Essentially, the game is solved backward from the endpoints of the game, up through successive subgames, until we arrive at the beginning move of the game. When the solutions to all the subgames are determined the game is solved. The equilibrium strategy is a full description of how the players choose—what action each takes—under each contingency. An equilibrium strategy is one in which the players cannot obtain better outcomes from the game by altering their play. Each player's choice of the action to take at a given choice node is equivalent to a choice of which subgame to play out from that node forward. To make this choice, the player must know the equilibrium outcomes in the subgames and find these equilibria in like manner until all the choices are determined. The basic intuition is that the players are sufficiently farsighted to see their antagonists' responses to their actions and that they, like their antagonists, base their choice of strategies on the anticipated consequences of their choice.[1] An example of a subgame perfect equilibrium should clarify the concepts and the method of solution.

1. When players are uncertain about the responses of other players, the game is played out with imperfect information. In such cases, players hold beliefs, rather than certain knowledge, about how their rivals will respond to alternative actions. These beliefs provide the probabilistic bases for selecting among alternative actions in accordance with the axioms of rationality, as shown in subsequent chapters.

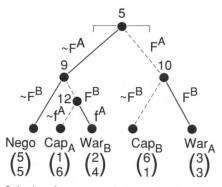

3.1: A subgame perfect equilibrium in the crisis subgame.

In figure 3.1 we have constructed the crisis subgame of our larger international interaction game with hypothetical numerical values supplied as the payoffs to each player at the terminal nodes. The first value listed at the terminal nodes is the payoff to player A from the resulting event; the second value is the payoff to player B. The crisis subgame can be further partitioned into three more subgames: the subgame that follows from node 9, which includes three terminal events, negotiation over the demands, the forced capitulation of A to B's demands, and war initiated by B; the game that follows from node 12, resulting in either a capitulation by A or war initiated by B; and the game that follows from node 10, which ends with either B's capitulation to A or with a war initiated by A. Each partition includes the rest of the game from that node onward, and because each information set includes a single node, we have broken no information sets by partitioning the game in this way. Taken together, the partitions form the crisis subgame. The solution of the game is that both players choose not to fight, resulting in negotiation as the outcome. We arrive at this equilibrium solution by beginning with the subgame at node 12.

Note that the subgames at nodes 12 and 10 are both degenerate subgames in that if the option is ever presented to the player who has the move at each of these nodes, that player can determine the outcome of such simple subgames merely by choosing the action leading to the preferred outcome—which at this point is no longer contingent on any other choices. The question then becomes whether that subgame will ever be reached.

At node 12 the player with the option is A. A would find himself making this choice after being attacked by B and would choose to fight back (F^A) rather than not fight back because of his preferences ($2 > 1$). Fully informed as to A's preferences, B understands A's choice is to fight back and knows that to arrive in this subgame by attacking A is equivalent to obtaining a war that B has initiated. At node 9, B is choosing between fighting and not fighting. B compares the value of the subgame at node 12 to the value of the outcome if she chooses to negotiate ($\bar{F}^B$). In this case, negotiation is preferred by B to a war that she initiates (5 > 4), and the equilibrium outcome of the subgame at node 9 is to negotiate. If node 9 is reached, we know the outcome. The question is, does A begin the crisis subgame by offering to negotiate such that node 9 will be reached? This depends on the strategy chosen by A at the beginning of the crisis. If A forgoes fighting, B will also forgo fighting and A will have the negotiation. Is $\bar{F}^A$ a rational choice for A? After all, A prefers a capitulation by B to negotiation (6 > 5), even though negotiation is preferred to War$_A$ (5 > 3). A knows, however, that B, preferring to fight back if attacked (3 > 1), will not capitulate in the subgame at node 10. Therefore, A will initiate the play of this crisis game by choosing not to use force, and B will respond by not using force.

In this hypothetical example both parties base their strategic choices on their own preferences, their full understanding of the game, and their complete knowledge of their opponent's preferences. Equipped with this information, they are able to reach a Pareto-superior outcome and to avoid turning down violent paths. Other equilibria are possible, given different preference orderings of the outcomes. What we have illustrated here is the method of solving full-information extensive form games. Now let us inject just a bit of uncertainty into our example. Suppose that we have the same game with the exception that at node 10, A is uncertain whether B will capitulate to an attack or retaliate. Let us say, for the sake of illustration, that A estimates that B will choose to capitulate. Then, A, preferring a capitulation by B over negotiation, chooses to fight. B fights back on the basis of its true preferences, and a war initiated by A ensues, a war that A would have avoided by negotiating had A understood that B would retaliate. In chapter 6 we discuss the background to the outbreak of the Sino-Indian War of 1962 and show how that conflict fit conditions very similar to those in this hypothetical example.

It is often stated, and has taken on the aura of folk wisdom, that in the interactions of nations desiring to negotiate their differences rather than wage war over them, some form of uncertainty (perhaps like the uncertainty in the present example) is required in order to have war. Is uncertainty always necessary for wars to occur between adversaries? Is the mutually acknowledged existence of some negotiated outcome that is superior to such horribly costly events as war sufficient to maintain peaceful relations? If uncertainties ensnare nations, can we describe more precisely what the uncertainties are and where they reside? The answers to these questions are critically dependent on whether we assume that the realpolitik or the domestic version of the game is operative. We begin with the realpolitik variant and inquire as to what the necessary and sufficient conditions are with full information for each possible outcome to result from an equilibrium strategy of the game.

REALPOLITIK EQUILIBRIA WITH PERFECT INFORMATION

In the realpolitik interpretation of international interactions, demands are selected to maximize expected utility within the game, without regard for external pressures to make alternative demands. The magnitude of any demand is, therefore, endogenous to the structure of the game. This means that demands, like actions, are chosen on the basis of a backward induction starting at the end of the game and working up to the very first move. Actor A will make a demand only if doing so yields a higher expected utility at the end of the game than is anticipated if no demand is made. And if A makes a demand, B will make a counterdemand only if doing so produces a higher expected utility than acquiescing. Looking down the game tree, we can determine the size of any demands made by A and B if they are fully informed and if the realpolitik version of the game is germane.[2]

If A makes a demand, how large will it be? A knows that for B, the expected utility from a negotiation is superior to acquiescence to A. Therefore, A knows that if B can steer A toward negotiation, then there must be a counterdemand for B that yields B greater expected utility than will result from acquiescence. Both A and B have an interest in steering one another toward a terminal node that maximizes the expected utility for the relevant actor. As we will see, B can maneuver to encourage A to negotiate if A makes an initial demand. In such a case, A typically—though not always—is in a position that encourages it to make a very large initial demand, larger than A can hope to realize through negotiation.

Because A knows that a fully informed B always has a counterdemand that improves B's welfare relative to acquiescing, A can anticipate that the crisis subgame that starts at node 5 will be reached if A

2. We assume that once a demand is made, it is of fixed magnitude for the duration of the game, although A and B are each prepared to settle for less than their demand at the negotiation stage.

makes a demand. If A makes a demand, then, it must pick one that maximizes its expected utility in the crisis subgame. By the assumptions we have already stated, it is common knowledge that the best that can happen to A in the crisis subgame is either a negotiated resolution of the dispute or a capitulation by B: A will pursue the attainment of one of these outcomes if A makes a demand. B strictly prefers a negotiated settlement to a situation in which it is compelled to capitulate to A.[3] Therefore, B's counterdemand will be chosen to ensure that A's utility for negotiation is just larger than its utility for compelling B to capitulate. This relative weighting assures B that A will not choose to use force, provided B has correctly sized its counterdemand. Given that A realizes B's concerns, A must pick a demand that will lead B to choose negotiation over the use of force if A makes a demand and offers to negotiate. What do these various restrictions look like, and how do their feasible combinations affect the possible equilibria for the realpolitik variant of the game? We answer these questions by stating and proving the first realpolitik proposition that results under full-information conditions in the international interaction game.[4]

REALPOLITIK PROPOSITION 3.1: THE NEGOTIATION/STATUS QUO THEOREM. *Under full-information conditions and with demands being endogenous to the international interaction game, only negotiation or the status quo can be an equilibrium outcome of the realpolitik variant of the game.*

Proof. The proof follows in terms of the various cases that are possible because of particular constraints on the policymakers.

We begin by considering the outcomes that are possible on the left

---

3. Strict preference rules out the possibility of indifference between two alternatives. A weakly preferred option is at least as good as the other alternative (and so satisfies the relation $\geq$), whereas a strictly preferred choice is better than the alternative (and so satisfies the relation $>$). When we say preferred, we mean strictly preferred unless otherwise noted.

4. Realist theorists do not assume full information, and so some may believe that a full-information evaluation of realism is inappropriate. However, the full-information analysis provides a benchmark against which we can begin to form expectations with regard to imperfect information. Indeed, of the three key propositions we deduce here regarding the realpolitik variant of the game, the second is shown to hold logically under any information conditions, and the third is shown to indicate the necessity of imperfect information of a particular kind in order for war to arise. Thus, the full-information investigation highlights some important ways in which behavior within the realist or neorealist perspective depends on uncertainty.

side of the tree. To reach the left side of the tree, A must prefer not making a demand to making a demand. If, as the proposition asserts, negotiation is the only possible outcome on the right side of the game, then $\bar{D}^A$ is possible only if an outcome superior to negotiation can arise for A by not making a demand. The assumptions delineated in chapter 2 restrict the payoffs associated with the terminal nodes of the game such that only three outcomes on the left can be superior for A to negotiation on the right. These are the status quo, a capitulation by B, or the negotiation on the left. Only a capitulation by B is inconsistent with the proposition, but this outcome cannot arise because B always prefers the status quo to capitulating. B, then, can prevent having to capitulate simply by not making a demand on the left side of the tree. In that way, the status quo will prevail. If we can prove that negotiation is the only outcome that can arise on the right, then we will have proved that A can choose not to make a demand only if the full-information outcome on the left is also negotiation or the status quo.

In the realpolitik version of the game, some incentives regarding the structure of demands hold under all circumstances, so we can say that under all circumstances one or another actor will be guided in the selection of demands by that incentive. Other incentives with regard to the magnitude of a demand are contingent on specific conditions, which we describe as alternative cases. The proof proceeds by going through each possible case one at a time. But first we note that if A makes a demand, B always has an incentive to select D^B such that for A, Nego $\geq$ Cap$_B$. This is true because negotiation is strictly preferred by B to having to acquiesce or capitulate. Therefore, B wants to steer A away from initiating the use of force, for it considers both outcomes that follow from F^A inferior to negotiation. By acting on this incentive, B ensures that A does not seek a capitulation rather than a negotiated settlement. B, as a realist, must pick a demand such that

$$U^A(\Delta_B) \geq U^A(\Delta_A) - \frac{\phi_A P^A}{1 - P^A}. \tag{3.1}$$

B can always meet these conditions, regardless of A's demand. Expression (3.1) stipulates simply that B cannot pick just any demand but rather is constrained to choose one that falls within the interval $U^A(\Delta_A)$ to $U^A(\Delta_A) - (\phi_A P^A)/(1 - P^A)$, an interval that is always available to B. B's particular incentive to maximize its own welfare dictates that B's demand be arbitrarily close to the right-hand side of expression (3.1) so that A will choose to negotiate and B will have made the largest demand it can consistent with its constraints. Similarly, if the left side of the game is reached and B makes a demand, A can always make a counterdemand such that $U^B(\text{Nego}) \geq U^B(\text{Cap}_A)$. Likewise, on the right side of the game, A can always (but need not) make an initial demand such that $U^B(\text{Nego}) \geq U^B(\text{Cap}_A)$. To meet these conditions requires that A makes a demand such that

$$U^B(\Delta_A) \geq U^B(\Delta_B) - \frac{\phi_B P^B}{(1 - P^B)} \, . \tag{3.2}$$

Case 1. Assume A can select D^A such that for A, War$_B$ is at least as good as or preferred to Cap$_A$. This condition requires that

$$U^A(\Delta_A) \geq U^A(\Delta_B) + \frac{(\tau_A - \gamma_A)(1 - P^A)}{P^A} + . \phi_A. \tag{3.3}$$

When the terms in (3.3) are satisfied, a particular backward induction on the right side of the game tree follows. If node 12 of the game is reached, A chooses to retaliate. At node 9, B must therefore choose $\tilde{F}^B$, for this is strictly preferred to War$_B$ according to assumption 2.A4. Whichever choice B makes if node 10 is reached, A prefers to select $\tilde{F}^A$ at node 5. We know this because B has chosen D^B to ensure that $U^A(\text{Nego}) > U^A(\text{Cap}_B)$, and A always prefers negotiation to initiating war. Because reaching node 5 implies the choices $\tilde{F}^A$, $\tilde{F}^B$, we know that B will make a demand at node 3, for B prefers negotiation to acquiescence to A. Thus, if A makes a demand, the equilibrium is D^A, D^B, $\tilde{F}^A$, $\tilde{F}^B \to$ Nego. If A does not make a demand, A must prefer either the status quo or negotiation on the left side of the tree.[5] Therefore, the only equilibrium outcomes that are possible are negotiation or the status quo.

Case 2. Assume that the conditions of expression (3.3) cannot be met. Before proceeding with the proof, we pause to note the circumstances that would preclude satisfying (3.3).

Expression (3.1) provides the minimum value that A associates with B's demand. This, combined with expression (3.3), gives us

5. We conjecture, but do not prove here, that A is always better off in a negotiation that it initiated on the right side of the tree than a negotiation initiated by B's demand on the left side of the tree. We believe this is so because of the constraint imposed by expression (3.2). When A makes an initial demand, the magnitude of the demand generally is unconstrained, whereas when it makes a counterdemand, the magnitude of the objective that is sought is constrained to fall within a specified interval.

$$U^A(\Delta_A) \geq U^A(\Delta_A) - \frac{\phi_A P^A}{1 - P^A} + \frac{(\tau_A - \gamma_A)(1 - P^A)}{P^A} + \phi_A. \tag{3.4}$$

Expression (3.4) tells us whether A can make a demand that convinces B to respond by negotiating if A offers to negotiate. We note that $U^A(\Delta_A)$ appears on the left and right sides of (3.4) so that the terms cancel out. This mutual annulment means that whether A has a credible retaliatory threat does not hinge on the value of the prospective gain per se. Rather, A's ability to threaten credibly that $F^B \to f^A$ requires that the right side of the inequality in (3.4) be greater than or equal to zero. We solve (3.4) in terms of P^A to determine the conditions under which A satisfies the incentive expressed in (3.2) and so makes a demand accompanied by a credible threat of retaliation if B tries to exploit A:

$$\frac{P^A(2P^A - 1)}{(1 - P^A)^2} \geq \frac{\tau_A - \gamma^A}{\phi_A}. \tag{3.5}$$

If the inequality in (3.5) is not met (and we discuss the conditions under which it is not met later), then $U^A(Cap_A) > U^A(War_B)$.

Assume B is prepared to retaliate if A uses force. Then, on the right side of the game, $\bar{F}^A \to Cap_A$ or Nego (whichever is preferred by B), and $F^A \to War_A$. On the left side of the game, if A does not make a demand and B does, then by (3.2), A selects a counterdemand that ensures that B prefers to negotiate rather than compel A to capitulate. If B is prepared to retaliate whenever A uses force, then B can be certain to avoid exploitation by A because A will respond to $\bar{F}^B$ by negotiating. Negotiation on the left side of the game will then be the outcome unless B prefers the status quo, in which case the status quo will result. Thus, the two possible equilibria if $U^B(Cap_A) > U^B(Nego)$ under case 2 are $\bar{D}^A$, $\bar{D}^B \to SQ$, and $\bar{D}^A$, D^B, d^A, $\bar{F}^B$, $\bar{F}^A \to$ Nego. If B prefers a negotiated settlement to a capitulation by A, then another possible equilibrium is D^A, D^B, $\bar{F}^A$, $\bar{F}^B \to$ Nego.

Case 3. Assume the conditions of expression (3.3) cannot be satisfied. Assume that B is not prepared to retaliate if attacked. Then $F^A \to Cap_B$, and $\bar{F}^A$ implies Cap_A or Nego, whichever B chooses. If B prefers negotiation to a capitulation by A, then (3.1) is sufficient to guarantee that A will opt to negotiate rather than accept the inferior outcome associated with compelling B to capitulate. But if B prefers a capitulation by A to a negotiation, then D^A, $D^B \to (F^A, \bar{F}^B)$, which is inferior for both A and B to a negotiation. The problem is that A cannot risk exploitation by B. However, A can avoid this problem by choosing its initial demand to satisfy (3.2) on the right side of the tree. A constrains its demand on the right side of the tree only if case 3 arises and A prefers a negotiated settlement on the right of the game to negotiation or the status quo on the left of the tree. With B choosing its counterdemand to satisfy (3.1) and A selecting its initial demand to satisfy (3.2), the equilibrium outcome is negotiation if that is preferred by A to the status quo or negotiation on the other side of the game.

These three cases are exhaustive and so complete the proof. QED

The first realpolitik proposition suggests a very stable world under full-information conditions. Only negotiation or the status quo prevails. These implications are similar, though not identical, to the system-stability and resource-instability results derived by Niou, Ordeshook, and Rose (1989). In our realpolitik game, resources or valued goods can be exchanged through negotiation, or the system can remain fixed through maintenance of the status quo, but other outcomes are precluded under full-information conditions. The proposition suggests several possible empirical tests. Using the measurement procedures described in detail in appendix 1, we now describe these tests and report the results.

According to realpolitik proposition 3.1, only negotiation or the status quo can be the outcome of an international interaction if demands are endogenous to the international context and there is full information. The proposition implies that, on average, as uncertainty diminishes, the likelihood of negotiation or the status quo increases if the realpolitik variant of the game is an accurate description of behavior. The first test, then, compares the frequency of negotiation or status quo outcomes to the degree of uncertainty in the international environment. Figure 3.2 depicts the association between this frequency and our measure of uncertainty, which is defined in appendix 1. For purposes of the figure, the uncertainty variable has been divided into four quartiles, from most information (that is, least uncertainty) to least information. The figure is accompanied by a logit analysis in which the dependent variable is coded as 1.0 if the outcome is the status quo or a negotiation and as zero otherwise. We call this dependent variable Nego/SQ. The independent variable again is Uncertainty. The expectation for the figure and for the logit analysis is that Uncertainty is inversely associated with the dependent variable.[6] Yet both

6. Strictly speaking, the theory does not require a monotonic decline in the likelihood of negotiation or the status quo as uncertainty increases but rather that, on average, the likelihood of negotiation or the status quo is lower with any degree

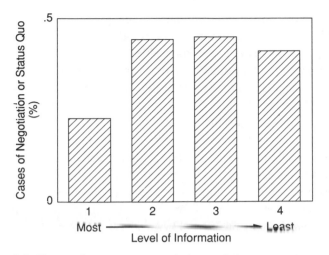

3.2: Uncertainty versus negotiation and the status quo.

results show that this is not the case. The weak association between Nego/SQ and Uncertainty is positive, indicating that there is some tendency for the incidence of the predicted outcomes to rise rather than fall as uncertainty increases.[7] In the logit analysis, then, Nego/SQ $= -.660 + 0.806$ Uncertainty, $\chi^2 = 1.69$, $P \le .193$, and $N = 686$.

An alternative measure of uncertainty was also investigated to evaluate the stability of this and other results reported below. Here, we estimated A's perception of uncertainty as the product of $P^A \times (1 - P^A)$. A comparable indicator was constructed to evaluate B's subjective estimate of uncertainty. The notion is that as A's or B's chance for success approaches .5, the expected outcome becomes increasingly uncertain. With a larger probability of success, the relevant actor can be fairly confident of attaining the desired goals. With a smaller probability of success, the relevant actor can be fairly confident of failure. At .5, the relevant actor's uncertainty is maximized.

These two subjective estimates represent measures of uncertainty

---

of uncertainty than without. In reality, of course, it is unlikely that uncertainty is ever completely absent, making such a test impossible to conduct.

7. Alternative operational definitions of negotiation or of acquiescence are possible. We have reanalyzed all acquiescence or negotiation related propositions using alternative definitions. The results are strongly robust. Coefficients that were significant with one specification remain significant with other specifications, with signs and the magnitude of coefficients remaining the same. Coefficients that were not significant remain insignificant. Consequently we report results only using the operational procedures detailed in appendix 1, but we remind the reader that our results hold across alternative specifications of negotiated or acquiescent outcomes.

that are independent of the variable we call Uncertainty. The correlation between A's subjective estimate and our other indicator, Uncertainty, is only .07 (N = 686). The comparable correlation between B's subjective estimate of uncertainty and our variable, Uncertainty, is .09 (N = 686). The correlation between the two subjective indicators themselves is .49 (N = 686). Substituting either or both of these subjective indicators for the variable Uncertainty in the above logit analysis yields essentially the same results. The relevant logit analyses are not statistically significant, and the coefficients are generally in the wrong direction from the (neo)realist perspective. The failure of the first realpolitik proposition is sustained if we restrict the test to just those cases in which the stakes at risk are very high, that is, to the cases in which the realist focus on external considerations is probably most germane.

The failure across the alternative specifications to find support for the realist hypothesis calls into question the realpolitik version of the game. Nego/SQ should always be satisfied when information is complete and perfect, with the likelihood of mistakenly arriving at some other outcome generally increasing as imperfect information leads to the mistaken selection of demands and counterdemands. Yet this is not what has been observed.

A second set of tests is also implied by proposition 3.1. Regardless of which case in our proof holds, expression (3.1) must be satisfied according to proposition 3.1 if A makes an initial demand. That is, under all such circumstances, B picks its counterdemand to ensure that A prefers negotiating rather than compelling B to capitulate. As B becomes uncertain about critical features of A's decision calculus, B is more and more likely to fail to induce $U^A(\text{Nego}) > U^A(\text{Cap}_B)$ by making a mistake in selecting its demand. Therefore, if the realpolitik variant of the game is correct, we should expect the satisfaction of (3.1) to be inversely related to Uncertainty. This hypothesis is tested in figure 3.3 and in an additional logit analysis. The dependent variable, called Exp (3.1), is coded as 1.0 if $U^A(\text{Nego}) > U^A(\text{Cap}_B)$ and is coded as zero otherwise. The test is performed only on that subset of cases that remains on the right side of the tree, for expression (3.1) is germane only in those cases: Exp (3.1) = −3.298 + 3.745 Uncertainty, $\chi^2 = 8.65$, P ≤ .004, and N = 448.

Figure 3.3 and the logit analysis both reveal a highly significant association between the degree of information in the international environment and the propensity for expression (3.1) to be satisfied. However, the relationship is in the opposite direction of that predicted by the realpolitik version of the international interaction game. On the

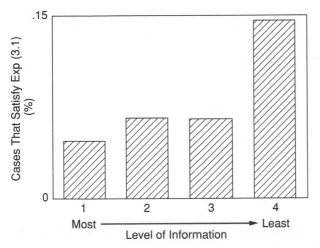

3.3: Uncertainty and the probability of a counterdemand by B.

strength of these and the previous tests, we must conclude that realpolitik proposition 3.1 is not supported by the evidence. The validity
of this variant of the game appears to be in serious doubt.

WAR, ACQUIESCENCE, AND THE REALPOLITIK VARIANT

Perhaps the doubts cast on the realpolitik version of the game are
offset by successful predictions about behaviors other than negotiation
or the status quo. In this section we turn to two additional propositions
implied by the development of proposition 3.1. These pertain to acquiescence by actors A or B and to certain characteristics of war. We
state the following two additional realpolitik propositions:

REALPOLITIK ACQUIESCENCE IMPOSSIBILITY PROPOSITION 3.2: *If demands
are endogenous to the international context of the international interaction game, then regardless of information conditions, neither A nor
B ever acquiesces.*

Proof. In proposition 3.1 we showed that for any demand made by
A, B has a counterdemand such that $U^A(\text{Nego}) > U^A(\text{Cap}_B)$, and for
any demand made by B, A has a counterdemand such that $U^B(\text{Nego}) >
U^B(\text{Cap}_A)$. Regardless of A's or B's belief about the other player, there
is always a counterdemand that B or A thinks satisfies the conditions
of (3.1) or (3.2), respectively. Therefore, when confronted with an
initial demand, each actor believes it has an appropriate counter-

demand that will induce negotiation. *B* strictly prefers to negotiate rather than acquiesce to *A* just as *A* strictly prefers to negotiate rather than acquiesce to *B*. Therefore, under the realpolitik variant in which demands are endogenous to the international setting, neither *A* nor *B* ever has an incentive to acquiesce to the rival. QED

This implication of the realpolitik version of the game, like the implications of proposition 3.1, does not withstand empirical scrutiny. Of the 707 observations in our data set, 101 represent acquiescence by *B,* and 8 acquiescence by *A*. As these conditions can never arise under the realpolitik variant of the game, regardless of uncertainty or misperception, the existence of 109 such cases is strong evidence that the realist version of the game structure proposed here is empirically mistaken. Indeed, this is particularly strong evidence because the (neo)realist, structuralist perspective implies that acquiescence is impossible under any and all circumstances of the game. Thus, the only way to explain the incidence of even one acquiescence is that such cases are miscoded. All 109 cases would have to have been in actuality some other terminal event of the game. Indeed, if we apply a more stringent definition of acquiescence than that proposed in appendix 1—so that *A* or *B* do not counter in any way when *B* or *A* makes a demand of the highest level short of using force—we still observe seventy ostensibly impossible events.

REALPOLITIK WAR PROPOSITION 3.3. *If* $\tau_B \geq \gamma_B$, *then* $P^B \geq .5$ *is necessary but not sufficient for War$_A$ to arise as the equilibrium outcome in the realpolitik version of the game.*[8]

Proof. *A* always believes that it has picked a demand such that $U^B(\text{Nego}) \geq U^B(\text{Cap}_A)$. If *A* believes that $U^B(\text{War}_A) \geq U^B(\text{Cap}_B)$, then it always prefers $\tilde{F}^A$ to F^A. Therefore, in choosing between $\tilde{F}^A$ and F^A, F^A is only possible if *A* believes that *B* mistakenly failed to satisfy expression (3.1) in its counterdemand. In that case, $U^A(\text{Cap}_B) > U^A(\text{Nego})$. For war to arise, *A* must mistakenly believe that *B* prefers to capitulate rather than retaliate when faced with F^A, whereas $U^B(\text{War}_A) > U^B(\text{Cap}_B)$. If we substitute the right-hand side of (3.2) for

8. Although our assumptions do not require that $\tau_B \geq \gamma_B$, we believe that this is the typical circumstance. This condition states that the expected costs in lost life, credibility, and property from sustaining an unreciprocated first strike are generally smaller than or equal to the same costs associated with absorbing a first strike and then fighting back.

$U^B(\Delta_A)$, then $U^B(War_A) \geq U^B(Cap_B)$ is necessary for War_A to be the equilibrium outcome. This implies

$$\frac{P^B(2P^B - 1)}{(1 - p^B)^2} \geq \frac{\tau_B - \gamma_B}{\phi_B} . \tag{3.6}$$

Given that $\tau_B \geq \gamma_B$, as assumed in the proposition, then the right side of (3.6) is not negative. The left side is not negative only if $2P^B \geq 1$, which means that $P^B \geq .5$. This is necessary but not sufficient for war because not only must the left side be nonnegative, but it also must be as large or larger than the right side. Thus, under the stipulated conditions of the proposition, $P^B = .5$ is the minimal value for P^B under which it is possible to satisfy the conditions of expression (3.6). QED

Proposition 3.3, and a companion condition for War_B that follows from expression (3.5), replicates a well-known realpolitik hypothesis: a perceived balance of power (or the misperception that one's own side is weaker than the rival's) tends to promote peace, whereas war tends to follow when each side to a dispute believes its chances for success are greater than fifty-fifty. Indeed, we alluded earlier in this chapter to a proposition put forward by Blainey (1973) that is almost identical to our realpolitik proposition 3.3. That we have deduced this hypothesis from the realpolitik variant of the game encourages us to believe that we have captured central features of the realist or neo-realist perspectives. We are particularly heartened by the realization that the specific realist threshold value for the relative power of the competing sides—.5—is derived from the game despite our making no obvious assumptions that focus on this number. Although we will have occasion to investigate this central realist claim at much greater length in chapter 6, here we provide a preliminary test of the hypothesis.

We define two dependent variables, WAR and BIGWAR, to be all of those instances of reciprocated European-state-directed violence that involved at least some fatalities during the years 1816–1970 or that satisfied the Singer and Small criteria for an interstate war. WAR, then, includes events that do not meet the commonly used Correlates of War Project fatality threshold of at least one thousand killed, whereas BIGWAR does satisfy this criterion. Using the operational definitions of WAR and BIGWAR set out in appendix 1, we display in tables 3.1 and 3.2 simple cross-tabulations of the incidence of war in relation to the frequency with which P^B is or is not greater than or equal to .5. If proposition 3.3 is supported empirically, then all (or

Table 3.1
WAR and P^B

WAR	$P^B \geq .5$	$P^B < .5$
No	290	228
Yes	107	82

χ^2	.022
$P \leq$	.881
Yule's Q	-0.013^*

*Not significant. Unless otherwise noted in the text, significance levels are assessed using one-tailed tests.

Table 3.2
BIGWAR and P^B

BIGWAR	$P^B \geq .5$	$P^B < .5$
No	345	273
Yes	52	37

χ^2	.214
$P \leq$	.644
Yule's Q	-0.053^*

*Not significant.

nearly all, given measurement error) cases that became wars should have arisen when $P^B \geq .5$, although meeting this requirement does not preclude the possibility of an outcome other than war.[9]

Neither table reflects a significant association, measured in terms of Yule's Q (a measure of necessary but not sufficient conditions) or χ^2. What is more, several other tests were also performed, focusing on subsets of the data in which the disputes involved higher and higher stakes. The realist propositions failed to find support no matter how stringent the criteria were for including or excluding cases. As in Bueno de Mesquita and Lalman (1988), the evidence here strongly suggests that the generic features of realism—that demands and inter-

9. As appendix 1 details, we are able to observe War$_A$ with our data set but not War$_B$.

national interactions are shaped primarily by external, structural features of the international system—are not a reliable representation of international affairs.

We have deduced three critical realist propositions and failed to find support for any of them. Perhaps the general structure of the international interaction game is not a useful vehicle for investigating international affairs. Or perhaps the realpolitik variant of the game, with its reliance on the assumption that demands are endogenous to the international setting, does not capture an essential feature of reality. If the former explanation is correct then the domestic variant of the game will also fail to produce propositions that prove empirically reliable. If the latter explanation is correct and the domestic/constrained assumption that foreign policy demands are endogenous to the domestic political setting to a significant degree is correct, then we should expect to find strong empirical support for that version of the game. We turn now to the central full-information propositions of the international interaction game in its domestic version.

DOMESTIC EQUILIBRIA WITH PERFECT INFORMATION

War

Our first domestic politics proposition states that war is a possible equilibrium outcome of our game of international interactions (figure 2.1), even under the restrictions placed on the preference orders described in chapter 2. If war is never a full-information equilibrium outcome, as in the realpolitik version, we might reasonably ask whether its absence is due to the structure of the game or to the restrictions we have imposed on the preferences of the players. The presence of war as an equilibrium behavior indicates that we have not begged the question as to whether war is a possible culminating event arrived at through a sequence of rational choices. Furthermore, in finding the necessary and sufficient conditions for war, we do not find that any lack of information is required as to the choices available to the players or their preferences. Misperceptions by the players are neither necessary nor sufficient for war to occur in the domestic version of the game. This conclusion directly contradicts a finding of the realpolitik variant, thereby facilitating the possibility of one or more severe tests. What is more, we can see from the conditions for war in the domestic interpretation of the game that the equilibrium is not optimal in that both players prefer to negotiate, but they are not able to.

This is an unpleasant finding. The players do not find themselves in war because they are confused or misinformed—the equilibrium conditions are obtained with complete and perfect information. Each player knows the options and the intentions of the opponent exactly. War need not be a mistake in this sense. Also, the war is not due to warmongering. The players are not particularly bloodthirsty, they both prefer to negotiate their differences rather than settle them on the battlefield, and they both are aware that the opponent holds a similar desire to resolve their differences peacefully. The search for ways to avoid suboptimal outcomes, in this case the search for ways to avoid "unnecessary" war, seems more difficult than we thought. Let us state our proposition more precisely and prove it before returning to speculate about the significance of the result.

DOMESTIC PROPOSITION 3.1: BASIC WAR THEOREM. *With perfect information, War_A is a pure strategy equilibrium outcome if and only if we add to the restrictions on the preference orders delineated in chapter 2 (including 2.A7b but not 2.A7a) that for A, $Cap_A > War_B$, $War_A > Acq_A$, and for B, $Cap_A > Negotiate$, $War_A > Acq_B$.*

Proof. To show that the restrictions we have laid out are necessary and sufficient for a subgame perfect equilibrium of war, we first show that the conditions are sufficient to induce war. We then demonstrate their necessity by showing that removing any of the conditions results in an equilibrium outcome other than war.

The subgame at node 10 is equivalent to a choice by B between Cap_B and War_A. As implied in domestic proposition 3.1 (for B, $War_A > Acq_B \rightarrow War_A > Cap_B$), B prefers to fight a war initiated by A rather than to capitulate ($War_A > Cap_B$), hence B's strategic choice is to strike back, F^B. At node 12, A's choice is between capitulating to B's use of force and waging a war initiated by B. According to the conditions of the proposition, A prefers to capitulate, and hence the equilibrium strategy at node 12 is $\bar{f}^A$. B would certainly like to take advantage of A's unwillingness to retaliate, and B prefers a capitulation by A to the anticipated results from negotiating ($Cap_A > Nego$). Therefore B's equilibrium strategy at node 9 is F^B. A's choice at the beginning of the crisis subgame at node 5 compares the equilibrium outcomes of the subgame at node 9 (Cap_A) to the equilibrium outcome of the subgame at node 10 (War_A). In preferring War_A to Cap_A, A's equilibrium strategy is F^A, and the equilibrium outcome to the crisis subgame is War_A.

Is the crisis subgame at node 5 itself in equilibrium? After all, there is the crisis subgame at node 6, and there are strategy sets that avoid military crises. The nodes terminating at acquiescence (by A or by B) and the status quo are all outcomes where crises are avoided. B values acquiescing less than fighting a war initiated by A ($War_A > Acq_B$); at node 3, B's strategy is to counter A's demand with a demand of its own (D^B). Once A has started the game by making a demand (D^A), we are led to the equilibrium outcome of War_A. Is D^A part of the equilibrium strategy? Which subgame does A prefer to play out from node 1? To determine A's choice, we find the equilibrium outcome to the subgame at node 2 and compare it in terms of A's preferences to War_A, the outcome to the subgame at node 3.

A is not the type to fight back if attacked. At node 8, A prefers Cap_A to War_B. At node 11, B prefers War_A to Cap_B, so at node 7, A compares War_A to negotiating. Given A's preferences, the equilibrium strategy is $\bar{F}^A$, and the outcome is negotiation, suggesting a ray of hope for peace. Alas, at node 6, B, knowing that A is unwilling to retaliate at node 8, can seize the advantage by using force first and compelling A to capitulate. B prefers Cap_A to negotiating, and the equilibrium outcome to the crisis subgame at node 6 is Cap_A. A prefers to avoid capitulating by acquiescing ($Acq_A > Cap_A$) and has the opportunity to do so at node 4 by choosing the $\tilde{d}^A$ strategy. At node 2, B prefers Acq_A to the status quo and chooses the D^B strategy. The equilibrium outcome to the subgame at node 2 is Acq_A. A prefers the subgame to the right over the subgame to the left on the basis of the equilibrium outcomes ($War_A > Acq_A$ for A). Using the conditions set out in proposition 3.1, we see that they are sufficient to produce War_A as the outcome.

Are the conditions necessary for war as an outcome? If they are not necessary, dropping them will not alter the outcome, but as we will see, dropping any of the additional restrictions we have made does alter the outcome. Note that changing a strict preference to a weak preference on the part of one player induces a mixed strategy rather than a pure strategy for the other. We will now reverse the strict preference conditions in the proposition.

If A prefers War_B to Cap_A at node 12, then B chooses $\bar{F}^B$ at node 9, preferring to negotiate rather than initiate a war ($Nego > War_B$). By assumption 2.A4, A, too, prefers negotiation to initiating war. At node 5, A therefore chooses $\bar{F}^A$, and the outcome is altered. Suppose that A's other preference is reversed such that $Acq_A > War_A$. If the equilibrium to the subgame at node 6 is War_A, A's choice at node 4 is to acquiesce. If the equilibrium at node 3 is War_A, A's preference upsets the equilibrium. By choosing $\bar{D}^A$, A can ensure at least its own acquiescence, which it prefers to initiating war.

What about B's preferences? If it prefers negotiation to a capitulation by A, then at node 9, B chooses $\bar{F}^B$, and at node 5, A can avoid war by choosing $\bar{F}^A$, for negotiation is preferred to war. Now let B prefer Acq_B to War_A. Even if the equilibrium outcome at node 5 is War_A, B can avoid it at node 3 by acquiescing to A's demand. No matter what the equilibrium at node 2 may be, Acq_B is superior to it for A. Thus War_A does not remain as the outcome if we alter B's preferences. QED

This demonstration highlights several features of the game. When we identified the pure strategy equilibrium conditions for a war initiated by A, we used full information. The players know the other player's preferences and use that knowledge to assess the consequences of the actions they choose. Misperceptions of an adversary's intentions or available options are not necessary to obtain war in equilibrium. The puzzle of wars between nations is not simple. It is not necessarily escapable by merely finding mechanisms to reveal to the players the precise values held by their antagonists. We have interpreted the concept of misperception as a mistaken belief about the intentions of other decision makers. Here we can at least see that such mistaken beliefs need not reside within this game structure in order to obtain war in equilibrium. The mistaken beliefs could reside in some super game of which our already fairly large game is only a part (one like the domestic political game that produces a choice of national foreign policy objectives). That is, some larger game containing our structure as a subgame will not produce war as an equilibrium, because the players will not desire to play out a subgame resulting in war. In this case, perhaps misperceptions would be required to obtain war. But notice that such misperceptions as these are becoming remote from the event, and we are stretching the notion of misperceptions quite far. We can also see, on the basis of domestic proposition 3.1, that the restrictions on preferences we set out in chapter 2 are not overly restrictive in that they rule out war. Should we wish to retain the notion that misperceptions are necessary for war, we will need more restrictive assumptions, not less. In particular, making the realist assumption that demands are endogenous to the international setting is sufficient to rule out war as a full-information equilibrium outcome of the game structure we have proposed.

War initiated by A is not, as we mentioned above, something that either player wants. Both players prefer negotiating to waging war, but they cannot always get what they want: Even if both players prefer the status quo to War$_A$, we would still arrive at war under the conditions of domestic proposition 3.1, for the players' preferences with respect to the status quo and a war initiated by A are not part of the argument. So the decision makers could face each other in a situation where each values the two peaceful outcomes of the status quo or a negotiated settlement to War$_A$ and nonetheless obtain War$_A$. We return to this observation in several subsequent chapters.

Consider further the preferences of the decision makers in order to see whether their preferences are intuitively reasonable. Is it difficult to imagine national leaders holding such preferences? Let us begin with A, the party initiating the war. Although A is unwilling to acquiesce rather than fight a war it initiates and is not so pacifistic as to forswear all violence (War$_A$ > Acq$_A$), A is also unwilling or unprepared to retaliate against an initial use of force by B (Cap$_A$ > War$_B$) and fight a war on B's terms. Nation A, however, is confronted by an adversary who holds something like a first-strike advantage in that if B uses force first, A will capitulate. In equilibrium and with full information such an A would never actually capitulate, for it can choose actions that preclude the need to give in peremptorily to B during the crisis subgame. B, while desirous of negotiating, prefers to take advantage of the opponent and force a capitulation by A if given the chance.

What we have here is a failure by A to deter. A's inability or unwillingness to resist the initial use of force by B gives B an incentive to initiate force. A would do well to remember Vilfredo Pareto's admonition: "The efforts of men are utilized in two different ways: they are directed to the production or transformation of economic goods, or else to the appropriation of goods produced by others."

Should B not be the type that would capitalize on a capitulation by A, then A need not fear B's actions. But there are many potential opponents with different value systems. There are those who would exploit the opportunity to appropriate another's goods. From an Arab perspective, this ordering of preferences may be a reasonable characterization of relations between and expectations by the Arab states and Israel. Negotiation is difficult to attain because the Arab states fear exploitive reactions by Israel if they offer to negotiate. They are ill prepared to retaliate effectively if attacked by the Israelis' superior air and ground forces. Thus they live much of the time uncomfortably with the status quo, tacitly acquiescing to Israel's existence, or they strike first, seeking whatever advantage can be gained from seizing the initiative.

Domestic proposition 3.1 raises a troubling and, to some, surprising observation about international relations. This first result of the domestic variant of the international interaction game, however, may be a mere quirk of the structure we propose, rather than a germane feature of international affairs. As one of us noted elsewhere, a theory may be true in a logical sense and trivial from an empirical perspective (Bueno de Mesquita 1981). Thus far, our assessment of the realpolitik version of the game suggests that it is not an empirically useful representation of international affairs. The degree to which domestic proposition 3.1 is an important starting point for evaluating war depends, consequently, upon an assessment of its empirical relevance. Therefore, we propose the following empirical evaluation.

We define two dependent variables as before: WAR and BIGWAR. Using the operational procedures elaborated in appendix 1, we estimate three independent variables: War_A, $War_A \times$ Uncertainty, and Uncertainty. War_A is a dummy variable that equals 1.0 if the conditions of proposition 3.1 are satisfied by our operational criteria and otherwise is coded as a zero.[10] Uncertainty is evaluated in terms of the variance in risk-taking propensities across European nations in each year as detailed in appendix 1. The interaction term and the variable Uncertainty are included to evaluate the effects of full-information conditions on the prospects of war. Because the conditions of the theorem are necessary and sufficient for war under full-information conditions, we expect War_A to be positively associated with the likelihood of war, the interaction term to be negatively associated with the risk of war, and Uncertainty by itself to be positively associated with the danger of war.

That War_A should be positively associated with the incidence of war follows directly from proposition 3.1. Because the interaction term $War_A \times$ Uncertainty equals zero under full-information conditions, it evaluates the impact of Uncertainty when the theorem's non-informational conditions are met but uncertainty is present. Because the theorem theoretically guarantees war when its conditions are met and uncertainty is not present, the risk of war can only decline as uncertainty enters the picture, given that the conditions of the theorem are otherwise satisfied. When, however, the conditions of the theorem are

10. In actuality we are unable to distinguish the expected utility for A (or B) of the outcomes War_A and War_B. We can only assess three of the four conditions of the theorem. We cannot assess whether $Cap_A > War_B$ for A. Therefore, our test is weakened beyond the already crude nature of many of the indicators. Consequently, in this, as in our other empirical tests, we are concerned primarily with the central tendency of the theory to provide a significant accounting of relations.

Table 3.3
War with Full Information

	WAR		BIGWAR	
	Coef.	P	Coef.	P
Constant	−2.29	.000	−2.93	.000
War$_A$	0.58	.094	0.95	.027
War$_A$ × Uncertainty	−2.48	.065	−5.05	.004
Uncertainty	3.37	.001	4.69	.000
χ^2	11.10		19.44	
P ≤	.015		.000	
N	625		686	

not met, then Uncertainty can only increase the likelihood that war
will result as a mistaken consequence of someone's misjudgment,
misperception, or miscalculation. Therefore, the Uncertainty variable
by itself should be positively associated with the danger of war,
whereas the interaction term should be negatively associated with war.

Domestic proposition 3.1 is evaluated through the use of logit analysis. As we can see in table 3.3, the proposition is supported by the
historical record. One-tailed significance levels are reported next to
the logit coefficients. All signs are in the anticipated direction, with
modest significance levels for the more inclusive WAR variable and
substantial significance in the case of BIGWAR.

Domestic proposition 3.1 reflects the dangers that can arise when a
prisoner's-dilemma situation prevails in the crisis subgame of the international interaction game. Although such conditions need not arise
in that subgame, the basic war theorem highlights possible risks associated with such situations. In chapter 4, when we explore possible
norms of behavior that might avoid war we return to the subset of
cases that satisfy the definition of a prisoner's dilemma. Then we
evaluate the tit-for-tat reciprocity norm as a possible means of escaping
violence in this specific context. In the meantime, table 3.4 offers a
small sampling of the disputes in Europe that appear by our operational
criteria to satisfy or at least closely approximate the conditions of the
basic war theorem and that eventuated in war.

The first constrained, domestic proposition indicates that decision
makers have a basis for fearing even those nations that are not particularly belligerent. It is a direct contradiction of the first realpolitik

Table 3.4
Wars Apparently Consistent with the
Basic War Theorem and Apparently
with Nearly Full Information

Year	Nation A	Nation B
1849	Austria	Papal States
1849	Prussia	Denmark
1870	France	Prussia
1876	Russia	Turkey
1939	Germany	England
1940	Italy	England

Note: This is a small sample of the
cases for which the uncertainty
indicator fell in its lowest quartile,
where uncertainty is nearly zero.

proposition, which indicates that war cannot arise under full-information conditions. The evidence supports the domestic perspective over the realist outlook. Thomas Hobbes warns, perhaps correctly, that *homo homini lupus* (all men are wolves), but one need not be surrounded by wolves to see the need to prepare defenses in a world in which attentiveness to domestic affairs helps shape foreign policy objectives.

THE IMPOSSIBILITY OF OBTAINING CERTAIN OUTCOMES IN PURE STRATEGIES

DOMESTIC PROPOSITION 3.2: SECONDARY WAR THEOREM. *A war initiated by B is not a complete information equilibrium in pure strategies, given the assumptions of the domestic version of the game.*

Proof. War$_B$ arises as a possible terminal event of the game in two distinct places. We show that neither of these terminal nodes can be reached under the conditions of full information (and strict preferences).

The outcome War$_B$ contained in the subgame at node 9 cannot survive as an outcome. Although it is possible that A prefers War$_B$ to Cap$_A$ at node 12 and chooses f^A, B, according to assumption 2.A4, prefers negotiation to War$_B$. Thus B will choose $\tilde{F}^B$ at node 9.

It is possible that the other War$_B$ could survive as an equlibrium outcome as far as node 2 if it is an equilibrium outcome at node 6 and if A prefers it to acquiescing at node 4 and B prefers it to the status quo. For the War_B contained in the subgame at node 8 to survive as an equilibrium at node 6, several conditions have to be met. At node 8, A must prefer War_B to Cap_A. At node 6, B's choosing War_B implies that at node 11, B prefers Cap_B to War_A. Otherwise, according to assumption 2.A4, A would choose to negotiate at node 7. This, in turn, would induce a choice at node 6 for negotiation over War_B (assumption 2.A4). So our conditions for War_B at node 6 are that A prefer War_B to Cap_A and that B prefer Cap_B to War_A. These preferences also induce negotiation in the crisis subgame at node 5. At node 3 the only outcomes are either Acq_B (which by assumption 2.A6 is better for A than negotiation) or Nego. Therefore, A can guarantee itself at least the value of negotiation by playing the subgame at node 3. By assumption 2.A4, negotiation is preferred over War_B, removing it as an equilibrium outcome. Neither of the paths to a war initiated by B can be supported in equilibrium under full-information conditions. QED

DOMESTIC PROPOSITION 3.3: BASIC CAPITULATION THEOREM. *Capitulation is not a pure strategy equilibrium outcome for fully informed players.*

Proof. Begin with capitulation by A. It is possible for Cap_A to survive as an outcome to the subgame at node 3, but A will not choose to play this subgame. Player A can guarantee itself at least the value of its own acquiescence in the subgame at node 2. By choosing not to make a demand, $\tilde{D}^A$, A would face the possibility that B will respond either by making a demand or by not making a demand upon A. If B were to choose $\tilde{D}^B$, the status quo would be preserved, which A prefers over capitulating (assumptions 2.A5 and 2.A6). Even if B were to make a counterdemand, A would have the opportunity to acquiesce at node 4. By assumption 2.A6, players would rather acquiesce to demands peacefully than have to capitulate after the use of force and suffer the additional costs of an attack. If the other Cap_A were to be the equilibrium outcome to the crisis subgame at node 6, A, disliking capitulation, could escape this outcome by acquiescing at node 4. Thus A has sufficient control of the game to avoid being forced to capitulate.

Capitulation by B does not occur as a pure strategy outcome. If B understands the outcome to the crisis subgame at node 5 to be Cap_B, then at node 3, B chooses $\tilde{D}^B$ and acquiesces to A's demand (assumption 2.A6). The other capitulation by B can be an outcome as far as node 4. At node 2, B can prevent being forced to capitulate to actor A by choosing $\tilde{D}^B$. By making no demand upon A at node 2, B terminates the game and secures the value of the status quo, which B prefers to capitulating (assumptions 2.A5 and 2.A6). B also has suffi-cient control of the game to avoid its own capitulation. QED

CONDITIONS FOR PURE STRATEGY EQUILIBRIA LEADING TO THE OTHER TERMINAL NODES

Next we assess the conditions that would produce an acquiescence by A under full information.

DOMESTIC PROPOSITION 3.4: ACQUIESCENCE BY A THEOREM. *The neces-sary and sufficient conditions with full information, assumption 2.A7b (the domestic variant), and strict preferences for an acquiescence by A are the same as in the basic war theorem except that for A, $Acq_A > War_A$ or Cap_A is the subgame perfect equilibrium outcome in the crisis subgames.*

Proof. For Acq_A to be an equilibrium outcome, A must associate a value with it that is superior to the value of the equilibrium to the subgame at node 6, and node 4 must be reached. At node 6 one of the outcomes—negotiation—is restricted such that it is always preferred to acquiescing (assumption 2.A6). Negotiation as an equilibrium out-come at node 6 is never a condition for A's acquiescence. Yet as-sumption 2.A6 stipulates that A always finds acquiescing better than capitulating. Under our assumptions, A is allowed to prefer acquiesc-ing to any of the other crisis outcomes. If any of these other crisis outcomes are in equilibrium at node 6 and A prefers to acquiesce, then A will choose $\bar{d}^A$ at node 4. The remaining conditions are those re-quired to reach node 4.

If Acq_A is the outcome to the subgame at node 4, it will always be reached from node 2. At node 2, B will choose D^B because according to assumption 2.A5 any nation B prefers acquiescence by A to the status quo. When Acq_A is the outcome to the subgame at node 2, A will choose to make no demand only if the outcome to the subgame at node 3 is an outcome that is less preferred than Acq_A. For A, neither negotiation nor acquiescence by B is ever inferior to acquiescing. The remaining candidates are the conflictual crisis outcomes: Cap_A, War_B, Cap_B, and War_A. Cap_A is already restricted by assumption 2.A6 to be less preferred than Acq_A, and we need make no additional restrictions. War_B does not survive at node 9 (assumption 2.A4) and need not be compared to Acq_A. Cap_B cannot be an equilibrium to the subgame at node 3 (assumption 2.A6), nor does it get compared to Acq_A. The only remaining outcome is War$_A$. As we see in proposition 3.1, War$_A$ is a possible equilibrium to the full game, and consequently, it can be an outcome to subgame 2. To obtain Acq$_A$ as an outcome, we must add the condition that A prefers Acq$_A$ to War$_A$. This condition causes A to initiate the game by not making a demand at node 1. And, as mentioned previously, assumption 2.A5 gives us D^B at node 2. These conditions, taken together, allow us to reach node 4.[11] QED

DOMESTIC PROPOSITION 3.5: Acquiescence by B THEOREM. *With full information conditions, assumption 2.A7b (that is, the domestic variant), and strict preferences, Acq$_B$ is a full-information equilibrium outcome of the international interaction game if and only if the equilibrium outcome of the crisis subgame at node 5 is either Cap$_B$ or War$_A$, and for B, Acq$_B$ > War$_A$.*

Proof. If the outcome to the subgame at node 3 is Acq$_B$, our assumptions indicate that node 3 will be reached. In table 2.3 we see that the assumptions of the game cause Acq$_B$ to be preferred by A to all other outcomes. No matter what the equilibrium to subgame 2 might be, A would rather that B acquiesce, and therefore A will make a demand at node 1. Next we find the conditions for B to favor acquiescing at node 3 rather than playing out the game. These conditions have to do with the possible equilibrium outcomes to the crisis subgame at node 5. Again, negotiation is valued over Acq$_B$ according to assumption 2.A5, and its presence as the outcome to the crisis subgame at node 5 prevents Acq$_B$ as an outcome. In the conditions for Cap$_A$ above, we see that Cap$_A$ is not a supportable outcome with perfect information because at node 1, player A would always choose $\bar{D}^A$ to obtain at least Acq$_A$, which is superior to Cap$_A$. War$_B$ is not a supportable outcome, as we saw above, because assumption 2.A4 rules it out at node 9. A capitulation by B, should it be the outcome at node 5, is prevented as an outcome at node 3 by assumption 2.A5 (as in the conditions for Cap$_B$ above). This leaves only War$_A$. To obtain Acq$_B$ at node 3 when War$_A$ is the outcome at node 5, we must add the condition that B values Acq$_B$ more highly than War$_A$. QED

Before turning to a systematic analysis of proposition 3.5, we pause to illustrate the proposition with an historical example, the events surrounding the Fashoda crisis from July through November of 1898.

---

11. Unfortunately, our data set does not contain a sufficient number of cases of acquiescence by the initiator of the dispute to permit any statistical assessment of these conditions. There are only eight instances of Acq$_A$.

In doing so, we recognize that the conflict over Fashoda was not devoid of imperfect information. Still, the essential preferences of the British and French became clear and were consistent with those delineated in proposition 3.5 and, we believe, help illustrate how the logic of the proposition operates. The outcome was consistent with the proposition as well.

French Acquiescence in the Fashoda Crisis

The British and French rivalry over the Sudan and Egypt evolved over decades. French and British technology and financial interests were involved in the region through the construction of the Suez canal and the Egyptian railroad system. Egyptian policy, developed to protect Anglo-French investments, resulted in a nationalist backlash that was put down when British forces bombarded Alexandria in 1882. Using the British presence to resist nationalist movements and Turkish challenges, Egypt became, in effect, a British protectorate. Wishing to prevent Egyptian vulnerability to hostile control of the Upper Nile, Britain expanded its concerns to the Sudan as well. By 1895 Britain's sphere of influence encompassed the entire Nile basin according to declared British policy.

Denied a foothold along the Lower Nile, the French set out to establish a presence on the Upper Nile. A small expeditionary force led by Jean Baptiste Marchand arrived in July 1898 from Gabon and raised the French flag over Fashoda, in the Sudan. A fortnight later, the risk of a military confrontation arose over French and British colonial policies when Horatio Kitchener arrived with greatly superior force from Omdurman, where the British had recently defeated the Sudanese dervishes. Kitchener, pursuing Britain's declared policy, was under orders to take control of as much of the Upper Nile as possible. Both Marchand and Kitchener were aware that bloodshed at Fashoda could set their countries at war. They arrived at a temporary, local, and amicable compromise by agreeing that Kitchener's forces could raise the Egyptian flag over an outlying part of the fort while waiting for the situation to be resolved in Europe.

When the news of a possible clash at Fashoda arrived in Paris sometime later, Foreign Minister Théophile Delcassé, the former colonial minister, was forced to reconcile two major concerns in French foreign affairs: the competition with Britain over colonial interests and the desire for a rapprochement with Britain to bolster the French diplomatic position on the Continent. The Fashoda crisis also occurred

at an awkward time for the French government, coming as it did on
the heels of revelations of the army's involvement in the Dreyfus affair.
It was thought at the time that the fall of the cabinet was imminent.
Now Delcassé had to try to negotiate with the intransigent and militarily superior British. René Albrecht-Carrié describes the French
position:

> France soon found out the extent of her isolation; Russia and Germany,
> each for her own and different reasons, saw an Anglo-French clash without
> reluctance. If it came to considering an isolated conflict between the two
> countries, then the British naval superiority furnished a ready answer.
> Delcassé wanted negotiation, not war, but the uncompromising attitude of
> Britain made it difficult to find a face-saving solution, and for the moment
> the tension was acute and war seemed even probable. (1973, 224)

On the basis of such a weak military position the French could
entertain only very small expectations from negotiating. Given domestic dissatisfaction with the cabinet and the small advantages of
negotiation, the French were in a vulnerable position indeed. Even
giving in looked more attractive than prolonging a crisis in which they
would probably have to face capitulation or war in the end anyway.
Concomitantly, Britain had little incentive to offer a compromise and
was more inclined to enforce its will, even if doing so meant violence.
In accordance with our formulation of proposition 3.5, Britain preferred to compel France to yield rather than negotiate, and the French
recognized that they had no viable alternative to accepting Britain's
demands.

Lord Salisbury clarified the British position and defused domestic
fears that he might be too accommodating to the French by the extraordinary step of issuing a blue book on the Fashoda crisis prior to
its resolution, a highly "undiplomatic" action (Grenville 1964). The
firmness of the British position was perceptibly reinforced when Britain spurned an offer by the French to quit Fashoda in return for
commercial uses of the Nile. The British were unyielding in the crisis;
no negotiation was possible as long as the Marchand expedition was
in the Sudan. The British apparently wanted nothing less than a full
acquiescence and were prepared to go to war to enforce their will.

In the meantime, Marchand had taken it upon himself to leave
Fashoda for Cairo in order to communicate with Paris. He was ordered
to return to his troops immediately, but the British sent their gunboats
south of Khartoum so that no transportation would be available to

take him back. The French mission in Fashoda was without its commander. Paris notified London of its decision to recall the Marchand
expedition on November 3, thereby yielding to the British position.
The French had acquiesced, and the immediate crisis passed.

Later, the British and French held discussions over related technical
issues in which Britain secured the watershed between the Congo and
the Nile valleys as the boundary of its sphere of influence. Not wishing
to further humiliate the French after the British had secured their
claims and the French had withdrawn, the British renamed Fashoda
to avoid unpleasant associations in the public mind.

In our view, the Fashoda crisis illustrates proposition 3.5 clearly.
The French feeler as to whether the British would consider even some
small concession in the form of commercial access to the Nile brought
no hope. The British flatly refused and were convincing in their willingness to use force. Both the government and the opposition in Britain
had warned Salisbury against accepting any part of the French position. French isolation was nearly complete, the Russians and Germans
being reluctant to lend support. Thus, the British held preponderant
power in the crisis, and they were willing to use it. Consistent with
proposition 3.5, Delcassé, contrary to his protestations that he saw
"war as preferable to national dishonour," chose to acquiesce (Grenville 1964, 227). Although tensions remained high between the two
nations for some time, they were not the issue for an Anglo-French
war.

Fashoda illustrates the main features of proposition 3.5, but the
question still remains whether the proposition is broadly supported by
the historical record. We can test it empirically. We define a dummy
variable $BACQ$ to satisfy the theoretical conditions of the Acq_B theorem (3.5). The details of the operationalization are in appendix 1. We
define a dependent variable, ACQ_B, which equals 1.0 if actor A made
a demand and B did not respond and the incident ended without
fatalities. According to the theorem, when $BACQ$ equals 1.0, so that
the conditions of proposition 3.5 are satisfied, then ACQ_B should tend
to equal 1.0 as well.

Table 3.5 depicts a cross-tabulation of $BACQ$ and ACQ_B. The logit
analysis of these variables is as follows: $ACQ_B = -2.31 + 1.10\,BACQ$,
$\chi^2 = 23.94$, P $< .001$, N $= 707$.

Given the difficulties inherent in measuring the concepts and the
prevalence of uncertainties in international politics, table 3.5 and the
associated logit analysis stand as a strong endorsement of proposition
3.5. Acquiescence by B is substantially more likely when the condi-

Table 3.5
B's Propensity to Acquiesce

Actual ACQ$_B$	Predicted ACQ$_B$	
	No	Yes
No	442 (90%)	170 (76%)
Yes	44 (10%)	51 (24%)
χ^2	25.69	
P ≤	.001	

tions of the theorem are approximated in reality. What is more, table 3.5 and its associated proposition represent a contradiction of real-politik proposition 3.2, which states that acquiescence cannot arise under any circumstances in the realist interpretation of the game.

The Status Quo

To reach the status quo, *A* must initiate the game by making no demand, and *B* must respond by making no demand. In proposition 3.6 we specify the full-information conditions under which the status quo can arise as the equilibrium outcome of the domestic account of the international interaction game.

DOMESTIC PROPOSITION 3.6: BASIC STATUS QUO THEOREM. *With complete information and assumption 2.A7b, the status quo is the equilibrium outcome of the game if and only if A prefers the status quo to negotiation and A and B satisfy one of the following four cases of additional restrictions on their preferences over outcomes:*

  Case 1. For A, Cap$_A$ > War$_B$.
     For B, War$_A$ > Cap$_B$, Nego > Cap$_A$, SQ > Nego.

  Case 2. For A, Nego > Cap$_B$, Cap$_A$ > War$_B$.
     For B, Cap$_B$ > War$_A$, Nego > Cap$_A$, SQ > Nego.

  Case 3. For A, War$_B$ > Cap$_A$.
     For B, War$_A$ > Cap$_B$, SQ > Nego.

  Case 4. For A, Nego > Cap$_B$, War$_B$ > Cap$_A$.
     For B, Cap$_B$ > War$_A$, SQ > Nego.

Proof. We will look first at the conditions that support the status quo as an equilibrium in subgame 2. Then we will check to see whether these same conditions are consistent with a status quo outcome in the larger game and, if they are, whether other conditions need be added to support the status quo in the full game.

For B to choose to make no demand on A at node 2, B must prefer the status quo over any of the possible equilibrium outcomes to the subgame at node 4. War$_A$ fails as an outcome at node 7 (assumption 2.A4), and therefore, War$_A$ cannot be an outcome to subgame 4. There is no need to make any comparisons between how B values War$_A$ and how B values the status quo.

An outcome of capitulation by A at node 6 induces A's acquiescence at node 4 (assumption 2.A6). Acq$_A$ at node 4 in turn prevents the status quo at node 2 because B prefers Acq$_A$ to all other outcomes (see table 2.3). Any preferences leading to Cap$_A$ as the outcome to partitions of the subgame cannot support the status quo.

In contrast to Cap$_A$, Cap$_B$ does support the status quo in subgame 2. It does not support the status quo in the full game, however. By assumption 2.A6, conditions on the preferences of the players leading to capitulation by B as the result at node 4 will lead to the status quo at node 2. The specific conditions required for Cap$_B$ to be the outcome at node 4 are for A, Cap$_B$ > Nego, War$_B$ > Cap$_A$, and Cap$_B$ > Acq$_A$, and for B, Cap$_B$ > War$_A$ and Cap$_B$ > War$_B$. But node 2 cannot be reached with these restrictions. These conditions induce Cap$_B$ as the outcome to subgame 5. But at node 3, assumption 2.A6 indicates that B will choose to acquiesce rather than suffer the additional costs of a capitulation. With Acq$_B$ now as the equilibrium to subgame 3, assumptions 2.A5 and 2.A6 stipulate that A prefers Acq$_B$ to the status quo and therefore will choose to initiate the game by making a demand. This leaves negotiation and a war initiated by B as outcomes that can rise as far in the game as node 2.

For the status quo to be in equilibrium it must be preferred to negotiation or War$_B$, if either is in equilibrium at node 4 and node 3. We will have sets of conditions. For War$_B$ to survive as far as node 4, it must survive at nodes farther down. At node 8, War$_B$ must be preferred by A to Cap$_A$. At node 6 the only possible comparisons to War$_B$ are negotiation and Cap$_B$, because War$_A$ fails as an equilibrium at node 7. Assumption 2.A4 already restricts negotiation to being superior to War$_B$, and we need introduce only the additional restriction that B prefers War$_B$ to Cap$_B$. The assumption will yield War$_B$ at node 6. At node 4, A must also prefer War$_B$ to Acq$_A$. And B must prefer the status quo to War$_B$. With respect to War$_B$, then, the added restrictions are for A, $War_B > Cap_A$, $Cap_B > Nego$, and $War_B > Acq_A$, and for B, $Cap_B > War_A$, $War_B > Cap_B$, and $SQ > War_B$. These conditions induce Acq_B as the outcome at node 3. Because A prefers that B acquiesce over all alternative outcomes, including the status quo, at node 1 we must expect D^A, thereby precluding the status quo as the equilibrium outcome.

Consider negotiation now and what is required for this outcome to be compared to the status quo outcome. There are two combinations of preferences that yield negotiation at node 7. If B's choice at node 11 is War_A, we know that negotiating is preferred and is the outcome at node 7. Also, if Cap_B is B's choice at node 11 and A prefers negotiating over B's capitulation, then negotiation will be in equilibrium at node 7. At node 6, negotiation could prevail if two conditions are met in the subgame at node 8. Either A prefers War_B to Cap_A, in which case we know negotiation to be better than War_B at node 6, or A prefers Cap_A to War_B and B prefers negotiation over a capitulation by A. Whenever negotiation is the outcome at node 6, assumptions 2.A5 and 2.A6 ($Nego > Acq_i$) will make it the outcome at node 4. We then have four cases where negotiation supports the status quo at node 2.

Case 1. For A, $Cap_A > War_B$.
    For B, $War_A > Cap_B$, $Nego > Cap_A$, $SQ > Nego$.

Case 2. For A, $Nego > Cap_B$, $Cap_A > War_B$.
    For B, $Cap_B > War_A$, $Nego > Cap_A$, $SQ > Nego$.

Case 3. For A, $War_B > Cap_A$.
    For B, $War_A > Cap_B$, $SQ > Nego$.

Case 4. For A, $Nego > Cap_B$, $War_B > Cap_A$.
    For B, $Cap_B > War_A$, $SQ > Nego$.

Each of these cases also supports negotiation as the outcome at node 5 on the right side of the game structure. With negotiation at node 5, Nego being better than Acq_i leads to negotiation as the outcome at node 3. To have A initiate the game by making no demand upon B, we need add only the further restriction that A prefers the status quo to negotiating. That B holds this preference is already stated in the four conditions delineated above. These are the conditions of the theorem. QED

Because there are four different sets of restrictions and because numerous pairs of complete orderings can satisfy any one of them,

Table 3.6
Predicted and Actual Status Quo

	Predicted status quo	
Actual status quo	No	Yes
No	436 (68%)	33 (52%)
Yes	208 (32%)	30 (48%)
χ^2		6.03
$P \leq$		.014

there are many ways to arrive at the status quo. Indeed, with uniformly distributed preferences 232 possible pairings of preference orders (or 8.6 percent of all possible orderings on outcomes) lead to the status quo. But, as with each of our other propositions thus far, we must wonder whether these particular conditions, when approximated in the real world, disproportionately increase the prospect that nations will abide by the status quo. We turn to an empirical assessment of the Basic Status Quo Theorem to evaluate its usefulness.

We define a dummy variable, SQ, coded 1.0 if, by our operational procedures, A preferred the status quo to negotiation and A and B satisfied one of the four cases of the theorem that support the status quo as the equilibrium outcome. Otherwise, SQ is coded as zero. We define a dependent variable, STATUS QUO, which is coded 1.0 if nations A and B made no demands on each other and coded zero otherwise. That is, STATUS QUO is coded 1.0 for the subset of cases in our data set that represents randomly paired European nations in years when they did not engage each other in an event in which at least one of them made a demand of the other accompanied by a threat.

Table 3.6 provides a cross-tabulation of the results of the test, and we also offer a test based on a logit analysis of the relation between theoretically predicted and observed instances of the maintenance of the status quo. The logit result is STATUS QUO $= -0.74 + 0.64$ SQ, $\chi^2 = 5.76$, $P < .016$, $N = 707$. Clearly, the theorem is supported by the empirical record. Given the crudity of our data, the prevalence of measurement error, and the undoubted presence of imperfect information in international affairs, the central tendency in support of the theorem is encouraging indeed.

Table 3.7
The Expectation of Negotiation

	Negotiation is expected	
Actual negotiation	No	Yes
No	596 (96%)	76 (88%)
Yes	25 (4%)	10 (12%)
χ^2	9.28	
$P \leq$	.002	

Negotiation

In the sections above we have described the conditions on the preference orders of the players that lead to the outcomes of the game other than negotiation. Any pairing of orderings not meeting one of these sets of restrictions will lead the players to negotiate their differences rather than settle them in some other way. Whether actual behavior is consistent with the expectations of the game, as with each other outcome that is feasible under full-information conditions, is an empirical question. Here we offer three tests of the predictions regarding the advent of negotiation. In one test we define a dummy variable, PredNego, that is coded 1.0 when the conditions of the game lead to the prediction that an interaction will culminate in negotiation and coded zero otherwise. We cross-tabulate that variable with the dependent variable, NEGO, which equals 1.0 when the interaction did lead to negotiation and equals zero otherwise. The cross-tabulation, found in table 3.7, is accompanied by a second test, consisting of a logit analysis of the relation between these two variables. The expectation is that PredNego is positively associated with the dependent variable. The logit result is NEGO = $-3.17 + 1.14$ PredNego, $\chi^2 = 7.21$, $P < .007$, $N = 707$.

Once again, the direct evaluation of the conditions identified in the theory provides support for the belief that the domestic version of the international interaction game represents a structural scaffold for understanding relations among nations. Negotiation is three times more likely when the full-information conditions of the theory are met for such an outcome than when they are not satisfied. Even without controlling for imperfect information, nearly 30 percent of actual negotiations were expected to have ended in that way.

In the third test of conditions leading to negotiation, reported in

Table 3.8
Negotiation and the Basic Theorems

| | Nego | |
| |------------|-------|
	Coef.	P
Constant	-2.22	.000
War$_A$	-0.79	.037
AAcq	-0.85	.068
BAcq	-1.20	.010
SQ	-0.11	.421
χ^2	6.00	
P	.10	
N	707	

table 3.8, we conduct a logit analysis that relates NEGO to the previously specified dummy variables BAcq, War$_A$, and SQ, as well as a dummy variable, AAcq, coded 1.0 if the conditions for an acquiescence by actor A are satisfied. Because these four variables each predict an event other than negotiation as the equilibrium outcome under conditions of full information, each should be inversely related to the likelihood that an interaction culminates in a negotiated settlement.

Our final test further highlights the potential predictive and explanatory capacity of the game. Here we undertake a multivariate analysis of the relation between negotiation and the necessary and sufficient full-information conditions for each other feasible outcome of the domestic version of the international interaction game.

Only the status quo variable in table 3.8 does not meet or approximate normal standards of statistical significance. The status quo is the political circumstance in the international interaction game that is closest in its promotion of peace and harmony to the outcome of negotiation. All of the other variables appear to be significantly associated with the likelihood of resolving a dispute through negotiation. Each variable has the predicted direction of impact, with most also having a statistically strong influence on the prospects for a negotiated settlement.

We have now completed the assessment of the basic structure of the game. Several fundamental full-information theorems have been set out and evaluated empirically. Each one represents the full-information conditions that are necessary and sufficient for each possible outcome of the international interaction game under the two principal interpretations of the game: the realpolitik perspective and the domestic perspective. We have found that in either version of the game, three events—capitulation by A or by B and a war started by B—cannot arise without some incomplete information or uncertainty on the part of at least one player. We see that five events—negotiation, the status quo, acquiescence by A or by B, and a war started by A—can each arise under full-information conditions (as well as under conditions of imperfect information) in the domestic variant of the game. Only negotiation or the status quo are possible with full information from the realpolitik perspective. Acquiescence is never possible within the realpolitik perspective.

Some of the domestic/constrained deductions, most notably those concerned with war, represent a significant departure from views previously stated by students of international affairs. In that sense, the empirical evaluation of the basic war theorem may well represent what Karl Popper (1963) has termed a severe test of the theory. What is more, we know of no other theory that sets out explicit, axiomatic proofs for the circumstances for such a wide variety of international interactions and then goes on to provide empirical evaluations (and support) for the theoretically derived expectations. To the best of our knowledge, these theorems represent the first statements of precise conditions required for the preservation of the status quo, for the promotion of negotiation, or for the acquiescence of one nation to the demands of another. In that regard, they provide the broadest clues yet to the circumstances that lead some disputes to escalate into violence while others are resolved peacefully or avoided altogether. The significant empirical support for the domestic explanation of international interactions and the absence of such support for the realpolitik version of the game causes us to forswear, albeit cautiously, our initial agnosticism with regard to these two perspectives on international affairs. We now have serious doubts about the efficacy of the predominant realist perspective.

Having said that, we are mindful that the basic theorems discussed here are restricted by a very demanding condition—the presence of full information. That such conditions are often violated in reality almost goes without saying and certainly is reflected in all of the empirical results reported thus far. In the remaining portions of this study we will be increasingly attentive to the evaluation of the international interaction game in the face of imperfect information and particularly attentive to some surprising implications for behavior that arise in the face of uncertainty about one's opponent.

We will proceed with the domestic interpretation of the game unless otherwise stipulated. Two factors push us in that direction. First, the conditions of the realpolitik version, especially as reflected in expressions (3.1) and (3.2), highlight an important distinction between realism and the constrained, domestic perspective. Expressions (3.1) and (3.2) show that in choosing demands, realist decision makers are attentive to the domestic political constraints faced by their adversaries but that they need not be attentive to their own domestic political constraints. The domestic theory, in contrast, consistently reflects the notion that decision makers are attentive both to their own domestic constraints and to those of their rivals. The domestic version, which links national actions to internal and external considerations, strikes us as more believable than the implication from the realist point of view. Second, the empirical evidence indicates that the domestic perspective appears to be the version that best fits the historical record.[12] This pertinence reinforces our conviction that the domestic theory is more believable.

12. The realist perspective might be rescued if we assumed that some stochastic process at the outset of the game perturbs the realist's selection of demands. However, such an argument is difficult to sustain because random shocks to the system would have to be very large indeed to produce results consistent with the empirical record. The significance tests and the evidence in general all point away from such a strained interpretation of realism. That this is so can most easily be recognized by examining the complex and substantial ways in which realist preferences over outcomes have to be reshaped to yield the results reported here. Yet the results are consistent with the constrained, domestic interpretation of the game, despite being quite far afield from realist expectations, even with random perturbations around the realist predictions. Any random shocks to the system would have to be consistently large enough to produce a selection of demands very different from those anticipated by the realist theory.

Part II

Domestic Constraints and Foreign Policy

Chapter 4

Norms, Beliefs, and International Cooperation

Jethro Tull tells us that "it's hard to find true equilibrium when you're looking at each other down the muzzle of a gun." And so it may be. Yet, while the lyric succinctly characterizes the traits of the anarchic international system, more often than not, even nations looking down the muzzles of great guns appear to abide by precepts of international law and custom and are expected to honor the agreements they make. Indeed, we are more likely to be surprised by breaches of international accords than by the honoring of such arrangements.

Common experience indicates that international anarchy is not accompanied by international chaos. The absence of a recognized monitor of international affairs apparently need not mean that there are no clear norms and rules governing international interactions. The presumption that we live in a world characterized by anarchy, coupled with compelling observations of cooperative behavior among nations, obliges us, therefore, to inquire into the norms of behavior, if any, that prospectively account for cooperation among sovereign, self-interested states. To do so, we must first define what we mean by the concept of a norm of cooperation.

In the context of this inquiry we mean by a norm of cooperation a generally agreed-upon set of values that restricts preferences over the outcomes of the domestic/constrained international interaction game such that negotiation is held to be a more desirable way to settle disputes than are alternative means of resolution. Two particular distinctions implied by this definition warrant further elaboration.

First is the recognition that norms are not universally adhered to but rather are the commonly accepted values or behaviors in a community.[1] In the Judeo-Christian world (indeed, among most of humanity), for instance, the ten biblical commandments represent norms of behavior. Some of the commandments are very widely obeyed (for example, "Thou shalt not kill"); others are frequently observed in the breach (for example, "Thou shalt keep the Sabbath"). Norms are less

1. In our context the community is the set of nations that constitute the international system. In other contexts the individual units in a community and the magnitude of a community will vary from the application of the concept here.

interesting if they represent patterns of interaction that necessarily are universal. Then they simply represent background assumptions—constants rather than variables in the swirl of international affairs. Norms are of interest if they represent common—usually socially induced—restrictions on actions that otherwise would be unconstrained. They are akin to the notion that certain orderings of preferences are simply unacceptable bases for interactions between leaders of "civilized" states.

Second, we concentrate on the preferences of actors regarding outcomes rather than on their actions per se. In game theory—and, we assume, in life—actions are chosen as means to attain ends. To be sure, not all means are justified by their ends in life or in our theory. That is why, for instance, we assume there is a political cost associated with the use of force, even the successful use of force. Ends, constrained by costs, dictate the choice of actions. Therefore, when we speak of a preference over outcomes, it is in terms of assumed restrictions on the expected value of one outcome versus another. By imposing such limitations on the value attached to outcomes, we also impose constraints on the chosen behaviors of the actors in our game. Later, for example, we will discuss a norm that assumes a general tendency for national leaders to prefer to resolve disputes through negotiation rather than through the use of force. We do not particularly question how such a norm might arise in the international community but rather what the consequences for behavior would be if such a norm existed. Our abiding, fundamental concern is, How might particular restrictions on most leaders' preferences influence the prospects of cooperation between states? We begin our investigation of norms of cooperation with two parables from the life of Chingis Khan.

Early in the career of the great Mongol leader an episode occurred that highlights the potential benefits and pitfalls of social norms—or patterns of expected behavior—for peacefully resolving disputes. The incident involved a discussion in the family of Old Man Shirgugetu concerning how best to encourage cooperation and concessions from Chingis Khan. Like many other accounts in *The Secret History of the Mongols,* the story of Shirgugetu leaves little doubt that norms of cooperation influenced the international affairs of the day. Alas, the discussion also leaves little doubt that there were competing norms; that norms of action then, as now, involved common but certainly not universal patterns of interaction. The story highlights the risks of misjudgment about the expected behavior of a rival in warlike, life-or-death circumstances.

Consider the calculations of the old man and his sons as they

approached the camp of Chingis Khan after the defeat of their own
clan by Chingis's army:

> The Tayichigud leader Targhutai Kiriltugh had escaped into the forest,
> but he was seized there by Old Man Shirgugetu,
> one of his own servants,
> and the Old Man's sons, Alagh and Nayaga.
> Old Man Shirgugetu thought:
> "Chingis Khan has good reason to hate Targhutai.
> If I bring him to Chingis he'll surely reward me."
> Targhutai was too fat to put on a horse
> so they loaded him into a cart and rode off toward Chingis Khan's camp.
>
> So the Old Man and his two sons continued along
> until they reached Khutukhul.
> Here they stopped and Nayaga said:
> "We've seized Targhutai and decided to take him to Chingis Khan.
> When we get there Chingis will say to himself,
> 'These people have laid hands on their khan.
> How can I trust them?
> These aren't the kind of men I want in my camp.
> People who rise up against their own khan should be killed.'
> When we get there Chingis will have us executed for our troubles.
> Instead we should let Targhutai go back by himself
> and when we get to Chingis Khan's camp we'll say to him,
> 'We've come with nothing but the clothes on our backs
> to offer our services to Chingis Khan.
> We captured Targhutai Kiriltugh and were bringing him to you
> but as we approached your camp we thought to ourselves,
> "How can we do this to our own khan?
> How can we watch him die before our very eyes?"
> So we let him go.
> Believing in your wisdom
> we've come to offer our strength in your service.'"
> His father and brother agreed with Nayaga's advice
> so they set Targhutai free at Khudukhul [sic]
> and went on to the camp without him.
> When Old Man Shirgugetu, Alagh, and Nayaga arrived
> Chingis Khan asked them:
> "Why have you come?"
> Old Man Shirgugetu answered:
> "We captured Targhutai Kiriltugh and were bringing him to you,

but as we approached your camp we thought to ourselves,
'How can we let our khan die before our very eyes?'
So we let him go free and came here without him, saying,
'We'll offer our strength to serve Chingis Khan
and trust in his wisdom.'"
Hearing this Chingis said to him:
"If you'd come here bringing your own khan as a captive
I'd have had you all killed, you and your children.
That's what happens to people who lay hands on their khan.
So you made the right choice." (Kahn 1984, 66–68)

Because Nayaga had understood the norm of behavior appropriate for a servant to a khan, the norm of conciliation and respect, Chingis rewarded him, making Nayaga a commander in his army. Old Man Shirgugetu and his sons had wisely chosen not to exploit their momentary advantage over their own khan. Had they followed their first inclination by delivering the hated Targhutai Kiriltugh to Chingis, they would have died for their effort. Yet rewarding Chingis with the capture of Targhutai, his rival, might reasonably have been thought to be a way to gain favor with the great khan. Hence, Shirgugetu first thought of the possible rewards he would receive for delivering Targhutai to Chingis. Clearly, Shirgugetu and his sons could not be certain whether Chingis would reward them for capturing or releasing an enemy. Death might as readily have been the reward for freeing Targhutai as for surrendering him to the great Mongol leader.

Chingis, by sparing the lives of the old man and his sons and by rewarding Nayaga, reinforced the view that it pays to be conciliatory, noting: "If you'd come here bringing your own khan as a captive I'd have had you all killed, you and your children. *That's what happens to people who lay hands on their khan*" (emphasis added). Yet on other occasions, Chingis would exploit a momentary advantage rather than pursue conciliation. His behavior was influenced by, but not governed by, norms of action. Consider the tale of Chingis and his brother Khasar:

Teb Tengri arrived at the tent to speak with Chingis Khan.
"These are the words of Eternal Blue Heaven," he said.
"I have heard commandments from above about the Khan.
Once I heard voices say, 'Let Temujin rule the Nation.'[2]
Then I heard voices say, 'Let Khasar rule the Nation.'

2. Temujin was Chingis Khan's given name.

If Chingis Khan doesn't strike first at Khasar
none of my powers can predict what will happen."
Chingis Khan set out that night to arrest Khasar,
and two of the chiefs Chingis had given to Mother Hogelun
went to her and told her:
"He's gone to arrest Khasar."
When she heard these words, even though it was the black of night,
the mother had a white camel harnessed to her black cart
and she set out travelling through the darkness.
As the sun was rising,
just as Chingis Khan was tying back Khasar's sleeves,
taking off his hat and his belt,
questioning Khasar about his words and his motives,
Hogelun arrived at the camp.
Chingis Khan was terrified at the sight of her.

                              .   .   .

Chingis Khan let his mother speak till her anger died down,
then he said:
"Seeing how angry our mother is, We're afraid of her.
We're ashamed of what We've done.
We'll take our leave," and he left the camp.
But without telling his mother
he took many of the people away from Khasar
and left his brother only one thousand four hundred households.
When Hogelun finally heard about this it brought on her old age.
And the man who had been appointed chief of Khasar's people
fled in fear to the West. (152–54)

The confrontation between Khasar and Chingis shows an alternative
norm of action, albeit not a norm of cooperation: carpe diem, seize
the day. Not only did Chingis exploit the advantage he had over his
brother in yet another life-or-death situation, but he also exploited the
good faith of his own mother. He promised conciliatory action but
instead deprived Khasar of his wealth and power, driving his mother
to her grave and driving Khasar's chief westward in fear for his life.
He spoke like a dove but acted like a hawk.

Which norm of action, conciliation or exploitation, was the expected
pattern of action? If the former, then being conciliatory in response
probably would have fostered cooperation; if the latter, then a more
militant, defensive posture might have been suitable for promoting
peace. In searching for cooperative solutions to conflicts, which norms

were or are most likely to arrest violence in a world in which one is
rarely certain of a rival's precise intentions?

The stories of Old Man Shirgugetu and of Khasar, like so many
other anecdotes of decision making during crises, call for an explanation. How did Nayaga know what action was appropriate to induce
Chingis Khan to offer a cooperative gesture toward himself and all of
his kin? Why did similar gestures of conciliation not work for either
Khasar or Mother Hogelun? How does cooperation emerge in an
inherently noncooperative and uncertain world?

In this chapter we hope to offer insights into the norms of behavior
that are likely to produce cooperation and avoid violent confrontation.
We have in earlier chapters established the full-information conditions
required for the occurrence of each outcome in the international interaction game. With that information in hand, we can probe the means
by which the prospects of peace can be heightened. In doing so, we
are mindful that we live in a world in which most of the time most
disputes are peacefully resolved but in which failures to attain nonviolent settlements can have cataclysmic consequences. For many,
the duality of peaceful conflict resolution in a world of egoistic leaders
is a fundamental puzzle. Perhaps by the conclusion of this chapter we
will have helped fit some pieces of that puzzle together.

The prevalence of cooperative interactions among states seems
surprising to many observers of international affairs (Keohane 1984;
Gilpin 1981; Keohane and Nye 1977; Kegley and Raymond 1990). If,
as suggested by so many realist theorists, the international system is
comprised of autonomous actors functioning in an anarchic environment, then why is the world not more in line with the brutish state of
nature envisioned by Hobbes? Why are so many trade, investment,
monetary, organizational, and even military international interactions
cooperative rather than conflictual? Why do nations honor commitments in an anarchic world in which promises are never binding and
alliances are often believed to be worth no more than the paper on
which they are written? Why might nations abide by such agreements
even if the agreements have become burdensome for one or another
of the adherents?

Why, for instance, did the United States stand by Pakistan in its
1971 war against India? It was obvious at the outset that Pakistan
could not win and that support for Pakistan could only alienate India
without being popular at home. Yet the inconveniences of support
notwithstanding, the United States remained a loyal, cooperative ally.

Why does OPEC survive despite blatant cheating by its members?
Might petroleum production be even greater without the constraining

influence of OPEC? Is there some compelling norm of behavior that discourages nations from breaking completely with OPEC, encouraging some modicum of cooperation despite the apparent economic incentives for more independent action?

Why was the United States willing to give up the territory of El Chamizal to Mexico in 1963 after refusing to do so on terms favorable to the Mexicans for more than fifty years (Lamborn and Mumme 1988)? What norm of action prompted President Kennedy to sacrifice this territory to a weaker opponent who could not have enforced its will against U.S. intransigence? What in each of these and countless other instances prompts cooperation even when a state can at the moment gain greater welfare from being uncooperative? Such cooperation is difficult to understand with a model of the world that is solely focused on narrow, short-term calculations of self-interest. Yet each instance of cooperation may be explicable in terms of a more sophisticated perspective on rational action.

One solution to the puzzle of cooperation might be that the international environment is not anarchic and that international interactions do not preclude enforceable contracts. Such a response may well be correct for some interactions, but it assumes away the puzzle for those interesting cases where commitment is not assured and cooperation still persists. Although the legal doctrine *pacta sunt servanda* (pacts made in good faith are binding) seems a reassuring depiction of international law and is not wholly inconsistent with observed behavior, still if such good faith behavior is common even when adherence to the contract seems ill advised, then it cries out for a coherent explanation. Likewise, if the doctrine *rebus sic stantibus* (as matters stand) is an acceptable standard for terminating agreements, then we must explain the persistence of cooperative behavior even when such action has become costly and inconvenient (Kegley and Raymond 1990; Keohane 1986). This puzzle of cooperation in a noncooperative world is the subject to which we now turn our attention.

NORMS AND THE INTERNATIONAL INTERACTION GAME

The international interaction game provides clues to the paths expected to lead to or away from cooperation. We explore here a set of strategies and norms that ensure the cooperative resolution of conflicts of interest and offer some hints regarding the threats to the survival of such behaviors. We begin by exploring the meaning of cooperation, being careful to distinguish between the normative connotations of cooperation and the strategic implications of cooperative action. Then we assess the international interaction game to evaluate several prospective norms by which conflict might be hypothesized to be diminished. Each norm is evaluated in terms of its impact on the generation of cooperative equilibria in the game. When appropriate, some of the norms are assessed not only under full-information conditions but also under imperfect information.

Robert Keohane (1984) has suggested a useful definition for cooperation that helps inform our analysis. Following Keohane, we distinguish cooperation, coercion, and harmony. Harmony arises whenever an agreement is reached between putative adversaries without either party sacrificing any of its interests. Coercion occurs if one party surrenders any part of its interests to an adversary while the adversary benefits from the sacrifice without giving up anything. Cooperation entails concessions by each participant to a dispute in exchange for the avoidance of a conflictual, violent escalation of the interaction.

In terms of the international interaction game, cooperation is a strategy for resolving a conflict of interests in a peaceful way. A conflict of interests arises whenever a crisis subgame is reached. Without the sequence of interactions denoted by the strategic choices D^A, D^B or $\tilde{D}^A$, D^B, d^A, there may be a tacit conflict, but there is no overt conflict of interest. Consequently, failure to reach a crisis subgame does not ensure harmony, just as entry into a crisis does not ensure cooperation.

A harmony of interests exists in the international interaction game whenever the status quo prevails as the equilibrium outcome, so that harmony arises whenever $\tilde{D}^A$, $\tilde{D}^B$ represents the strategic path of nations A and B. Yet states may have harmonious interests, meaning they each value the status quo very highly, without enjoying harmonious relations. We will show that harmonious relations imply harmonious interests, but harmonious interests do not necessarily imply harmonious relations.

Coercion arises under two quite distinct sets of circumstances within the confines of our model. Whenever one actor acquiesces to the demands of another actor, then we say that the acquiescing party has been (tacitly) coerced. Such coercion may be accompanied by little or no empirical trace of a threat. All that may be observed is that one state has surrendered some portion of its interests to another without compensation. Coercion may, however, also occur within the context of overt pressure as when one state capitulates to the demands of another during a crisis. These latter instances of coercion leave greater empirical traces, for they involve the direct use of violence by one adversary. Such violence is the means by which one state enforces its demands and persuades the other to capitulate.

If a crisis subgame is reached, there can be no doubt that a conflict of interest exists. Rivals table competing demands, with neither side showing a willingness to give in to the other. The relationship between the opponents can take any of three basic directions: they may wage war; one state may be coerced into capitulating to the other; or they may reach a compromise settlement of their differences. Cooperation occurs if the sides eschew the use of violence, agreeing instead to negotiate. Thus, cooperation is characterized by the strategic sequence D^A, D^B, $\bar{F}^A$, $\bar{F}^B$ or $\bar{D}^A$, D^B, d^A, $\bar{F}^B$, $\bar{F}^A$. In our model, as in Keohane's view, cooperation ends with each side expecting to give up some of its interest in exchange for the avoidance of violence. In that sense, cooperation is always burdensome relative to coercing an adversary into acquiescing to one's demands. That is why the payoffs to the game stipulate that

$$U^i(\Delta_i) > P^i U^i(\Delta_i) + (1 - P^i)U^i(\Delta_j).$$

Yet cooperation also has an inherent attraction: it is always better than waging war. Additionally, cooperation through a negotiated settlement may be better than living with the status quo or forcing an adversary to capitulate in a crisis.

Our interest here is in identifying strategies that may foster cooperation. In doing so, we distinguish sharply between a positive and a normative view of cooperation. In the positive sense, cooperation arises whenever a crisis is resolved by negotiation. Of greatest normative interest are those circumstances that lead to cooperation even though one or both actors prefer to coerce the other into capitulating to its demands. In these circumstances, cooperation is not attained by the coincidence of a common preference for conciliatory gestures but rather as a result of strategic interaction. Thus, of greatest normative concern are those cases in which negotiated settlements of disputes can be reached even though the disputants are not filled with goodwill toward one another.

The positivist view of cooperation focuses exclusively on the set of strategic paths that lead to negotiation. It distinguishes between mutual harmony, coercion, and cooperation. The normative view of cooperation is more restrictive. It gives greatest importance to the attainment of compromise through negotiation in those situations where both actors prefer to coerce their counterpart into submission and least importance to those circumstances in which actors make concessions because they value compromise above efforts to get their own way through coercion. Surely, cooperation is more difficult to achieve when the rivals lack goodwill toward one another. We will, then, toward the end of this chapter, evaluate the alternative norms we examine from this rather narrow perspective: which norm is best suited to encouraging cooperation even when the rivals take a hardened, self-interested view lacking in goodwill toward one another?

We begin our inquiry with an assessment of the prospects of cooperation when both sides to a dispute prefer compromise to coercion. Then we evaluate the prospects for cooperation when compromise is preferred but information about that preference is imperfect.

COOPERATION IN A WORLD OF DOVES

How difficult is it to avoid violence or coercion if all parties to a dispute would rather compromise than fight? To address this question we assume for the moment that for all i,

$$P^i U^i(\Delta_i) + (1 - P^i)U^i(\Delta_j) > U^i(\Delta_i - \phi_i P^i).$$

We define a dove as a nation (or even coalition of nations) that, in its relation with some other nation (or coalition of nations) prefers to negotiate rather than use force to compel capitulation to its demands. This auxiliary dovish assumption—that negotiation is preferable even to coercing a rival into capitulating to one's demands—in conjunction with the assumptions delineated in chapter 2, is sufficient to ensure that there will be no coercion provided that this auxiliary restriction, this norm of cooperation, is known to hold universally. If such a conciliatory attitude toward foes is known to be universally adhered to, then all foreign policies will culminate either in negotiation or in the maintenance of the status quo. Indeed, with the norm universally known to be operative, negotiation is the only possible solution to an interaction between states unless both parties prefer the status quo over a negotiated compromise settlement of their differences. We prove these claims.

COOPERATION PROPOSITION 4.1. *If it is common knowledge that negotiation is universally preferred to coercing an adversary into a capitulation (that is, $P^i U^i(\Delta_i) + (1 - P^i)U^i(\Delta_j) > U^i(\Delta_i - \phi_i P^i)$), for all nations i) and if for at least one actor negotiation is preferred to the status quo, then negotiation represents the equilibrium outcome of the domestic variant of the international interaction game.*

Proof. At node 9, B chooses between $\tilde{F}^B$ and F^B. F^B implied A's choice at node 12 will be $\max[U^A(\text{War}_B); U^A(\text{Cap}_A)]$. By assumption 2.A4, negotiation is preferred to either type of war. By the auxiliary assumption of the proposition—the putative norm—negotiation is also preferred to forcing an adversary to capitulate. Therefore, regardless of nation A's expected choice at node 12, B is better off choosing $\tilde{F}^B$ at node 9. By the same logic, A is better off selecting $\tilde{F}^A$ at node 5. Because negotiation is always preferable to acquiescence, the leader of nation B chooses D^B at node 3. If A chooses D^A, the equilibrium is D^A, D^B, $\tilde{F}^A$, $\tilde{F}^B \rightarrow$ Nego. If A does not make a demand at node 1, what happens? If the crisis subgame is reached at node 6, then both actors choose $\tilde{F}$. The logic is the same as for the crisis subgame beginning at node 5, except that the order of choices for nations A and B is reversed. Similarly, at node 4, A will make a demand rather than give in to B, for the negotiation outcome is always preferred to acquiescing. If A prefers negotiation over the status quo, then A can ensure that there will be negotiation by making a demand at node 1. If A prefers to maintain the status quo, then it may chose $\tilde{D}^A$ at node 1. However, the status quo will be preserved only if B also expects greater welfare from the status quo than from negotiation. Otherwise, B will respond to $\tilde{D}^A$ with D^B, and, as already shown, the equilibrium will be $\tilde{D}^A$, D^B, d^A, $\tilde{F}^B$, $\tilde{F}^A \rightarrow$ Nego. QED

Cooperation Proposition 4.1 is testable in terms of the central tendency of interactions between doves. It is highly unlikely that such a dovish form of behavior is universal; because of uncertainty, we should expect many deviations from cooperative behavior even between doves. The presence of uncertainty, as is proved later, fundamentally alters our expectations regarding the behavior of doves. Indeed, in the next section we turn to an investigation of variants of the first cooperation proposition in the face of uncertainty. But first we provide a preliminary assessment of the deduction that doves are likely to behave cooperatively, bearing in mind that the common knowledge that foes are doves is sufficient for cooperation or harmony, but it is not necessary.

In the international interaction game, full information is sufficient to guarantee that Cap_A, Cap_B, and War_B cannot arise as equilibrium outcomes. Thus, with our model a war begun by nation A is the only possible violent event under full information. The cooperation proposition tells us that this particular event is also prohibited as a possible equilibrium outcome under full information when A and B are doves. As the information conditions in the international environment deviate from the requirements of the proposition, the opportunity to engage in violence increases.

We acknowledge that decision makers are unlikely to possess full information in the real world, but we hypothesize that some environments provide clearer information than others regarding the preference structures of adversaries. As our measure of uncertainty decreases in value—approaching its full-information limit—we expect that real-world circumstances are more in line with the stipulations of the proposition. The cooperation proposition leads us to anticipate that doves will have virtually no proclivity to engage each other in violent conflict as those perfect information conditions are approached.

Using the operational procedures specified in appendix 1, we construct two logit analyses to assess Cooperation Proposition 4.1. With the dependent variable we evaluate whether the one feasible violent event under perfect information arose or not. This variable, WAR, is coded as 1.0 if there was violence by nations A and B and is coded as zero otherwise. In partial anticipation of the next section, each of the logit analyses controls for the level of uncertainty prevalent in the European international system on a year-by-year basis. In the first assessment of the proposition we utilize three independent variables: Uncertainty; Doves; and the interaction of the two. Doves is a dummy variable coded as 1.0 if nations A and B each satisfy our definition of a dove. Uncertainty is evaluated as the variance in risk-taking propensities for the European nations in the year of the observation. Large values reflect high uncertainty while a value of zero indicates full information about each state's willingness to engage in risky behavior. The interaction term assesses the relation between violence and joint dovishness when uncertainty is present. As is evident from Cooperation Proposition 4.1, the dummy variable Doves should be inversely associated with the likelihood of violence, whereas the interaction of this variable with the indicator of uncertainty should be positively associated with the risk of war. After all, with full information, the interaction term and Uncertainty equals zero, so that the expected level of violence is a function of only the variable Doves and the constant term.

The second logit analysis examines Cooperation Proposition 4.1 from a slightly different angle. Here we assess the relation between the likelihood of war and the magnitude of uncertainty given that we are examining only that subset of dyads in which both nation A and nation B satisfy our criteria for being called doves. The details of the logit analyses can be found in the notes, and figure 4.1 depicts the association between variations in the information conditions con-

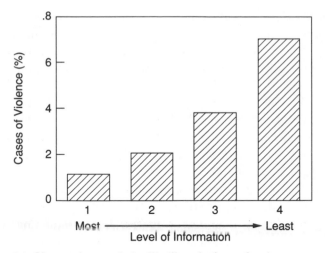

4.1: Uncertainty and the likelihood of war for doves.

fronted by doves and the likelihood of war. The figure shows dramat-
ically what the logit analyses reveal in greater detail: that the first
cooperation proposition is supported by the historical record for interactions in Europe between 1816 and 1970.[3]

COOPERATION, DOVES, AND UNCERTAINTY

The first cooperation proposition does not require perfect information
about all aspects of an interaction between states but only about
whether one's rival shares the preference for negotiation over capitulation. Knowledge of such a preference might arise as a result of a
universal behavioral inclination favoring the avoidance of violence and
the pursuit of conciliation. Such a conciliatory norm ensures either

3. War = $-1.23 - 3.46$ Doves + 9.89 Uncertainty $\times$ Doves + 1.14 Uncertainty,
$\chi^2 = 9.78$, P $< .021$, and N $= 686$. The probabilities for the terms, in order, are
.057, .038, and .055. War = $-4.69 + 11.03$ Uncertainty, $\chi^2 = 5.89$, P $< .015$, and
N $= 36$ Doves. The probability for the term is .027.
   It is important to realize that the percentages in figure 4.1 and other figures are
useful for comparison to one another only. The data we use include a comprehensive representation of violent disputes in Europe but only a sample of randomly
paired dyads that were not engaged in a dispute with one another. The random
sample represents only a fraction of the total number of nonconflicting dyads in
the years included in our analysis, whereas the conflict data are much closer to a
complete set, thereby overrepresenting cases of disputatious behavior compared
to cases in which the status quo prevailed. Fortunately, results are not distorted
in logit analysis by combining the population of one subset of cases and a random
sample of another subset. See Achen 1990.

harmony or cooperation if it applies universally and if it is known to do so. But the conciliatory norm should not be expected to hold without exception. It does not prove robust enough to ensure cooperation if there is some uncertainty about whether a rival is a conciliator or not.

Suppose that A, like Old Man Shirgugetu, does not know whether B is the type that abides by the conciliatory norm or the type that exploits offers to negotiate. A's decision to offer to negotiate depends, then, on how confident A is that B will not resort to force if A yields the first strike advantage.

Let A believe that B is a dove with probability π^A. Let A and B each be the purest type of dove: a state that would capitulate if coerced and that would negotiate rather than coerce another into capitulating. We call such actors pacific doves, and we assume that A can observe B's own exploitability, although dove A has a decided distaste for taking advantage of this feature of B's makeup. Thus, we assume that A knows that B prefers Cap_B to War_A (later we relax this condition) but does not know whether B prefers Nego to Cap_A. If A and B are pacific doves but each is uncertain of the other's dovishness, then A will gamble on negotiating if the expected utility of the lottery in which A offers to negotiate—not knowing whether B will also reject the use of force or will exploit its momentary advantage—is superior for A to choosing the use of force:

$$\pi^A > \frac{U^A(\Delta_A - \Delta_B) + \gamma_A(1 - P^A) - \phi_A P^A}{P^A U^A(\Delta_A - \Delta_B) + \gamma_A(1 - P^A)} = \pi^{*A}. \tag{4.1}$$

The benefits from negotiation are worth the risk of exploitation for A under rather constrained circumstances. For instance, the critical threshold value for A's belief that B is a dovish type, π^{*A}, increases as A's expected domestic penalties for using force decrease.[4] Indeed, if $\phi_A \leq [(1 - P^A)U^A(\Delta_A - \Delta_B)]/P^A$, then no level of belief about B by A is sufficient to warrant risking exploitation. A will use force. In this case, domestic political considerations are central in determining a critical foreign policy choice.

Actor B appears to be less constrained. For B, the risk of exploitation is worthwhile so long as the gamble that A will choose to be conciliatory versus the danger that A will force a capitulation by B is superior to acquiescing to A's initial demand:

---

4. $\dfrac{\partial \pi^{*A}}{\partial \phi_A} = - \dfrac{P^A}{P^A U^A(\Delta_A - \Delta_B) + \gamma_A(1 - P^A)} < 0.$

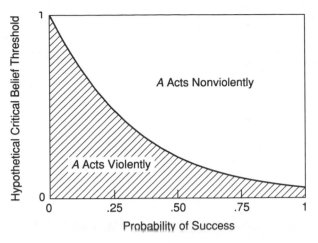

4.2: Pacific dove A's critical belief threshold.

$$\pi^B > \frac{\gamma_B(1 - p^B)}{P^B U^B(\Delta_B - \Delta_A) + \gamma_B(1 - P^B)} = \pi^{*B}. \tag{4.2}$$

This ratio is always less than 1.0, ensuring that π^B at least can always hold a feasible value.[5] For dove B, domestic factors apparently do not enter into this foreign policy decision. The domestic cost term appears nowhere in expression 4.2.

Of course, war is an impossibility if neither A nor B would retaliate if attacked. But how likely is cooperation between such pacific doves if each is uncertain only of the other's willingness to refrain from exploitation in favor of negotiation? Just how willing are they to gamble on the dovishness of the rival? We evaluate the relation between dovishness and the prospects of cooperation as a function of the probability of success by A and its coalition of supporters. Figures 4.2 and 4.3 plot the functional form of expressions (4.1) and (4.2) with respect to the subjective probability of success. The figures map the critical thresholds π^{*A} and π^{*B} for increasing values of P^A (as subjectively estimated by A and B, respectively).

B gambles on A's dovishness so long as its belief is above the critical threshold value depicted in figure 4.3 and delineated in expression 4.2. Likewise, A gambles on B's goodwill provided its actual belief about B is above the critical threshold line depicted in figure 4.2 and derived from expression 4.1. For B to gamble means that it does

5. For purposes of this analysis, the probability of success P is assumed to be common knowledge, so that $P^B = 1 - P^A$.

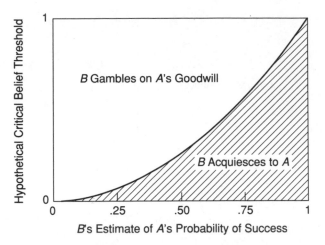

4.3: Pacific dove *B*'s critical belief threshold.

not acquiesce to *A*'s initial demand. For *A* to gamble means that it offers to negotiate, risking that *B* will seize the initiative and exploit *A*'s offer. Because both parties are actually doves, if both gamble, then, cooperation and negotiation ensue. However, if either chooses not to gamble, then coercion ensues.

If *B* does not gamble on *A*'s dovishness, then the resultant coercion is tacit and nonviolent. *B* acquiesces under the belief that *A* will exploit *B* if the opportunity arises. If *A* does not gamble and *B* does, then *A*, despite its distaste for exploiting *B*, coerces *B* into capitulating to *A*'s demand under the perhaps mistaken belief that the alternative was for *A* to be coerced. As is evident from figures 4.2 and 4.3, one or another form of coercion may be likely. What is more, there is a wide range of circumstances in which pacific dove *A*'s coercion of *B* involves violence.

The case of two pacific doves is instructive. As figures 4.2 and 4.3 reveal, such a dovish *A* is more and more willing to gamble on *B*'s goodwill as *A*'s probability of success (that is, *A*'s power or that of *A*'s coalition of supporters) increases, but *B* is less and less inclined to gamble on *A*'s goodwill under these conditions. Thus, *B* is increasingly willing to submit to tacit coercion as *A* gets stronger, whereas *A* is increasingly inclined to resort to force rather than risk exploitation as it gets weaker.

The intuition behind these results is straightforward despite their seemingly counterintuitive nature. The stronger *A* is relative to *B*, the worse *B* can expect to do even if the two nations reach a negotiated settlement. Therefore, because negotiation is not all that attractive, it is not worth B's while to risk exploitation and the outcome of capitulation. As B's power (or, more precisely, its own power and that of its coalition of supporters) increases relative to A's, the value of a negotiated settlement also rises for B, making the gamble more attractive. At the same time, the value of the gamble becomes less attractive for A because A does not stand to gain much from a negotiated settlement. A simply does not bring much leverage to the bargaining table. Having less power inclines A not to risk being exploited by B, for the positive side of the risk (that is, a negotiated settlement) is of diminishing worth. Therefore, A becomes more inclined to take an action it finds distasteful: attacking B. By gambling, A can end up doing poorly in a negotiation or, even worse, can end up being attacked and having to capitulate (remember A is a *pacific* dove). Weak A's only real chance at a significant benefit arises, paradoxically, if A attacks B and B turns out to be the pacific type who gives in. That is A's incentive for using force when A is weak and pacific.

The more inclined one pacific dove is to gamble on the other's goodwill, the less so inclined is the other pacific dove. Depending on the magnitude of the expected costs of coercion, the inverse relations between A's and B's willingness to take a chance on the other's goodwill can be a recipe for substantial coercion.

Figures 4.2 and 4.3 suggest counterintuitive, testable hypotheses that represent modifications of Cooperation Proposition 4.1 under conditions of uncertainty.

COOPERATION PROPOSITION 4.1A. *Expression 4.1 indicates that if A and B are doves uncertain of each other's type and if B is not expected to retaliate if attacked, then the coercive use of force by A is most likely if A is weak compared to B. Weak dovish As are more likely to initiate violence than are strong dovish As, with the likelihood diminishing asymptotically as A's subjective estimate of its probability of success increases.*

COOPERATION PROPOSITION 4.1B. *Expression 4.2 indicates that if A and B are doves uncertain of each other's type and if B is not the type that retaliates if attacked, then the likelihood that B acquiesces to A's initial demand increases exponentially as B's subjective estimate of A's probability of success in a confrontation with B increases.*[6]

6. The shape of each function is ascertained by finding the partial derivative of the relevant belief with respect to A's probability of success. The partial derivatives are presented below.

We subject these two propositions to empirical tests. We cannot measure the actual beliefs of A or B about the other's type, although we do estimate their beliefs about A's probability of success in a confrontation. Also, we estimate for each side whether it was a pacific dove. We assume that true beliefs, on average, are more likely to fall above the critical threshold, facilitating cooperation, as the critical threshold value falls lower and lower. That is, the lower the critical threshold, the more likely that, on average, the required level of belief is satisfied. Then we can test the central tendency of the expectations from propositions 4.1a and 4.1b.

We define all of the necessary variables—whether A and B are doves, whether B is a tough, retaliatory dove or a pacific, exploitable dove, and whether A has much probability of success—in accordance with the procedures described in appendix 1. As figure 4.2 indicates, A's gambling threshold falls asymptotically as A's power rises. We capture this nonlinear, asymptotic expectation by taking the logarithm of side A's probability of success. Our test of proposition 4.1a, then, is a logit analysis. The dependent variable, ViolentA, recognizes that the theory predicts the conditions under which A will use force. This variable is coded as 1.0 so long as A uses force, regardless of B's ultimate response. The independent variable is the natural logarithm of A's probability of success. This is a function that emulates our theoretically derived expectation that the relation between P^A and the likelihood of violence by A is asymptotic.

In keeping with A's hypothesized uncertainty, we include all cases in which nation B was paired with A when A was, by our operational procedures, a pacific dove. That is, we do not segregate cases for this test on the basis of whether B was a dove, for that information is the source of A's uncertainty. We have sixty-seven observations of European disputes that satisfy these requirements. The hypothesis is that $\ln(P^A)$ is inversely related to the likelihood of A using force.

The result of the logit analysis is ViolentA $= -1.06 - 0.83 \ln(P^A)$, $\chi^2 = 5.89$, P $< .015$, and N $= 67$. Figure 4.4 depicts the theoretically derived expectation and the empirically observed reality. The observed relations in the logit analysis and in the figure are consistent with the surprising expectation from Cooperation Proposition 4.1a that weak pacific doves faced with uncertainty are more likely to coerce their rivals than are strong pacific doves. Figure 4.4 makes clear how well the theoretically derived functional form of expression 4.1 fits the actual relation between A's subjective estimate of its probability of success and the incidence of violence.

Cooperation Proposition 4.1b is evaluated by specifying a dummy

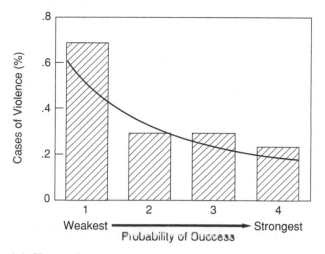

4.4: Uncertainty and violence for pacific dove A.

variable, Gamble/Acq$_B$, which is coded as 1.0 if B made a demand and is coded as zero if B acquiesced to A's demand. Using the cases in which our measures indicate that B was a dove, we estimate the square of B's subjective estimate of A's probability of success $(1 - P^B)^2$ as the independent variable in keeping with the functional form of expression 4.2 and as shown in figure 4.3. We again perform a logit analysis, this time in keeping with proposition 4.1b, with the expectation that $(1 - P^B)^2$ is positively associated with the dependent variable Gamble/Acq$_B$. The cases utilized for this analysis are those in which nation B was a dove by our estimation. In keeping with the uncertainty conditions of the proposition, B knows that it is a pacific dove but does not know whether A is a dove, so all nations A paired with dove B are included. Furthermore, the proposition assumes that A has already made a demand to which B can respond by acquiescing or by making a counterdemand. Therefore, we examine only those cases in which A in fact made a demand, with the dependent variable assessing whether B gambled that A was a dove or B acquiesced. The logit results are Gamble/Acq$_B$ = 0.76 + 2.61 $(1 - P^B)^2$, χ^2 = 2.66, $P < .10$, N = 32. The significance level for the independent variable is .083.

Figure 4.5 depicts the theoretically expected functional relation between B's belief about A's chances of success and B's likelihood of gambling that A is a dove. The histogram shows the distribution of observed gambles by B in relation to B's belief about A's chances

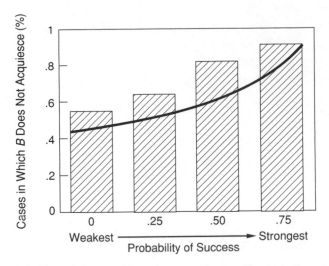

4.5: Uncertainty and acquiescence for pacific dove *B*.

of success. The statistical results and the representation in figure 4.5 modestly support the expectations derived from expression 4.2.

The results displayed in figures 4.4 and 4.5 are sobering reminders of the inadequacies of a conciliatory norm in an environment of uncertainty. It is hard to sustain a dovish perspective when so many interactions between the most pacific doves end in violence or coercion. At the same time, the results are encouraging to the extent that they reflect the existence of a norm that would always prohibit violence if it were universally applied and if that were common knowledge.

The Punktation of Olmütz

Propositions 4.1a and 4.1b represent severe tests of the theory. These specific hypotheses do not arise (or, to our knowledge at least, have not arisen) in other theories, and they represent previously unsuspected relations. Severe tests represent important evidence about a theory and its progressive content. Although we have offered systematic evidence for the phenomena described by propositions 4.1a and 4.1b, a brief, illustrative historical account of an appropriate event will facilitate a fuller understanding of the subtleties of these deductions.

Following the revolutions of 1848–49, the German Confederation underwent a difficult period of adjustment. Austrian prestige was on the ascent by the summer of 1849. The Habsburg monarchy found itself again at the head of a restored German Diet, despite the dissenting voices and rival constitution promulgated in Frankfurt on

May 28, 1849. Alas, the restoration of the German Diet was viewed as provocative by the Prussians. They, as well as a few smaller German states, supported dual leadership in Germany, thereby hoping to give greater prominence to Prussia. Gen. Joseph Maria von Radowitz, the key adviser of Frederick William IV, pressed firmly for Prussian pursuit of parity with Austria in a newly constituted confederation (Mowat 1932, 172, 174). Although his approach was popular with the king, Radowitz's position was opposed by leading Prussian conservatives, including the young rising star Otto von Bismarck. Restitution of the pre-1848 organization of the German states, Austria's declaration that the resolutions of the Erfurt Parliament were null and void, and the reassertion of the authority of the German Diet led to rising animosity between Prussia and much of the rest of Germany. These tensions arose initially over the Treaty of Berlin, by which Prussia intended to resolve the Schleswig and Holstein dispute with Denmark and, not incidentally, to assert its rights outside the Federal Diet. Austria claimed that only the reconstituted German Diet had authority to ratify the treaty, thereby leading to a direct confrontation of wills.

The tensions escalated, reaching a head when Austria and its allies confronted Prussia over a dispute centered on Electoral Hesse. The elector was locked in a struggle with the Hessian Parliament. In the contest of wills, the Parliament was dissolved even before it could authorize a budget. Much of the Hessian officer corps resigned, as did many judges and other key officials, creating a power vacuum. Fearing for his security, the elector sought military assistance from the Diet. The grant of assistance provoked a strong negative reaction in Prussia, where there were fears that the circumstances in Hesse would be used to consolidate the German Confederation at Prussia's expense. Prussia declared that it did not recognize the Diet's authority and that it would not permit the Hessian frontier to be closed.

On October 8, 1850, the Erfurt Union, which included several German states as well as Prussia, determined to treat the union as an alliance and to back Prussia in its struggle. This action provoked the Kings' Alliance to pursue the interests of Austria and its allies. The kings of Austria, Bavaria, and Württemberg met on October 11–12 and agreed, by the Punktation of October 12, that Bavarian troops and an Austrian rifle battalion would march into Hesse. By late October 1850, Bavarian troops, acting in response to the Punktation, entered Hesse to protect against a Prussian incursion.

At the same time, Prussian forces approached Hesse. War seemed imminent. So dangerous had the situation become that the Russians, who had been trying to mediate the dispute in a conference at Warsaw, declared that any armed resistance by Prussia to any other German troops in Hesse would constitute a declaration of war against Russia. Nevertheless, 140,000 men of the Prussian army were mobilized (*Times* [London], Nov. 4, 1850). To make matters still more threatening, it looked as though the dispute would spread. The French also gave indications of entering the conflict, with some ambiguity as to which side they favored. On November 2 the *Economist* reported that the French were prepared to assist the Russians in "dismembering" Prussia. Indeed, by November 23 the French were reportedly calling up an additional forty thousand conscripts and amassing a large army on the Rhine. Historians, with the benefit of perspective that time renders, suggest that the French tried to negotiate a treaty with Prussia (Mowat 1932, 183). Wherever the truth lies, it was widely believed that should a war begin, it probably would involve Russia, France, and also England. By November 1850 there was serious danger of a Europe-wide war.

By November 1, eight thousand Bavarian troops and one thousand Austrian Rifles entered Hanau in Hesse, with about half the Austrian Rifles sent to occupy Gelnhausen. With Prussian troops close at hand, an accidental, if not intentional, confrontation seemed inevitable. The immediate Prussian reaction to the incursion was to issue orders not to resist the occupation of Hanau but not to permit the occupation of the provinces of Cassel or Fulda, which were strategically important to Prussia. On November 8, Bavarian troops, under the leadership of Prince Taxis, advanced against Fulda. In the village of Bronzell—near Fulda, territory the Prussians had orders not to cede—the Bavarians encountered Prussian troops, and the greatly feared collision of the two armies took place. Shots were exchanged, with several soldiers seriously wounded and some killed. It appeared that war had broken out.

Yet Otto von Manteuffel, the new Prussian minister president and foreign minister did not call for an escalation against the Bavarian forces. Rather, he ordered an evacuation, and no further fighting took place. Indeed, Manteuffel's ascent to power was largely sparked by his dovelike desire to avoid a war—a war described by "an eyewitness, who is neither a Prussian nor a Bavarian," as "the beginning of a bloody drama that is now unfolding itself, and that nobody will triumph in except Germany's enemies" (*Times*, Nov. 13, 1850).

Following Manteuffel's display of restraint, Prince Felix Schwarzenberg, Austrian minister president, offered Manteuffel guarantees

concerning Prussia's right of way over the military road of the elec-
torate and concerning the duration of the occupation of Electoral
Hesse. Manteuffel rejected these promises, requesting a meeting instead. Prussia and Austria met at Olmütz, and reached a settlement
on November 29, one that largely represented a capitulation by Prussia. As Agatha Ramm explains it, the capitulation at Olmütz came
about because "the King's fundamental wish for peace [brought] Prussia to concede the whole of Schwarzenberg's demands" (1967, 221).

The events leading up to the Punktation of Olmütz fit the conditions
of propositions 4.1a and 4.1b. It is important to recognize that events
such as those that occurred between Prussia and the Federal forces in
Hesse are scarcely written about at length by historians.[7] This is
because, *ex post*, little comes of disputes like this one. The international interaction game instructs us as to why such events do not
escalate into wars, even when, *ex ante*, an event looks very threatening.

It is apparent from the contemporaneous journalistic accounts,
which did not have the benefit of hindsight, that the events leading to
the Punktation of Olmütz portended a war between the great European
powers. The representatives of Austria, Bavaria, and Württemberg
demanded Prussian acquiescence to the authority of the German Diet
(D^A), but they were not sure how Prussia would respond. The truth
of Prussia's intentions was unknown. On the one hand, it was possible
that Prussia was a hawk bent on exploiting the lesser German states.
Such a view squared with the formation of the Erfurt Union and the
accompanying efforts to deny Austria its historic position in Germany.
On the other hand, the Prussians acted in a restrained manner while
pursuing a reconciliation through the Russian-sponsored discussions
in Warsaw. Indeed, on November 2, 1850, the *Times* reported: "The
ceremonious attention shown to the Austrian Emperor [during the
meetings in Warsaw] must have made an unusual impression on public
opinion. . . . Prussia exhibited a disposition to mediate and come to a
better understanding with the Government of Vienna, although it adheres firmly to its protest, on principle, against every general interpretation of the Austrian Bund." Furthermore, it was clear that there
were divisions within Prussia over how to approach the crisis. Even

7. The Punktation of Olmütz is much more extensively discussed by German and
Austrian historians than by historians writing in English. Even among German and
Austrian scholars, however, Olmütz is discussed more in terms of its impact on
subsequent German policy than in terms of the events in Hesse per se.

Radowitz—a relative hawk—had declared that Prussia's displays of armed power were meant only to encourage negotiation, not to show any intention of fighting. Here, then, was the crux of the matter for the German Federal forces, consisting of Austrian and Bavarian soldiers. They could not tell whether Radowitz's actions and those of Manteuffel after him were intended to encourage negotiation or were preparatory to an attack against the Federal army. If the latter case, as noted by proposition 4.1a, it was better for the Federal forces to move first.

The Prussians also must have been uncertain of the intentions of the Federal army. The troops were undeniably placed to prevent Radowitz and Frederick William, who desired greater influence in Germany, from realizing their goals. Yet the pro-Austrian factions in greater Germany had gone to great lengths in Warsaw and even later to try to provide Prussia with a face-saving way out of the impasse. Perhaps they were only trying to gain additional leverage in future negotiations—behavior consistent with dovishness—or, more ominously, perhaps they believed Prussia was only bluffing, and they intended to exploit Prussian reluctance to fight other Germans.

The Prussians, being much stronger than the Bavarian force sent to resist them, did not acquiesce but rather demanded Prussian rights as they understood them (D^B). That is, the Prussians, in accordance with proposition 4.1b, believed that they were strong enough to gamble on the dovish orientation of the Federal army, even at the risk of having to capitulate later. The evidence that their adversaries would actually fight was not sufficient to warrant a Prussian decision to acquiesce without testing the waters.

The mobilized Austro-Bavarian forces were weaker than the mobilized Prussian army.[8] What is more, the Austrians had been careful to minimize their own military involvement. In the event of a direct confrontation, the overwhelming bulk of the Federal forces would be Bavarian. Table 4.1 displays our estimates of the subjective probability of success of each of the key rivals in this dispute, taking into account not only their own strength but that of potential third-party supporters and opponents. The estimates are done in accordance with the procedures delineated in appendix 1. Apparently, the Federal forces were less well prepared to cede the first-strike advantage by gambling on Prussia's good intentions. Not being sure of Prussia's true type and

8. The Prussians did worry about the threatened intervention of Russia. Still, that intervention might have been offset by the anticipated support of other powers for Prussia's claims.

Table 4.1
Subjective Probabilities of Success for
Key Players in the Punktation

Nation A	P^A	Nation B	P^B
Austria	.25	Prussia	.73
Bavaria	.23	Prussia	.73
Württemberg	.23	Prussia	.73

knowing themselves to be too weak in the field to relinquish whatever small advantage was to be had by seizing the initiative, the Bavarian forces struck out, leading to the violent collision in Bronzell.[9]

By our estimation, the confrontation between the German Federal forces and the Prussians was a confrontation between states that were pacific doves vis-à-vis one another.[10] In fact, as would be the case if the Prussians were pacific doves, the Prussians capitulated when faced with a military confrontation by the Bavarians.

With some befuddlement, the *Times,* a source generally hostile to Prussia's ambitions and sympathetic to those of the German Confederation, summarized the unfolding events of the conflict in this way:

> There remains still a subject of mortification in the fact that Bavaria should now be playing the part of an intervening Power, even though it is manifestly under the wing of Austria. That Bavaria, the subordinate state, which [sic] wishes to assert its place as one of the first rank. According to the theory of the Confederation, its army, formed of the contingents from the several states, is considered as one, and it is difficult to discover how, in this case, Prussia is entitled to resolve the occupying force now in Hesse into its national elements, and attribute the entry to the "too great haste" of the least influential of them. (Nov. 8)

9. The exact details of the confrontation are not known. Pro-Austrian reports indicate that the Bavarian soldiers marched with their muskets unloaded and with their swords sheathed, whereas Prussian accounts state that the Prussians had their swords sheathed and their muskets unloaded. Nor has anyone established who fired the first shots. Some accounts indicate that the Prussians fired some volleys over the approaching troops, presumably to signal them to halt or retreat. Other accounts indicate that the Bavarians shot at the Prussians as soon as they saw them in Bronzell. In either case, the Bavarians certainly knew that they were proceeding into sensitive territory as they approached Fulda, inevitably coming face to face with the Prussian forces.

10. In our conceptualization of dovelike or hawklike behavior, these characteristics are specific to the particular rivalry and not necessarily general characteristics of one or another state's foreign relations.

Yet propositions 4.1a and 4.1b seem to provide an accurate description of how Prussia is entitled to resolve the occupying force in Hesse. Manteuffel simply was not prepared to fight a war against fellow Germans over so small an issue. Consequently, he ordered the Prussian forces to capitulate when the weaker Bavarians used force—the precise action anticipated by the propositions. War did not materialize apparently because Prussia was a pacific dove at that time and in that place.

WHAT IF B IS A TOUGH DOVE?

Perhaps the previous analysis asks for too strong a norm of conciliation in requiring that neither A nor B will retaliate if attacked. Here we investigate the robustness of the conciliatory norm when both actors are doves: whether they are doves is uncertain, and B is known to retaliate with force if attacked. That is, A knows that if it tries to coerce B, then a war will ensue. There is no prospect that B will capitulate to A's demands. In that case,

$$\pi^A > \frac{P^A U^A(\Delta_A - \Delta_B) + \gamma_A(1 - P^A) - \alpha_A(1 - P^A) - \phi_A P^A}{P^A U^A(\Delta_A - \Delta_B) + \gamma_A(1 - P^A)} = \pi^{*A},$$

(4.3)

and

$$\pi^B > \frac{\tau_B(1 - P^B) + P^B[\phi_B - U^B(\Delta_B - \Delta_A)]}{\tau_B(1 - P^B) + \phi_B P^B} = \pi^{*B}.$$ (4.4)

In expressions (4.1) and (4.2), in which the choices involve only cooperation or exploitation, the partial derivative of π^{*A} with respect to P^A is negative, and the partial derivative of π^{*B} with respect to P^B is also negative (and positive with respect to P^A or $1 - P^B$).[11] However, if nation B is a tough dove—one who prefers to negotiate rather than

11. The respective partial derivatives are

$$\frac{\partial \pi^{*A}}{\partial P^A} = -\frac{[U^A(\Delta_A - \Delta_B)]^2 + \gamma_A \phi_A}{[P^A U^A(\Delta_A - \Delta_B) + \gamma_A(1 - P^A)]^2},$$

and

$$\frac{\partial \pi^{*B}}{\partial P^B} = -\frac{\gamma_B[U^B(\Delta_B - \Delta_A)]}{[P^B U^B(\Delta_B - \Delta_A) + \gamma_B(1 - P^B)]^2}.$$

exploit but who retaliates if attacked—then the more likely A is to succeed in pressing its demands, the higher the threshold of confidence is likely to be before A will risk exploitation.[12] At the same time, B's threshold for gambling on A's goodwill rises as A's probability of success increases, meaning that B is decreasingly willing to take a chance on A. The relevant partial derivatives are

$$\frac{\partial \pi^{*A}}{\partial P^A} = \frac{[U^A(\Delta_A - \Delta_B)](\alpha_A) - \phi_A\gamma_A}{(P^A[U^A(\Delta_A - \Delta_B)] + \gamma_A(1 - P^A))^2} , \tag{4.5}$$

and

$$\frac{\partial \pi^{*B}}{\partial P^B} = - \frac{[U^B(\Delta_B - \Delta_A)]\tau_B}{[\tau_B(1 - P^B) + \phi_B P^B]^2} . \tag{4.6}$$

Here we can see the horns of the cooperation dilemma faced by uncertain doves. A's threshold of confidence is usually rising asymptotically as P^A increases (the inverse of the situation when A is a pacific dove).[13] We can state the dilemmas as propositions.

COOPERATION PROPOSITION 4.1C. *The stronger pacific dove A becomes relative to tough dove B, the less willing generally that A is to gamble on B's dovishness and the more inclined dovish A is to strike first, launching a war that neither A nor B wants. This inclination on A's part rises especially quickly when A's power is growing from a weak base.*

At the same time, B is between a rock and a hard place. If B does not gamble on A's goodwill, then B must acquiesce to A's demand, thereby losing for sure. If, however, B gives A a chance to cooperate, A may interpret such action as a signal that B is hawkish, making A likely to start a war.

COOPERATION PROPOSITION 4.1D. *The stronger pacific dove A is, the more inclined tough dove B is to give up, appeasing A by allowing itself to be tacitly coerced by the mistaken belief that A is hawkish.*

Alas for nation B, propositions 4.1c and 4.1d indicate that A's increased belief threshold enhances the prospect that B's mistaken belief about A will be reinforced by A's actions: A is increasingly likely

12. Unless the unusual circumstance holds in which $\phi_A\gamma_A \geq U^A(\Delta_A - \Delta_B)$. Then the partial derivative is negative.

13. We say usually because of the exception detailed in note 12.

to attack *B*. Unlike the case of two pacific doves, here dove *A* is confronted with an adversary believed to be willing to resist *A*'s use of force. In this instance, the more powerful *A* is, the more likely it is that there will be a war.[14] The prospects of cooperation diminish even though both nations would rather negotiate than exploit or fight one another, except under the unusual circumstance delineated in note 12.

In expressions (4.5) and (4.6) we see an explanation of Chingis Khan's behavior toward his brother Khasar. Chingis may well have been the conciliatory type he appeared to be to Old Man Shirgugetu, but in Khasar he faced a tougher rival. The powerful Chingis Khan was willing to gamble on the cooperative intentions of Shirgugetu and his family. They were in no position to retaliate against Chingis if he exploited them, and Chingis surely knew that. But he was not willing to gamble on Khasar, a rival with the means to strike back.

A conciliatory norm that favors negotiation over the use of force appears to diminish in its effectiveness if there is uncertainty about a rival's likelihood of following the norm. Although perfectly effective if universally applied, it rapidly deteriorates as a source of cooperation if, as with all norms, it is applied probabilistically. Even doves who are almost certain of each other's goodwill may nevertheless engage in tacit or violent coercion or even war with one another, particularly if there is a substantial asymmetry in their subjective chances for success. The inadequacy of the conciliatory norm is succinctly captured by a favorite maxim of the late Japanese admiral Isoroku Yamamoto, architect of the attack on Pearl Harbor: "An efficient hawk hides his claws" (Prange 1981, 13). In a world of limited information, vulnerable doves are especially fearful of just such hidden claws.

THE SELF-DEFENSE NORM

We have seen several of the strengths and weaknesses of dovish behavior. Often, especially in journalistic discussions, the dovish, conciliatory approach to foreign policy is poised against a more hawkish

---

14. We return to this point in chapter 6 when we discuss the theories of power transition and hegemonic stability. Unfortunately, the specific functional forms of expressions (4.3) and (4.4) cannot be tested because of a lack of data. Although we have numerous cases in which both *A* and *B* appear to be doves and several instances in which *B* appears to be a tough, retaliatory dove, the intersection of cases in which *A* seems to be a dove and *B* seems to be a tough dove is nearly empty. There are only two such instances in our data set, thereby precluding any assessment of these propositions.

attitude that emphasizes strong retaliatory capabilities. We turn now to the prospects of cooperation emanating from a purely retaliatory, self-defense norm.

Few would dispute that the right to self-defense is one of the oldest principles of human interaction. As John Locke maintained, "The law, which was made for my preservation where it cannot interpose to secure my life from present force, which if lost is capable of no reparation, permits me my own defence, and the right of war, a liberty to kill the aggressor, because the aggressor allows not time to appeal to our common judge, nor the decision of the law, for remedy in a case where the mischief may be irreparable" (1937, 15), and again, "Whosoever uses force without right, as everyone does in a society who does it without law, puts himself into a state of war with those against whom he uses it, and in that state all former ties are canceled, all other rights cease, and everyone has a right to defend himself and to resist the aggressor" (155). Here, then, is a widely accepted norm of conduct. But what relation does it bear to the prospects for peacefully resolving disputes?

Thucydides suggests an answer to our question. Speaking through the Corinthians, he makes the claim that self-defense is an essential norm of action if there is to be peace. The Corinthians, in the debate at Sparta over the declaration of war, say: "The likeliest way of securing peace is this: only to use one's power in the cause of justice, but to make it perfectly plain that one is resolved not to tolerate aggression. On the contrary, your idea of proper behaviour is, firstly, to avoid harming others, and then to avoid being harmed yourselves, even if it is a matter of defending your own interests" (1954, 76). In other words, the Corinthians believed the Spartans to be nonretaliatory doves, whereas they were convinced that the threat of retaliation was essential to the preservation of peace. Indeed, the Corinthian argument explicitly contends that the use of force in self-defense is always in the cause of justice.

A norm of self-defense is more consistent with a realist view than a liberal view of foreign policy, and a conciliatory norm is more consistent with a liberal perspective than a realist perspective. Acting in accordance with the conciliatory norm shows a reliance on the goodwill of others, and acting in accordance with the self-defense norm shows a reliance on one's own capabilities. Those who pursue Vegetius's well-known dictum "Those who desire peace, prepare for war" take as axiomatic that states should maintain a military capability sufficient to persuade any rival that attempted coercion will lead to war.

Such a militaristic posture is sometimes conceived to be incompatible with a dovish perspective, but this is not necessarily so, at least not in terms of how dovish behavior has been defined here. Recall that a dove is an actor that prefers to negotiate rather than exploit a rival. Such an attitude has been shown in proposition 4.1 to be generally conducive to the avoidance of violence, although in specific circumstances (that is, propositions 4.1a–d), dovishness is consistent with the risk that force will be used. The norm of self-defense is compatible with dovish behavior of the type we have called tough dove. The norm of self-defense can also exist without such an attitude of dovishness. One can be prepared to retaliate if attacked, whether one is a hawk or a dove. As the security dilemma highlights, a prospective difficulty with a self-defense norm is that the acquisition of arms—even defensive arms—may be misconstrued by the rival as a signal of aggressive intentions. However, as we show in the second cooperation proposition, so long as it is evident that both side's forces are adequate for retaliation, it does not matter whether either side believes the other has dovish, conciliatory or hawkish, exploitive motives.

We propose as the second cooperation proposition the following self-defense norm.

COOPERATION PROPOSITION 4.2. *If both parties to a conflict of interest are known to be prepared to retaliate if attacked, then cooperation or harmony is guaranteed, regardless of whether either or both adversaries are believed to be exploitive or conciliatory.*

Proof. At node 12 of the international interaction game, $f^A > \bar{f}^A$ by the assumption of the norm that retaliation is preferred to capitulation. At node 9, $\bar{F}^B > F^B$ by our assumption that negotiation is always preferred to war. At node 10, $F^B > \bar{F}^B$ by the retaliation assumption of the proposition. Thus, at node 5, A's choice is between offering to negotiate or waging war. Because negotiation is preferred to war, A offers to negotiate. In anticipation of this choice by A, $D^B > \bar{D}^B$ at node 3, for negotiation is always better than acquiescing. The same reasoning leads to the following choices from node 4 forward: d^A, $\bar{F}^B$, $\bar{F}^A$. At node 2, then, the choice is between negotiation or the status quo. If A prefers negotiation to the status quo, then A chooses D^A at node 1, precluding the selection by B of the status quo at node 2. If A prefers the status quo, then A chooses $\bar{D}^A$ at node 1. If B also prefers the status quo to negotiation, then the equilibrium is the status quo.

If B prefers negotiation to the status quo, then B selects D^B at node 2, which implies negotiation at node 7. Consequently, if A and B are known to be retaliators, then regardless of any other characteristics they may possess, only negotiation or the status quo can be an equilibrium outcome. QED

Proposition 4.2 demonstrates that if A and B prefer to retaliate rather than capitulate and that if each knows the other is a self-defender, then only cooperation or harmony can ensue. As with the conciliatory norm, the self-defense norm ensures a peaceful outcome if it is universally applied. Unlike the conciliatory norm, the self-defense norm does not require faith that the rival has good intentions but rather requires that each state be clearly and adequately prepared to defend itself. In that sense, the self-defense norm comes closer to meeting the normative standards for cooperation raised at the outset of this chapter than does the conciliatory norm. Even hawks confronting one another will behave cooperatively if the self-defense norm is known by each party to be operative.

The threat to cooperation when this norm is enforced is the risk that one or another rival will mistakenly believe that the adversary is not adequately prepared militarily or is too severely constrained by domestic costs to use force. It may well have been just such uncertainty that encouraged the mistaken belief by the Japanese in 1941 that the United States could be forced to capitulate in the Pacific. Recall, for instance, that in August 1941, despite the dual threats to American interests in the Pacific and the Atlantic, the Congress extended the Selective Service Act only by the narrowest of margins. In the House, the vote was 203 to 202. It is little wonder that the Japanese ambassador to the United States failed to persuade his foreign minister that the United States could not be coerced. "Talk and bluster were cheap, but when it came to a hard vote to lay before their constituents, Congress felt safe in nearly scuttling the draft" (Prange 1981, 178–79). Apparently, the president was believed to be facing substantial domestic political costs if he used force.

The self-defense norm, like the conciliatory norm, guarantees peace if universally applied. Of course, the prospect of uncertainty is always present. What, then, are the conditions that lead to cooperation if the self-defense norm is only probabilistically employed? To answer this question, we let π^A and π^B equal, respectively, A's and B's belief that their opponent is the type who will retaliate if attacked. Similarly, we let ω^A equal A's belief that B is the type who will gamble on using force against A if A offers to negotiate so that this is the risk A takes of ending up with the outcome War$_B$ if A does not resort to force. For negotiation to be the equilibrium outcome if demands have been made when A and B actually are self-defenders who will retaliate if attacked, the following conditions must hold:

$$\pi^A > \frac{(1 - P^A)[U^A(\Delta_A - \Delta_B + \omega^A \tau_A)] - \phi_A P^A(1 - \omega^A)}{(1 - P^A)[(U^A(\Delta_A - \Delta_B) + \alpha_A]} = \pi^{*A}, \quad (4.7)$$

and

$$\pi^B > \frac{(1 - P^B)U^B(\Delta_B - \Delta_A) - \phi_B P^B}{(1 - P^B)[U^B(\Delta_B - \Delta_A) + \alpha_B]} = \pi^{*B}. \quad (4.8)$$

How is the prospect of negotiation influenced by changes in A's and B's subjective estimates of their respective probabilities of success? To answer this, we first derive the partial derivatives of (4.7) and (4.8) with respect to P^A and P^B. These are

$$\frac{\partial \pi^{*A}}{\partial P^A} = - \frac{\phi_A(1 - \omega^A)}{(1 - P^A)^2 U^A(\Delta_A - \Delta_B + \alpha_A)}, \quad (4.9)$$

and

$$\frac{\partial \pi^{*B}}{\partial P^B} = - \frac{\phi_B}{(1 - P^B)^2 U^B(\Delta_B - \Delta_A + \alpha_B)}. \quad (4.10)$$

Each of these partial derivatives tells an important story about the prospects for negotiation as a function of the size of the belief threshold required for negotiation and the actor's subjective estimate of the probability of success. As A's power increases, its required threshold of confidence in B's capability for self-defense, not surprisingly, decreases. The stronger A is, the more willing it is to gamble on offering to negotiate and risk attack. What is more, the magnitude of the effect is nonlinear and is dependent on A's belief that B acts like the dovish type who prefers negotiation to a chance at exploitation.[15] That is the meaning of the term $1 - \omega^A$ in the numerator of (4.9).

A similar pattern of expected behavior is revealed with regard to B in (4.10). The greater the magnitude of P^B, the more willing B is to respond to an offer of compromise by negotiating rather than exploiting

15. This statement should not be construed to mean that A believes B is a dove. There are two reasons for $1 - \omega^A$ to be large: A believes B is a dove, or A believes that B expects A to retaliate and therefore believes that B will negotiate even if B is a hawk.

A. Thus, the theory implies that self-defenders *A* and *B,* when faced with uncertainty about their rival's ability or willingness for self-defense, are each less likely to use force as their probability of success in war and in negotiation rises. This means that if there is uncertainty, but not about each other's capabilities, then the self-defense norm will minimize the risk of war when the adversaries are equally powerful. The domestic variant of the game, then, provides logical support for a balance-of-power perspective on the risk of violence under some contingent circumstances. In chapter 6 we will have occasion to explore more closely contingent circumstances related to power distributions that are believed to encourage or discourage violence.

The partial derivatives we have just discussed imply testable hypotheses. We can estimate virtually all of the terms in (4.9) and (4.10) so that we can test directly whether the functional form of the partial is significantly associated with the likelihood that *A* offers to negotiate. To do so, we use the operational forms described in appendix 1.

The value of *A*'s belief about *B*'s dovelike character $(1 - \omega^A)$ has not previously been estimated, but it can be. *A* knows that the opportunity cost for *B* associated with giving up the chance to exploit *A* increases as *B*'s chances for success in negotiation and war go down. Indeed, in the limiting case, as *B*'s chances for success approach zero, *B* has little to lose and potentially much to gain by gambling that *A* is not the type to retaliate. *A* does not know *B*'s belief about its own chances of success. But *A* does know its own estimate of *B*'s chances for success. *A* can reasonably be expected to assume that *B*'s belief is approximately equal to $1 - P^A$. *A*'s belief that *B* is dovelike should thus be inversely related to P^A. A logit analysis with DOVE$_B$ as the dependent variable and P^A as the independent variable serves to generate continuous estimates of $1 - \omega^A$.[16] These estimates are used in creating an independent variable that is a specification of equation (4.9).[17] The dependent variable in the first test is called NEGO$_A$, which is coded as 1.0 if *A* made a demand and did not use force and is otherwise coded as zero. The independent variable, PARTIAL$_A$, is expected to be positively associated with negotiation (because it is negatively associated with the threshold to gamble on negotiation,

16. The results of that logit analysis are DOVE$_B$ = $-1.24 - 3.82\ P^A$, χ^2 = 28.02, P < .000, N = 655. The significance levels for the two coefficients are .000 and .000.

17. Recall that we do not have an estimation procedure for α_A or α_B, so these terms are dropped from our empirical assessment of (4.9) and (4.10).

meaning that the lower the threshold is, the more likely A is to offer to negotiate). The subset of cases for the test of the expectation derived from (4.9) includes only those instances for which we estimate that A is the type that will retaliate if attacked (that is, $War_B > Cap_A$) and for which A and B each make a demand such that we are at the top of the crisis subgame initiated by A. The logit result is as follows: $NEGO_A = -0.508 + .500\ PARTIAL_A$, $\chi^2 = 5.32$, $P < .02$, $N = 423$, with significance levels of .000 and .038 for the constant and the independent variable.

The expectations derived from the game with respect to A are supported by the evidence. Indeed, the support is stronger than one might realize at first blush. The test we have performed is very stringent. It specifies not only the variables of relevance but also the precise functional relation among those variables. A logit analysis of these same variables, but examined in an atheoretical linear, additive fashion is not significant across the same exact cases. Apparently, the significance comes not just from the variables but also from the deduced functional relation, and the shape of that function is not likely to have come to mind without the formal derivation provided here.

A test of the predictive potential of partial derivative (4.10) is similarly possible. We expect a positive association between the partial derivative and the likelihood that B returns A's offer of negotiation. The subset of cases is necessarily smaller than for the test of (4.9). After all, (4.10) becomes operative further down in the crisis subgame. Therefore, the test is on all cases in the game that fall beyond the point at which A has offered to negotiate. That is, the test includes cases of negotiation, capitulation by A, and war.[18] The results point in the right direction, but less strongly than for A: $NEGO_B = -1.80 + 0.01\ PARTIAL_B$, $\chi^2 = 5.2$, $P < .025$, $N = 228$. The significance levels for the constant and the independent variable are .000 and .087. Again the test is stringent in that we have specified the precise functional form of the partial derivative rather than merely assessing the impact of each variable.

The evidence highlights strengths and weaknesses of the self-defense norm. Like the conciliatory norm, the self-defense norm provides a hypothetical guarantee of cooperation or harmony if it is known to be universally applied. As in the conciliatory norm, uncertainty introduces the risk of violence. The conditions under which that risk

18. Regrettably, our data do not permit us to distinguish between War_A and War_B, so both must be included here, making it more likely that the test will result in a failure for our theory.

Table 4.2
Violence and Norms of Cooperation for Self-Defense and Conciliation

	Self-defenders	Conciliators	Neither
No violence	149	21	212
Violence	109	16	200
χ^2	2.65		
P	—*		

Note: "Neither" means neither A nor B was a dove, or neither was a retaliator.
*Not significant.

Table 4.3
War and Norms of Cooperation for Self-Defense and Conciliation

	Self-defenders	Conciliators	Neither
No war	191	24	303
War	67	13	109
χ^2	1.43		
P	—*		

*Not significant.

is heightened, however, are different from those that raise the risk of violence among pacific doves. Is either norm more efficacious in promoting peace? It is difficult to say.

Probably less uncertainty surrounds the self-defense norm than the conciliatory norm, but both still begin to break down markedly under uncertainty. Tables 4.2 and 4.3 summarize the comparative efficacy of these two norms within our data set. Neither norm seems especially effective in averting violent confrontations. However, if the premise is correct that uncertainty is not equally likely under each norm, then these tables may distort the efficacy of one or the other of these central approaches to foreign policy. Fortunately, a partial test of such distortion is possible by examining a broader sweep of history.

The self-defense norm is driven by maintenance of adequate capabilities to retaliate and, tacitly, to enhance one's negotiating position (Downs and Rocke 1990). In a world in which demonstrations of retaliatory capabilities diminish uncertainty about a state's willingness to fight fire with fire, the incidence of war should diminish markedly. This observation and important historical developments in the technology of warfare provide the basis for our final tests of the efficacy of the self-defense norm.

Prior to the seventeenth century, most polities did not have the necessary means to signal their rivals that retaliation was a virtual certainty in the event of attack. Indeed, a very common form of conflict—the siege—revolved around this very weakness. Poorly protected towns, incapable of imposing a costly retaliatory strike against their foes, were frequently subjected to military coercion. The fundamental issue in a siege was always whether the besieged would capitulate without fighting or whether they could defend themselves effectively. Frequently, the leaders of a town were given a choice at the inception of a siege: surrender and be shown mercy, or resist and, if defeated, all in the town will perish ($\gamma < \tau$). The crucial issue for the townsfolk lay in the word *if*. If their defenses were adequate, then victory or a compromise settlement might be possible, and so they might be expected to resist. If their defense were not adequate, then capitulation was the best choice.

The dilemma of the besieged is explained in Shakespeare's *Henry V*. The king says:

> How yet resolves the Governor of the town?
> This is the latest parle we will admit.
> Therefore to our best mercy give yourselves,
> Or, like to men proud of destruction,
> Defy us to our worst; for as I am a soldier,
> A name that in my thoughts becomes me best,
> If I begin the battery once again,
> I will not leave the half achievèd Harfleur
> Till in her ashes she lie burièd.
>
>   .   .   .
>
> Therefore, you men of Harfleur,
> Take pity of your town and of your people
> Whiles yet my soldiers are in my command,
> Whiles yet the cool and temperate wind of grace
> O'erblows the filthy and contagious clouds
> Of heady murder, spoil and villainy.
> If not, why, in a moment look to see
> The blind and bloody soldier with foul hand
> Defile the locks of your shrill-shrieking daughters;
> Your fathers taken by the silver beards

And their most reverend heads dashed to the walls;
Your naked infants spitted upon pikes,
Whiles the mad mothers with their howls confused
Do break the clouds, as did the wives of Jewry
At Herod's bloody-hunting slaughtermen.
What say you? Will you yield, and this avoid,
Or, guilty in defense, be thus destroyed? (3.3.2–43)

And to the king's entreaty, what says the governor of Harfleur?

Our expectation hath this day an end.
The Dauphin, whom of succors we entreated,
Returns us that his powers are yet not ready
To raise so great a siege. Therefore, great King,
We yield our town and lives to thy soft mercy.
Enter our gates, dispose of us and ours,
For we no longer are defensible. (3.3.44–50)

By the end of Shakespeare's lifetime, sieges as instruments of war were entering their declining decades of usefulness.[19] In the latter half of the seventeenth century came a turning point in warfare. The widespread adoption of two technological innovations greatly expanded the ability of states to defend themselves against attack. States raised peacetime standing armies and drilled their members in the techniques of warfare.

The existence of standing armies enhanced a state's ability to attack and to defend. As we have seen, even hawkish exploiters are unlikely to use force in a dispute if they are convinced that the adversary has the ability to retaliate effectively.

The large peacetime standing army became a common feature of the European scene during the reign of Louis XIV of France. Although prototypes of such armies existed to the benefit of the Italian city-states centuries before and could also be found in France as early as 1369, the decision by King Louis to maintain his army after the completion of the French campaign against Spain in 1659 improved immeasurably the ability of states to defend against assault. The insti-

19. In the nuclear era, in which adequate self-defense against strategic nuclear war seems to be a contradiction in terms, the siege appears to be making a comeback. In its modern manifestation—economic embargoes and blockades—it was the tool of choice during the 1962 Cuban missile crisis and during the crisis following Iraq's 1990 invasion of Kuwait. In the latter case, nuclear war was not a threat, but gas and chemical warfare—approximate equivalents—were.

tution of such armies became a regular, widespread feature of the European landscape in the mid-seventeenth century.[20]

A standing army was a highly visible means of potential self-defense. The standing army of the seventeenth century was visible not only because of its peacetime existence but also because of the widespread adoption of new techniques of preparedness through military drill. As with the standing army itself, there were well-drilled armies prior to the seventeenth century. The Romans and even the Sumerians utilized drill techniques, many of which seem to have been forgotten or lost for centuries after them. In more recent times Swiss pikemen were likewise noted for their high level of skill and proficiency. As William McNeill notes, "One aspect of the new standing armies of Northern Europe, however, was without clear parallel in earlier times. . . . Drill, day in and day out, practiced year round when on garrison duty, and occupying spare time even when on campaign and in the field, was something earlier armies had not, so far as one can tell, found either necessary or sensible" (1982, 126).

The development and adoption of drill techniques formed soldiers into highly skilled, coordinated units of action. They learned to synchronize the loading and firing of muskets with great efficiency, thereby permitting rapid-fire volleying, which meant that one rank of soldiers could fall back safely while another rank came forward and fired. Prior to the introduction of such drills, soldiers operated largely as individuals once battle ensued. Success depended on individual valor and prowess, not on coordination and routinizing of tactics. Europe had for centuries lost the military arts of coordination so perfected by the Romans.

Drill enhanced the efficiency of warfare. The ideas of the prince of Orange, Maurice of Nassau, in the early 1600s, including the forty-two steps he identified for loading and firing a musket, and of Lt. Col. Jean Martinet (whose name has come down to us as a synonym for a strict disciplinarian) in the 1660s made it possible for common people, lacking physical prowess or special martial orientations, to defend hearth and home with skills superior to those of the most highly touted knights of old.

20. We are indebted to Robert Pahre for pointing out several earlier instances of efforts to establish a ready military capability. Charles V of France had a permanent army on horse and foot by the mid-fourteenth century. Similarly, the British established permanent garrisons, particularly in Calais, early in the fifteenth century. The technological advantages of standing armies, however, do not seem to have been widely employed prior to the seventeenth century.

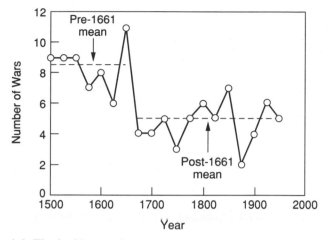

4.6: The incidence of wars, 1500 to the present.

The combination of peacetime standing armies and skilled, drilled personnel represented a technological change in warfare that must have made retaliation much more feasible and attractive than capitulation had been in the past. In the absence of adequate defensive capabilities, states are, according to the international interaction game, more likely both to face the threat of exploitation and to behave offensively, seeking out the enemy on the adversary's turf to hold down the costs of war or exploitation. Therefore, the introduction of the drilled, common-man standing army should have, on average, diminished the fear of being defenseless and the expectation of being exploited.

As states become more confident that their choice is to negotiate or to wage war, rather than to force or be forced into a capitulation, the likelihood of war should fall. This hypothesis follows directly from the self-defense norm and can readily be tested by comparing the incidence of war prior to and after Louis XIV's introduction of the peacetime standing army in 1661.

Figures 4.6 and 4.7 display the incidence of war and of great-power war drawn from Jack Levy's (1983) survey of European wars from 1500 to 1975. The patterns demonstrate clearly that war was twice as frequent and major-power wars were about three times more frequent before the mid-seventeenth century than they have been since.

When there was a quantum diminution in uncertainty regarding a state's ability to defend itself, there also was a quantum decline in the incidence of war. Indeed, in the case of the most dangerous and costly

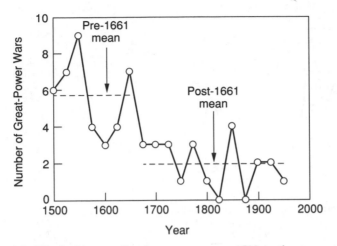

4.7: The incidence of major-power wars, 1500 to the present.

of conflicts—wars between the major powers—the decline is dramatic (Wang and Ray 1991). At a time when the opportunities for such disputes increased by 250 percent, the actual incidence of such wars fell by a factor of three.[21] This figure perhaps understates the strength of the association, for many of the wars after 1661 involve the Turks, who were slow to adopt the new techniques of training that had become common throughout Europe. Indeed, the janissaries, who steadfastly resisted the use of drill and training techniques developed by European "infidels," did not have their hold broken by the Turkish sultan until 1826. The delay was accompanied by a large number of wars that were disastrous for the Ottomans (McNeill 1982).

History provides additional instances of technological innovations associated with a nation's ability to retaliate if attacked and with the decline in warfare. We do not wish to ignore the important impact of the development of large, accurate, and mobile cannons used to such great effect by Gustavus Adolphus during the Thirty Years' War or the improvements in the use of gunpowder, and so forth. These innovations are also intimately tied to the theoretical notion set out in the self-defense norm. Technological improvements helped make visible the national preparations for self-defense and retaliation. It appears that confidence in the ability of rivals to retaliate played a significant role in diminishing warfare between nations.

21. The increase of 250 percent takes into account the changes in the number of major powers over the time span.

THE CONSERVATION NORM AND COOPERATION

Change is often thought to threaten peace. General favor with the status quo, in contrast, is often thought to preserve peace and avoid war. Jacek Kugler and Kenneth Organski, for instance, observe that "the international order is, as it should be, stable, as it has been since 1945 because of this massive power preponderance in support of the status quo" (1989, 175). Robert Gilpin, paraphrasing Thucydides, similarly places great emphasis on the destabilizing influence of change and on the benefits of a secure status quo for promoting peace. He claims that "the differential growth of power in a state system would undermine the status quo and lead to hegemonic war between declining and rising powers" (Gilpin 1988, 20). Such a perspective endorses the notion that harmony, if not cooperation, grows out of satisfaction with existing circumstances and that cataclysmic wars eventuate if a preponderant power's satisfaction with the status quo is not shared by a rising challenger. We have already seen in proposition 4.1 that harmony can follow if both parties to an interaction are satisfied with the status quo. Here we inquire whether such satisfaction guarantees the avoidance of conflict.

COOPERATION PROPOSITION 4.3. *Mutual regard for the status quo is not sufficient to ensure peace. Even mutual disdain for the status quo does not preclude cooperation.*

Proof. We begin by showing that war can arise even though the status quo is the jointly most preferred outcome of the international interaction game. Then we demonstrate that even when the status quo is jointly disliked as much as possible, cooperation can still be the equilibrium outcome of the international interaction game. We propose the following preferences that are consistent with the restrictions of our game as delineated in table 2.3: For A, let $U^A(Acq_B) > U^A(SQ) > U^A(Nego) > U^A(Cap_B) > U^A(War_A) > U^A(Acq_A) > U^A(Cap_A) > U^A(War_B)$, and for B, let $U^B(Acq_A) > U^B(SQ) > U^B(Cap_A) > U^B(Nego) > U^B(War_B) > U^B(War_A) > U^B(Acq_B) > U^B(Cap_B)$.

Although maintenance of the status quo is the jointly most preferred outcome and War_A is one of the least preferred outcomes for A and B, still the full-information subgame perfect equilibrium is D^A, D^B, F^A, $F^B \rightarrow War_A$. At node 9, B chooses F^B because at node 12, A's choice will be to capitulate to B, an outcome preferred by B to negotiation. If A uses force at node 5, then B strikes back, yielding War_A. If A

does not use force at node 5, then A is forced to capitulate to B. Because A prefers War$_A$ in this example to Cap$_A$, $F^A > \bar{F}^A$ at node 5. Because B prefers its chances in a war with A to giving in to A's demands, B chooses D^B at node 3. Thus, if A chooses D^A, the equilibrium is D^A, D^B, F^A, $F^B \rightarrow$ War$_A$. If A does not make a demand at node 1, what happens? If the crisis subgame is reached at node 6, then B chooses F, exploiting A. A's only means of avoiding this outcome is to acquiesce to B's demand at node 4, thereby precluding B's selection of the status quo at node 2. Acquiescence by A is the only outcome B prefers to keeping the status quo. But even a war begun by A is better for A than giving in to B at node 4. Therefore, at node 1, A makes a demand, precluding the maintenance of the status quo and preventing B from coercing A into acquiescence. The equilibrium outcome is War$_A$, a doubly Pareto-inferior outcome. Both A and B would have been better off negotiating a settlement or living with the status quo than they are by waging war.

We have just proved that satisfaction with the status quo is not sufficient to guarantee either cooperation or harmony. Now we show that such satisfaction is not necessary for the attainment of cooperation, although, as noted in chapter 3, love of the status quo is necessary for its preservation. Harmony requires an affinity for the status quo but is not guaranteed by it; cooperation can arise whether the status quo is highly valued or disdained.

We pick as our example a case in which war is more preferable to A and B than in the previous instance and in which both A and B are so hawkish that each prefers to exploit the other rather than cooperate. Still, despite the disdain each has for the status quo and despite their relative dislike of cooperation, negotiation—the cooperative solution to the game—is the equilibrium outcome: For A, let $U^A(\text{Acq}_B) > U^A(\text{Cap}_B) > U^A(\text{Nego}) > U^A(\text{War}_A) > U^A(\text{War}_B) > U^A(\text{SQ}) > U^A(\text{Acq}_A) > U^A(\text{Cap}_A)$, and for B, let $U^B(\text{Acq}_A) > U^B(\text{Cap}_A) > U^B(\text{Nego}) > U^B(\text{War}_B) > U^B(\text{War}_A) > U^B(\text{SQ}) > U^B(\text{Acq}_B) > U^B(\text{Cap}_B)$.

We omit the straightforward proof through a backward induction that the equilibrium outcome in this case is for D^A, D^B, $\bar{F}^A$, $\bar{F}^B$ to imply a cooperative, negotiated settlement of the dispute between A and B regardless of whether A chooses to make an initial demand. The method is the same as in the previous example. QED

The conservation norm has been shown not to be germane to guaranteeing peace. We will return to this observation when we investigate the relation between the international interaction game and theories of hegemonic war or power transition. Then we will see that the results here show that certain conditions stipulated by those theories as being either necessary or sufficient for a system-transforming war are neither.

TIT FOR TAT AND COOPERATION DURING REPEATED INTERACTIONS

Recent research suggests that a norm of cooperative behavior is expected to arise when nations follow a strategy of reciprocal interaction (M. Taylor 1976, 1987; Axelrod 1984; Gowa 1986). If nations are punished for defection and if they are immediately forgiven for their past sins once they turn toward cooperation, then sustained cooperation seems possible provided interactions are structured as an indefinitely repeated prisoner's dilemma. The one caveat that appears necessary is that the actors hold the expectation of valuable future interaction over a potentially unlimited time horizon (the so-called shadow of the future).

Yet the requirements that make cooperation possible are restrictive. For a broad class of iterated, infinite prisoner's-dilemma games that arise within the context of the international interaction game, the shadow of the future cannot be long enough for cooperation to be the expected equilibrium outcome. As with other prospective norms we have examined, there is a domain of circumstances for which the norm of reciprocation might help foster cooperation provided there is virtually no uncertainty. We prove that for a broad class of dynamic prisoner's-dilemma games—a class we call the prisoner's-dilemma, alternation game—the tit-for-tat strategy does not induce cooperation. Quite the contrary, the expected equilibria are defection or alternation between cooperation and defection—war or coercion in the context of the international interaction game—no matter how large is the shadow of the future.

Reciprocity is the key to many arguments that suggest that infinitely iterated prisoner's dilemmas yield cooperative interactions. Indeed, reciprocity is the unique feature of tit for tat that makes it the cornerstone strategy for those who seek a way to attain cooperation among self-interested actors. The notion behind tit for tat is that a decision maker will initially cooperate, signaling goodwill, and subsequently follow suit by adopting whatever strategy the opponent selected in the prior period of play. Thus, a tit-for-tat player that has just experienced exploitive behavior will defect in its next move. If the efforts at exploitation persist, the tit-for-tat player will persist in punishing the adversary. But should the adversary ever elect to cooperate by ending its efforts at exploitation, the tit-for-tat player will immediately return to cooperative play. Because cooperation is worth more than defection, the belief is that if the game is played indefinitely and if the future is valued sufficiently, then cooperation may ensue. This belief is sustainable under a set of restrictive assumptions focused on the initial move of the game and on the interval or cardinal value of the payoffs and not focused just on the length of the shadow of the future.

Before turning to an analytic demonstration that no possible attribution of value to future interaction is large enough to yield cooperation in some infinitely repeated prisoner's-dilemma games, we clarify the conditions of the prisoner's dilemma and how this class of games fits into our theory of international interactions.

The prisoner's dilemma is a two-player game with two strategies available to each player in any single round of play: cooperate or defect. The key characteristic of the game is that joint defection is the single-play Nash equilibrium even though it is Pareto inferior to joint cooperation. Following convention, let T represent the temptation payoff to a player who defects while the other actor in the prisoner's-dilemma situation continues to cooperate. R is the reward obtained for cooperating when the other player also cooperates. Suckers who cooperate when their fellow player defects receive S, and when each player defects, the punishment payoff to each is P. The necessary and sufficient conditions for creating a prisoner's dilemma are that $T > R > P > S$ (Ordeshook 1986; Brams 1975; Rapoport and Guyer 1966; Rapoport and Chammah 1965).

In the context of our theory, a prisoner's dilemma arises within the crisis subgame that begins at node 5 provided that

$$U^B(Cap_A) = T^B > U^B(Nego) = R^B > U^B(War_A)$$
$$= P^B > U^B(Cap_B) = S^B,$$

and

$$U^A(Cap_B) = T^A > U^A(Nego) = R^A > U^A(War_A)$$
$$= P^A > U^A(Cap_A) = S^A > U^A(War_B).$$

Under these conditions, war is the equilibrium outcome of the crisis subgame, although negotiation is Pareto superior. War, being equivalent to joint defection, has a value of P. The sucker payoff, S, is equivalent to having been coerced into capitulating or acquiescing to a rival's demands, and the temptation payoff, T, is attained when one's foe acquiesces or capitulates. The payoff from joint cooperation, R, arises when the adversaries resolve their differences by negotiating.

Table 4.4
Cooperation and Alternation Variants of the Prisoner's-Dilemma Game

| | Player B | | | |
| | Alternation game | | Cooperation game | |
Player A	Cooperate	Defect	Cooperate	Defect
Cooperate	40, 40	0, 100	60, 60	0, 100
	(R, R)	(S, T)	(R, R)	(S, T)
Defect	100, 0	20, 20	100, 0	20, 20
	(T, S)	(P, P)	(T, S)	(P, P)

Note: High payoffs are preferred to low payoffs. $100 > 60 > 40 > 20 > 0$.

A common auxiliary assumption in studies of indefinitely repeated prisoner's dilemmas is that $2R > T + S$ (Rapoport and Chammah 1965; Axelrod 1984). We distinguish two versions of the prisoner's dilemma as a function of whether this restriction is satisfied or not. When the restriction applies, we call the game the prisoner's-dilemma cooperation game. When the restriction does not apply (that is, when $2R \leq T + S$), we call the game the prisoner's-dilemma alternation game. Table 4.4 displays examples of each version of the prisoner's dilemma. The distinction between them is most important.

If any variant of the prisoner's-dilemma game is to be played once and only once, the Nash equilibrium strategy is for both players to defect, yielding war in the context of the crisis subgame. Should the players confront each other more than once but with the knowledge of when they will cease to confront one another, the finitely repeated version of the game unravels back to the beginning so that the equilibrium strategy is still to defect, leading to the punishment payoff (P) during each episode of play (Luce and Raiffa 1957). But if the game is expected to be indefinitely repeated, then cooperation is one possible equilibrium outcome.

Let w represent the weight or discount a player places on receiving benefits in the next move of the game compared to the value attached to receipt of those same benefits during the current move. The term w is what Robert Axelrod calls the shadow of the future. Assume that $0 < w < 1$, so that the postponement of benefits is always inferior to receiving the benefits now. If w is large enough, it is possible for the equilibrium strategy in an indefinitely repeated prisoner's-dilemma game to be joint cooperation, hence supporting the sanguine outlook among some students of international relations that egoistic actors can find a path to mutual cooperation through reciprocation.

Although such a path can exist in some prisoner's-dilemma situations, it does not exist in general. Quite the contrary. For those circumstances that satisfy the restrictions of the prisoner's dilemma alternation game, cooperation as equilibrium behavior is unlikely or impossible, regardless of the shadow of the future. Even for some circumstances that satisfy the restrictions of the prisoner's-dilemma cooperation game, cooperation is not assured even under full-information conditions. Indeed, an exploration of the precise conditions that are conducive to cooperation reveals how great are the temptations to defect and how tenuous or "knife-edge" are the circumstances under which cooperation is expected to be sustained (Bianco 1988; Bendor and Mookherjee 1987; Goldstein and Freeman 1990; McGinnis 1986).

Axelrod (1984) has shown that the strategy of tit for tat has special properties that make joint cooperation possible. For a strategy to take hold, it is necessary that it be able to invade rival strategies and gain a foothold. Tit for tat has this capability. Over the long run, tit for tat is collectively stable, meaning that an individual following this strategy can do better, on average, than a population following some alternative strategy. Axelrod proves that tit for tat is collectively stable if and only if it cannot be invaded by a player who always defects or by a player who alternates between cooperation and defection. The conditions required for noninvadability are

$$w \geq (T - R)/(T - P); \ w \geq (T - R)/(R - S). \tag{4.11}$$

If these conditions are met, then tit for tat can gain a foothold and, in time, can come to dominate interactions. Thus, tit for tat can lead to the evolution of cooperation (Axelrod 1984). Not all infinitely repeated prisoner's dilemmas are capable of satisfying the conditions of expression (4.11), however.

As noted earlier, many investigations of repeated prisoner's-dilemma games, including Axelrod's, assume that the reward payoff, R, must be greater than half the sum of the value of temptation and the sucker's payoff. That is, $R > (T + S)/2$. This restriction, used in virtually all experimental research on the iterated prisoner's dilemma, is equivalent to imposing the following auxiliary assumption on the international interaction game:

$$\phi_i + \gamma_i > (1 - 2P^i)U^i(\Delta_i - \Delta_j). \tag{4.12}$$

If the expected domestic costs for using force and the costs for absorbing a first strike without retaliating are smaller than the right-hand side of the inequality in (4.12), then tit for tat cannot induce cooperation, regardless of the shadow of the future.

To see that this is true, recall that the shadow of the future, w, is defined to be a positive fraction. This means that receiving a benefit in the future has some value but not as much as receiving the same benefit today. Such an assumption is entirely plausible, for it recognizes opportunity costs without denying the possibility of investing in the future. Now, suppose we relax the restriction that $R > (T + S)/2$, assuming instead that $R = (T + S)/2$ while still preserving the ordering $T > R > P > S$ that defines the generic game known as the prisoner's dilemma. Without loss of generality, assume $S = 0$, so that $R = T/2$, then the conditions under which tit for tat is collectively stable (expression 4.11) can be rewritten as

$$w \geq T/[2(T - P)], \tag{4.13}$$

and

$$w \geq (T/2)/(T/2) = 1. \tag{4.14}$$

Expressions (4.13) and (4.14) remind us that we are now examining the subset of repeated prisoner's dilemma games with alternation. Expression (4.13) substantially alters the prospects that the tit-for-tat strategy can invade the all-defect strategy, requiring that the shadow of the future is at least as large as .5. Condition (4.14) violates the restriction that $0 < w < 1$. That is, simply by relaxing (4.12) or its generic form, $R > (T + S)/2$, even slightly, it becomes impossible to satisfy the noninvadability requirements stated in (4.11). The relaxation of the assumption that $R > (T + S)/2$ eliminates the circumstances under which tit for tat can replace the all-defect strategy and thereby induce cooperation instead of war.

Tit for tat as a norm of interaction appears to require very special circumstances to make cooperation possible. Even when those conditions are satisfied and it is universally known that they have been met, the all-defect strategy remains an equilibrium approach to the iterated prisoner's dilemma. Thus, unlike the conciliatory norm or the self-defense norm, even full information is not adequate to ensure cooperation under the reciprocity norm. In that sense, it is a weaker prospective source of cooperation than the first two norms evaluated here.

The prisoner's dilemma is but one of many games that can emerge within the structure of our larger game or in the broader context of international affairs. It is not the sole characterization of relations among nations. Indeed, in the context of the 707 observations in our data set, the subset that meets prisoner's-dilemma cooperation conditions in the crisis subgame represents thirty-nine observations. Of these, twelve ended in war. For the additional 119 prisoner's-dilemma circumstances in the crisis subgame for which neither actor met the auxiliary condition of expression (4.12), twenty-six became wars. The difference almost meets the conventional standard of statistical significance ($z = 1.35$, $P < .10$), with mutual defection—war—being more common when the conditions conducive to tit for tat are met than when they are not. We do not know whether the rivals anticipated indefinite interaction or what the magnitude of their "shadow of the future" was, so this analysis is necessarily tentative. Still, it is not encouraging for those who are sanguine about the evolution of cooperation through reciprocity under prisoner's-dilemma circumstances between nations.[22]

We have assessed several prospective norms for inducing cooperation among self-interested decision makers in the anarchic international environment. Two norms, the conciliatory norm and the self-defense norm, ensure cooperation if it is common knowledge that they are obeyed. From the positivist perspective, each is equally effective given universal adherence. From the normative perspective, the self-defense norm may be more attractive, for it represents a means of enhancing the chances for cooperation when adversaries are not filled with goodwill toward one another, indeed, even when they may both have hawkish inclinations. With full information, it theoretically assures cooperation as readily when hawks confront one another, when a hawk and a dove are engaged, as when self-defense is redundant with the conciliatory behavior of two doves. The conciliatory norm enhances the chances for cooperation only in the case of interactions among doves. Each of these norms, as we have seen, breaks down to some extent in an uncertain environment.

Our statistical analyses support the expectations of the international

22. In an interesting and highly innovative formal analysis of repeated prisoner's dilemmas, Jean Pierre Langlois shows that the probability of cooperation, though above .5, is not near 1.0 under most circumstances. He claims that "in an imperfect world where disturbances of even minute sizes are bound to occur this [cooperation by A and B with probabilities of about .51 each] is the likely spontaneous outcome of this system of rational expectations" (1990, 24). Langlois's result is suggestive of the empirical observations reported here.

interaction game with respect to how these norms fare as the probability of success of one or another rival changes or as the degree of uncertainty changes. Some of the theoretical expectations are surprising (at least to us) and yet are supported by the historical record. For instance, weak pacific doves are more likely than stronger actors to initiate the use of force.

One norm, the reciprocity norm, can, but need not, yield cooperation under full information when the precise circumstances of an indefinitely repeated prisoner's-dilemma game are satisfied. This norm is unlikely to induce such behavior under uncertainty. Historically, situations that seem to satisfy the particular restrictions required for tit-for-tat effectiveness seem to evolve into wars more often, rather than less often, than other prisoner's-dilemma circumstances.

The conservation norm that places special emphasis on the maintenance of the status quo was found to be neither necessary nor sufficient to attain cooperation. This is true even if adherence to that norm is universal and if adherence is common knowledge.

Of the norms we have assessed, the self-defense norm and the conciliatory norm are the most practical, at least in the sense that they require minimal auxiliary assumptions about national behavior. They apply to any form of international interaction that can arise in our game. When universally applied, neither norm requires the presence of a particular game nested within the structure of the international interaction game. Neither the conciliatory norm nor the self-defense norm requires, for instance, that an international interaction satisfy the conditions of the prisoner's dilemma, the battle of the sexes, chicken, stag hunt, or any other specific two-player game. Rather, they truly apply universally if adhered to universally.

The reciprocation norm can also foster peace, but it appears to be limited to much narrower circumstances than the self-defense or conciliatory norms. Tit for tat appears to require the presence of an indefinitely iterated prisoner's-dilemma game, as well as the auxiliary condition that negotiation is twice as desirable as the difference between exploiting a rival and being exploited. And it requires that the stream of future benefits be particularly highly valued relative to current gains. Because tit for tat can be effective under more constrained conditions, it appears to be a less practical means of attaining international cooperation than either the self-defense or the conciliatory norm.

Norms of action may exist in international relations, but they are unlikely to be universally applied. This is the lesson to be drawn from the parables of Old Man Shirgugetu and of Khasar, Chingis Khan's

brother. Even openness and the avoidance of uncertainty cannot assure cooperation if one adversary is pacifically oriented and the other
is exploitive. Yet when foes recognize that their adversaries are prepared to protect themselves, peace is highly likely. The diminution of
the frequency of war since the advent of drilled standing armies is as
testament to the effectiveness of the crucial norm of self-defense. In
situations where misplaced trust might have cataclysmic consequences, reason dictates the wisdom of the dictum "Those who desire
peace, prepare for war."

Chapter 5

Five Democratic Puzzles

A house divided against itself cannot stand.
—Mark 3:25; Abraham Lincoln

Domestic politics has long been the stepchild of research into international conflict. To be sure, important hypotheses have now and then
been investigated with regard to linkages between critical aspects of
domestic and foreign affairs. Rudolph Rummel (1963), Raymond Tanter (1966), Jonathan Wilkenfeld (1972), Geoffrey Blainey (1973), and
others have explored the empirical relation between domestic violence
and foreign conflict behavior but have found little support for the
scapegoat hypothesis, which suggests that nations pursue aggressive
foreign policies as a means of deflecting attention from domestic problems.

Another fruitful area of research concerns Kant's claim that liberal
republican institutions induce nations to behave in a pacific manner
toward like-minded states.[1] Michael Doyle (1986), Rummel (1979,
1983), Zeev Maoz and Nassin Abdolali (1989), and others have noted
that democracies do not fight with one another, although they do fight
with nondemocratic states. This observation seems consistent with
Kant's view of *homo politicus* and calls for a logical demonstration of
a mechanism that leads liberal republics not to fight with one another.
We develop such a mechanism here, one that also addresses other
features of the foreign policy behavior of democracies (and nondemocracies, too).

The sundry observations about democratic politics and international

---

1. We use the terms *democracy, liberal democracy, republic,* and *liberal republic*
interchangeably throughout this discussion. Although distinctions can be made
among these categories, for our purposes they are sufficiently alike to use as
synonyms. We have in mind in this discussion the definitions and the set of states
identified in Doyle 1986 as liberal democracies.

conflict are rich with empirical puzzles but are not yet similarly en-
riched by an encompassing theory that helps make sense of the seemingly disparate, anomalous, and even contradictory observations that
have been made. We believe that the international interaction game in
its domestic version provides a theoretical framework from which to
make sense of the diverse empirical findings reported thus far on this
important topic. As we will try to show, the game replicates Kant's
expectations of peace between liberal republics and of a higher risk of
war when both sides are not liberal republics. The game, however,
shows when liberal democracies are expected to use force even against
one another and how liberal democracy is neither necessary nor sufficient to guarantee peace. Rather, liberal democracy naturally installs
institutions that encourage peace between such states and that encourage war and other forms of behavior otherwise.

We begin by summarizing the central puzzles and the principal
observed regularities that relate democratic or republican forms of
government to the prospects for war or peace. We identify five puzzles
and show how each is resolved theoretically by the international interaction game. We also provide empirical assessments of the explanations derived from the game and from alternative sources.

Most notable among the puzzles is the observation that liberal
democracies have not fought a war with each other. Later we will
suggest that this claim of no wars is questionable insofar as it is not
robust in the face of small changes in the definition of war or liberal
democracy. However, the general thrust of the observation is worth
taking seriously. Liberal democracies certainly do not fight with one
another very often. The international interaction game provides an
informational or signaling explanation for this phenomenon that we
believe is logically consistent and empirically dependable.

A second puzzle emanates from the first. Given that liberal republican governments rarely fight with one another, how are we to explain
the fact that they wage war with other types of states with as much
frequency and vigor as do nondemocratic regimes (Small and Singer
1976)? Whatever there is about democracies that leads them to avoid
war with one another, it is not sufficient to make such states immune
from using or even initiating violence in other contexts. The same
signaling explanation that accounts for the first puzzle appears to
resolve the second as well.

The third puzzle of interest is that more powerful democratic states
seem more responsive to constraints against the use of force than are
their weaker counterparts. This puzzle suggests the seeming paradox

that the states most capable of winning in a violent confrontation are least likely to resort to that means of settling their differences. As T. Clifton Morgan and Sally Howard Campbell note, "Higher political constraints reduce the probability of war for major powers. . . . For minor powers, however, our expectations are fully disconfirmed. . . . It appears that high levels of constraint *increase* the probability of war for minor powers" (1991, 21–22, emphasis in original). We will show that this reversal in behavior between relatively strong states and relatively weak states is what is expected in the international interaction game. We elaborate the observation further to make additional distinctions that are relevant to resolving this puzzle.

A fourth puzzle arises from the observations of Randolph Siverson and Juliann Emmons. They report "three facts, which taken together form an interesting observation: (1) allies have a higher propensity for war than is expected; (2) democracies have a higher propensity to ally with each other than is expected; BUT (3) democracies do not fight each other. This final point stands in stark contrast to the logical conclusion that obviously follows from the first two points" (1991, 24, emphasis in original). The international interaction game explains, we believe, why it is that allies are capable of fighting with one another and why it is that such a capability is diminished in the case of democratic allies. The explanation hinges on the resolution of the first puzzle and the game's account for the circumstances under which allies are likely to fight with one another.

Finally, we present and try to resolve a fifth puzzle. Can nations convince rivals that they possess the characteristics that stymie the use of violence, or is it too difficult to convey such an impression? Are democracies well positioned to convey such an impression, or are they disadvantaged in this regard? Are all republican governments fundamentally different from all nondemocratic states on a dimension that is relevant to the promotion of peace? Does republican governance determine behavior, or are republican governments just more likely to possesses one or more characteristics that encourage peace (or war)? Can such characteristics be missing from democracies and be present in nondemocratic regimes?

In addressing this puzzle we turn to an extensive assessment of an informational component of the game and of our solution to several earlier puzzles. In doing so, we show how difficult it is to alter a rival's beliefs about the domestic political constraints a nation faces for using force.

COMMON HUNCHES ABOUT THE DEMOCRACY PUZZLES

Several explanations of one or more of the empirical puzzles of interest to us have been suggested in studies of the relation between democratic or republican government and the risks of war. Most prominent among these hunches are the following claims.

1. Nations with like-minded, liberal economic and political policies are less likely to fight with one another than are nations lacking such an outlook. Democracies tend to be like-minded in their orientation toward individual freedom and in their belief in property rights. Consequently, liberal republican governments are less likely to fight each other than are other pairings of regimes.

2. The democratic political culture places a high value on individual rights and freedoms. This attachment to human rights leads to the abhorrence of the use of violence as a means of settling disputes. Consequently, liberal democracies are culturally biased in favor of peaceful means of conflict resolution.

3. Liberal democratic institutions ensure that opponents of government policies incur lower costs for their actions than in nondemocratic states. This makes it easy for domestic political opponents to mobilize, including mobilization to oppose the use of force. Such mobilized opposition increases the political constraints in democracies. Leaders in republican states, on average, expect to incur higher political costs for using force than do their counterparts in nondemocratic states and so are more reluctant than nondemocratic leaders to do so.

   Each of these three explanations is consistent with the observation that democracies do not fight with each other. However, we must also recall that democracies are no less likely to participate in or initiate wars—though not against each other—than are other states. The argument favoring like-mindedness (Rummel 1983) can be comfortably maintained in light of these two observations, although it remains to be seen how effective it is as an explanation for some of the other puzzles. The claim that democratic political culture abhors the use of force (Mill 1937; Schumpeter 1955) is certainly strained by the observed behavior of democratic nations (Small and Singer 1976). If such abhorrence is a characteristic of liberal democracies, then we must wonder why they are as likely to resort to violence as are other states. Still, it might be the case that democratic political cultures, if confronted with like-minded perspectives, are averse to war but that they are often confronted with hostile perspectives that necessitate defensive action. If so, then the abhorrence explanation can be sustained so long as democratic states use violence only in self-defense.

Likewise, one might think that the third explanation, which focuses on domestic political constraints arising out of the institutions of democracy, would also act equally against participation in wars directed at other democracies or wars against nondemocratic states. Indeed, the quotation from Morgan and Campbell was made in the context of observing that minor-power democracies facing the same constraints as major-power democracies behave differently with regard to the likelihood of engaging in the use of force.

We will see in a moment that the international interaction game can sort out the mistaken hunch that domestic constraints should have a uniform impact on behavior, so that the third explanation is not inconsistent with the observed tendency for democracies to fight wars every bit as often as other states. Indeed, we will show that explanation 3 virtually ensures that democracies will not fight with one another but will fight against other states, sometimes defensively (as in the abhorrence hypothesis) and sometimes aggressively. At the same time, explanation 3 will be shown to account for all of the empirical puzzles to which we have referred. It does so without altering the international interaction game at all while providing an explanation, grounded in beliefs, for the observation that democratic politics do not guarantee large constraints against the use of force (Domke 1988).

FUNDAMENTAL SUPPOSITIONS AND THE EMPIRICAL RECORD

Each of the three prospective ad hoc explanations of the behavior of democracies during international conflicts is predicated on fundamental postulates. Before exploring a theory to account for the five puzzles, we will appraise their empirical foundations. In this section, we investigate these assumptions as a means to inform and guide our subsequent theoretical and empirical assessments. The three assumptions of greatest interest to us are

1. Democracies are disproportionately likely to associate themselves with like-minded states.

2. Democratic states manifest an abhorrence of violence.

3. Democratic leaders face larger political costs for using violence than do their nondemocratic counterparts.

Each of these assertions is susceptible to empirical validation. Such validation is appropriate here in that these conjectures are not proposed in the literature as simplifying assumptions from which propositions are deduced but rather are submitted as if they are themselves an explanation for the behavior of democracies in international affairs. We turn therefore to the task of empirical validation.

In each of the empirical tests presented below, we compare liberal democracies to other states. We are particularly interested in whether democracies can be differentiated from other states with regard to the characteristics of like-minded alignments, abhorrence of violence, and constraints on the use of force. In each test, we define a state as being a liberal democracy in accordance with the rules set out by Doyle (1986). Even though we disagree with some of his decisions and view others as influenced by ex post considerations, we do not alter his coding decisions at all.[2] The relevant independent variables are explained as they are used.

What is the evidence for continuing to pursue the first proposed explanation, which claims that democracies disproportionately seek out relationships with like-minded states? The like-minded affinities for individual freedom and for property rights are believed to discour-

2. We find several of Doyle's coding decisions to be questionable in terms of the consistency with which criteria for inclusion or exclusion are applied. We find it peculiar that Switzerland, which until quite recently denied the vote to half of its population (that is, women) is classified as a liberal democracy but South Africa is not. South Africa's denial of the vote to its black majority is reprehensible, but then so was Switzerland's denial of suffrage to women. Similarly, it is difficult to understand why the Confederate States of America is not treated as a liberal democracy. By the standards of the day it had a fairly wide suffrage and certainly met Doyle's criteria in all other respects. Was the suffrage in the Confederate States narrower than the suffrage in Britain during the same period or than in Italy even decades later (Gaubatz 1991b)? We also find it peculiar that Doyle codes Germany as being nondemocratic in 1933. Given a knowledge of subsequent events, it is uncomfortable to refer to any part of Hitler's Germany as democratic, but we cannot escape the fact that Hitler and the National Socialist Party were elected to the German Parliament in 1933 and that Germany continued to function as a democracy for a while beyond that date. It was not until later that Hitler, as chancellor, ended competitive, multiparty politics in Germany. Furthermore, if the suspension of normal democratic processes is sufficient to reclassify a state (as seems reasonable), then it is difficult to understand why Great Britain's status as a liberal democracy was not questionable during the Second World War. Mitigating circumstances existed, but we cannot escape the fact that with parliamentary acquiescence, elections were suspended during the war. Indeed, in this regard we cannot help but recall that at the first electoral opportunity after the start of the war, even while Churchill was negotiating at Potsdam, he and his party were turned out of office.

age violence among the democracies but also to account for the greater degree of violent behavior between democracies and nondemocracies (and between nondemocratic states).

Siverson and Emmons (1991) note that in the years since the end of World War II, democratic states have had a significant propensity to ally with one another. They also note that whereas *The War Trap* (Bueno de Mesquita 1981) reports a distinct tendency for allied states to fight with one another, that tendency does not carry over to democracies (hence, puzzle 4). They also report that U.S. hegemony in the post–World War II years cannot be dismissed as an explanation for the alignment of democratic states. In this connection they observe that democratic major powers currently show a proclivity to ally with democratic minor powers. Siverson and Emmons find much weaker support for the contention that democracies seek out like-minded states as allies when they examine relations during the interwar years.

We are interested in assessing the general tendency for democracies to reveal a preference for like-minded states. The correlation of alliance portfolios (K_{AB}) that we discuss in appendix 1 is a useful tool for evaluating this tendency. If the like-mindedness argument is to explain at least some of the five empirical puzzles we have addressed, then the shared pattern of foreign policy commitments of democratic states during the years 1816–1970 should be greater than the shared patterns of foreign policy commitments among nondemocratic states during the same extensive period. That is, the mean value of K_{AB}—the correlation of alliance commitments—among randomly evaluated pairs of democracies should be higher than the mean for randomly evaluated nondemocratic states.

Our subsample of 238 randomly associated European states provides an appropriate testing ground for the hypothesis. Of the 238 randomly linked European states in that sample, 56 dyads are made up of democratic states. Another 104 dyads are comprised of one democratic and one nondemocratic state. The remaining 78 dyads have two nondemocratic members. To evaluate the fundamental assumption of the like-mindedness argument, we compare the means for the sample of 56 democratic dyads and the sample of 78 nondemocratic dyads. Because the democracies are supposed to value individual freedom and property rights more than the nondemocratic states, they should disproportionately seek each other out in pacts oriented toward the protection of such freedoms and so should have more similar alliance profiles than their nondemocratic counterparts. Presumably these other, nondemocratic states are motivated more by traditional realist or neorealist goals of power or security and less by liberal notions of shared values and interdependence (Keohane and Nye 1977; Waltz 1979). The respective means are .114 and .112. That this difference arose by chance is virtually a statistical certainty. In light of this observation, we must be extremely cautious in attaching significance to the first commonly proposed account for the behavior of democracies. It does not appear to be the case that their international ties are more like-minded than are those of nondemocratic states.

The second common explanation suggested by students of democratic politics and international conflict is that the political culture of democracies leads to an abhorrence of violence. There is some striking evidence to support this perspective, but there is equally striking evidence to suggest that such a cultural abhorrence of violence does not exist.

Of the 238 dyads that accepted the status quo in our data set, 23.5 percent (56) consist of two democracies. Of the dyads that engaged in some level of dispute, 7.5 percent (35) involved two democracies; and of the 325 dyads that involved the use of violence by at least one member, 6.8 percent (22) comprise two democratic states. That 6.8 percent drops to 4.8 percent (9) of the 189 disputes that involved reciprocated violence (that is, war). Finally, that percentage is zero for the 89 dyads that satisfy the criteria for our variable BIGWAR.[3] Clearly, as we move up the violence ladder, the observed likelihood that the relevant dyad is made up of two democracies becomes smaller and smaller, eventually reaching zero. It appears that democracies do abhor even low levels of violence toward one another.

This evidence suggests a strong distaste for violence as a means of resolving differences between democracies. However, as noted by Melvin Small and J. David Singer (1976), such distaste seems less evident when contemplating relations between democratic and nondemocratic states. It is true that 67.2 percent (160) of the 238 dyads that retained the status quo contained at least one democracy, and 53.9 percent (253) of the 469 disputatious dyads included at least one democracy. Of the dyads entailing violence by at least one party, 37.8 percent (123) involved the use of force by a democracy, and 43.9 percent (83) of the 189 cases of WAR or reciprocated violence saw the

3. Note that there are nine small reciprocated uses of force between democratic adversaries in the data set. Although the threshold for BIGWAR apparently has not been crossed by democratic rivals, the threshold for smaller wars has been, at least using Doyle's definition for liberal democracy. The number of such cases satisfying the WAR, but not BIGWAR, criteria becomes zero if Gurr's (1978) coding scheme is used, as in Maoz and Abdolali (1989).

use of force by a democracy. These numbers are discouraging for those who believe that democratic political cultures abhor the use of force. Especially troubling is the fact that twenty-two cases entail the use of force by a democracy against a nondemocracy when the nondemocratic state did not itself initiate the use of force or retaliate with force. Another thirteen cases involve the use of force by one democracy against another that did not reciprocate in kind. Such cases seem more in line with Machiavelli's notion of republican expansionism or J. A. Hobson's and Lenin's views on imperialism than John Stuart Mills's view or Joseph Schumpeter's rational, democratic capitalists who abhor war. The abhorrence argument seems to hinge on democratic uses of violence arising as self-defense. This claim is difficult to support when the use of force is unprovoked by a similar action by the adversary and when such uses of force even occur when the adversary is itself a democracy.

The third hunch suggests that domestic political constraints make the use of force particularly problematic for democracies.[4] As we noted in chapter 2, Kant argues that

> if . . . the consent of the citizens is required in order to decide whether there should be war or not, nothing is more natural than that those who would have to decide to undergo all deprivations of war will very much hesitate to start such an evil game. For the deprivations are many, such as fighting oneself, paying for the cost of war out of one's own possessions, and repairing the devastation which it costs, and to top all the evils there remains a burden of debts which embitters the peace and can never be paid off on account of approaching new wars. (Kant 1977, 438)

It is appropriate to inquire whether Kant's initial supposition is correct. Do democratic political leaders face a greater political cost for using force than their nondemocratic counterparts? This is an empirical question of considerable importance to the debate on the apparent existence of a tacit pacific union among democracies. If democratic leaders do not generally face a higher level of constraint than nondemocratic leaders do, then we can dismiss this account of the observed peacefulness of relations among democracies.

We assess the empirical merits of the claim by comparing the mean ratio of expected political costs from using force to the expected benefits from a negotiated resolution of a dispute, controlling for

---

4. Or for any other state that endures a high level of domestic political opposition to the use of force.

whether the initiating state was or was not a democracy. Recall that
what distinguishes the expected utility from war and the expected
utility from negotiation in our game is the costs that must be borne if
force is used. Therefore, the ratio of expected domestic political costs
to expected gains (or losses) from negotiation captures the magnitude
of the presumed democratic constraint, normalized by the expected
stakes in the dispute.[5] If Kant's argument has merit, then we should
observe a higher political cost-benefit ratio for democracies than for
nondemocracies. The ratio of expected political costs to the expected
value of negotiation is estimated in accordance with the method for
operationalizing each component discussed in appendix 1.

Our data set includes 254 instances in which nation A was a liberal
democracy according to Doyle and 453 instances in which A was not
a liberal democracy. The mean expected political cost-benefit ratio for
the democracies is 1.113. The comparable mean for the nondemocratic
states is 1.019. Are these means different? Yes, they are, with the
difference being statistically significant at the .003 level. Democratic
leaders, on average, apparently expected to experience greater political opposition to the use of force than did their nondemocratic counterparts. Furthermore, this result remains remarkably robust as we
move up the dispute ladder.

For those instances in which no dispute took place (so that the
status quo prevailed), democracies were more constrained than their
nondemocratic counterparts. The mean of the cost-benefit ratio is
1.173 for democracies. The comparable mean for nondemocracies is
1.044. These means are significantly different from each other (P <
.015, with 104 democracies and 134 nondemocracies). Eliminating the
238 instances in our data set in which there was no dispute, democracies still face a significantly higher constraint than nondemocracies.[6]

5. We ignore here expected losses of life and property that are independent of the
expected political costs associated with the use of force, for it is the latter that is
of relevance to this discussion. We also remind the reader that our indicator of
expected domestic costs, explained in appendix 1, is coarse and is not intended as
an ex post indicator of actual costs.

6. It is interesting to note that democracies also face a political cost constraint that
is, on average, larger that the expected utility from negotiating, making the use of
force, on average, unattractive. That is, for democracies the average ratio is greater
than 1.00. In this regard, we gain some confidence in our crude indicators from
the observation that the combined mean for democracies and nondemocracies
diminishes as we assess the ratio at higher and higher levels of the conflict ladder.
On average, the political constraint is lower in those cases in which force was used
as compared to those in which force was not used. That is, when the constraint
was particularly large, it helped, on average, to forestall the use of force. Domestic

The respective means are 1.071 and 1.004 (P < .050, with 150 democracies and 316 nondemocracies). Among events that involved the use of force at least by side *A,* the respective means are 1.097 and .996 (P < .034, with 86 democracies and 213 nondemocracies). Apparently, the common and crucial assumption that democratic leaders anticipate, on average, higher domestic political costs for the use of force than do nondemocratic leaders is supported by the evidence.

These observations provide a foundation for continuing to pursue the role of domestic constraints as a potential source of explanation for the empirical puzzles we have identified. We focus now on this feature in the international interaction game.

PUZZLE 1: WHY WAR IS ABSENT BETWEEN DEMOCRACIES

How does the presence of a large domestic political constraint influence behavior? Given the assumptions of the international interaction game, large expected domestic political costs decrease the attraction of strategies that involve the use of force, including war or compelling a rival to capitulate. Because we now know that democratic leaders, on average, bear a higher cost-benefit ratio than nondemocratic leaders, we know that, on average, they should be more constrained in their ability to choose violent strategies. This is akin to suggesting that democratic leaders, on average, are more likely to follow dovelike policies than are nondemocratic leaders. All else being equal, the greater the constraint in terms of anticipated domestic opposition to the use of force, the more attractive it is to negotiate rather than try to force a capitulation. This conclusion leads us to propose an explanation of puzzle 1 as follows:

DEMOCRATIC CONSTRAINT PROPOSITION 5.1. *Democracies confronting one another are less likely to engage in violence than are mixed dyads because each believes the other is likely to be averse to using force (that is, to be dovelike), and each state is more likely to be dovelike. Leaders averse to using force who confront rivals also believed (with sufficient confidence) to be averse to using force do not use force.*

Discussion. In chapter 4 we proved that if nation *A* is a dove and nation *B* is a dove and each knows the other is dovish, then negotiation

---

political opposition apparently can be very important in shaping foreign policy behavior. For a sampling of other evidence that domestic politics is important in foreign policy choices see, for instance, Russett 1990, Ostrom and Job 1986, James and Oneal 1991, and Morrow 1991.

and the status quo are the only possible equilibrium outcomes of the game. The proof, however, depended critically on there being common knowledge that the rivals were sufficiently averse to using force to be doves. In general, leaders cannot know the political costs that their opponents anticipate from using force, nor can they know that their opponents are doves. The presence of the constraint is not alone sufficient to ensure cooperation or harmony. However, it is common knowledge whether a given state is a liberal democracy. We also know that the common supposition that leaders in such states bear higher costs than their counterparts in nondemocratic states is generally true. As a matter of prior beliefs, a rival facing a democratic opponent can be expected to assume that the democracy is more likely to be averse to using force than would be the case for a nondemocratic regime. This assumption follows directly from the empirical evidence in support of the key supposition. Apparently, the institutions that make a state a liberal democracy provide information to other states about the likely constraints on the leadership. Adoption of those institutions sends the signal that the leadership is more likely to face higher costs for using force than are leaders in states without democratic institutions. Therefore, the prior belief that a democratic state behaves in a dovelike manner is higher than it is for nondemocratic regimes. In chapter 4 we proved that under imperfect-information conditions such states are less likely to use force against one another than other states for whom the belief that they are dovelike is lower. The proofs of those propositions serve to prove proposition 5.1, thereby concluding our discussion.

Being a liberal democracy does not guarantee that a nation behaves like a dove, just as failing to be a liberal democracy does not guarantee that a nation is hawklike. But the highly visible characteristic of regime type does influence the odds or the risk of facing a state averse to the use of force. Suppose A is a democracy and B is a democracy. Then there is a higher prior belief that they are both averse to the use of force than would be true for any other mix of regime types. Because the evidence adduced here in support of the supposition that democratic leaders face high political constraints is as readily apparent to any leader as it is to us, we must conclude that, on average, pairs of democracies with a conflict of interests are more likely to resolve it through negotiation or maintenance of the status quo than are other types of states. When democracies confront one another, it is common knowledge that each has unusually high confidence that the other is likely to be constrained to be averse to the use of force. And that common knowledge about the magnitude of the prior belief encourages states under all but the most unusual circumstances to negotiate with one another or to accept the status quo. In the limiting case of complete confidence about the dovish intentions of the rival, war becomes an impossibility. In the more realistic case in which the probability that either side supports exploitive behavior is low, the likelihood of war is extremely low. One side might still be sufficiently fearful of being exploited that it launches a preemptive strike (see proposition 4.1a), or one actor, believing its rival is a dove, might offer to negotiate, only to find that its democratic rival is an exception that does not face unusually high costs for using force. Still, it is true that democracies face higher costs on average.

Doyle, Maoz and Abdolali, and others maintain that no war has occurred between liberal democracies. Indeed, no war as defined by Singer and Small (1972) has occurred between liberal democracies, at least during modern times. There have, however, been nine instances of reciprocated violence between democracies and an additional thirteen instances in which one or the other member of a liberal democratic dyad used force to get what it wanted from another democratic state. These are still rather small numbers, and the events themselves were small in terms of loss of life or duration.[7] These observations are consistent with our expectation from the game that violence between democracies is expected to occur very rarely, if at all.

Further evidence can be adduced for the proposition. We define a dependent variable, as used in chapter 3, called Nego/SQ. This variable equals 1.0 in all cases in our data set in which negotiation or the status quo prevailed. We construct a simple logit analysis in which the independent variables DEM_A and DEM_B are coded as 1.0 if the relevant state satisfied Doyle's criteria for a liberal democracy and coded as zero otherwise. If the claim of proposition 5.1 is correct, then each of these variables should be strongly associated with Nego/SQ. That is in fact the case. Table 5.1 summarizes the statistical associations. The evidence supports the contention that democracies are generally averse to using force.

Puzzle 1, then, can be explained by the difference in the magnitude of the domestic political cost associated with using force in democracies and in other regimes. The presence of democratic institutions provides a basis for rivals to have an above-average prior belief that

7. For instance, the average duration of a violent event involving two democracies is 253 days. For mixed or nondemocratic dyads, the average duration of such an event is 366 days. This difference is significant ($P < .045$, with 22 and 303 such events, respectively).

Table 5.1
Democracy and Negotiation or the
Status Quo

	Nego or SQ	
	Coef.	P
DEM$_A$	.497	.001
DEM$_B$	.769	.000
Constant	−.933	.000
χ^2	31.77	
P≤	.000	
N	707	

the potential foe is restrained from using force too readily. When this restraint exists for both sides, amicable settlements of disputes are more likely. Consequently, democracies are unlikely to fight with one another.

PUZZLE 2: WHY DEMOCRACIES FIGHT WITH OTHER NATIONS

DEMOCRATIC CONSTRAINT PROPOSITION 5.2. *Nations like the average democracy that face a high and visible domestic political cost for using force utilize force to avoid exploitation either by initiating violence or by retaliating for the use of force by rivals who do not face a relatively high domestic political constraint.*

Proof. Figure 5.1 displays the international interaction game, with hypothetical admissible numerical payoffs assigned to each terminal node of the game. Each branch that would be chosen in accordance with subgame perfection is in solid lines in the figure. This illustrative application of the game is consistent with the discussion of puzzle 1 in that we have made nation *A*—a democracy facing high domestic political costs—a dove. It is also consistent with the problem raised in puzzle 2. Nation *B,* the adversary, is not a democracy or a dove in this example. Notice that democratic state *A* is expected to initiate the use of force, and *B* is expected to retaliate, leading to war. The backward induction of figure 5.1 constitutes an existence proof for the use of force by *A,* a democracy, against *B,* a nondemocracy with a relatively small expected domestic political cost for using force. In

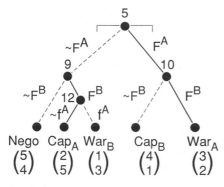

5.1: Crisis subgame when constrained A uses force against B.

this example, A uses force as a preemptive strategy to avoid exploitation.

Even if A mistakenly believes that B will negotiate if given the opportunity, it is possible for war to ensue. Suppose B mistakenly thinks that A's domestic cost will be so high that A will fear retaliating if attacked. Then B will use force because it prefers to force A to capitulate and because it believes that A's offer to negotiate signals weakness. Democratic A, despite a large domestic political cost for using force, can still prefer the gamble of war to the sure defeat associated with capitulation. To have such a preference it must be true that

$$U^A(\Delta_A) - U^A(\Delta_B) + \tau_A - \gamma_A - (\tau_A - \gamma_A)/P^A > \phi_A. \qquad (5.1)$$

Under these conditions, A can offer to negotiate, B uses force, and dovish, democratic A retaliates, yielding War_B.

The two examples just presented demonstrate the possibility of democratic A starting a preemptive war or waging a war in self-defense against B, which used force for its own aggrandizement. Other examples can readily be offered to show that the game also permits the possibility of war when A is not a democracy and B is. These existence proofs, however, are sufficient to establish the claims of proposition 5.2. QED

The point of these illustrations is to provide logical evidence for the observation that democracies, though unlikely to fight with one another, are capable of fighting with nondemocratic states. Indeed, the high domestic political constraint faced by democracies makes them vulnerable to threats of war or exploitation and liable to launch preemptive attacks against presumed aggressors. After all, if B is not a democracy, then B is drawn from a pool of nations facing, on average, small domestic political costs for using force. B is therefore more likely than a democracy to force a capitulation if the opportunity presents itself. Furthermore, because A is a democracy, A is drawn from a pool with a higher than average cost for using force. B's prior belief, then, is that there is a higher-than-normal chance that A is exploitable. A's prior belief is that B is likely to be a hawkish exploiter. If the first-strike advantage is large enough, A will prefer to initiate the use of force rather than risk being compelled to capitulate or to fight under the most adverse conditions. Thus, A's democratic institutions make it susceptible to exploitation and incline it toward preemption. Puzzle 2 is apparently resolved by the same informational quality that makes the presence of democratic institutions act as a restraining feature when democracies confront one another.

Turkish-Greek Relations in Two Cyprus Crises

Propositions 5.1 and 5.2 focus on the role that domestic political constraints play in helping to shape foreign policy crises. We now turn to an application of those propositions to two crises over Cyprus, one in 1967 and the other in 1974.

Long before Cyprus was granted its independence from Great Britain, political and economic animosities divided the island along ethnic lines. The majority of the population on Cyprus is of Greek extraction, and a substantial minority is Muslim of Turkish lineage. Although the sources of dispute are diverse, complicated, and interesting, we do not attempt to address the causes of the conflict here. Rather, our interest is in the fact that the Greek-Turkish crisis over Cyprus in 1967 ended with a negotiated settlement, whereas the Greek-Turkish crisis of 1974 culminated in a military invasion of Cyprus by Turkish forces following a Greek-inspired coup that overthrew the government of Archbishop Makarios.

At the outset of the 1967 dispute, both Greece and Turkey were democracies. By the time the dispute seemed headed for war, a group of Greek colonels had overthrown the government in Greece and replaced it with a military dictatorship. By contrast, when violence broke out between Greek and Turkish forces in 1974, Turkey still maintained a democracy and Greece retained its military government. In the midst of the dispute, the Greek government was returned to civilian rule and was committed to the restoration of democracy, but the fighting continued unabated until the Turkish army had achieved most of its objectives. How well do these two critical episodes in

Cyprus's history comport with the expectations derived from the international interaction game? Recall our expectation that war is unlikely between two rivals facing high domestic constraints and is more likely when one adversary has a high constraint and the other has a lower constraint.

From a realist perspective, international structural circumstances must have looked much the same to the Greeks and Turks in 1967 and in 1974. In both instances, NATO's hegemon, the United States, was largely preoccupied with other problems. At the time of each crisis the U.S. president faced a collapsing presidency and pressing foreign policy problems that pushed Cyprus to the back burner. On both occasions the Turks were greatly advantaged militarily, with more armed forces than Greece. Our estimates give the Turkish military about a three-to-one advantage. Furthermore, Turkey possessed airfields a scant forty miles from Cyprus, whereas Greek aircraft were barely within range. Greek aircraft could expect to be over Cyprus for only about two minutes before fuel requirements would necessitate a return to home base (Foley and Scobie 1975).

The structure of the international system and the relative strength of the adversaries was essentially invariant across the two disputes, but the outcomes were completely different. It appears that a realpolitik or realist account is unlikely to explain the variation in outcomes given the constancy of international structural circumstances.

Domestic political considerations in Greece, Turkey, and Cyprus were important factors that varied between 1967 and 1974, especially concerning the interests and constraints facing the Greek government. In particular, it appears that the Greek regime of 1974 was less constrained than the government in 1967 and that it was more willing to pursue *enosis,* the union of Cyprus with Greece, in 1974 than it had been in 1967, even at the risk of violence.

A poll of Cypriots showed in 1965 that barely 18 percent of the Greek-Cypriot population supported enosis at that time (Markides 1977). The pro-enosis candidate for the presidency of Cyprus in 1968, Dr. Takis Evdokas, received only 2 percent of the popular vote, compared to 98 percent for President Makarios. On Cyprus, at least, enosis seems to have been an increasingly unpopular dream by the late 1960s. Yet we can reasonably portray the principal cause of the 1967 dispute as agitation among a segment of Greek-Cypriots and Greek army officers for enosis.

Attitudes toward enosis within Greece differed markedly in 1967 and in 1974. In 1967 a major factor contributing to the conflict on Cyprus was the attack by Gen. George Grivas against the Turks in

Kophinou on November 15. Grivas, born on Cyprus, was a long-standing, fanatic advocate of enosis. He also was at the time a high-ranking officer in the Greek army. His return to Cyprus marked an intensification of the Greek military's pro-enosis campaign. Yet the democratic Greek government, which was soon to be overthrown by the military, seemed itself to be cooling toward enosis.

In 1967 the Turkish government responded to the attacks by Grivas and others against Turkish-Cypriots by preparing for war. Secretary General U Thant of the United Nations reported on November 24, 1967, that "Greece and Turkey are now on the brink of war" (Foley and Scobie 1975; Markides 1977; Crawshaw 1978; Hart 1990). Yet war did not begin. Instead, a settlement was negotiated with the able assistance of the U.S. special envoy Cyrus Vance. As a gesture to lower tensions, the Greek junta recalled General Grivas from Cyprus, and a strained peace prevailed until the 1974 crisis.

What was the role of the views of the domestic elite and the masses in Greece and Turkey in 1967? Parker Hart, the U.S. ambassador to Turkey in 1967, reports in his assessment of the crisis that "there were strong forces for peace in both Ankara and Athens. In Ankara, [Foreign Minister] Çağlayangil had the invaluable help of Türkmen and the broad support of Prime Minister Demirel and Defense Minister Ahmet Topaloğlu" (1990, 90). On Athens, he reports,

> As [then U.S. ambassador to Greece] Talbot told me later, there was a "sea change" in Greek public opinion, discernible notwithstanding censorship by the colonels. *Enosis* would still be regarded as a natural and indeed inevitable course of history, which would come about some day because of the ties of Hellenism, of common language and culture, shared by the large majority of the population of Cyprus with "Mother Greece"; but it was not to be gained by war with Turkey. Such a war risked Greece itself, as well as NATO and the protection which NATO offered Greece. The colonels knew the cost. (103)

The Greek government of 1967 faced important opposition to war from within elite circles, as well as from segments of public opinion. The Turks could not help but recognize the heavy constraint under which the newly empowered military junta operated. If they had any doubts on this score, those doubts must have been mitigated by the Greek decision to recall General Grivas during the dispute, thereby abandoning their principal military trump card on Cyprus. The high domestic constraint more typical of a democracy operated in this case against the Greek colonels in the early days of their leadership, just as elite sentiments in Turkey also militated against warfare. Democratic Turkey and authoritarian Greece, each confronted with the expectation of high political costs from the use of force in 1967, chose a peaceful path and negotiated a resolution of their dispute.

By 1974 the Greek military government was well ensconced, more inclined toward enosis than it had been in 1967, and more skilled at suppressing the views of political opponents. The military leadership of 1974 had long experience with censorship and with suppressing opposition views. It was better prepared to promote its policy goals on Cyprus than had been true in 1967, when it had just come to power. Indeed, the junta had already permitted General Grivas, the staunch advocate of enosis, to return secretly to Cyprus in 1971. As one observer has noted, "Greek policy on Cyprus remained basically the same, with one exception. The colonels had no scruples over the use of violence against the Cypriot government to force it to accept the dictates of Athens. . . . The Greek military government claimed commitment to Cypriot independence, while the real covert policy appeared to have been different, as the events of 1974 proved" (Markides 1977, 130). In 1974 the Greek government, now headed by Gen. Demetrios Ioannides, apparently led a military coup that overthrew Makarios and installed a puppet regime amenable to the Greek military dictatorship in Athens. In accordance with the Treaty of Guarantee, Turkish Prime Minister Bülent Ecevit called on the Greek government to cooperate in restoring order to Cyprus. General Ioannides refused, declaring the dispute a purely internal Cypriot concern. Seeing that the Greeks apparently discounted the prospects of a counterthreat from democratic Turkey, Ecevit responded by sending a large military force to Cyprus. The swift and decisive Turkish military response led to the collapse of the Ioannides dictatorship as his military colleagues abandoned his policy, which they could now see was leading to disaster. "The option of war with Turkey was rejected by the junta, which unconditionally withdrew from power in favor of a return to a civilian regime headed by former Prime Minister Constantine Karamanlis" (Hart 1990, 131).

The dictatorship, which in 1974 no longer benefited from the moderating influence of opposition voices, chose a calamitous strategy, a strategy that brought about its downfall on Greece and a substantial reduction in Greece's influence on Cyprus. The expectation of small constraints in Greece and high constraints in Turkey forced the hand of the superior Turkish forces and triggered an event that neither side really wanted.

Turkey, anticipating further expansionist designs by the Greek military against Turkish Cypriots, chose the path of force in 1974 as is all too common when democracies come into conflict with nondemocracies. In 1967 a negotiated settlement arose, apparently in part because the then-new military junta on Greece was unable to quell opposition elements effectively and was unprepared to bear the high political costs of a war. In both cases behavior seems to have followed closely the logic of the international interaction game, once with happy results and once with violence and bloodshed.

PUZZLE 3: DEMOCRATIC MICE ROAR, DEMOCRATIC LIONS SQUEAK

Puzzle 3 seems especially paradoxical. Apparently, among nations facing substantial domestic political constraints against the use of force, major powers are more likely to be responsive to the constraints than are their weaker counterparts. Weak highly constrained states are more likely to use force, albeit the effect is not substantial (Morgan and Campbell 1991). Proposition 4.1a, which predicts an unusual proclivity for violence among weak pacific doves, foreshadows puzzle 3. We can readily shed light on this puzzle—including the weakness of the statistical results observed by Morgan and Campbell—by specifying the conditions under which the crisis subgame can eventuate in violence (that is, end in Cap_A, War_B, Cap_B, or War_A).

DEMOCRATIC CONSTRAINT PROPOSITION 5.3. *The probability that A will resort to the use of force depends on A's probability of success and on A's domestic political constraints such that these two variables bear an inverse relation to each other if B is expected to capitulate to A's use of force or if B expects A to capitulate to its use of force. If B anticipates a war begun by A, then B's probability of success can be positively or negatively associated with its domestic political constraints.*

Proof. In the first case we examine, assume that nation A believes B will try to coerce it into giving B what it wants so that A does not anticipate a negotiated settlement to the dispute. Assume further that A, facing high domestic constraints, prefers to capitulate if attacked rather than fight at a disadvantage. Then A will use force (F^A) if it believes that either of the two outcomes associated with its initiation of force is superior to Cap_A. If Cap_B is expected, then A will choose to initiate violence if

$$\frac{U^A(\Delta_A - \Delta_B) + (1 - P^A)\gamma_A}{P^A} > \phi_A. \tag{5.2}$$

If A anticipates a retaliatory strike by B, then A will still choose F^A provided that

$$U^A(\Delta_A - \Delta_B) + \alpha_A - \gamma_A - \frac{\alpha_A + \gamma_A}{P^A} > \phi_A. \tag{5.3}$$

Finally, A also will use force at a later node if it mistakenly concludes that B is interested in negotiating, finds itself under attack, and prefers to retaliate rather than capitulate. In this case, it must be true that

$$U^A(\Delta_A - \Delta_B) - \gamma_A + \tau_A - \frac{\tau_A + \gamma_A}{P^A} > \phi_A. \tag{5.4}$$

In the case covered by (5.2), it is evident that the larger P^A is, the more difficult it is to satisfy the required inequality, and so the lower is the probability of A's initiating the use of force—part 1 of the Morgan and Campbell result. Under the conditions of (5.3) and (5.4), the opposite is true. The larger A's probability of success against B, the larger the domestic cost factor that can be tolerated. Thus, conditions akin to (5.2) must obtain for weak As to be more likely to initiate violence and for strong As to be likely to eschew such action in the face of domestic political costs. Under other circumstances, weak As are disadvantaged by their willingness to use force in the face of specific domestic costs. Interestingly, this result is precisely what we find in the data on disputes. Yugoslavia's decision to confront the Soviet Union with a display of force in 1948 and to break with Stalin during the formative phase of the Warsaw Pact occurs, by our operational estimates, under the conditions stipulated in (5.2).

What about nation B? In the crisis subgame, B will fight back against A if A initiates the use of violence and if for B it is true that

$$U^B(\Delta_B - \Delta_A) + \tau_B - \gamma_B - \frac{\gamma_B - \tau_B}{P^B} > \phi_B. \tag{5.5}$$

B will initiate the use of force even after A offers to negotiate provided that

$$\frac{(1 - P^B)U^B(\Delta_B - \Delta_A)}{P^B} > \phi_B. \tag{5.6}$$

Inequality (5.6) clearly is more likely to be satisfied for smaller values of P^B than for larger values. In fact, in the limiting case in which P^B equals 1.0, it is impossible for (5.6) to be satisfied, and as P^B approaches zero, it is nearly impossible for the inequality not to be satisfied. In the cases reflected by expression (5.5), the relation between relative capabilities (P^B) and the magnitude of acceptable domestic political costs is indeterminate. It can go either way, depending on the relative magnitudes of the costs associated with loss of face, reputation, and so forth that accompany capitulation and the costs associated with lost life and property in a defensive war. Expressions (5.2) to (5.6) are proof of proposition 5.3. QED

Morgan and Campbell (1991) found some support for the hypothesis that strong states are unlikely to engage in violence if they face unusually large domestic constraints; they found a slight tendency for weak but highly constrained states to be more violent than strong, constrained states. Such results are consistent with the implications of inequalities (5.2), (5.6), and possibly (5.5). The anticipated strength of association is reduced by (5.3) and (5.4), as reflected in the results reported by Morgan and Campbell. The international interaction game provides a basis for comprehending puzzle 3, the Morgan and Campbell observations.

PUZZLE 4: WHY DEMOCRATIC ALLIES DON'T FIGHT EACH OTHER

Puzzle 4 really is a special case of the first puzzle. It arises from a set of observations: democracies do not fight with one another; they tend to ally with each other; and allies have a propensity to fight with one another. We have already shown that the second part of the argument—that democracies tend to pursue like-minded foreign policies—is questionable. However, for the sake of resolving the theoretical aspect of this puzzle, we will proceed as if it were true that democracies generally have a propensity to ally with one another over the long haul.

Recall that in chapter 4 we demonstrated that even with full information, nations that are fond of the status quo are not immune from war with each other. Allies are more likely to be satisfied with the status quo between them than are other states. This fondness, however, is not a guarantee of peaceful relations. Indeed, allies fighting with each other are unlikely to expect third parties to make a significant contribution to the effort to help one or the other side win. Consequently, a very powerful member of an alliance has something of a free hand to bully its friends over any small differences. Likewise, weak friends have incentives to act preemptively to prevent such bullying. Such circumstances foster prisoner's-dilemma conditions that encourage wars. Fortunately, if such wars arise, they are likely to be small, with few casualties and of short duration. The proof for these claims is found in chapters 6 and 7.

Wars among allies are diminished in likelihood if each party to the alliance faces a substantial political cost for using force and if each believes that the other also has a large domestic constraint. We have already noted that the presence of democratic institutions conveys exactly this information. Although that information is probabilistically conveyed—it is not a certainty—on average it means that democracies confronting each other as allies are more likely to be types who do not bully one another. Therefore, they are unlikely to satisfy the necessary prisoner's-dilemma conditions that foster violence even among allies. Indeed, puzzle 4 does not require a more formal statement or proof. It is a corollary of proposition 5.1. We can also see readily why such bullying or violence is not uncommon in mixed alliances. This follows as a corollary of proposition 5.2.

PUZZLE 5: ARE NATIONS WHO THEY SAY THEY ARE?

The fifth and final puzzle is concerned with whether uncertainty about the magnitude of domestic political constraints is likely to be beneficial or costly for those who seek to avoid war. Recall that democracies, on average, face high constraints. But, the constraints need not be so high for all democracies as to make all republican governments dovish. Nor are the constraints for all nondemocratic regimes necessarily so low as to guarantee that nondemocratic institutions always imply low domestic costs and invariably result in aggressive policies.

Choices of actions in the international interaction game frequently are shaped by beliefs about the domestic constraints faced by a rival. We have seen that this is true in both versions of the international interaction game. How, then, does uncertainty about the constraint of domestic costs influence the choice of actions, particularly in situations where war is threatened?

To introduce uncertainty about an opponent's domestic opposition into our game structure, let us suppose that some decision makers believe there is some possibility that the conditions of domestic proposition 3.1—the basic war theorem—hold during an international confrontation. That is, each decision maker knows his own preferences and thinks that the other may have an ordering of preferences such that their combined actions will lead down the path to war. Is it possible for him to induce in his opponent a belief about payoffs such that the course toward war can be averted?

Assume that B is uncertain about the domestic opposition faced by A. Specifically, let B believe that A faces domestic opposition either at the level ϕ_A or at the lower level $\delta\phi_A$, where $0 < \delta < 1$. Leaders facing the lower cost of $\delta\phi$ are less constrained by domestic opposition within their own country when considering the use of force in pursuing their demands than leaders facing ϕ, the higher cost.

It is a paradox that under full information, leaders facing such high political opposition at home that they are willing to capitulate to the use of force are also likely to initiate war. Those who anticipate little domestic opposition to their use of force are conversely more likely to obtain a negotiated settlement in international disputes than those who do not. The prospects for a negotiated settlement are enhanced for leaders bearing a low opposition to their use of force because their threat of retaliation if attacked is more credible. In contrast, those with high domestic costs can less credibly threaten to escalate if attacked. As their threat of retaliation is reduced, states facing higher political costs for escalating crises are pushed either to accept exploitation (Cap_i) or to preempt the opponent and strike first (War_i). Highly credible threats to retaliate if attacked encourage opponents to negotiate rather than to resolve differences through force.

The preceding discussion is a direct implication of the basic war theorem. It suggests that in the absence of uncertainty dovish states are likely to escalate disputes with hawkish states, and in doing so, they appear to be the aggressors. Of interest here, therefore, is the effect of uncertainty on strategic behavior when that uncertainty influences beliefs about how leader A will respond to nation B's use of force. Whether leader A is the type that will capitulate to or retaliate against the use of force is the critical uncertainty. If A is the type who will capitulate, B has a strong incentive to exploit offers by A to negotiate, striking first against A and forcing its capitulation. A, anticipating this exploitation, has an incentive to attack B first, given the restriction in domestic proposition 3.1 that A prefers War_A to Cap_B. If A is the type that will retaliate if attacked, then B has no incentive to try to exploit an offer by A to negotiate. B is known to prefer to negotiate rather than fight a war (2.A4). Therefore, the course of action B selects if A offers to negotiate depends critically upon whether B believes A is the type to capitulate or to retaliate.

The cost term δ can be fixed at the level that creates this uncertainty:

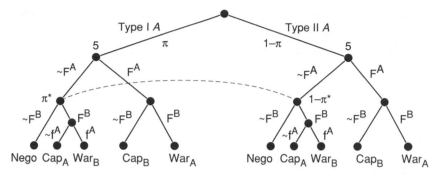

5.2: Crisis subgame with uncertainty about A's domestic costs.

$$\delta\phi_A < U^A(\Delta_A - \Delta_B) - \frac{(\tau_A - \gamma_A)(1 - P^A)}{P^A} < \phi_A. \qquad (5.7)$$

These two inequalities indicate that for type I As (those whose domestic opposition costs are smaller, discounted by δ), War$_B$ is preferred to Cap$_A$, whereas type II As (those without discounted domestic political costs) prefer Cap$_A$ to War$_B$. Type I actors are expected to retaliate if attacked, whereas type II actors concede an advantage to the opponent by not retaliating if attacked.

Figure 5.2 depicts the decision problem confronted by nations A and B within the crisis subgame that begins at node 5. In the event that A offers to negotiate, B does not know whether it would be better off negotiating (as it would if A is type I) or pursuing its demands forcefully and compelling A to capitulate (which type II As will do). It is assumed in this game that the probability that A is type I (π) is common knowledge shared by both players. A knows its own type and knows B's beliefs about A's type. B, too, knows that A understands that B will make decisions based on the probability that A is type I or type II, π and $1 - \pi$, respectively. In accordance with Bayes's rule, B updates its beliefs (π^*, $1 - \pi^*$) about A's type at the information set indicated by the broken line in figure 5.2.[8]

In accordance with the basic war theorem (domestic proposition

8. Bayes's rule provides a method that can be used in game theory to reflect learning. According to the rule (theorem), an initial, or prior, probability is changed, or updated, to a posterior probability based on the observation of conditional events. The rule is

P(event|observation) = [P(observation|event) P(event)]/([P(observation|event) P(event)] + [P(observation|not the event) P(not the event)]),

with "|" meaning "conditional upon."

3.1), we stipulate that B prefers Cap_A to negotiation and that B prefers to retaliate if attacked rather than capitulate to A ($War_A > Cap_B$). For simplicity in notation, we rename the variables here:

$U^B(Cap_A) = a$,

$U^B(Nego) = b$,

$U^B(War_B) = c$,

$U^B(War_A) = d$,

$U^B(Cap_B) = e$,

where $a > b > c > d > e$.

We are interested here in how B's beliefs about the political opposition faced by A influences decisions leading to war. We select values for the terminal outcomes for player B such that war is a possible sequential equilibrium outcome to the crisis game (Kreps and Wilson 1982; Cho and Kreps 1987).

Whether there is war or negotiation depends upon the choice made by B at the information set in figure 5.2. Should B's leadership believe that the nation will be better off negotiating than risking retaliation from A, then B will choose to negotiate; otherwise, B will use force to gain a capitulation to its demands. To choose to negotiate is for B to calculate that

$$b > \pi^*c + (1 - \pi^*)a. \tag{5.8}$$

Inequality (5.8) implies that B's action will be $\bar{F}^B$. With large-enough π^*, B's updated belief that A is a type I, the lottery becomes too risky for B, and it will negotiate. A simple backward induction will convince the reader that for large-enough values of π^*, nation A, regardless of whether it is type I or type II, will negotiate the dispute rather than use force. Provided that π, the initial belief about A's type, is large enough, type II has no incentive to call attention to its high domestic costs by behaving differently from type I nations, where high enough means $\pi > (a - b)/(a - c)$. In such circumstances type I nations act just like type II nations; there is no separation (that is, difference) in their behavior. As a consequence of this lack of separation in behavior, B has no way to update its initial belief about A's type when the information set is reached, leading to one pooling, sequential equilibrium in the game:

$$\bar{F}^A, \; \bar{F}^A, \; \bar{F}^B; \; \pi^* > (a - b)/(a - c). \tag{5.9}$$

The equilibrium is read, type I A offers to negotiate, type II A offers to negotiate, B offers to negotiate at the information set, B believes that A is type I with probability greater than $(a - b)/(a - c)$.

This first equilibrium condition reveals that if B is sufficiently confident that nation A is not very constrained by domestic opposition in its use of force, then B will not wish to challenge A during the crisis. Notice that B's choice to negotiate rather than fight is based on its belief that the adversary is hawkish in its responses. Now this decision-making rationale suggests that dovish leaders have an incentive to pretend hawkishness to avert conflict—an incentive that accentuates a central substantive concern in the study of crisis behavior. Can dovish nations successfully feign hawkishness? Can they deceive their opponents into thinking that the price of force will be retaliation? This ability on the part of dovish nations would help them to avoid conflicts and improve their prospects for ending crises through negotiation. Our analysis of the equilibrium conditions allows us to address this question directly. What we find is that nations cannot profitably engage in this kind of behavior if one side has private information and the other side does not.

The second equilibrium, like the first, is also a pooling equilibrium in which both type I and type II nations respond in the same way to the anticipated behavior of the opponent. But this equilibrium, in which B has greater doubt about whether nation A is a hawkish type I state, supports war as the equilibrium outcome. If $b < \pi^*c + (1 - \pi^*)a$, then B's choice will be F^B. Type I and type II As will each, though for somewhat different reasons, choose to initiate war rather than offer to negotiate.

Type II fights at this juncture because if it offered to negotiate, nation B would be able to exploit its unwillingness to retaliate. And because type II prefers War_A to Cap_A, A precludes capitulation by initiating the use of force. In contrast to type II, type I retaliates if attacked. Thus, for type I A, the choice is between War_B and War_A. Because $\tau > \alpha$, War_A is preferable, and type I will choose to fight rather than offer to negotiate. The second possible equilibrium is

$$F^A, F^A, F^B; \pi^* < (a - b)/(a - c). \tag{5.10}$$

In this equilibrium, player B does not reach the information set depicted in figure 5.2. Instead, both types of A anticipate that B will elect to use force if they offer to negotiate, and as noted, because both types are better off acting preemptively than they are by turning over the initiative to B, either type will attack B given the initial beliefs. In these cases the nations end up waging a war when both would have been better off negotiating.

The two equilibria just reported show that if nation A is type II, it has an incentive to try to encourage the belief that it is the more hawkish type I. If nation A can raise nation B's initial belief, $\pi < (a - b)/(a - c)$, so that its updated belief $\pi^* \geq (a - b)/(a - c)$, then A can reduce the risk of war and enhance the prospects of resolving such crises through negotiation. Dovish As, wishing as they do to avert war, do have a strong incentive to act hawkish.

This strong incentive to act like a hawk has to be balanced against the high domestic costs incurred for such behavior, and the negative consequences of having its bluff called must also be weighed in. Nations of type II are not free to engage in unlimited hawkish behavior. The leadership is constrained by the internal costs and by the rational expectation that B will test the waters, challenging them from time to time to see if they really are hawks or if they are bluffing. A mixed strategy equilibrium, when it exists, reveals the extent to which dovish nations can raise B's belief that they are a hawkish type I state.

A's objective in following a mixed strategy is to raise π^* sufficiently that B's belief at the information set equals at least $(a - b)/(a - c)$. In doing so, A would successfully alter B's behavior. In order to do so, As of type II must act as if they are more willing to counteract force with force than B otherwise would have expected. By picking the right mix of behaviors, A hopes to appear like type I to B. By deceiving B in this way, at least some violent conflicts would be avoided and replaced by negotiation. We let the probability that A selects the strategy $\tilde{F}^A$ be λ. The term λ is chosen by A to induce an updated value of $\pi^* = (a - b)/(a - c)$. The value of λ depends upon A's expectations regarding B's reaction to A's strategy. To be effective, A must be convincing in its efforts to appear hawkish.

B understands A's incentives and knows that A may be bluffing. Consequently, A can anticipate that B will also mix its behaviors to take account of the chance that A is bluffing. So, from time to time B will negotiate when it reaches the information set and from time to time it will challenge A to see if A capitulates or retaliates. In this way, B forces A to be cautious when choosing its actions. In particular, B selects a mixed response (with ρ being the probability with which B negotiates) when A offers to negotiate, placing a limit on A's willingness to risk exploitation. This boundary is created by making A indifferent between initiating the use of force on its own (F^A) and facing the risk of B's calling its bluff [$\tilde{F}^A$, $\rho\tilde{F}^B$, $(1 - \rho)F^B$]. The probability with which B will not call A's bluff is equal to ρ, such that

$$\rho[U^A(\text{Nego})] + (1 - \rho)U^A[(\Delta_B) - \gamma_A(1 - P^A)] = P^A U^A(\Delta_A)$$
$$+ (1 - P^A)U^A[(\Delta_B) - \alpha_A(1 - P^A) - \phi_A P^A]. \qquad (5.11)$$

Expression (5.11) is equivalent to the statement that

$$\rho = \frac{P^A[U^A(\Delta_A) - U^A(\Delta_B)] + (\gamma_A - \alpha_A)(1 - P^A) - \phi_A P^A}{P^A[U^A(\Delta_A) - U^A(\Delta_B)] + \gamma_A(1 - P^A)} . \qquad (5.12)$$

Type II A in selecting a mix of strategies—$\lambda \tilde{F}^A$, $(1 - \lambda)F^A$—and B in selecting its response must both consider how type I will respond to B's anticipated strategy. Type II A is aware of this factor because it is trying to look like a type I. B considers this factor because challenging A too often is inefficient, given the possibility that A is the hawkish type I who will retaliate if attacked. If B's mixed strategy challenges A too often, then if A is type I, B will always face a preemptive attack. Thus, for A's and B's mixed strategies to be effective, it must be true that if A is of type I, then

$$\rho \geq \frac{(\tau^A - \alpha^A)(1 - P^A)}{\tau^A(1 - P^A) + \delta\phi^A P^A} . \qquad (5.13)$$

Expression (5.13) tells us that if the probability that B will not try to exploit A by using force is large enough, then actors of type I will always offer to negotiate. This feature is critical if type II As are to benefit from efforts to deceive B into thinking they are type I. Given a ρ large enough that type I will always elect $\tilde{F}^A$ rather than F^A, then for type II, the probability with which it chooses $\tilde{F}^A$ is

$$\lambda = [\pi(b - c)]/[(1 - \pi)(a - b)]. \qquad (5.14)$$

From this, the mixed-strategy sequential equilibrium would appear to be

$$\tilde{F}^A, [\lambda\tilde{F}^A, (1 - \lambda)F^A], [\rho(\tilde{F}^B), (1 - \rho)F^B]; \pi^*$$
$$= (a - b)/(a - c). \qquad (5.15)$$

This equilibrium appears to suggest that type II As have an opportunity to engage in strategic deception that will make their crises more likely to be resolved peacefully than otherwise would be the case. However, we will prove that such a strategy is not available. We state this as proposition 5.4. The proof can be found in the second appendix.

DOMESTIC CONSTRAINT PROPOSITION 5.4. *If type II A nations hold the preferences delineated in the basic war theorem, and if type I A prefers War$_B$ to Cap$_A$, then there is no value of δ (0 < δ < 1) such that* *expression (5.13) can be satisfied. In other words, type II As cannot engage successfully in strategic deception to induce negotiation when war would otherwise have occurred.*

According to proposition 5.4, when the actors have entered the crisis subgame, no level of deception about domestic opposition to threats of escalation can be used to communicate a revised image that will influence an adversary's course of action. We conclude that B's uncertainty over whether A is greatly or only mildly opposed at home cannot be manipulated to deflect B from its intended course of action. So long as B believes A has a high probability of being type I, $\pi^* \geq (a - b)/(a - c)$, then it will negotiate rather than fight. Regardless of whether the initiator offers to negotiate, B will use force so long as it holds a sufficiently high belief that A, the initiator of the dispute, is type II, $\pi^* < (a - b)/(a - c)$. No amount of effort by A to alter B's beliefs regarding domestic costs will be sufficient to induce negotiation where force might otherwise have been used. Such efforts are doomed to being ineffective because they necessarily lack credibility.

The problem for type II As is that once the prior belief is no longer greater than $(a - b)/(a - c)$, any display of toughness is too risky. By bluffing in such circumstances, the probability of being exploited by nation B is just too great. If A really were a type I hawkish state, then, under the stipulated conditions, it would fight for sure. If B witnesses an effort by A to negotiate, then B knows that A is type II. A type II can only raise B's initial beliefs by acting out of character. Regrettably for type II nations, in this instance acting out of character means fighting rather than offering to negotiate. Consequently, dovish As cannot encourage negotiation by persuading their rivals that they are hawkish under the conditions set out in proposition 5.4. Rather, type II nations, with relatively dovish populations, paradoxically face a greater risk of war—wars that they themselves start—than do hawkish nations.

UNCERTAINTY ABOUT THE TARGET'S DOMESTIC COSTS

We now examine those circumstances under which state A, facing the choice between using force or offering to negotiate, is uncertain about the reaction of the domestic population in the rival state. Will its rival find that fighting back involves minimal political costs, or will it confront strong opposition from within? How will A's uncertainty about rival state B influence the equilibrium of the crisis game?

Inasmuch as our specific interest here is in strategies to avoid war

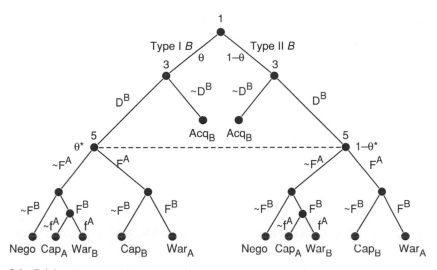

5.3: Crisis subgame with uncertainty about B's domestic costs.

during crises, we restrict our attention to those cases in which state A's preferences are consistent with the conditions in the basic war theorem from chapter 3. Let us condense the notation for A's utility for each outcome in figure 5.3, which depicts the game between A and B when there is uncertainty about B:

$U^A(Acq_B) = a$,

$U^A(Negotiate) = b$,

$U^A(Cap_B) = c$,

$U^A(War_A) = d$,

$U^A(Cap_A) = e$,

$U^A(War_B) = f$,

where $a > b > c > d > e > f$.[9]

Nation A's uncertainty about B's preferences for certain outcomes is indicated by the information depicted in figure 5.3. Suppose that type I B has a dovish population and that, therefore, B is constrained by high domestic costs for using violence. Suppose Bs of type II face little domestic political opposition to forceful foreign policies, so that $\delta\phi_B$ is the domestic cost for type II and ϕ_B is the cost for type I. Let

9. Although we stipulate these preferences throughout the remainder of our analysis, all of the results hold with the same proofs if A prefers that B capitulate rather than negotiate.

A's prior belief that B is type I equal θ (so that $1 - \theta$ is the probability that B is type II) and A's updated belief at A's information set (indicated by the dotted line in figure 5.3) equal θ^*.

DOMESTIC CONSTRAINT PROPOSITION 5.5. *If type II B bears* $\delta\phi_B$ *and type I B incurs* ϕ_B, *with* $0 < \delta < 1.0$ *and if for both types of B,* $U^B(War_A)$ *>* $U^B(Cap_B)$, *then there is no level of strategic deception that can sufficiently revise A's belief about B's type to induce negotiation when war or acquiescence by B to A would otherwise occur.*

Proof of this proposition can be found in appendix 2. Proposition 5.5 mirrors from nation B's standpoint the result found in proposition 5.4 for nation A. Taken together, we see that neither party to a dispute of the sort modeled here can communicate a belief about hawkishness or dovishness of its domestic opposition that will alter the course of a crisis, steering events away from war and toward a negotiated settlement. Successful bluffing can occur in the sense that A's initial belief may be wrong about B (or B's initial belief may be wrong about A). It is evident from the equilibria of the game that estimates about the level of domestic opposition do alter the prospects of war or peace. But neither party can signal new information that alters the behavior of the other party from what that behavior is expected to be given the initial beliefs about one another and the asymmetric information conditions we assume. Our analysis of the equilibria in this model shows that uncertainty can sometimes foster peaceful resolutions of disputes but that uncertainty about domestic constraints cannot be subjected to artful strategic manipulation during a crisis to make peace more likely.

The linkage between domestic opposition to conflictual foreign policy initiatives and the expectation that disputes will escalate to violence or be resolved peacefully has been examined in a general context and in the specific context of democratic institutions. Beliefs about domestic political opposition to conflict prove not to be easily manipulated but do prove to be crucial to choices for war or peace, in accordance with puzzle 5. Our results for all five puzzles are germane to any leader who must confront domestic political constraints, whether those constraints arise through democratic processes or otherwise.

Democratic processes convey information about domestic constraints, and they are designed to make leaders pay attention to them. But democracy does not determine the magnitude of such constraints, nor does it guarantee their effect on preferences among foreign policy outcomes. The information embedded in democratic institutions helps demonstrate whether a nation's population is likely to be hawkish or dovish. Such knowledge is a good thing when democracies confront one another, as we saw in puzzles 1 and 4, but can endanger peace when at least one party to a dispute is not democratic, as indicated in puzzle 2. We have found that powerful nations are more constrained in the use of force by their domestic opposition than are weak states, as in puzzle 3.

Initial beliefs about the magnitude of a state's domestic opposition profoundly influence the course of events in international affairs. The size of the domestic constraints and the institutions that influence those constraints provide important clues to the solution of the five empirical puzzles posed here. The proposed solutions that are testable with the available data are found to be consistent with the notion that constraints, rather than like-mindedness or a cultural abhorrence of violence, are at the root of conflict behavior.

Part III

Power and Foreign Policy

Chapter 6

International Power Relations and War

What king, going to make war
against another king, sitteth not
down first and consulteth whether
he be able with ten thousand to
meet him that cometh against him
with twenty thousand.

Or else, while the other is still
far away he sends a delegation
and asks terms of peace.
—Luke 14:31

We have emphasized the roles of power and preference in forging war
or peace. These two prongs of political life have nowhere been more
important or received more attention than in the investigation of wars
of enduring consequence. Here we focus on prospective constraints
on preferences and on the distribution of power that may shape the
size and effects of conflict.

A central debate in the study of conflict and cooperation highlights
the role of balanced power or power preponderance in promoting
peaceful or violent resolutions of disputes. Variants of a balance-of-
power theory have been central to the thinking of policymakers and
at the core of much postwar analysis. A perspective that emphasizes
peace through power preponderance has been the principal alternative
theory, gaining eminence in the past decade of speculation about the
possibly declining hegemony of the United States (Keohane 1984;
Russett 1985; Kugler and Organski 1989; Kennedy 1987). These apparently competing theories of international politics have generally
been viewed as positing irreconcilable approaches to international
interactions. One—the balance-of-power theory—implies that state actions are dictated by a universal preference and insatiable national
appetite for power. The other—the theory of power transition or he-

gemonic war—contemplates states that vie for control over the rules and norms of international intercourse, for control over the values by which nations live and interact. Here we propose to investigate these contending theories with the international interaction game. We deduce propositions regarding power relations between rivals and the likelihood of war, and we contrast those deductions to expectations extracted from the balance-of-power and power preponderance perspectives. Empirical tests accompany the propositions to evaluate the relative merits of the alternative points of view and to identify commonalities, complementarities, and differences.

We begin by reviewing the arguments of balance-of-power theorists and of power transition or hegemonic-war theorists, first with respect to the motivation for war, especially—but not exclusively—wars of sufficient consequence that they might transform the fundamental functioning or structure of the international system. Then we assess these theories in terms of the power relations that are expected to promote such wars or to encourage peaceful relations among states.

THE BALANCE OF POWER AND WAR

It is difficult to point to a definitive statement of the balance-of-power theory. Indeed, there are so many variants of this perspective that it is difficult to speak of it as a single theory at all. Still, there appears to be a set of assumptions common to the many proponents of the view: a rough equality of power among rival states discourages any from risking war, whereas an approximate shift to preponderance by any is a *causus belli*. Seemingly fundamental to all such arguments are the following assumptions.

1. States try to maximize their power (or their security), so that gaining power (or security) is always preferred to maintaining power (or security), and maintaining current levels of power (or security) is always preferred to losing power (or security).

2. If a state threatens to become preponderant, then other states coalesce to prevent the threatening state from gaining any more power, and if possible, those aligned against the threatening state seek to aggrandize themselves at the expense of their putative opponent.

3. Nations augment their power (or security) through several means, of which the most prominent is the formation of power-seeking alliances.

4. The sovereignty of key states—those that are critical to redressing potential imbalances in the distribution of power—is preserved even if these states are defeated in war.

From these assumptions, or variants of them, balance-of-power theorists argue that alliances are short-term, nonideological arrangements geared toward increasing one's own power or diminishing the power of some rival(s). Balance-of-power theorists also hypothesize that an approximate equality in the distribution of power makes war unlikely, whereas a shift that threatens to give one state a potential preponderance of power exacerbates the prospects of war. The theory suggests that although the overall status quo of the international system is not assured of preservation, still the status quo in terms of countervailing power (or security) among the key states—those essential for building "winning" coalitions (Niou, Ordeshook, and Rose 1989)—is guaranteed by a balance of power. Indeed, using cooperative game theory, Emerson Niou, Peter Ordeshook, and Gregory Rose prove this latter expectation as a theorem from their game.

The general viewpoint of balance-of-power theory is elegantly and succinctly summarized in the following passage from *Europe's Catechism,* published in London in 1741.

> *Catechist:* Hold, my pretty Child—one Word more.—You have been ask'd concerning the Ballance of Power.—Tell me what it is?
> *Europa:* It is such an equal Distribution of Power among the Princes of Europe, as makes it impracticable for the one to disturb the Repose of the other.
> *Catechist:* Pray who was it that formed that excellent Plan?
> *Europa:* The immortal King *William,* the *Dutch,* and other wise Men.
> *Catechist:* Tell me wherein consists the Safety of Europe?
> *Europa:* In this same Ballance of Power.
> *Catechist:* What is it that generally causes War in her Bowels?
> *Europa:* It is occasion'd by the Ballance of Power being destroy'd.
> *Catechist:* And how may that Ballance be destroy'd?
> *Europa:* That Ballance may be destroyed by Force or Fraud; by the Pusillanimity of some, and the Corruption of all.
> *Catechist:* When any Potentate hath arriv'd to an exorbitant Share of Power, ought not the Rest to league together in order to reduce him to his due Proportion of it?
> *Europa:* Yes, certainly.—Otherwise there is but one Potentate, and the others are only a kind of Vassals to him. (Gulick 1955, 2)

This notion that balanced power fosters peace enjoys widespread acceptance among policymakers and in the councils of states. It finds expression in such diverse documents of diplomacy as the Treaties of Utrecht and the NATO alliance; it is taken as a received wisdom and universal truth of international relations. As Eyre Crowe said about the impending First World War,

> History shows that the danger threatening the independence of this or that nation has generally arisen, at least in part, out of the momentary predominance of a neighboring State at once militarily powerful, economically efficient, and ambitious to extend its frontiers or spread its influence. . . . The only check on the abuse of political predominance derived from such a position has always consisted in the opposition of an equally formidable rival, or of a combination of several countries forming leagues of defence. The equilibrium established by such a grouping of forces is technically known as the balance of power. (Hartmann 1978, 316)

This sentiment continues to be echoed today, although the proposition itself cannot be derived from the assumptions typically made by balance-of-power theorists (Riker 1963; Bueno de Mesquita 1980). Yet it does follow under specific (and fairly typical) conditions within the deductive structure of the realpolitik version of the international interaction game.[1]

Unlike most theories of power preponderance, balance-of-power theory is not exclusively concerned with the causes of wars of large consequence. The theory is as readily adapted to giving an account of small conflagrations as it is to explaining wars of such import that they transform the international system. Like the theory of power transition or hegemonic war, however, the balance-of-power theory does not explain large wars according to the same logic as it accounts for small wars.

For balance-of-power theorists, a fundamental feature of interactions among states is that there is a substantial motivation to preserve the sovereignty and integrity of key actors. These key nations are seen as crucial to the ability of governments to redress future threats to the power status quo (Gulick 1955; Kaplan 1957; Morgenthau 1973; Claude 1962; Niou, Ordeshook, and Rose 1989). Their sovereignty is essential

---

1. As proved in chapter 3, P^A and P^B must each be believed to be greater than or equal to .5 for war to be possible, provided that the realpolitik variant of the game is operative and provided that $\tau_i \geq \gamma_i$. This latter condition, we believe, is typical of international affairs. When it is not satisfied, P^i need not be as large as .5. In all cases, the exact threshold value of P^i depends on the specific values of the relevant cost terms. For the specific condition that must be satisfied, see expressions (3.5) and (3.6) in chapter 3.

for preserving the flexibility needed in the formation of alliances that can ensure stability and preserve the peace. States small enough that they are not essential for redressing potential shifts in power are viewed as expendable. Small wars over the sovereignty of these states are not likely to end with generous, restorative settlements, although for balance-of-power theorists, wars among key states are likely to be resolved through compromises that restore the central role even of defeated essential powers. It appears, then, that for balance-of-power theorists, big wars differ from small wars in their consequences: big wars are oriented toward restoring or preserving the status quo; lesser wars may or may not be.

Wars among key states, from a balance-of-power perspective, necessarily involve circumstances in which at least one side is dissatisfied with the existing power status quo; if this were not so, there would be no reason to fight. As Morgenthau notes, "The opposition, under the conditions of the balance of power, between one status quo nation or an alliance of them and one imperialistic power or a group of them is very likely to lead to war" (1973, 217). Neorealists hold similar though subtler views. In the neorealist perspective, the status quo is evaluated in terms of national security, with dissatisfaction rising as the sense of security falls. Balance-of-power theorists and power preponderance theorists agree about the importance of the status quo, although they disagree about the feature of the status quo that engenders dissatisfaction. As we will see, the domestic variant of the international interaction game does not share the expectation that wars that transform the international system must involve dissatisfaction with the status quo.

Unlike power preponderance theories or the international interaction game, balance-of-power theory collapses motives of action and prospects for success into a single indivisible category: the quest for power (or security). As Morgenthau contends, "The concept of interest defined as power imposes intellectual discipline upon the observer, infuses rational order into the subject matter of politics, and thus makes the theoretical understanding of politics possible. . . . A realist theory of international politics, then, will guard against two popular fallacies: the concern with motives and the concern with ideological preferences" (5–6). For balance-of-power advocates, nations have only one motive and only one preference: "Since the desire to attain a maximum of power is universal, all nations must always be afraid that their own miscalculations and the power increases of other nations might add up to an inferiority for themselves which they must at all costs try to avoid" (215). Waltz (1979), the foremost neorealist theorist, expresses a closely related view, his focus being on security, which itself derives largely from power.

This balance-of-power perspective is inconsistent with our domestic/constrained version of the game and with theories of hegemony. To be sure, the international interaction game does not preclude the possibility that nations are trying to maximize power (or security), but neither does it insist upon that goal as a primary and universal objective of all states. Rather, it enthusiastically embraces the notion that motives or preferences might be crucial in foreign policy choices. Indeed, that is one regard in which the domestic interpretation of the international interaction game departs from a classical realist or neo-realist theory of international affairs.

Theories of power transition or hegemony also diverge from balance-of-power expectations. These power preponderance theories insist that "it is not a desire to maximize power or a single-minded urge to guarantee security in the narrow sense that leads nations to start major wars, . . . it is a general dissatisfaction with its position in the system, and a desire to redraft the rules by which relations among nations work, that move a country to begin a major war" (Organski and Kugler 1980, 23). Through this argument, power preponderance theorists avoid conflating power as an instrument for achieving objectives and power as the objective itself. We turn now to a more careful development of their arguments.

HEGEMONIC WAR AND THE STATUS QUO

Theories of hegemonic war can be traced back to Thucydides, but their modern manifestations and the current debate are clearly rooted in the research of Organski, Kugler, Gilpin, and Paul Kennedy, among others. The essence of the chief variants of the theory is that differential rates of growth lead some nations to rise in power and others to fall. When the dominant state in an international system is being surpassed in power by a rival that is dissatisfied with the international order—the prevailing status quo—then the risk of hegemonic war is great. Such power transition wars, in turn, culminate in a restructuring of the international system around the leadership of the newly emergent hegemon (Thucydides 1954; Carr 1951; Organski 1958; MacKinder 1962; Organski and Kugler 1980; Doran and Parsons 1980; Doran 1989; Gilpin 1981; Kennedy 1987; Modelski 1987; Thompson 1988).

Questions of who fights in hegemonic wars and when such wars are fought are at the heart of theories and historical evaluations of relations

among competing great powers. Organski and Kugler, Gilpin, and
Kennedy offer remarkably similar answers to these questions. Recall
that Organski and Kugler contend that power transition or hegemonic
wars arise because great powers "desire to redraft the rules by which
relations among nations work" (1980, 23). Gilpin says of such disputes:
"The war determines who will govern the international system and
whose interests will be primarily served by the new international order.
The war leads to a redistribution of territory among the states in the
system, a new set of rules of the system, a revised international
division of labor, etc." (1981, 198).

Organski and Kugler maintain that the aggressor in a power transition war "will come from a small group of dissatisfied strong countries" (19). In a similar vein, Gilpin argues that "the fundamental issue
at stake is the nature and governance of the system" (198) and that

> the disequilibrium in the international system is due to increasing disjunc-
> ture between the existing governance of the system and the redistribution
> of power in the system. . . . From the perspective of dominant powers, the
> costs of maintaining the international status quo have increased. . . . From
> the perspective of rising powers, the perceived costs of changing the inter-
> national system have declined relative to the potential benefits of doing
> so. . . . Thus, in accordance with the law of demand, the rising state, as
> its power increases, will seek to change the status quo as the perceived
> potential benefits begin to exceed the perceived costs of undertaking a
> change in the system. (186–87)

Apparently, conflicting views of the international status quo are hypothesized to be a key cause of system-transforming wars.

Students of hegemonic or power transition wars also agree broadly
in the specification of criteria for identifying the events that could
transform the international system. As Gilpin notes, "The most important consequence of a hegemonic war is that it changes the system
in accordance with the new international distribution of power," and
therefore, "such a war . . . becomes total and in time is characterized
by participation by all the major states and most of the minor states
in the system. . . . For this reason, hegemonic wars are unlimited
conflicts; they are at once political, economic, and ideological" (198–
99). Organski and Kugler observe that such wars must include major
power participation in each opposing coalition, with the major powers
making "an all-out effort to win" so that "the number of battle deaths
reached higher levels than in any previous war" (46). Such wars not

only involve great stakes but also expand to encompass many, if not all, of the great powers (Siverson and Starr 1990).[2]

The transformation of the international order through a large-scale bloody war is believed to be a consequence of hegemonic decline.[3] In the balance-of-power theory, such wars are the consequence of emerging hegemony, not decline. Yet within the structure of our game-theoretic model, system transformation can occur without a large-scale bloody conflict or even without such a transformation being the ex ante objective of the relevant disputants. A system transformation may fail to materialize, even though it was the intended objective.

If our model is germane, then theories of system transformation may offer a somewhat misleading view because of a tendency to study only those cases in which a large war was motivated, at least partially, by a desire to redraft the rules of the international system. By selecting cases only from such wars, researchers risk misstating the conditions that are either necessary or sufficient for such events, although they may have identified conditions that are likely to be correlated with the advent of cataclysmic wars. To delineate more fully the necessary and sufficient conditions under which system-transforming wars can occur, we turn to the international interaction game, which we will evaluate in accordance with concepts that are central to theories of power transition or balance of power.

THE INTERNATIONAL INTERACTION GAME AND THE STATUS QUO

Theories of power transition emphasize power parity and dissatisfaction with the existing status quo as crucial elements contributing to the risk of a system-transforming war. Balance-of-power theory emphasizes power imbalance and dissatisfaction with the status quo as crucial elements contributing to the risk of a system-transforming war. Our first concern here is with the possibility of a system-transforming war when the status quo is highly valued, a condition explicitly ruled out by the theories of hegemonic war and power transition and, when focused on key states, by balance-of-power theory. The condition is also ruled out by the realpolitik account of the international interaction game if it is common knowledge that the status quo is highly valued.

2. Our operational specifications for P^A and P^B specifically draw attention to the expectation that a dispute will involve third parties.

3. For similar views of the causes of systemic wars see, for instance, Midlarsky 1988, Thompson 1988, or Doran 1989.

If such wars are possible according to the domestic version of the international interaction game when the status quo is known to be highly valued, then it is possible to construct a test of the game vis-à-vis that aspect of the other, realist theories. Clearly, the expectations of the game contradict the suppositions based on the theory of the balance of power or the theories of the power transition or hegemonic war.

Once the evaluation of the role of the status quo or other sources of dissatisfaction is completed, then we can turn to an assessment of the role of specific power relations as influence on the likelihood of war according to balance-of-power theory, power preponderance theories, and the international interaction game.

We have already seen in our investigation of the conservation norm (in chapter 4) that war can be a full-information equilibrium outcome of the domestic/constrained international interaction game even if the status quo is highly valued. Recall our basic war theorem from chapter 3, restated here partially in terms of beliefs to acknowledge effects that could arise under limited information conditions.

BASIC WAR THEOREM. *War initiated by side A is the equilibrium outcome of the international interaction game if side A prefers to initiate a war rather than acquiesce to its rival's demands; side B prefers to try to force the adversary to capitulate rather than offer a negotiated settlement; B believes (and A believes B believes) A will capitulate rather than retaliate if B strikes A; and B is prepared to strike back at its opponent rather than give in to the opponent's demands.*

With expected costs being a function of the relevant actor's subjective probability of success, as assumed earlier, the basic war theorem can be restated:

$$\frac{\tau_A - \gamma_A}{U^A(\Delta_A - \Delta_B) + \tau_A - \gamma_A - \phi_A} > P^A > \frac{\alpha_A}{U^A(\Delta_A - \Delta_B) + \alpha_A - \phi_A}, \quad (6.1)$$

and

$$\frac{U^B(\Delta_B - \Delta_A)}{U^B(\Delta_B - \Delta_A) + \phi_B} > P^B > \frac{\tau_B}{U^B(\Delta_B - \Delta_A) + \tau_B - \phi_B}. \quad (6.2)$$

The theorem gives several important clues about war. First, the value attached to the status quo does not enter into the theorem at all. Consequently, whether a war is system transforming or not, the claim of some theorists that dissatisfaction with the international status quo is a necessary condition is contradicted by the domestic international interaction game. In chapter 4 we offered an existence proof that a highly valued status quo does not guarantee peace, just as a poorly valued status quo does not ensure war. In the next chapter we provide a historical demonstration of the importance of this implication of the theorem. Here, however, we state it as the first testable' proposition in our comparison of the international interaction game and the theories of power transition and the balance of power.

STATUS QUO PROPOSITION 6.1. *Dissatisfaction with the status quo is unrelated to the likelihood of war.*

If proposition 6.1, which disconnects the status quo from the likelihood of war, is correct, we should not expect a statistical tendency for wars, including potentially system-transforming wars, to arise in conjunction with a low valuation of the status quo by A (the challenger) and a high valuation by B (the challenged state). That is, we should not expect challengers to launch wars only when they are dissatisfied with the status quo, nor should we expect most defenders to be satisfied with the existing order of things. A pattern of insignificant relations is consistent with the game-theoretic expectations and is inconsistent with the expectations of power transition and hegemonic war theory or of balance-of-power theory when applied to conflicts among key states.

Because our indicators of utility, including $U^i(\Delta_i)$, $U^i(SQ)$, and $U^i(\Delta_j)$, are based on similarities and differences in alliance portfolios, they are good tools for assessing hypotheses that are specifically about values attached to the overall structure of the international system. The indicators are constructed, after all, to reflect not only the bilateral associations between states but the commonality in their perspective on the overall array of commitments in the international system—the extent to which they share a set of alignments that constitutes the international order.

We test proposition 6.1 with a set of simple logit analyses. In the first set, we evaluate the likelihood of war between pairs of major powers in light of our estimation of their utility for the status quo. We define two dependent variables: WAR, as previously specified to mean reciprocated use of force, and BIGWAR, defined, using the Small and Singer (1982) criteria, as a conflict involving at least one hundred regular troops on each side or one thousand battle-related fatalities. In the second set of tests, we assess the relation between the value attached to the status quo and the likelihood of war for all disputes,

Table 6.1

The Likelihood of War and the Value of the Status Quo

	A and B are major powers				A and B are states of any size			
	WAR		BIGWAR		WAR		BIGWAR	
	Coef.	P	Coef.	P	Coef.	P	Coef.	P
$U^A(SQ)$	−.92	.08	−.84	.14	−.18	.18	−.41	.06
$U^B(SQ)$	−.25	.33	.14	.42	.04	.24	.60	.01
Constant	−1.07	—	−1.71	—	−1.00	—	−1.95	—
χ^2	2.60	.27	1.20	.55	.89	.64	7.78	.02
N	109		109		707		707	

whether they involved major powers on each side or not. The results of the logit analyses are summarized in table 6.1. Before turning to those results, however, we note that the correlation between $U^A(SQ)$ and $U^B(SQ)$ is only .10 for all of our observations (N = 707) and .18 for the cases in which nations A and B were each a major power (N = 109). These correlations provide assurance that there is little colinearity to distort the coefficients in table 6.1.

Only the logit analysis reflecting the relation between all Small-Singer wars and the valuation of the status quo is statistically significant. In one of the four logit analyses—including all cases of reciprocated violence between major powers—not only is the overall relation insignificant but even the sign of $U^B(SQ)$ is opposite to the expectations of balance-of-power and hegemonic war and power transition theories. The results in table 6.1 are generally consistent with our basic war theorem and inconsistent with either classical realist theories or our own realpolitik version of the international interaction game. The value of the status quo does not appear to be strongly or consistently related to the likelihood of war, at least not in ways anticipated by balance-of-power or power preponderance theorists.

Perhaps our investigation has taken too literally the claim that dissatisfaction with the international status quo is essential for disputes with the potential to become system-transforming wars. Perhaps what is meant by discussions of dissatisfaction with the status quo is that the potential stakes of a system-transforming dispute must be very large rather than that the overall value of the status quo is low for the challenger and high for the defender. The relevant theorists may have in mind that wars that alter the international order involve such disparate demands that the marginal utility for obtaining one's objectives is large compared to the utility associated with giving in to the opponent's goals (that is, $U^A(\Delta_A - \Delta_B)$ and $U^B(\Delta_B - \Delta_A)$ are large). Expressions (6.1) and (6.2) can shed considerable light on this viewpoint.

Certainly both can be satisfied if the stakes are large, and neither can be satisfied if the stakes are especially small. Specifically, if $U^A(\Delta_A - \Delta_B) \leq \phi_A$, then war for A is possible only if $P^A \geq 1$, which is not possible. Similarly for B, if $U^B(\Delta_B - \Delta_A) \leq \phi_B$, then war is possible only if $P^B \geq 1$, also an impossibility. Thus, the conditions of the game and the conditions stipulated in power transition or balance-of-power theory are only partially in agreement on the stakes surrounding a potential war. The game does not indicate that the stakes must be especially large; rather, it suggests that they cannot be especially small. The anticipated gains must be larger than the expected domestic costs, or else a rational actor will not wage war.

The game provides a somewhat different perspective on the belief of some theorists that wars involving large stakes must be large, costly wars in particular. Recall, for instance, that Organski and Kugler (1980) and Gilpin (1981) maintain that system-transforming wars are unlimited contests involving great losses of life and destruction of property. A focus now on the partial equilibrium conditions identified on the right-hand side of expressions (6.1) and (6.2) call this generalization into question. Note that in the limit, as the stakes approach their lower feasible bound, the expected costs of the war must approach zero for the inequalities to hold. Wars with small expected stakes necessarily are expected to be low in costs, with the anticipated costs approaching zero as the stakes approach their lower limit. By contrast, as the stakes increase—suggesting growing dissatisfaction—it is possible for the expected costs to be large or small. Large stakes do not necessitate large expected costs in the way that small stakes do necessitate small expected costs. Rather, wars expected to be high in costs necessarily must be expected to involve large potential net benefits. The opposite is not true. Wars expected to yield large net benefits need not be expected to be costly. Contrary to those who argue that dissatisfaction, at least between essential great powers, leads to cataclysmic wars, disputes involving even great dissatisfaction, as indicated by the magnitude of the difference in the value of demands, need not, according to our theory or any basic cost-benefit analysis, be large costly wars. Rather, large costly wars will always involve such dissatisfaction. In that sense, Organski and Kugler's contention that great dissatisfaction is necessary but not sufficient for cataclysmic wars is modified by the

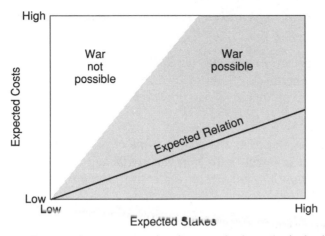

6.1: Expected costs and stakes in war: the hypothetical relation.

game to say that large stakes are necessary but not sufficient for wars expected to be costly, whether such costs are a characteristic of system transformation or not.

The argument is summarized by a diagram of the game-theoretic relation between expected costs and dissatisfaction as indicated by the magnitude of the stakes. Figure 6.1 depicts the general form of the expected costs-stakes relation for either *A* or *B*. As is clear in the figure, the distribution of expected costs is heteroscedastic with respect to the expected stakes.[4] The variance in expected costs rises like a funnel pinched shut at the origin (the lower bound for the stakes) and spread widest at the upper bound for the stakes.

Figure 6.1 implies several testable hypotheses, which we can evaluate by adding an operational assumption. To investigate the accuracy of figure 6.1, we assume that the costs actually experienced in war are highly and positively correlated with expectations. We contend that for a fixed set of demands, if the incurred costs rise to exceed the expected benefits, then the war ends. With the assumption that expectations are correlated with experience, we can test the following corollaries of the basic war theorem.

HETEROSCEDASTICITY PROPOSITION 6.2. *The distribution of costs with respect to stakes should be heteroscedastic and assume the general shape depicted in figure 6.1, in which all wars with low stakes are*

4. Heteroscedasticity arises when the statistical assumption of constant variance is violated.

small wars and wars with high stakes can be large or small in expected costs.

ZERO-INTERCEPT PROPOSITION 6.3. *As the stakes approach the lower limit, the expected magnitude of costs is zero, so that the intercept of a regression analysis of stakes on costs should not be significantly different from zero.*

POSITIVE-SLOPE PROPOSITION 6.4. *The slope for the observed costs with respect to the stakes is positive, so that the coefficient for $U^i(\Delta_i)$ is positive and larger than the coefficient for $U^i(\Delta_j)$, which is expected to be negative.*

To test propositions 6.2–4—all of which are implied by the basic war theorem (and its partial representation in figure 6.1)—we utilize two distinct measures of costs, testing the hypotheses on the sixty-two Small-Singer warring dyads for which we have complete data on battle deaths and on war duration. Because the general form of the propositions is expected to apply both to actor A and to actor B, we split each dyad into two individual observations with the nation-state as the unit of analysis. This gives us 124 observations, twenty-six of which satisfy the additional stipulation that A and B were both major powers. For half of the observations, the costs refer to those incurred by A, and for the other half, to those incurred by B.

We expect no difference in the consistency between the propositions and the analyses across the data sets. Although our theory makes no statement one way or the other about the magnitude of stakes in wars that are putative candidates for causing a system transformation—for instance, those involving at least one major power on each side—power transition and hegemonic war theorists expect such disputes to involve higher stakes than the other wars. Apparently, balance-of-power theorists share this expectation. Our model anticipates that wars with higher stakes, on average, involve higher costs, as should be clear from the expectation that the regression line is positively sloped. However, we do not expect that all major-power wars involve large stakes or large expected costs, hence our expectation that the distribution of costs is heteroscedastic with respect to stakes. These additional hypotheses are tested below.

Costs are defined as the duration of the war in days and in terms of battle deaths per million of population for each participant. The dependent variables that evaluate costs are called Deaths and Duration. The correlations between these alternative dependent variables are .70 (N = 124) for all the cases for which we have complete cost data and .64 (N = 26) for the subset in which both nation A and nation B were major powers. There is a substantial correlation between the two alternative indicators of costs. Still, in neither data set do the two dependent variables share as much as 50 percent of their variance in common. Thus it is safe to say that they are measuring related, but still different, aspects of the costs of war.

The goodness of fit, measured as R^2, for the proposed regression analyses, is not expected to be large. There are several reasons for the R^2 to be depressed. First, the hypothesized relation is heteroscedastic, with little variance anticipated in the dependent variable as the stakes approach their lower bound. By implication, the regression line is expected to fit the data better for small-stakes wars than for large-stakes wars. Second, because with the available data we cannot distinguish the subtleties in costs that are identified in the international interaction game, we can test only partial equilibrium conditions, rather than the entirety of expression (6.1). If the theory is correct, part of the variance, even under full information, is not being accounted for simply because we are unable to estimate adequately the left-hand side of the inequalities in the expression. Third, the conditions being tested assume full information, a condition that is undoubtedly violated in reality. The hypothesized relations do not take into account the ways in which uncertainty might shift the specified association between expected costs and stakes, moving the tolerable costs up or down in response to beliefs about the costs or benefits of the dispute. Finally, we treat the utility for costs as linear with their expected value, while treating anticipated gains and losses in a nonlinear manner, to figure risk-taking propensities. It is likely that the utility of costs is not linear with the value of costs, but we have no adequate way to estimate the shape of the cost function.

What, then, are the observed relations between the costs of war and the expected gains and losses? The utility for success and the utility for failure are measured in the manner described in appendix 1. For the subset of cases involving a major power on each side, we construct the independent variable called Stakes as the difference between the utility an actor attaches to gaining its demand and the utility it attaches to giving in to its rival's demand. We do so to conserve degrees of freedom, for the number of observations for this subset of events is small (N = 26). Because this variable is simply the difference in the two utilities [$U^i(\Delta_i)$ and $U^i(\Delta_j)$], we expect, in accordance with proposition 6.4, that the regression coefficient is positive. Table 6.2 summarizes the relation between costs and stakes for the

Table 6.2
Expected Stakes and Observed Costs for War

	All war				Major-power war			
	Death		Duration		Death		Duration	
	Coef.	P	Coef.	P	Coef.	P	Coef.	P
$U_i(\Delta_i)$	7897	.00	613	.00	—	—	—	—
$U_i(\Delta_j)$	−2152	.03	−242	.00	—	—	—	—
STAKES	—	—	—	—	7669	.05	475	.01
Constant	−1982	.27	14	.90	126	.99	362	.39
F		12.36		25.46		2.90		6.03	
P≤		.00		.00		.10		.02	
N		124		124		26		26	
R^2		.17		.30		.11		.20	

two alternative dependent variables and for the two alternative data sets.

Proposition 6.3 anticipates that the estimated costs of war when the stakes approach zero will be zero, meaning that the constant term in the regression analyses should not be statistically significant. As predicted, none of the constant terms is significantly different from zero, a highly unusual finding. Proposition 6.4 makes several specific predictions: the coefficient β_1 for $U^i(\Delta_i) > 0$; the coefficient β_2 for $U^i(\Delta_j) < 0$, and $\beta_1 > |\beta_2|$; or the coefficient for the variable Stakes [which equals $U^i(\Delta_i - \Delta_j)] > 0$. Each of these predictions is borne out.

Proposition 6.2 contends that the distribution of costs with respect to the stakes in war is heteroscedastic and funnel shaped, with the funnel pinched closed as the stakes approach zero. Figure 6.2 displays the actual distribution of costs in terms of duration with respect to stakes for all wars as reported in table 6.2. The figure shows the anticipated characteristics, as do the relations in the other regression analyses, not displayed here. All the observations of costs, whether in terms of duration or deaths, are clustered around the origin when the stakes are close to zero. As the stakes rise, some wars continue to involve low costs while others lead to high costs. The data are distributed in the shape of a funnel pinched closed at the origin. The funnel shape is also highly significant.

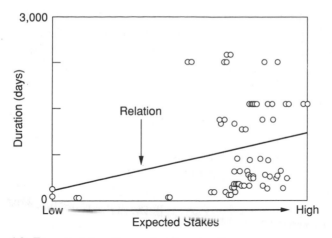

6.2: Expected duration and stakes in all wars.

As we have noted, theories about wars that have transformed the international system focus on dissatisfaction between rivals as a necessary condition for such wars. The basic war theorem agrees that dissatisfaction (conceptualized as large stakes) is necessary for large costly wars but disagrees with the contention that high costs are either necessary or sufficient specifically for system-transforming wars. Here we test to see whether costly wars involved unusually high stakes and then to see whether high-stakes wars were necessarily system transforming. The tests represent some commonality of outlook between a rational-choice perspective and a power transition or balance-of-power perspective: high-stakes wars should incur a higher average level of costs than low-stakes wars. They have. Dividing our sample of the 124 warring nations for which we have complete cost data at the median for stakes, we find that the average number of battle deaths per million population in the low-stakes disputes was under three thousand, whereas the average for the high-stakes subsample was nearly five thousand. The Kruskal-Wallis test for equality of populations yields a χ^2 of nearly 21 (P $\leq$ .001). The comparable difference is even greater when duration is the measure of costs. Then $\chi^2 = 41.4$ with one degree of freedom.

The difference in the stakes for participants in warring dyads in which each actor was a major power as contrasted to the stakes for participants in warring dyads in which at least one actor was not a major power is also significant. The difference in means is so large, and in the direction predicted by hegemonic war and power transition theorists, that it would have occurred by chance less than one time in ten thousand (t = 4.57, N = 124). Thus, wars that could transform the system do, on average, involve substantially greater dissatisfaction, as indicated by the magnitude of the stakes, than do other wars. These results are consistent with the power transition, balance-of-power, and the game-theoretic perspectives delineated here.

The international interaction game further indicates that the ranges of stakes and costs are likely to be large whether major powers are involved or not. Hegemonic war theory is unclear about expectations on this issue, and balance-of-power theory appears to disagree with the international interaction game. Concern over preserving or defending the status quo apparently is less important in small-power wars than in wars among key states, according to balance-of-power theory. If large stakes are purported to be necessary or sufficient for system transformation, then we cannot agree. Large stakes are necessary for war when costs are expected to be high, but nothing in our model suggests that large consequences cannot follow from disputes involving small stakes or small costs.

We find that the stakes can vary enormously both in the case of wars between major powers and in the case of warring dyads not involving two major powers. In both types of wars we observe cases for which the stakes approach a value of zero. We also find that the highest values the stakes reach are about the same, as is also true for battle deaths and war duration. Although, as anticipated, the means are different, wars, whether involving major powers or not, have enormous variance surrounding the stakes and the costs. This is expected from proposition 6.2 and seems inconsistent with balance-of-power expectations.

By treating the magnitude of competing demands as an indicator of dissatisfaction, we have found support for some expectations of power transition theory and our game-theoretic model. We have also found places of disagreement between theories that focus on dissatisfaction with the status quo and our own model of international interactions. In every test, the specific, often detailed predictions of the international interaction game were supported with respect to the role of dissatisfaction in influencing the likelihood of war. Thus far, when balance-of-power theory and power preponderance theory have diverged in their hypotheses, the theory supported, if either, tended to be based on the notion that a preponderance of power encourages peace.

POWER AND WAR

A source of disagreement among several scholars interested in system-transforming wars is whether the dissatisfied challenger of the existing order strikes before or after surpassing the capabilities of its foe. Organski and Kugler (1980) and others, for instance, expect the challenger to attack before overtaking the hegemon in power. Gilpin (1981) maintains that the challenger waits until it has surpassed the heretofore dominant state. Charles Doran and Wes Parsons (1980) associate periods of high risk of war with rapid changes in expected power, whether for the better or the worse. Woosang Kim and James Morrow (1991), using a game-theoretic approach, contend that risk-averse challengers tend to strike before the transition and more risk-acceptant challengers wait. Balance-of-power theorists like Morgenthau (1973) seem to expect the likelihood of attack to increase as the disparity between the power of the challenger and the power of the hegemon (erstwhile or otherwise) increases.

The international interaction game may illuminate this controversy. The basic war theorem suggests a proposition:

PROBABILITY PROPOSITION 6.5. *For any probability of success for A or B, there is a feasible mix of costs and benefits such that war is possible. There are situations, such as those involving large stakes and small expected costs, in which A, the challenger, can initiate the use of force even though it expects to lose (implying that the power transition war begins before the transition). There are also situations in which A will not initiate a war unless its probability of success is fairly large (implying that the power transition war begins after the transition). Such cases involve high expected costs and only slightly larger potential net benefits.*

Proof. Let τ_A be large. Let α_A, γ_A, and ϕ_A approach zero, with $\alpha_A < [U^A(\Delta_A - \Delta_B) + \phi_A]$, and let $U^A(\Delta_A - \Delta_B)$ be arbitrarily close to but greater than $(\gamma_A + \phi_A)$. Then the left-hand side of 6.1 is approximately 1.0, and the right-hand side is approximately zero, so that $0 < P^A < 1.0$. Therefore, for any given value of P^A, there are conditions under which A can initiate a war against B. QED

Proposition 6.5 identifies circumstances under which even a very weak state might provoke a war against a more powerful adversary, especially if the stakes are perceived to be high and the costs to be low. In chapter 3 we presented a case study of the Fashoda crisis. In doing so, we illustrated how weakness led France to give in to Britain's demands rather than risk a crushing defeat in war. Here we present a case in which a weak state, India, repeatedly behaved forcefully toward its more powerful rival, China, for regional preeminence, leading to the outbreak of war in 1962. The difference between the Fashoda crisis and the Sino-Indian interaction seems to reside in each side's preferences and in its beliefs about the preferences of the other. In the case of Fashoda, the preferences were consistent with the conditions of the international interaction game for an acquiescence. With India and China, the preferences appear to be consistent with the predictions of the game for war in general, and they highlight features of proposition 6.5 in particular.

The Sino-Indian War

On October 20, 1962, the Indian army confronted a massive assault by soldiers of the Chinese army, resulting in a decisive defeat of Indian forces. India, which had persisted in its territorial claims along the Thag La Ridge, near the McMahon Line, had maneuvered itself into a humiliating and politically devastating failed war against China. What happened, and how can the international interaction game account for the central events?

The territorial dispute over the McMahon Line that precipitated the war was long-standing. India demanded that China accept its claims to the border while China persisted in its own claims. Considerable evidence suggests that the Chinese were not eager to fight over the border, placed as it was near remote military outposts. They gave every indication that a negotiated settlement or the persistence of the status quo was better from their perspective than a war. As early as 1959, the Chinese appeared willing to accept the McMahon Line in the east in exchange for Indian recognition of China's claims to the Aksai Chin (Maxwell 1970, 160). Through their concrete proposals, the Chinese also made clear that they preferred to negotiate a compromise settlement, rather than use force to compel the Indians to accept their initial claims.

The Indians, like the Chinese, indicated a preference for negotiation over war. Unlike the Chinese government, the Indian government saw negotiations as talks in which the Chinese would be made to recognize the rightness of the Indian claims and the incorrectness of their own position. There was no thought of concessions and compromise. In a 1960 press conference, for instance, Prime Minister Jawaharlal Nehru was asked, "Is it still the Indian stand that our frontiers are not negotiable?" He replied: "That is our stand. . . . At the same time there is nothing that is not negotiable. . . . It seems to be contradictory. But there is no question of negotiation or bargaining about the matter. But . . . one cannot refuse to talk to another country" (Maxwell 1970, 140–41). This attitude persisted throughout the crisis. Even in its final stages "China was again urging the early opening of negotiations; India was refusing" (431). India's position was that China must accept India's claims, by acquiescence if possible but through the use of force if necessary. Nehru preferred to force a capitulation rather than negotiate a compromise settlement. For him, the stakes were high in terms of his personal political fortunes and in terms of India's valuation of success in this dispute (Lebow 1981).

India introduced its forward policy to demonstrate its resolve. The forward policy intruded Indian forces forward of Chinese outposts, thereby asserting India's claims to territory in Arunachal Pradesh (then the North East Frontier Agency), which was under the physical control of China. The forward policy was a means of demonstrating how strongly India sought its objectives. Even when the policy heated up the dispute in 1961–62, China showed remarkable restraint (Whiting 1975). Repeatedly, the Chinese threatened to crush India's advances, only to back away each time from stepping over the brink. Nehru assured the Indian Parliament that forces were ready if it should come to a fight. Indian forces sometimes fired on and killed Chinese soldiers on patrol; naturally, the Chinese responded with a sharp condemnation of India's actions and with threats of dire consequences.

The Indian government dismissed Chinese warnings as mere bluff and bluster. There were good reasons for the Indian leadership to believe the Chinese threat was not credible. The Chinese had backed down from a confrontation in the Chip Chap Valley in May 1962 and again at the Galwan River in July (Maxwell 1970; Vertzberger 1984). They had sustained losses without retaliatory strikes. Thus, the Indian government was confident that the Chinese would choose capitulation over war, making the dispute a high-stakes, low-cost enterprise from their perspective. As Gen. J. N. Chaudhuri noted, "It was a game of Russian roulette, but the highest authorities of India seemed to feel that the one shot in the cylinder was a blank. Unfortunately for them and for the country it was not so. The cylinder was fully loaded" (Maxwell 1970, 171).

As the crisis unfolded, India's actual military position was very weak compared to China's. Indian soldiers were ill equipped for fighting in the frozen, rough terrain of the high mountain passes. They had not even been issued uniforms suitable for the cold climate. Chinese soldiers, by contrast, were well equipped and provisioned. The Indian government should have believed that its chances for success in war were slim. Yet it persisted in a very aggressive policy, presumably because it did not believe the Chinese would fight.

From the Indian perspective, a capitulation by China seemed likely. The Chinese were fully aware of this belief and tried to disabuse the Indians of it. In response to the forward policy, the Chinese announced: "The Chinese Government deems it necessary to point out that it would be very erroneous and dangerous should the Indian Government take China's attitude of restraint and tolerance as an expression of weakness" (Maxwell 1970, 225–26). Alas, China's repeated backing down in the face of Indian provocation was taken as the true signal of China's weak type.

Ultimately, India tried China's patience one time too many, and war erupted. All the conditions for war were there. India believed China preferred to capitulate rather than fight back. China knew India held this belief. China sought negotiation and offered concessions, whereas India sought capitulation or acquiescence. The Chinese were prepared to fight back, but India, a low probability of success in war notwithstanding, pursued the use of force through its forward policy. China ultimately met force with force. In the terms of proposition 6.5, a weak state with high stakes and expecting low costs initiated the use of force against a powerful adversary, anticipating a capitulation. Under circumstances consistent with the conditions of the international interaction game that lead to war, just such a tragic event took place.

Proposition 6.5 reminds us that in the context of the international interaction game, war can be initiated with any probability of success, provided the stakes and expected costs are appropriate. Recall that power transition and hegemonic war theories and balance-of-power theory specify that the stakes—the presumed manifestation of dissatisfaction with the status quo—must be large for a big system-transforming war to occur. Such theories also contend that the costs of the war are unusually large, perhaps even larger than in any previous dispute (Organski and Kugler 1980). These contentions can be restated in terms of expressions (6.1) and (6.2), permitting us to see what the implications of our game are under conditions stipulated by these theorists. Then we can test whether a rough equality of power makes a potentially major war more likely or less likely than a preponderance of power in the hands of a hegemon.

Neither balance-of-power theory nor theories of hegemonic war or power transition are attentive to potential domestic political costs associated with the use of force. In keeping with these theories we assume for the moment that such costs approach zero in magnitude.

Such theories are concerned with losses in life and property that are expected to be suffered during a system-transforming war. For nation A, in other words, α is the relevant cost, and for nation B, τ is. In the wars we are interested in—those expected to be unlimited—the costs are anticipated to be very high. Thus, we assume here, to echo the realist theories, that the expected magnitude of $\alpha_A \approx U^A(\Delta_A - \Delta_B)$ and that $\tau_B \approx U^B(\Delta_B - \Delta_A)$, so that the expected costs are large enough to almost equal the expected net gains. Then, according to expression (6.1), $P^A > .5$, and according to (6.2), $P^B > .5$.[5] Naturally, this situation can arise only if there is imperfect information on the true probability of success. Implied by power transition and hegemonic war theories, then, is the observation that there is uncertainty regarding the chances of success, with at least one of the combatants overestimating its prospects.

Surprisingly, this implication seems not to be adequately attended to by students of cataclysmic wars. Although the basic war theorem establishes that war can arise even under full-information conditions if demands do not arise as an endogenous function of international circumstances, uncertainty is a necessary condition for wars with high expected losses of life and property and with low expected domestic costs even in the domestic version of the game. Organski and Kugler are particularly attentive to this implication, noting:

> The power transition model postulates that the speed with which modernization occurs in big countries is also quite important in disturbing the equilibrium that existed theretofore. For if development is slow, the problems arising from one nation's catching up with the dominant one may have a greater chance of being resolved. On the other hand, if growth takes place rapidly, both parties will be unprepared for the resulting shift. The challenger may not have had the opportunity to develop a realistic evaluation of its position because its elites will be strangers to power, and the sources of new-found strength are almost entirely the result of internal changes. It seems plausible to think that the chances for miscalculation consequently increase. (1980, 21)

Blainey, too, is attentive to this issue when he hypothesizes that wars start only when both sides expect to win. This is not supported by our

5. If the expected costs are not as large as assumed, then the greatest lower bound of P^i is diminished in the domestic version of the game. Recall that in the realpolitik variant, $P^i \geq 0.5$ under specific cost conditions. Under other cost configurations, P^i is unconstrained in either the realpolitik or the domestic account of international interactions.

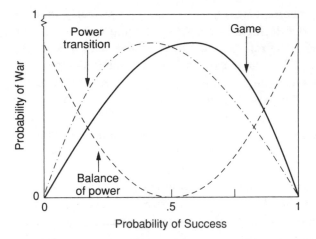

6.3: Theoretical probability of success for initiators of large wars.

domestic perspective on wars in general or by the example of the Sino-Indian War of 1962, but it is supported in the limiting case of wars in which the magnitude of costs (other than domestic political costs) is expected to approach available gains.

Our discussion suggests several testable hypotheses. Figure 6.3 approximates the Organski (1958) hypothesis that the risk of a major war peaks just before A's probability of success equals .5, the hypothesis of balance-of-power theorists that the risk of war is minimized when A and B both have about an equal chance of success, and the expectation derived from the international interaction game (and also by Kugler and Zagare, 1990) and stated here as two propositions:

DOMESTIC PROBABILITY-OF-SUCCESS PROPOSITION 6.6. *For wars that have the prospect of being very costly, the risk of war is maximized when side A believes its probability of success is greater than .5.*

DOMESTIC PROBABILITY-OF-SUCCESS PROPOSITION 6.7. *In disputes in which sides A and B each believe that its probability of success is greater than .5, there is a disproportionate tendency for the dispute to end in warfare.*

These alternative views and propositions 6.6 and 6.7, which are corollaries of expressions 6.1 and 6.2, are readily tested. We define the subjective probability of success for A and B as before. In keeping with our observation that high stakes are necessary (but not sufficient) for an expectation of a high-cost war, we test the arguments only on

Table 6.3
Expectations of Success in a High-
Stakes War

	BIGWAR	
	Coef.	P
P^A	24.95	.006
$(P^A)^2$	−18.16	.009
Constant	−9.15	.000
χ^2	17.39	.002
N	116	

disputes that involved high stakes, so high that the cases fall in the
upper 25 percent of stakes for all dyads in our data set. We also select
only disputes for which the rivals at least threatened the use of force.
In these ways we focus our analysis on disputes that were candidates
for meeting Organski and Kugler's or Gilpin's criteria for system-
transforming wars. In keeping with the empirical focus of most balance-of-power and power transition theorists, our dependent variable
for this analysis is BIGWAR, defined earlier. We use logit analysis to
test the likelihood of such conflicts given A's subjective estimate of
its probability of success. The competing expectations that are represented in figure 6.3 reflect the following functional relation between
P^A and the incidence of war:

Power transition: BIGWAR = $a + b_1 P^A - b_2 (P^A)^2$, $b_1 \leq b_2$.

Balance of power: BIGWAR = $a - b_1 P^A + b_2 (P^A)^2$, $b_1 = b_2$.

Game: BIGWAR = $a + b_1 P^A - b_2 (P^A)^2$, $b_1 > b_2$.

Table 6.3 summarizes the logit analysis that relates the likelihood
of BIGWAR to the challenger's subjective probability of success. The
observed functional relation is consistent with the expectations derived
from the international interaction game for high-stakes, high-cost wars
and also with results reported by Organski and Kugler (1980). The
peak probability of war arises when $P^A = .69$ for Small-Singer wars,
here called BIGWARs.

Proposition 6.6 is supported by the evidence. Wars with the potential to be cataclysmic—those for which the stakes and casualties are

high—tend to occur *after* the challenger believes it has surpassed its rival in power, taking into account its own capabilities and the anticipated help from its allies and opposition from its adversary's allies.[6]

Proposition 6.7 is also supported. Of the 109 disputes that involved a major power on each side, 16 escalated to the level of warfare, and 93 did not. In five of the sixteen wars, P^A and P^B were each greater than .5 by our estimates. Only fifteen of the ninety-three other disputes between two major powers satisfied that condition. The difference is statistically significant. In fact, the relation is even stronger than is reflected by this result.

Recall that we derived the expectation that P^A and P^B would each be greater than .5 through an analysis in which we imposed on expressions (6.1) and (6.2) the conditions stipulated by power transition and hegemonic war theorists. Included among those conditions was the assumption that domestic political costs for using force were irrelevant and approached zero. Yet in the test reported above, we have not controlled for the estimated magnitude of those costs.

We now split our sample into those cases in which the estimated domestic costs for using force were below the median and those for which they were above the median. In this way we have a subset that is the quartile of observations with low joint expected domestic costs. These 176 cases are compared to those in which at least one of the rivals anticipated high domestic costs for using force. As should be evident from the basic war theorem, it is generally true that, all else being equal, low domestic costs make waging war easier, not more difficult. One might intuitively anticipate, then, that wars expected to involve low domestic costs are more readily fought, even when a nation's subjective estimate of its probability of success is low. However, we have shown that under the special conditions stipulated by power transition theory, our theory requires that both rivals anticipate that their chances of success are greater than .5, a rather unusual circumstance.

In our entire data set of 707 dyadic interactions, there are eighty-nine cases in which P^A and P^B were each greater than .5. Sixty-eight

6. Proposition 6.6 reflects expectations derived from the international interaction game that are also broadly consistent with the empirical observations about warfare reported in Doran and Parsons (1980). Their theory concerns the relation between cyclical changes in power and the frequency and intensity of warfare. Support for proposition 6.6 reinforces some of their results and suggests that it would be useful to explore the complementarities and divergences between these two distinct theoretical perspectives on war.

Table 6.4
Domestic Costs and the Probability of Success in War

Year	A	B	P^A	P^B
Low				
1853	Russia	England	.68	.55
1853	Russia	France	.58	.71
1859	Austria-Hungary	France	.66	.75
1866	Germany	Austria-Hungary	.50	.50
1866	Italy	Austria-Hungary	.61	.69
1870	France	Germany	.76	.65
High				
1914	Austria-Hungary	Russia	.27	.34
1914	Germany	Russia	.35	.34
1914	Austria-Hungary	England	.32	.37
1914	Germany	England	.43	.37
1914	Austria-Hungary	France	.27	.29
1914	Germany	France	.36	.29
1939	Germany	France	.51	.29
1939	Germany	England	.65	.34
1940	Italy	England	.41	.62
1940	Italy	France	.14	.70

of them fall into the subsample with low combined estimated domestic costs. Of these, thirteen satisfy our conditions for being classified as BIGWARs. Consistent with proposition 6.7, eleven of the thirteen wars involved estimated domestic costs below the median for nations A and B. Of the sixteen wars between major powers, ten occurred when the estimated domestic costs were high for at least one of the two rivals. All of these cases arose in situations in which either P^A or P^B or both were less than .5. Of the six wars between major powers that arose when domestic costs were low, in all but one P^A and P^B were above .5. The apparently deviant case is the Seven Weeks' War between Austria and Prussia in 1866. We say "apparently deviant" because the estimate of Prussia's probability of success is .497, while Austria's is .503. This case is the topic of the next chapter. Table 6.4

shows the estimated probability of success for warring major powers
A and *B*, controlling for the size of expected domestic costs. Notice
the difference in estimated probabilities of success when the estimated
domestic costs are low or high.

The evidence indicates that the difficult-to-satisfy probability conditions expected in our theory under circumstances consistent with
power transition and hegemonic war theory are satisfied precisely.
They are satisfied even though the deduced conditions appear inconsistent with the expectation of power preponderance theorists, who
contend that such wars arise when one or the other of the rivals
appears to have the decided advantage.

COMPARISON OF THE COMPETING THEORIES

Before concluding this discussion, we examine one more set of propositions that provide each of the three theories assessed here an opportunity to compete in accounting for the escalation of international
disputes. In chapter 1 we mentioned a theorem by Banks (1990) that
establishes that the probability of using force in any Bayesian game
with asymmetric information is an increasing function of the expected
utility from doing so. Banks's theorem is driven by the ordinary assumption that the choice of actions is incentive compatible. His theorem is consistent with the assumption in our earlier research (Lalman
1985, 1988; Bueno de Mesquita and Lalman 1986) of just such a monotonic relation between expectations and the likelihood of violence.

In those studies we found a strong monotonic relation between our
estimates of expected utility and the incidence of war. There we used
a decision-theoretic framework with a rational expectations component embedded in it. Others have shown that such decision-theoretic
models are likely to have results that are convergent on game-theoretic
equilibria (Marcet and Sargent 1987a, 1987b). Consequently, our earlier findings were encouraging in terms of the game delineated here as
well. Still, the exact specification of the expected utility that accom-
panies the use of force in the international interaction game is different
from the precise specification in our earlier investigations. In the game,
the expected utility for nation *A* and nation *B* in a war initiated against
B is

$$P^A U^A[(\Delta_A - \alpha_A(1 - p^A) - \phi_A P^A]$$
$$+ (1 - P^A)U^A[\Delta_B - \alpha_A(1 - P^A) - \phi_A(P^A)], \qquad (6.3)$$

and

$$P^B U^B[\Delta_B - \alpha_B(1 - p^B) - \phi_B(P^B)]$$
$$+ (1 - P^B)U^B[\Delta_A - \tau_B(1 - P^B) - \phi_B(P^B)], \quad (6.4)$$

whereas in our earlier decision-theoretic formulation, the respective expected utilities were calculated as

$$(S^B[P^A U^A(\Delta_A) + (1 - P^A)U^A(\Delta_B)] + (1 - S^B)U^A(\Delta_A))$$
$$- (Q^A U^A(SQ) + (1 - Q^A)[T^A U^A(\beta_A) + (1 - T^A)U^A(\omega_A)]), \quad (6.5)$$

and

$$(S^A[P^B U^B(\Delta_B) + (1 - P^B)U^B(\Delta_A)] + (1 - S^A)U^B(\Delta_B))$$
$$- (Q^B U^B(SQ) + (1 - Q^B)[T^B U^B(\beta_B) + (1 - T^B)U^B(\omega_B)]), \quad (6.6)$$

where

S^j = the probability that the rival will resist a demand;

Q^i = the probability i attaches to the continuation of the status quo if no demand is made;

T^i = the probability i attaches to the prospect that the status quo will change for the better from i's perspective;

$U^i(\beta_i)$ = the utility i attaches to any anticipated improvement over the status quo; and

$U^i(\omega_i)$ = the utility i attaches to any anticipated deterioration from the status quo.

Because the decision-theoretic formulation is known to be significantly related to the likelihood that disputes escalate to war (Bueno de Mesquita and Lalman 1986; Lalman 1988), our first task is to see whether the game specification represents a step forward, backward, or sideways from our own previous decision-theoretic analysis. Once that task is completed, we can investigate the relative robustness of the game, power transition, and balance-of-power theories as competing or complementary explanations of the escalation of interactions to war. To undertake this comparison, we first transform expressions (6.3) through (6.6) so that they fall within the interval between zero and 1.0. In that form, as explained in Bueno de Mesquita and Lalman (1986) and given Banks's theorem, they serve as indicators of the probability with which nations A and B are expected to use force. Then we can construct the following variables. The term S_i is nation i's share of the European system's composite capabilities.

Table 6.5
Theoretical and Observed Probability of War

	χ^2	P
BIGWAR $= -2.99 + 6.06$ P(W)	7.36	.007
BIGWAR $= -2.50 + 6.30$ P(War)	7.69	.006
BIGWAR $= -3.20 + 3.99$ P(W) $+ 4.40$ P(War)	10.15	.006
WAR $= -1.57 + 4.66$ P(W)	5.92	.015
WAR $= -1.27 + 5.34$ P(War)	7.64	.006
WAR $= -1.72 + 2.68$ P(W) $+ 3.97$ P(War)	9.09	.011

Note: N = 467. In the final BIGWAR equation the significance of P(W) is .057, and the significance of P(War) .045. In the final WAR equation the significance of P(W) is .115, and the significance of P(WAR) .039.

$$P(War) = Exp\ (6.3) \times Exp\ (6.4),$$

$$P(W) = Exp\ (6.5) \times Exp\ (6.6),$$

$$Prep = \sqrt{\frac{\Sigma_{i=1}^{N}\ S_i^2 - (1/N)}{1 - (1/N)}}\ ,$$

$$Hegemony = |S_A - S_B|,$$

and

$$PowTrans = |S_A - S_B|/(S_A + S_B),$$

where P(War) is based on the game-theoretic specification, P(W) on the decision-theoretic specification, and S_i in Prep on the definition in the Correlates of War Project (Ray and Singer 1973).

We begin with the relations between P(W), P(War) and our two dependent variables, WAR and BIGWAR, for the subset of cases in which a dispute existed. First, note that the bivariate correlation between P(War) and P(W) is .51 (N = 467). The game-theoretic estimation and the decision-theoretic estimation, though clearly overlapping, share only about one fourth of their variation in common. Table 6.5 depicts the logit analyses that compare the formulation derived from our decision-theoretic approach and our game-theoretic approach.

What does table 6.5 tell us? First, P(W), which has not previously been tested on this extended data set, generally is significantly related to the likelihood of both reciprocated violence (WAR) and violence that passes the Small-Singer threshold for war (BIGWAR). Second,

P(War) is also significantly related to the likelihood of war and reciprocated violence. Third, when P(War) and P(W) are both included as potential explanations for the likelihood that an interaction will escalate to involve violence on both sides, P(War), as noted by the significance levels reported below the relevant coefficients, is more strongly associated with the ᵗpendent variables than is P(W), with the difference itself bordering on statistical significance. The game-theoretic specification improves distinctly upon the decision-theoretic explanation provided in earlier studies of war in general, improving on it modestly in the case of the big wars.

With this knowledge in hand, we now assess the explanatory power of key aspects of our game, the balance-of-power theory, and the theories of power preponderance. The expectations can be stated as propositions.

GAME PROPOSITION 6.8. *Even after controlling for the systemic and dyadic power relation, P(War) is expected to be positively associated with the likelihood of war.*

BALANCE-OF-POWER PROPOSITION (NOT FROM THE GAME). *As Prep approaches zero, the major powers are balanced in power, so the balance-of-power theory expects Prep to be positively associated with the likelihood of war.*

POWER PREPONDERANCE PROPOSITION 1 (NOT FROM THE GAME). *The variable Hegemony approaches zero when the challenger and the more powerful state in the dyad approach equality in power. Therefore, Hegemony is expected to be inversely related to the likelihood of war.*

POWER PREPONDERANCE PROPOSITION 2 (NOT FROM THE GAME). *The larger PowTrans is, the greater is the difference in the power of the two rivals, and therefore, the lower should be the likelihood of war.*

The variable Hegemony differs from PowTrans in that it evaluates the power differential without normalizing for the total power of the rivals, whereas PowTrans does normalize. Therefore, Hegemony can only be large if at least one of the adversaries in the dispute is very powerful, though this need not be true for the variable PowTrans itself.

Table 6.6, which summarizes the results of the relevant logit analyses, provides a very mixed picture with regard to theories of balance of power or power preponderance but offers a consistently confirmatory view of the international interaction game and Banks's theorem. P(War), the variable derived from the game, is generally quite signifi-

Table 6.6
Power Transition, Balance of Power, Monotonicity, and the Likelihood of War

	WAR				BIGWAR			
	ALL STAKES		HIGH STAKES*		ALL STAKES		HIGH STAKES*	
	Coef.	P	Coef.	P	Coef.	P	Coef.	P
Constant	−3.40	.00	−3.22	.00	−4.04	.00	−5.11	.00
P(War)	5.54	.01	5.09	.06	10.37	.00	10.87	.01
Prep	5.11	.00	4.25	.03	0.38	.43	1.05	.38
Hegemony	−11.60	.00	−12.80	.00	−8.77	.00	−25.08	.00
PowTrans	5.11	.00	2.61	.00	1.77	.00	4.90	.00
χ^2	57.71	.00	15.30	.00	28.84	.00	20.78	.00
N	415		165		415		165	

*The stakes were above the median for both A and B.

cant and in the predicted direction. Prep, the variable designed to evaluate the preponderance versus the balance of power among the major powers in the European system, is unstable with respect to its statistical significance, although it always points in the direction of preponderance increasing the likelihood of war. Prep works best when the dependent variable includes all forms of reciprocated violence (WAR). In that sense, balance-of-power proponents can find support in our broadest test, as shown in the first column of table 6.6.

Power preponderance theorists may be encouraged by the strong support given their thesis by our variable called Hegemony but are likely to be disappointed by the performance of the variable PowTrans. Both variables were expected to be inversely related to the likelihood of war, yet only Hegemony is. PowTrans is statistically significant but not in the direction apparently anticipated in power transition and hegemonic war theories. The smaller the proportionate difference in power between rivals, apparently, the lower the likelihood of war, whether a small one or a more serious event, a war of any level of dissatisfaction or a war with large stakes. Some additional support for the power transition and hegemonic war perspectives can be extracted from the results of the logit analysis. Recall that those who subscribe to the peace-through-preponderance perspective generally are interested only in disputes between the largest powers. Conflicts among lesser states are not a primary focus of their research.

We can solve analytically the results of the logit analyses to determine the combined power of A and B at which the likelihood of war begins to decline. Because the sign of the effect for Hegemony is opposite to that for PowTrans and because the coefficient for Hegemony is always larger than it is for PowTrans, it follows that there is a turning point in the power relation of A and B beyond which the risk of war begins to fall. This turning point can be seen most clearly by solving the denominator of PowTrans—the sum of the power of A and B. With β_1 = the coefficient for the variable Hegemony, β_2 = the coefficient for the variable PowTrans, and PowTrans = (Hegemony)/(Power$_A$ + Power$_B$), then

$$\text{Likelihood of War} = -\beta_1 \text{ (Hegemony)} + \beta_2 \text{ (Hegemony)/(Power}_A + \text{Power}_B), \qquad (6.7)$$

which, after factoring, is equal to

$$-\beta_1 \text{ (Hegemony)} \left[1 - \frac{\beta_2}{\beta_1} \frac{1}{\text{(Power}_A + \text{Power}_B)} \right]. \qquad (6.8)$$

Expression (6.8) makes clear that there are two circumstances under which (6.7) changes directions. If Hegemony equals zero, so that the power of nation A is equal to the power of nation B, then the entire expression is zero, which, in this case, indicates that the probability of war is maximized. Maximization is essentially consistent with the expectations from power transition and hegemonic war theory. The second turning point arises if β_2/β_1 = Power$_A$ + Power$_B$. In that case, the likelihood of war rises until the combined power of A and B equals β_2/β_1, with the probability of war falling if the combined power of the adversaries is greater than that ratio. The first condition—Hegemony equals zero—arises once in our data set. The one case led to the persistence of the status quo. To evaluate the effects of the ratio condition, we must first calculate the ratio as determined from the logit analyses in table 6.6. The relevant values across the four logit analyses are

	WAR	High-stakes WAR	BIGWAR	High-stakes BIGWAR
β_2/β_1	.44	.20	.20	.20

It is interesting that the threshold value at which the likelihood of war begins to fall is higher for the most encompassing dependent variable when there is the least apparent dissatisfaction (WAR regardless of the stakes). This is exactly what one would expect from the axioms of rationality. So long as expected gains (that is, the marginal gain discounted by the probability of obtaining it) exceed expected costs, war is possible. As the stakes rise, the magnitude of the probability of success can fall for a conflict of some constant cost level. Yet the observed result seems possibly at odds with theories of power preponderance insofar as they lead to the expectation that the risk of a big, costly war is constant with respect to the combined power of the rivals, regardless of the level of dissatisfaction.

For cases in which the power of the rivals is higher than in those noted above, the likelihood of war falls. Surely, these values represent the pinnacle of what Organski (1958) has called the power pyramid. Not surprisingly, such magnitudes of combined power rarely occur. Of the 415 cases analyzed in table 6.6 without regard to the magnitude of the stakes involved, only three reached a combined power threshold of at least .44. Of these, none became a serious war, although one satisfies the criteria for reciprocated violence, or small wars.

When we examine the events involving high stakes and adjust the threshold of capabilities to .20, as above, a more interesting pattern emerges. Of the thirty-nine high-stakes events in table 6.6 that satisfy or exceed the power threshold, eleven became at least small wars but only two satisfied the Small-Singer requirements to be classified here as BIGWARs. The incidence of either type of war is lower—significantly so in the case of big wars—when the power threshold is met or surpassed than when it is not. Thus, although the associations are weak, they are at least more supportive of the hegemonic war and power transition propositions than appears to be the case from a cursory evaluation of table 6.6. True, a small difference in power for large nations heightens the risk of war, but not if the combined power of the adversaries exceeds the stated thresholds. Then big wars, the particular concern of power transition and hegemonic war theorists, become less likely as one adversary tends toward hegemony over the other.

Before leaving this discussion of large-scale wars, we propose an additional set of tests that approximate still more thoroughly the equilibrium expectations derived from the international interaction game. In the tests presented so far, we have relied upon Banks's theorem to introduce a useful simplification of expectations that follow from the international interaction game. Now we assess more directly the equilibrium strategies of the game that imply war.

The basic war theorem delineated in chapter 3 specifies four conditions that are necessary and sufficient for war to be the equilibrium outcome of the game under full-information conditions. In chapter 3 we tested and found considerable support for the basic war theorem, controlling for uncertainty, with respect to the dependent variable BIGWAR. Now we replicate that test but expand it to include the balance-of-power and power transition variables discussed earlier. In this way we can test the robustness of the game's predictions when prominent alternative explanations are given the opportunity to overwhelm the relations deduced from the game structure. We state our expectations in proposition 6.9:

WAR PROPOSITION 6.9. *When War$_A$ indicates that the necessary and sufficient conditions for war under full information are met, then*

the likelihood of war should be higher than when War$_A$ indicates those conditions are not met;

War$_A$ × Uncertainty should be inversely related to the likelihood of war;

Uncertainty should be positively associated with the likelihood of war;

Prep, according to balance-of-power theorists, should be positively associated with the likelihood of war and, according to power transition theorists, should be negatively associated with war;

Hegemony, according to balance-of-power theorists, should be positively associated with the likelihood of war and, according to power transition theorists, should be negatively associated with war; and

PowTrans, according to power transition theorists, should be inversely associated with the likelihood of war. Balance-of-power theory does not appear to make a prediction about PowTrans.

We use logit analysis to test the above expectations. The observed relations across all cases of BIGWAR are presented in table 6.7. In the table we can see a severe test of the domestic account of the international interaction game. The conditions captured by War$_A$, War$_A$ × Uncertainty, and Uncertainty are specifically derived from this particular game structure. What is more, the logit analysis provides ample opportunity for the explanatory benefits of the game to be washed out by variables representing alternative theories. Yet the results are robust, and, as with table 6.6, there is little to encourage

Table 6.7
Power Preponderance, Balance of Power, and the Likelihood of War

| | BIGWAR | |
	Coef.	P
Constant	−4.10	.000
War$_A$	1.98	.001
War$_A$ × Uncertainty	−7.66	.000
Uncertainty	7.83	.000
Prep	−2.11	.150
Hegemony	−5.07	.023
PowTrans	1.41	.008
χ^2	39.57	
P≤	.000	
N	643	

confidence in the balance-of-power theory. Support for the power transition theory or the theory of hegemonic war is equivocal. With respect to the international interaction game, proposition 6.9 is fully supported in these tests.

The theoretical and empirical results of this chapter not only address general issues relating to our game-theoretic focus on wars but also provide a direct evaluation of the merits of the international interaction game as compared to balance-of-power and power transition theory under conditions assumed by those theories to be necessary for the occurrence of a system-transforming war. In every test performed here, the expectations deduced from the domestic version of the game-theoretic model are borne out. Sometimes those expectations were the same as those of the balance-of-power or power transition theories or even both. Sometimes the expectations were complementary developments based on the incorporation of features of balance-of-power or power transition theory into our game-theoretic approach. And sometimes the results reflect comparisons of competing expectations. When the alternative theories diverge in their expectations, the domestic rather than realpolitik variant of the game continues to perform well. Indeed, besides finding support in every empirical comparison to the balance-of-power or hegemonic war theories, the game also performed as well as or better than our own earlier decision-theoretic approach.

For the power-centered theories, we find that the power preponderance theory performs better than the balance-of-power theory. Greater gains may be obtained by linking more fully the power transition and hegemonic war theories to the international interaction game, building on the complementary features of each. We now turn to an assessment of the game and power preponderance theories through a more detailed examination of a single case history: the story of the Seven Weeks' War.

Chapter 7

The Seven Weeks' War and System Transformation

It is too true, however disgraceful
it may be to human nature, that
nations in general will make war
whenever they have a prospect of
getting anything by it.
—John Jay, *Federalist Paper* 4

Of all of the possible consequences of international interactions, none inspires greater apprehension or attention than wars of cataclysmic proportions. These wars are the focus of theories concerned with power transitions or hegemonic decline. Such theories generally assume that system-transforming wars must be large, costly conflicts between powerful adversaries who hold different views on how the international system should be run. As we saw in the previous chapter, the constrained, domestic interpretation of the international interaction game suggests a new angle of vision on such wars. We have established several of the important theoretical differences between the expectations derived from our model and from theories of power preponderance, and we have performed a variety of statistical tests to evaluate the competing expectations. In this way we have fostered confidence in the external validity, or generality, of the propositions that follow from the game. Now, in the interest of fostering a comparable level of confidence in the internal validity, or richness, of the game, we assess the implications of the theory through the close scrutiny of a single event: the Seven Weeks' War.

In important respects, the Seven Weeks' War approximates key conditions of power transition and hegemonic war theory, but in other essential ways, the war is inconsistent with the expectations derived from those theories. The Seven Weeks' War is an instance of a system-transforming conflict that was small and in which the rivals did not disagree markedly over the functioning of the international system.[1] We show how uncertainty about the prospects for success at war influenced the course of events in 1866 and led, ultimately, to a transformation of the international system.

We show how the removal of unintended biases in the selection of cases for study can expand the application of some important insights from theories of power preponderance. In particular, we try to illuminate the consequences that follow when theories of hegemony assume that only large events can have large consequences. We show that the Seven Weeks' War—a small event—fundamentally changed the international order by providing the foundation for German hegemony on the European continent.

To demonstrate the argument, we show that the push toward German hegemony following the Seven Weeks' War conforms to the expectations of the game-theoretic model. Yet the war is overlooked by hegemonic war theorists because they conflate the consequences of system-transforming wars with their causes and proximate conditions. Although they contend that large changes can arise after large events only, our game supports the belief that such changes can be spawned by small events or even without violence at all. We attempt to build an intellectual bridge between our game-theoretic perspective and key features of power transition theory, yielding, we believe, a richer and fuller understanding of the roots of cataclysmic war and system transformation.

THE ROLE OF UNCERTAINTY IN SYSTEM-TRANSFORMING WARS

The basic war theorem of the domestic version of the international interaction game is inconsistent with hegemonic war theories regarding the critical role of dissatisfaction with the international status quo but in other ways is consistent with important aspects of those theories. Recall that such theories contend that the risk of a system-transforming war is heightened when a rival increases in power sufficiently to challenge the hegemon. As the hegemon's preponderance is eroded, uncertainty increases regarding each actor's probability of defeating the

---

1. We intend to distinguish sharply the internecine disagreements between Austria and Prussia over the political order within Germany, their essential agreement on most fundamental issues regarding relations outside Germany, and the large consequences that German unification had for those external relations.

other in a confrontation. In the face of such uncertainty, each decision maker's expectations about each other's future actions are critical.

According to many theorists who contend that power preponderance encourages peace and that power parity exacerbates the risk of war, a critical issue is whether the rivals are about equal in power or not. Yet our game implies—and the evidence supports—the contention that wars expected to lead to many deaths and much destruction, and also expected to engender little domestic opposition, can occur only if each side believes its probability of success is greater than .5. As the level of political support for the war decreases, so that domestic opposition rises, then the probability-of-success threshold falls, so that the more opposed the domestic population is on each side of the war, the more willing are the political elites to wage war when the risk of defeat is believed to be high. This startling, even counterintuitive deduction is borne out by the evidence we have presented. It is a direct consequence of the observation that a commonly known increase in a nation's domestic opposition to the use of force enhances the risk for that nation of being exploited. That risk, in turn, makes initiating a war to avoid exploitation more likely. The surprising feature of this condition is that large, popular wars can apparently occur only if each side is confident of success.

This and other aspects of our game highlight an important difference between our expectations and those of power preponderance theorists. In our game, the difference in power—the probability of success—of the rivals is not particularly important. What is important is whether the expectation of success is large enough (or the relevant costs are small enough) that the rivals each believe the other will or will not retaliate effectively if attacked. If nation B does not think A can mount a potent counterattack and if B is not a dove, then B will exploit A if A cedes the initiative to B. Whether A is a dove or not, if A believes that B will exploit a first-strike advantage and if A believes its own first-strike advantage is large enough (either because it thinks B will capitulate if attacked or because it thinks it can do better by initiating a war than by giving in to its opponent's demands), then A will start a war rather than risk exploitation or having to fight a defensive, retaliatory war. According to our game, the central source of uncertainty concerns whether the adversary is believed to prefer to retaliate if coerced.

As was seen in chapter 5, nations known to bear high domestic costs are less likely to retaliate and therefore more likely to initiate war than are those for whom a prospective war is popular. The popularity of a prospective war can facilitate reaching a negotiated settlement. One possible source of uncertainty in choosing between violence and peace, then, is the level of domestic opposition to the use of force. However, another source of uncertainty, more in line with the concerns of power preponderance theorists, is the likelihood that one or the other side will succeed if a dispute turns violent. In keeping our discussion within the power transition perspective, we treat that uncertainty here as a function of the difference in the hegemon's (or the challenger's) beliefs about the chance for success.

Suppose, for instance, that nation A possesses private information that encourages its leadership to believe that it can wage a successful war even if B strikes first. Suppose that B is uncertain of A's relative power or prospects for success. This difficulty in calibrating the rival's power accurately might arise, as hypothesized by Organski and Kugler (1980), Gilpin (1981), William Thompson (1988), and others, during periods of rapid growth by the challenger. Alternatively, the difficulty in estimating one's chances for success might be the consequence of some combination of differences in rates of growth and shifts in alliances, as argued by Morrow (1991a), Kim and Morrow (1991), Grace Iusi-Scarborough and Bueno de Mesquita (1988), and others. For our purposes, it does not matter whether domestic changes or alliance politics is the fundamental source of changing prospects of success; what matters is that there is uncertainty about the relative power of the contending sides.

Assume that B believes with probability π^B that its chances to succeed in a war with A are large enough that A will prefer to capitulate to B rather than retaliate if attacked. Suppose, then, with probability $1 - \pi^B$, that B thinks its prospects of success are not so great—A has closed the gap—and therefore anticipates a retaliatory strike if it attacks A. The problem for B is that it does not know whether A's chance for success is small enough that A will capitulate if attacked or whether A will strike back, yielding a war. A does know this about itself. If A offers to negotiate with B, then B must choose between trying to exploit A but risking a war and trying to negotiate with A but possibly forgoing the benefits of exploitation. If B decides to respond to A's offer to negotiate by using force, then with probability π^B, B gains $U^B[\Delta_B - \phi_B(P^B)]$—the value for B of a capitulation by A—and with probability $1 - \pi^B$, B ends up starting a war with A. The gamble is worthwhile so long as its expected utility for B is superior to entering into negotiation with A.

The determination of the value of using force versus negotiating depends critically upon B's uncertainty about its own chances for success. Let P^{*B} be B's subjectively estimated probability of success if A, the challenger, is believed to have grown sufficiently powerful that it will retaliate if attacked. That is, P^{*B} is B's probability of success with probability $1 - \pi^B$, and P^B is B's estimate of its chance for success if A is the weak type that capitulates when attacked, a prospect believed to arise with probability π^B. $P^B > P^{*B}$. Then, if B mistakenly tries to exploit A only to find itself at war with A, its expected value from the war is

$$P^{*B}U^B[\Delta_B - \alpha_B(1 - P^{*B}) - \phi_B(P^{*B})]$$
$$+ (1 - P^{*B})U^B[\Delta_A - \alpha_B(1 - P^{*B}) - \phi_B(P^{*B})],$$

a value that arises with probability $1 - \pi^B$. If B chooses to negotiate with A rather than trying to coerce its adversary, B can expect

$$\pi^B [P^B U^B(\Delta_B) + (1 - P^B)U^B(\Delta_A)]$$
$$+ (1 - \pi^B) [P^{*B}U^B(\Delta_B) + (1 - P^{*B})U^B(\Delta_A)].$$

The value associated with negotiating is also dependent on the uncertainty. If B has the larger threat implied by a likelihood of success as large as P^B, then it can expect to cut a better bargain at the negotiating table than if its chances for success at war are only as large as P^{*B}. That is, as B's true chance for success approaches P^B, negotiation and war become more attractive for B.

What difference does the gap make between B's possibly higher prospect for success (P^B) and B's possibly lower prospect for success (P^{*B})? To answer this question—which is truly at the heart of power transition and hegemonic war theory—we restate the above expectations by solving for π^B. If

$$\pi^B > \frac{(1 - P^{B*})\alpha_B + \phi_B P^{B*}}{(1 - P^B)U^B(\Delta_B - \Delta_A) + (1 - P^{B*})\alpha_B - \phi_B(P^B - P^{B*})} , \quad (7.1)$$

then B attacks A in the hope of coercing it into a capitulation. If π^B is smaller than the right-hand side of (7.1), then B will pursue negotiation.

Expression (7.1) reveals several important features of prospective power transition wars and illuminates some aspects of the success enjoyed by Organski and Kugler, Woosang Kim (1989), Henk Houweling and Jan Siccama (1988), Erich Weede (1976), David Garnham (1976), and others in their empirical investigations of this theory. First, notice that there is a critical power transition, but it is not necessarily related to whether A's power equals and is overtaking B's power, as Organski and Kugler contend. Rather, the critical transition in our game structure occurs when B believes that A has achieved a chance for success large enough that it expects A to retaliate if attacked.

Just before that transition, A is likely to launch a preemptive attack against B to secure whatever first-strike advantage there is. Beyond that threshold, B will negotiate with A, setting the stage for a peaceful transition. Overall, A might pursue a purely preemptive strategy, a purely negotiating strategy, or a mixed strategy, depending upon the value A attaches to fighting a retaliatory war or negotiating versus the value of initiating the war (presuming that B is known to be the retaliatory type). The key is that B's critical belief threshold is not critically dependent on the difference between A's power and B's power, at least not in the international interaction game. The belief threshold is a complex mix of B's estimates of relevant costs, benefits, and probabilities. Whence, then, comes the belief of power transition theorists that the two rivals must be about equal in power?

Suppose $P^B = P^{*B}$. This can be true when P^B equals any value in the interval $(0,1)$, including but not limited to $P^B = P^{*B} = P^A = .5$. Suppose for the moment that large expected losses in life and property are a necessary condition for a system-transforming war, in keeping with the assumptions of Organski and Kugler (1980) and Gilpin (1981). In particular, let $\alpha_B = U^B(\Delta_B - \Delta_A)$ in (7.1), and let each of these be very large compared to anticipated domestic costs. Then, for a large, popular war, in which B is fighting to retain control over the international system and A is challenging that control, $\pi^B \geq .5$ for B to try to exploit A. If A is the type that will retaliate if attacked and A has gambled that B will negotiate rather than exploit A, then A, the challenger, will wind up fighting a war begun by the hegemon. If A does not gamble on B's willingness to negotiate, then A will launch the war. A can launch the war whether it is the type that will capitulate or retaliate if attacked. So, apparently, under conditions assumed by Gilpin (1981) and Organski and Kugler (1980), the critical belief threshold is at .5, although the power threshold or probability-of-success threshold need not be.

We propose that the circumstances of the initiation of the Seven Weeks' War were consistent with expression (7.1), given that $P^B = P^{*B}$. Austria was unsure of Prussia's chance for victory or of Prussia's willingness to fight the Austrians. The value $\pi^{Austria}$ was large enough that the Austrians were unlikely to make concessions to Prussian ambitions. Prussia's growth in power was critical, as suggested by hegemonic war and power transition theorists, and was the crucial factor pushing the rivals toward war even though they were satisfied with one another's view of the international status quo. We believe that it was just such uncertainty on Austria's part and private information on the probability of Prussia's success possessed by Bismarck and Moltke that were central to the decision to wage the Seven Weeks' War.

Before turning to the assessment of the Seven Weeks' War, recall from chapter 6 that the basic war theorem implies that wars in which the rivals are satisfied with the status quo have special characteristics. A partial equilibrium condition of the war theorem is that the probability of success must be greater than a positive function of the ratio of the expected costs to the expected stakes, with the stakes defined as the difference between the utility attached to obtaining one's objectives and the utility attached to giving in to the rival's demands. If the status quo is highly valued by both sides, then it is likely that the magnitude of either side's demands do not deviate much from the value of the status quo, so that the stakes are small. Under those circumstances, the condition just described can be satisfied only if the expected costs are small. Thus, when the status quo is highly valued, it is likely to be the case that the war will be fought only if the expected costs are small. If the battlefield costs rise above expectations without a concomitant increase in the stakes, then it seems likely that the war will end.

The partial equilibrium condition, then, shows that a war fought over small changes in the status quo must necessarily be expected to be a small war. These observations reflect on expression (7.1) and the theories of hegemonic decline and power transition. The probability π^B or $\pi^{Austria}$, for instance, remains constant as long as we sustain the assumptions of power transition and hegemonic war theorists that $P^B = P^{*B}$ and that the anticipated losses in life and property are as large as is feasible given the stakes and given that war is still an equilibrium outcome. "As large as is feasible," however, might indeed mean that the expected costs are very small. By contrast, the power transition view is that these costs must be expected to be very large.

THE SEVEN WEEKS' WAR: PRIDE OF PLACE AND THE STATUS QUO

In this section we show that the Seven Weeks' War was fought even though the rivals were satisfied with the international status quo. We do not argue that they were satisfied with the internal, German status quo, but we recognize that the internal status quo is not the focus of power transition or hegemonic war theorists. We go on to demonstrate that the Seven Weeks' War—more so even than the Franco-Prussian

War—transformed the international system. Finally, we show that Austria and Prussia were unwilling to bear high costs to preserve their position because the expected external stakes were small, and so they resolved their dispute quickly and cheaply.

Prior to the war, an Austro-Prussian crisis arose when each side made demands regarding the disposition of the Elbe Duchies, and neither was willing to accept the other's wishes. Recall that Prussia and Austria fought as allies in 1864 against Denmark during the Second Schleswig-Holstein War. As a consequence of that conflict, these two preeminent German states secured control over the disputed duchies of Schleswig and Holstein. Almost as soon as the war ended, Prussia and Austria began an internecine struggle over the governance of the captured territories. At stake for Prussia was access to a naval port, enhanced prestige among the lesser German states, and a demonstration that it was no longer decidedly weaker than Austria. At the same time, Prussia's ambitions within Germany were constrained by domestic sentiments against a fratricidal conflict and by Austria's favored position. Austria enjoyed the prestige it had earned as the predominant German power throughout the history of the German Confederation.

The Austro-Prussian conflict that surfaced after their joint success against the much weaker Danes was brought to an apparent end by late 1865 with the signing of the Treaty of Gastein. The treaty accommodated several of Prussia's ambitions and protected and preserved Austria's prestige and preeminence within the German Confederation. Yet in a few short months it became apparent that the treaty was not working. The immediate issues revolved around Bismarck's concern that Austria's right to administer Holstein was tantamount to sovereignty over the territory. Such an outcome—or even the right of the German Diet to decide Holstein's fate—frustrated Bismarck's immediate and long-term ambitions within the confederation. To rectify the situation from their perspective, the Prussians sought authority over Holstein, in partial violation of the Treaty of Gastein. The Austrians sought to extend their own control over Holstein and to further restrict Prussian aspirations by turning the resolution of the duchy's sovereignty over to the German Diet, a body more under Austria's domination than Bismarck's. This, too, was a violation of the Treaty of Gastein.[2]

2. The Treaty of Gastein was supposed to settle the remaining questions of sovereignty over Schleswig and Holstein that resulted from the Austro-Prussian defeat of Denmark in 1864. Article 1 of the treaty stipulates that "the common right obtained by the high contracting parties by Article 3 of the Treaty of Vienna of

The central demand of the Prussians amounted to a quest for pride of place within the leadership of Germany. As the *Economist* summarized the dispute on the eve of war, "The demand, therefore, is simply that the minor States [of the German Confederation] shall follow Prussian lead instead of Austrian lead." Likewise, the Austrian posture amounted to a desire to cling to the privileged position granted them by the Congress of Vienna, to hold on to their own pride of place as the leader of Germany. Again, as the *Economist* observed:

> Tradition counts for a good deal among nations, and the German tradition is that the leadership of Germany belongs *de jure* to the "Kaiser," that the King of Prussia is an overpowerful feudatory. . . . This demand [of Prussia] is, however, an assertion that the feudatory intends to rule, and . . . [it] will be resisted to the death by Austria, not only because it is inconvenient, not only because, like the claim to the Elbe Duchies, it greatly increases Prussian power, but because it terminates her own career as a German state, a career of which ruler and people are very proud, and also very jealous. (June 16, 1866, 699)

Prussian ambitions before the war of 1866 seem to have been modest in the greater European scheme of things, though most assuredly not in internecine Germany. Bismarck's energies before the war were largely concentrated on securing his and the king's political authority in the face of a reform-minded Parliament and an obstreperous Diet and on resolving the long-standing competition between Prussia and Austria for control over Germany (Hamerow 1973; Holborn 1960; Simon 1968). As W. M. Simon notes, many believed that "Bismarck had launched the war as a means of escape from his domestic difficulties" and that, even though the war culminated in *kleindeutsch* unification, "*Bismarck did not intend it as such*" (1960, 30, 29, emphasis added).

Whether Bismarck was motivated by a relentless desire to unify Germany is itself somewhat controversial. To be sure, he frequently remarked on the importance of this goal. In 1856, for instance, he commented to Otto von Manteuffel, minister president of Prussia, that "Vienna's policy being what it is, Germany is too small for the two of us. . . . For a thousand years Germany's dualism has from time to

---

the 30th of October, 1864, is transferred, as respects the Duchy of Holstein, to his Majesty the Emperor of Austria, and as respects the Duchy of Schleswig, to his Majesty the King of Prussia, *without prejudice to the continuation of these rights of both Powers to the whole of both Duchies*" (Malet 1870, 106–10, emphasis added).

time—and since Charles V once in every century—settled the mutual relationships of the German states through wholesale and radical internal war. And in this century as well, no other method will serve to set the clock of [Germany's] development to the correct time" (Bismarck 1924–35, 2:142, hereafter *GW*).[3] And in November 1862 he said: "I have set myself the goal of revenge for the humiliation of Olmütz, crushing this Austria that treats us with utter contempt" (*GW*, 7:66). Yet his actions suggested that some of this talk lacked credibility. Although subsequent events proved his willingness to fight, one can readily imagine that the Austrians doubted the sincerity of his threats. After all, his actions in early 1866 suggested that he was prepared to forgo the defeat of Austria (and subsequent German unification) in exchange for securing his limited goals regarding Holstein. Edward Crankshaw comments that "there was a moment when it looked as though Austria might be ready to sell Holstein to Prussia, as she had sold Lauenberg; Bleichröder was active in raising funds for this; Bismarck was ready for it." And, "Had Austria got rid of Holstein for cash and then sold Venetia to Italy, which she could also have done at this time, the face of history would have been changed. For Bismarck would have had no excuse to go to war and no Italian ally if he did so" (1981, 197, 200).

The demands of Prussia and Austria created an internal German crisis by casting doubt on the Treaty of Gastein. The crisis arose when Austria and Prussia faced the choice between negotiating a peaceful settlement of the dispute or resorting to arms to enforce their demands. Central to the argument here is the realization that, contrary to the assumptions of the theory of hegemonic war, even though Prussia and Austria valued the international status quo highly, they still reached the crisis stage and waged a war of such importance that it transformed the international system.

Recall that a necessary condition for war is that side A, the challenger, values initiating war more highly than it values offering to negotiate in the face of a significant risk that the hegemon (Austria) will exploit the offer and gain the upper hand. Recall also that the risk that this situation will arise would be heightened if the challenger's (Prussia's) power were underestimated by the Austrians (so that $P^{Austria}$ was thought to be considerably larger than the critical threshold value $P^{Austria*}$). That these were the circumstance as perceived by the Prussians is suggested by the following:

3. Translations from the collected works of Bismarck were graciously done by MacGregor Knox.

Agitation continued in Holstein, and matters arrived at a crisis which might easily lead to either peace or war. It was necessary to consider whether a lasting and sincere friendship with Austria might be obtained by further concession, not in this special case alone, but in the whole Holstein question, or whether it was the policy of Vienna here, as elsewhere, to suppress Prussia, and to prevent her free development in Germany by means of the press, the elements of revolution, the power of the Confederation, overtures for an alliance with France; in fact by every possible means. (Department of Military History of the Prussian Staff 1872, 123–38; see also A. J. P. Taylor 1976)

According to this account, the Prussian leadership was concerned about being exploited by the Austrians, about being suppressed by every means possible. The fear, in game terms, was that $\pi^{Austria}$ was larger than the right-hand side of the inequality in (7.1). This view is reinforced by Crankshaw's account. He notes that the Austrians, still believing that they possessed superior strength, were not prepared to negotiate with Bismarck in good faith. Thus, he reports, "in January 1866 Austria was given what looked like another chance—by Bismarck himself. . . . Surrender to us the primacy of North Germany and we will help you to reconquer Lombardy. But Francis Joseph refused to consider the matter: he still believed he could manage a two-front war if only Russia and France kept out of it" (1981, 201). Apparently Bismarck had reason to believe that an offer of concessions to Austria only invited exploitation and loss of the first-strike advantage.[4] He also had reason to believe that the Austrians underestimated Prussia's chances of waging a successful war.

As suggested in the game theory example based on uncertainty, Bismarck possessed information about Prussian power that was not available to the Austrians. He and Gen. Helmut von Moltke knew more about the benefits of the needle gun and about Prussia's superior skills in utilizing the railroads than was known to the Austrians (Showalter 1975, 52–73,105–39). The Austrians continued to rely on more traditional approaches to warfare. With regard to the needle gun, for instance, "the overwhelming weight of opinion at regimental levels in the Austrian army continued to regard the rifle as a glorified pike"

---

4. See A. J. P. Taylor 1976, 133, for an illuminating discussion of Francis Joseph's treatment of the Croats in negotiations in December 1866. Even after the Seven Weeks' War, Francis Joseph continued to use coercion rather than concessions in dealing with rivals perceived to be much weaker.

(123). The advantage of the railroads was even more central to Bismarck's choice for war.

Moltke's war plan hinged on the ability to mass troops at the scene of the central battle. Bohemia was selected as the site for that battle by the Prussians in part because they had multiple rail lines feeding to Bohemia. The Austrians did not. By fighting in Bohemia, the Prussians could utilize the railroads to facilitate a rapid mobilization and to avoid massing their troops until the last moment. In fact, Prussia waited to mobilize until long after the Austrians had already ordered the mobilization of their army. Prussia could assure itself of multiple avenues by which to resupply troops and replenish fighting forces with fresh soldiers. The Austrians had none of these advantages in Bohemia (52–73, 105–39). Had Bismarck sacrificed the initiative to the Austrians, this critical advantage in the selection of the venue of fighting would probably have been lost. That Bismarck was sensitive to such tactical considerations goes almost without saying. He frequently commented on the importance of gaining a tactical advantage over the Austrians in his oft-repeated—but not acted upon—reflections on a war with Austria. In 1854, for instance, he commented to the Russian representative at Frankfurt that "if we foresee the necessity for war against Austria, we must be in a position to attack her while she is still unprepared and before she can concentrate her troops on our frontiers" (Pflanze 1963, 101).

Bismarck and Moltke understood the crucial advantage of the railroads. Indeed, Moltke's war plans depended on exploiting the rail advantage, and it was the risk of losing this advantage that formed a core part of the argument to Kaiser Wilhelm that finally persuaded him to go to war. The Austrians, who greatly underestimated the role of railroads and other new technologies in future wars, may well have suffered defeat because of the first-strike advantage yielded in allowing the Prussians to dictate the main theater of combat.

Given Austria's perceived tendency to exploit adversaries that were perceived to be weak and given Bismarck's (and Moltke's) higher valuation of Prussia's chances of success, the Prussians chose war over further efforts at negotiation. Offering to negotiate brought the risk of both exploitation and the diminution or surrender of a crucial technological advantage.

What was the prewar view of the international status quo held by Prussia and Austria? Here we must carefully separate their disagreements within the confines of the German state system from their views on how the international order ought to have been functioning. The theories of hegemonic war and power transition emphasize the value the rivals attach to the international order, to the existing rules and practices that define the international status quo. These theories do not emphasize the local status quo between particular powers. Did Prussia and Austria differ regarding the rules by which the international system ought to have operated? The evidence suggests that they did not.

Austria's external policy, like Prussia's, was hostile to liberal reform and democratic sentiments. Both Prussia and Austria were concerned to keep French ambitions in check, as well as to counterbalance the Russians to the east. Prussia and Austria jointly waged war against Denmark in 1864 and remained allied with one another almost continuously from 1815 until the dissolution of the Habsburg empire at the end of World War I. Indeed, even the Seven Weeks' War produced just a brief interruption in their alliance of mutual defense. Bismarck strove to maintain good relations with Austria, even to the point of opposing Moltke and Wilhelm's desire to march on Vienna immediately after the decisive victory of the Seven Weeks' War at Königgrätz (Pflanze 1968; Simon 1968; Palmer 1976; Hamerow 1973; Grützner 1986).

The interests of Austria and Prussia external to Germany generally were jointly advanced during most of the nineteenth century prior to the 1866 war, even though the two great German states engaged in frequent internecine disputes. Austria's centrality to the maintenance of the European international order is well documented. As Paul Kennedy notes, "The general peace which prevailed in Europe for decades after 1815 was due chiefly to the position and functions of the Habsburg Empire" (1987, 163). In terms of the external affairs on which the power transition and hegemonic war theories focus there is little basis for arguing that Prussia and Austria were dissatisfied with the status quo.

In their own bilateral relationship there were considerable strains between Austria and Prussia, not over the international order but over pride of place in the German Confederation: the struggle for leadership within Germany. The Austrians presided over the German Diet in Frankfurt and steadfastly refused to share this privilege with the Prussians. Although of considerable symbolic importance to the Austrians and the Prussians alike, the actual decisions of the German Confederation seem to have been little affected by Austria's unwillingness to share authority. As the British envoy to the Diet observed, "In all matters upon which the two great Powers were agreed, the Diet's proceedings were marked by the most commendable activity and promptitude; if they differed . . . the game of official delays and chicanery of all kinds was played to the utmost" (Malet 1870, xxii). Still, it is likely that war would have been averted had the Austrians agreed to share leadership. Alan Palmer, for instance, reports that "if Mensdorff succeeded in calming the military party around Francis Joseph, there was every possibility of a change of front by Austria, as at Gastein the previous summer. Bismarck was, in consequence, determined to have ready an alternative policy which would provide for rapid Austro-Prussian reconciliation should Francis Joseph abandon the traditional Habsburg pretensions to dominate Germany. . . . Bismarck . . . was prepared for a dramatic change in policy right up to the moment the first troops crossed the frontier" (1976, 111).

After the war, when Bismarck had eradicated all belief that Prussia was a second-rate power, he again pursued peaceful relations with Austria. After Prussia's victory, after the establishment of the klein-deutsch policy that excluded Austria from Germany, "Bismarck wished to preserve Austria as she was in 1866—defeated, but still German" (A. J. P. Taylor 1976, 129).

Austria and Prussia disagreed very little over the operation of the international order, thus failing to satisfy a fundamental condition of the theories of hegemonic or power transition war. But in other important respects, the expectations of those theories were satisfied. Power transition and hegemonic war theorists contemplate that differences in rates of growth produce necessary conditions for war. If the weaker challenger is rising to equal and overtake the declining hegemon, then a fundamental condition for a power transition war is satisfied. As figures 7.1 and 7.2 make clear, there was a power transition between rising Prussia and declining Austria. Using pig iron production as an indicator of economic performance, figure 7.1 shows that Prussia's share of all production by major powers rose to equal Austria's around 1837, remained roughly equal to Austria's for another ten years, and then significantly overtook Austria's during the next two decades. By 1866, Prussia's economic capabilities had pulled far ahead of Austria's.

As is often the case, the military power transition lagged behind the economic transition. During the first half of the nineteenth century, Austria maintained a substantial advantage over Prussia in military might, measured as share of the total military personnel and military expenditures among the great powers. From the mid-1850s on, Austria began a precipitous decline in its military capabilities while Bismarck launched Prussia on a campaign of military expansion. With the indicators used here, the power transition actually occurred in 1866. Indeed, these data suggest that Bismarck's repeated threats of war with

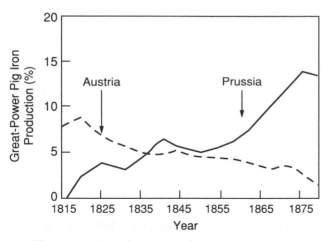

7.1: The Austro-Prussian economic transition. Pig iron data provided by J. David Singer and the Correlates of War Project.

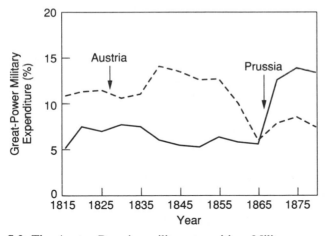

7.2: The Austro-Prussian military transition. Military expenditures data provided by J. David Singer and the Correlates of War Project.

Austria prior to 1866 may well have been empty threats, cheap talk
that served to lessen the credibility of his genuine and sincere threats
of 1866.

The evidence thus far suggests that the critical difference in growth
rates postulated by power transition and hegemonic stability theorists
was satisfied in 1866, but that the required disagreement over the
international status quo was not satisfied. However, two caveats are
in order.

First, the international interaction game focuses on a different transition. The relation between the challenger's power and the hegemon's
power is important insofar as it shapes the belief that the challenger
is exploitable. This transition can occur, but need not occur, when the
rivals are equal in power. It must occur when each thinks its chances
for victory are greater than or equal to fifty-fifty if domestic political
costs are expected to be small and expected losses in life and property
are expected to be about equal to the stakes. All of these conditions
probably obtain for the Seven Weeks' War, as noted in chapter 6.
Thus, the difference in power of the two sides was apparently consistent in this special case both with the international interaction game
and with the theory of power transition.

Second, although objective grounds exist for arguing that the two
sides shared a common view of the international status quo, still it
may be that there was a widespread perception of a sharp disagreement
between Austria and Prussia over the value of the international status
quo. We can never know with certainty what others believed at a given
time, but it is possible to develop sensitive indicators to reflect what
the prewar beliefs were about the impact of an Austro-Prussian war
on the international status quo.

The cost of money—the money market discount rate—in key financial centers reflects people's expectations about the future value of
that money. When, for instance, a government finds it difficult to
borrow money, then it is forced to raise the rate it pays for the money—
the discount rate—to attract lenders. Thus, a rising discount rate for
a national currency reflects a broad base of declining confidence in
that nation.

Just as the rise or decline in discount rates gives information about
expectations, so, too, do changes in discount rates across countries.
Where external conditions are expected to affect everyone about
equally, the money market discount rates for different currencies fluctuate about equally, with each responding equivalently to rising or
falling fears and uncertainties. But if some countries are expected to
be differentially affected by events, then their rates will rise or fall

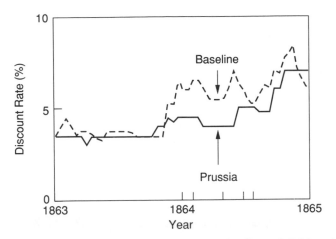

7.3: Money market discount rates and the Second Schleswig-Holstein War.

(depending upon the content of expectations) more than the rates of other, less affected, places.

Figure 7.3 depicts biweekly observations of the money market discount rate for Berlin and for a European baseline (which we have defined as the average of the discount rates for London and Amsterdam, two key financial centers in the nineteenth century) for the period from January 1863 to January 1865. The Second Schleswig-Holstein War began in early 1864, with a cease-fire interrupting the combat for all of May and most of June 1864. When the negotiations during the cease-fire failed, fighting resumed and Denmark was defeated, losing control over the Elbe Duchies. The Danes were expected to lose the war and territory to the Prussian-Austrian alliance. These expectations are clearly reflected in figure 7.3. The four small marks on the time line between 1864 and 1865 denote the beginning of hostilities, the interruption of war by the cease-fire (and the beginning of negotiations), the collapse of negotiation (and the resumption of fighting), and the conclusion of the war. The cost of money in London and Amsterdam rose at the outset of the war, responding in part to the general disquiet that war provokes in financial circles. The price of money fell just prior to the cease-fire, rising sharply in anticipation of the failed negotiations. Yet the price of Prussian money *fell* rapidly once the war got under way, rising to meet the European base rate only after the war ended. The clear separation in money discount rates, and the decline in the price Berlin had to pay for money compared to other money centers, suggests that the status quo was expected to change in Prussia's favor because of the Second Schleswig-Holstein War.

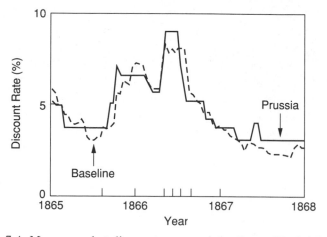

7.4: Money market discount rates and the Seven Weeks' War.

The mean spread between the base money market rates and Prussia's from January 1, 1863, to the outbreak of hostilities on February 1, 1864, when compared to the rates during the period of fighting (February 1 to July 20, 1864), makes it clear that the spread increased significantly during the war. The t-statistic is 4.42 (N = 42), indicating that the events of the war almost certainly influenced the competitive edge gained by Prussian funds.[5]

Figure 7.4 tracks the same variables as figure 7.3, but for 1865 to 1868. The small marks on the time line denote the signing of the Treaty of Gastein in August 1865, the announcement of the Italo-Prussian alliance on April 8, 1866, the mobilization of the Prussian army on May 5 (the Austrians having made their military preparations by early March), the recognition of the inevitability of war by June 16, and the conclusion of the war in late July. The uncertainties provoked by the expectation of war are reflected in the rising discount rate for money. That the great swings in the cost of money were driven by war fears is supported by the accounts in the *Economist* that accompany the weekly reportage of discount rates. On April 7, 1866, for instance, it is noted that "the Bourse has been greatly agitated every day . . . by the dread of war in Germany" (414). Again, on May 5, "The Bourse has been dreadfully agitated during the past week by the prospect of

5. Comparable indicators for Vienna cannot be utilized, for the Viennese discount rate was fixed by the government rather than by auction and was permitted to fluctuate relatively infrequently.

war, and prices have fallen heavily" (535). Similar reports can be found
nearly every week in the months preceding the outbreak of hostilities.

In spite of the great fears of war, and their reflection in the rising
cost of money, it is clear from figure 7.4 that the impact of the crisis
on expectations concerning Prussia was not substantially different
from the impact on the baseline. There was a small impact immediately
during the war. Although the cost of money rose markedly in London,
Berlin, and Amsterdam, it rose more in Prussia than in the base cities.
This rapid rise confirms the widely reported observation that Prussia
was expected to lose the war.[6] That the price differential between
Berlin and the other key financial centers was small supports, at the
same time, the belief that the perceived stakes in the war were not
very large. Immediately after the battle of Königgrätz the market price
of money fell rapidly. The decline in the cost of money in Prussia led
the baseline of London and Amsterdam. The expectations in the financial markets were updated to take account of the new information
revealed on the battlefield—the market had underestimated Prussia's
chance of victory. The prewar fears of postwar inflation or defaults on
money instruments by a defeated Prussia were allayed by Prussia's
decisive victory.

That Prussia's place in the European international system was not
expected, ex ante, to be fundamentally changed by the Seven Weeks'
War can be seen from a statistical assessment of the difference in the
price of money prior to the war compared to its price during crucial
events of the war. If rates during the period of the crucial events—
from the April 8 announcement of the Italo-Prussian alliance to surrender on July 28—reflect expectations of a fundamental change from
the status quo ante for Prussia, then the mean difference between the
Prussian and base discount rate for that period would be significantly
different from the mean difference for the prewar period. If the international status quo was not perceived to be at risk, then there would
not be a significant difference. Taking the mean difference between
Prussia's rate and the average rate for London and Amsterdam from
January 1, 1865, to April 1, 1866, as the baseline, we compare this
mean to the comparable mean price differential during the events of

6. Simon echoes the sentiment of many historians when he writes, "It is important
to remember that it was by no means a foregone conclusion that Prussia would
win; pessimism was widespread in the Prussian camp, and the Austrian government
was confident of victory" (1960, 30–31). See also A. J. P. Taylor 1976, 126, on
expectations from the Austrian perspective and Showalter 1975, 121, for a general
view of Prussian weaknesses.

crisis and war. The t-statistic for the difference is -1.054 (N = 43),
which is not significant. The money market data support the claim that
Prussia was not expected to be differentially affected by the war. The
status quo ante—in which Austria was the dominant German state—
was expected to prevail.

From this and the earlier discussion we can conclude that both on
objective grounds and on expectational grounds, the Seven Weeks'
War was not fought over an alteration of the international status quo.
The war was not fought to change the rules of the international order,
nor was it fought because one of the antagonists was dissatisfied with
that order. Thus, according to the theories of power transition and
hegemonic war, the Seven Weeks' War could not have been a system-
transforming war. Yet by the end of the war, nothing less than a major
reorganization of Europe was expected.

SYSTEM TRANSFORMATION

During the months remaining in 1866 after the war ended and through
1867, a sequence of events unleashed forces that shaped the course of
European history up to and beyond the outbreak of World War I.
These forces were all clearly visible and given intelligible shape well
before the outbreak of the Franco-Prussian War, itself made possible
by the events of 1866.

Austria, excluded from Germany by the Peace of Nikolsburg,
sought new arrangements in a greater Austro-Hungarian empire to
preserve its great-power status. As late as the spring of 1866, just on
the eve of a war that most expected to be won by Austria, the Austrian
government was intransigent in its negotiations with Hungary over
union. After the war, the Hungarians offered the same deal as before,
only by August 1866 the Austrians no longer had much choice in the
matter. As A. J. P. Taylor observes, "The Austria which emerged from
the war of 1866 was created by Bismarck as much as the Austria which
emerged from the Napoleonic Wars was created by Metternich" (1976,
127).

Francis Joseph's willingness to accept the establishment of Austria-
Hungary after the Seven Weeks' War was motivated by his desire to
secure Austria's position as a great power. For this purpose, he ceded
considerable power within the empire to the Magyars and helped
unleash the nationalist sentiments in eastern Europe that even today
jeopardize stability. As Herbert Michaelis observes, "While the revolution of 1848 had awakened the national consciousness of eastern

European peoples, the Prussian victory over Austria now provided them with the opportunity to fight actively for the realization of their national goals. Königgrätz set in motion the whole eastern realm of nationalities, both inside and outside the monarchy, a movement that was never again to cease" (Pflanze 1968, 106–13). Taylor makes a similar observation: "The settlement with Hungary could be challenged only if Czechs and Germans were reconciled, and any real concord among the peoples of Austria, though it would weaken the Magyars, would endanger also the supremacy of the Emperor. . . . Magyar hegemony was the price which Francis Joseph was willing to pay for the preservation of his own power; and since this Magyar hegemony brought the Habsburg Monarchy to destruction, Francis Joseph was the maker of his own ruin" (1976, 141).[7]

At least as significant as the forces unleashed in eastern Europe was the impact of the war on the balance-of-power system established by the Congress of Vienna. By September 1866 it was apparent that the European order established at the congress—an order that had generally preserved peace among the great powers of Europe since 1815—was at an end. As Friedhelm Grützner puts it, "A world collapsed, the world of the Congress of Vienna" (1986, 80).[8] France and Russia pressed for a new congress to establish order in the emerging Europe and to protect their position and the balance of power.

The collapse of the existing European order was neither planned by Bismarck nor recognized until several weeks after the war ended. Until Bismarck had achieved the moderate peace terms he desired, a peace that preserved Austrian sovereignty and left open the opportunity for realignment with Austria, the effects of the war remained unclear to Europe's other great powers. While negotiating with the Austrians, Bismarck wrote to Tsar Alexander that "he was not to worry; there would be no drastic change in the map of Europe, since all that Prussia asked was a reform of the Confederation with the expulsion of Austria from Germany, and a final accounting in the matter of the duchies" (Crankshaw 1981, 219). It was not until about a month later, with the war settled and Bismarck's possibilities clearer to him that France and Russia understood how fundamentally the balance of power had changed.

7. See also Simon 1960 on the formation of Austria-Hungary as a consequence of the Seven Weeks' War.

8. "Tatsächlich stürzte eine Welt ein, die Welt des Wiener Kongresses," translated by authors.

Then there was urgent talk of a European congress: if the Continental order established by the Congress of Vienna was to be replaced by a different system, then the signatories to the Treaty of Vienna must meet to sanction the changes—or to forbid them. . . . This time Bismarck, the man of moderation, snarled almost shockingly and showed his teeth. . . . He was the minister-president of a Prussia which had just revealed herself as the military superior of Austria and almost certainly of France as well. . . . Now he showed that if Prussia could not get her own way (meaning his, Bismarck's, own way), he was ready to plunge all Europe into revolutionary violence. (Crankshaw 1976, 220–21)

Between Prussia's victory at Königgrätz and the end of 1867, Bismarck's kleindeutsch policy was implemented, leading quickly to the unification of northern Germany. With the Treaty of Nikolsburg he had ended Austrian hopes for a *grossdeutsch* policy that envisioned a unified Germany including both Prussia and Austria. Bismarck's kleindeutsch policy dominated central European affairs until Hitler—an Austrian—launched the *Anschluss* that brought Austria back into greater Germany. Through a war fought over lesser issues, Bismarck had unified much of Germany, prompted the formation of Austria-Hungary, unleashed nationalist sentiments in Eastern Europe, and brought the Congress of Vienna system to a crashing end. No wonder that contemporary observers were startled by the consequences of the war:

Events of so startling a character have taken place in the theater of war and present such an aspect of importance toward the future that the mind is dizzied by its attempt to estimate their real importance. (*Illustrated London News,* July 14, 1866, quoted in Craig 1964)

Thirty dynasties have been swept away, . . . the fate of twenty millions of civilized men has been affected for ever, the political face of the world has changed as it used to change after a generation of war. . . . Prussia has leaped in a moment into the position of the first Power of Europe. (*Spectator,* July 7, 1866, quoted in Craig 1964)

The contemporaneous accounts reflect not only the flushed excitement of the moment but also give an enduring picture of the consequences of the Seven Weeks' War. It is worth contemplating Grützner's comparison of the Seven Weeks' War to the Franco-Prussian War. He argues that "the secular significance of 1866 has been underestimated by many German historians of the older generation. . . . In that regard, the Franco-Prussian War today would be classified as only an epilogue to the policies inaugurated in 1866" (1986, 80).

The Seven Weeks' War, *der Bruderkrieg,* as it is sometimes called, was motivated by Prussian ambitions within the German community. Prussia, in defeating Austria, however, overturned the international status quo. How can we explain the emergence of German hegemony and the reordering of the post–Congress of Vienna international system after a war fought over issues deemed by the theory of hegemonic war or power transition to be too limited to have such consequences?

The international interaction game provides a missing link in the puzzle of the Seven Weeks' War and the emergence of German hegemony. We have seen that war can be an equilibrium outcome even though the status quo is highly valued. But such a high valuation of the status quo imposes limitations on the expected size of the ensuing war. If the stakes are expected to be small—as with the Seven Weeks' War—then the expected costs of the war *must* be small. If we assume that expected costs are correlated with actual costs, then wars between rivals who value the status quo highly are likely to be small wars.

Austria's demands were minor enough in terms of the overall international order. Austria sought to hold on to its first place among the German states. The Habsburgs did not and were not expected to demand territory from the Prussians. Nor did they demand a change in Prussia's external policies or any diminution in Prussia's role in the German Diet. They did not demand any fundamental change in Prussian policy except to defer to Austria as the first among equals. Likewise, Prussia's demands *before* the war were modest, although Bismarck's accomplishments proved not to be.

Prussia demanded a share in the title of first among equals in the German Confederation, a leading role in Germany, but it did not demand an inch of Austrian soil. As Moltke notes, "The war of 1866 was entered on . . . not because the existence of Prussia was threatened, nor was it caused by public opinion and the voice of the people . . . but for an ideal end—the establishment of power. Not a foot of land was exacted from conquered Austria, but she had to renounce all part in the hegemony of Germany" (Craig 1964, 1–2). Notice that Moltke describes the goal as Prussian hegemony over Germany, not over Europe.

To be sure, acquiescence to Bismarck's original demands would have increased Prussia's influence within the Diet over the disposition of Holstein. Still, the demands themselves were not enough to alter fundamentally the perception of Prussian power in Europe, as suggested by the analysis of money market discount rates and by the review of Prussian policy before the war. That view is reinforced by the interpretation of several historians that the war, rather than the issues that produced the war, changed history (Simon 1968, 22–38; Crankshaw 1981, 189–223; A. J. P. Taylor 1976, 123–40; Grützner 1986, 80–117; Michaelis 1968). Thus it was that the German states could fight a war that ultimately transformed the international system over limited issues in the international context—issues limited enough that several authorities suggest war could have been averted by the purchase of Holstein from Austria, a purchase Bismarck was willing to make.

To say that the international status quo was reasonably well liked by the combatants and that the magnitude of the competing demands were fairly narrow is akin to saying that Prussia and Austria could satisfy the equilibrium conditions for war (and Austria could satisfy the inequality in expression [7.1]) only if the expected costs of the war were even smaller than the small expected stakes. According to the international interaction game, the Seven Weeks' War, although it transformed the international system, was likely to be a small war as far as costs are concerned.[9]

In fact, in terms of duration, total battle deaths, or thousands of battle deaths per million of population, the Seven Weeks' War is unusually small in scope as multilateral wars go. The battle deaths per million population, for instance, represent only about 1 percent of all such deaths in multilateral European wars since 1816. This level is approximately one tenth of the statistically expected level of losses for such a war based on data from Small and Singer (1982). Yet the war directly involved three great powers and eight lesser states, with a fourth major actor (France) playing a crucial role on the sidelines.

The relation between expected costs, stakes, and the status quo derived from the international interaction game shows a significant though unintended selection bias in some research on great-power wars. Some scholars mistakenly infer that events yielding major consequences must themselves have been major events. But big consequences can result from small causes. The conditions stipulated in theories of hegemonic war or power transition are not essential for the occurrence of system-transforming wars. The perspective that says system-transforming wars necessarily involve some combination of extended battle with many casualties involving many nations and usu-

9. Again, this statement is contingent on the assumption that actualized costs and expected costs are strongly and positively correlated with each other.

ally involving the exchange of territory conflates causes with consequences. Contrary to the expectations of these theories, a system-transforming war occurred in which the stakes were modest and in which, despite the many states involved and the great mass of troops assembled at the decisive battle, casualties were modest, and the fighting lasted only a short time.

The game-theoretic analysis suggests that by relaxing the assumptions that assign special significance to the satisfaction rivals have with the international status quo and that restrict the purview of researchers to large, costly wars, we can complement the explanatory potential of power preponderance theories. The game itself is not designed to account for war only among the great powers, nor even to account only for war. Rather, it is a general scaffolding for understanding a broad array of international interactions. In that regard, it differs markedly from the theories of power transition and hegemonic war. Yet it is a complement, rather than a substitute, for those theories.

Those theories, and attendant empirical assessments, have drawn our attention to the prospective importance of differential growth rates and to the existence of a critical power transition (albeit not necessarily related to parity between adversaries) in influencing the prospects of great wars (Garnham 1976; Weede 1976; Houweling and Siccama 1988; Kim 1989). The game-theoretic perspective has the added potential for explaining great shifts in the international order with or without war and certainly with or without much bloodshed. The game highlights the fact that the assumptions of power preponderance theorists have unnecessarily restricted their investigations to large, major-power wars and to differences in power between rivals, rather than to beliefs about such differences and the implications those beliefs have regarding prospective strategic decisions. The game emphasizes the consequences of treating satisfaction as a continuous concept instead of a dichotomous one; power transition or hegemonic war theorists have put forward the dichotomous view. Finally, the international interaction game identifies a different power transition as a critical variable in influencing the risk of war. Through the example of the Seven Weeks' War we have tried to clarify the value the game has for understanding how uncertainties about power have shaped events in the ever-changing international community.

Part IV

Foreign Policy Implications of the International Interaction Game

Chapter 8

Foreign Policy in the Post–Cold War World

When we began writing this book, the Cold War seemed an immutable fixture of international politics. Today, many analysts of the foreign policy scene are scrambling to understand the emerging reality. The bedrock under the systemic, structural determinants of international affairs has turned to quicksand. Balance-of-power theory and theories of bipolarity and multipolarity alike are at sixes and sevens. Proclamations of declining U.S. hegemony seem quaint in light of the general collapse of the Soviet Union's international sphere of influence. The vision of the world on which so many earlier conjectures were based is utterly transformed.

The predominant realist or neorealist viewpoint suggests that broad international structural characteristics overwhelm inconsequential variations in individual personalities, outlooks, and ambitions. System structure, not the individual qualities of decision makers or the particular domestic political institutions of states, is the essential explanatory factor in international affairs. The withdrawal of the Soviet Union from eastern Europe and its own implosion have challenged the view of system-oriented, structural realism that structure, not individual choices, is the foundation of international interactions. These changes have all taken place without having been anticipated by realist or neorealist theorists and without now having a coherent post hoc explanation of what structural features of international affairs encouraged or compelled such changes.

In spite of any external pressures markedly different from those that characterized the Cold War period, the Soviet Union of the late 1980s underwent a sudden, drastic, and mostly peaceful metamorphosis. In the span of fewer than five years the Soviet leaders transformed their country (or should we now say countries) from the archenemy of the United States into a nascent ally. With barely a whimper, the Soviet Union willingly endured and even encouraged political losses every bit as large as one might have expected if that superpower lay prostrate after total defeat in war. Many sacred pillars of Soviet defense and security policy are gone. Ideological fervor for the exportation of revolutions—except, perhaps, for liberal democratic revolutions—is gone, along with dreams of burying the United States with a Soviet economic miracle. The eastern European empire is gone; so are the beachheads in Central America and the Caribbean. Lenin and Marx are gone, at least for now.

Previous fluctuations in Soviet policy were often greeted with enormous skepticism in the West. Soviet proposals for advancing peace were viewed by many in the United States as tactics designed to lull naive Western leaders into a false sense of security. Perhaps, indeed, that was their intention. Today, however, no serious person can still characterize the altered behavior of the erstwhile Soviet leadership in that way. They have given up far too much, and much of what they have sacrificed could be regained at far too high a cost for anyone to deny that the concessions are real and far-reaching. Recent Soviet developments make more sense if understood from a domestic viewpoint than from a realist viewpoint, which interprets demands and foreign policy actions strictly in their international context. Internal imperatives, rather than external constraints, seem to have shaped the revolution in Soviet foreign policy and the struggle out of domestic chaos and economic collapse.

During the Persian Gulf War of 1991, for example, the Soviet Union gave the secrets of its missile computer programs as a gift to the United States to assist in the struggle against Saddam Hussein. These programs had long been an objective of the U.S. intelligence community. They represent an essential sacrifice of air combat capabilities by the Soviet Union to a nation that a few scant months before was understood to be the primary threat to Soviet security. Obviously, the equilibrium behavior has changed; critical belief thresholds have been crossed; critical variables have been altered enough to transform fundamental relations.

Such change is exactly the sort of metamorphosis that the domestic version of the international interaction game can help us understand. A central emphasis of game-theoretic analysis is that changes in equilibria can follow from small variations in variables. The selection of strategies is always seen in this context as a function of the comparison of expected values. In game-theoretic terms, a course of action is chosen because the anticipated consequences on the chosen side of the ledger are thought to be more attractive than those on the other side. Whichever side has the greater expected (subgame perfect) value will be chosen without regard to how much larger or smaller the expected value is. Thus, the accumulation of small changes in beliefs or expectations do sometimes grow large enough to cause one or another decision maker to turn down a radically different path, to seek a new solution to old problems. The proximity of choices for violent conflict or for negotiation that we have highlighted throughout this investigation frequently hinged just on such small changes in expectations. The observed changes in eastern Europe and in the Soviet Union may likewise have hinged on just such small shifts in key variables.

There was no cataclysmic precipitating event to account for the drastic reorientation of Soviet policy. Rather, there was a gradual withering of the Soviet economy, a slow erosion of the Soviet ability to compete simultaneously on the dimensions of guns and butter, and a gradual alteration of Soviet political institutions. These small, cumulative changes apparently grew large enough to alter the preferred strategy of the Soviet leadership in a seemingly discontinuous way.

The unleashing of opposition sentiments, beginning slowly and haltingly with the Helsinki Accords of 1975, has steadily lowered the cost to opponents of the Soviet and east European regimes. As opposition movements gained strength and momentum, first in Poland and Czechoslovakia through Solidarity and watchdog organizations formed in response to the Helsinki accords, later elsewhere in eastern Europe and ultimately within the Soviet Union itself, the calculus of acceptable foreign policy behavior changed. Where, before, rebellion could readily be crushed by force when necessary, a forcible response became unacceptable. By 1990, Mikhail Gorbachev had to apologize publicly and distance himself from the use of Soviet military might in the Baltic republics. Domestic opposition to force had become a powerful restraint, just as the stakes for competing with the United States were falling steadily.

Game theory helps us understand this important aspect of behavior: apparently discontinuous changes in behavior often follow in a highly predictable way from small alterations in expectations. The collapse of the Soviet empire has dealt a devastating blow to many contemporary theories of international affairs. It has not done the same to the international interaction game, which is, in principle, just as readily applicable to biblical war, decision making among the Mongolian hordes of the twelfth century, Cold Warriors of the 1945–89 period, or the emerging international order. The game does not depend upon particular power distributions, cultural affinities, or global structures—though its specific equilibria are intimately shaped by such considerations—but rather on supposedly universal features of reasoned decision making. Consequently, the current debate over whether the world is still bipolar, has entered a multipolar period, or is ensconced in a unipolar system led by the United States influences our judgments about the future indirectly, if at all.

The international interaction game suggests some general principles regarding war and peace that may help form expectations about the future and that imply policy prescriptions for that future. Here we explore some of those expectations and prescriptions in an informal, speculative way. Perhaps some will help inform discussion and debate in the new world order.

ARMS CONTROL, ARMS RACES, DISARMAMENT

To state it crudely: national leaders wage war when the expected gains minus the expected costs for doing so outweigh the net expected consequences of alternative choices. War can be stumbled into when one nation judges the intentions of a rival too optimistically. War can begin even with full information if it is motivated by a fear of ceding any advantage, however small, that is attached to the first use of force. The anticipated net gains from war may be real and tangible acquisitions, or they may be the avoidance of a future expected to be worse than the one anticipated through warfare. Therefore, expected gains are always viewed relatively—relative to the expected costs of acquiring them and relative to the state of affairs expected to prevail in the absence of the chosen course of action. In that sense, and as noted in chapter 6, the probability of obtaining benefits, whatever their content, must necessarily exceed the ratio of costs to benefits expected in the war. Naturally, the actual costs or benefits may not match expectations. That is why leaders sometimes enter wars they expect to win only to discover that they have lost. Arms control and disarmament are strategies for reducing the expected costs of war, though not necessarily for lowering the risk that war will take place. Consequently, arms reduction policies are rarely, if ever, discussed in the context of relations among friends and allies. Almost as rarely are arms reduction strategies contemplated in a unilateral framework that is motivated by domestic political considerations untempered by security interests. Arms reduction policies are in the domain of rivalry and have relevance only in relationships characterized by mutual fear and distrust. Although this idea may seem obvious, a little exploration will help clarify important features of the past and the evolving world. Some of those features encourage hope, but others give cause for alarm among those who desire a world devoid of violent international interactions and equally devoid of exploitive relations among states.

If one nation reduces its preparedness to fight and its adversary does not, then the nation adopting a unilateral policy of arms reduction makes war cheaper for its adversary. Unilateral reductions in arms naturally help an enemy by lowering the losses that it can expect to endure. The impact of unilateral reductions can be further enhanced by raising the expected costs to the disarming state, by diminishing its own credibility, and by reducing its deterrent posture. Such a unilateral policy of unpreparedness raises the risks of war or exploitation. Doves in a hostile world leave themselves open to blackmail and exploitation or set themselves up to act preemptively and violently. When they do so, sometimes their actions are aimed at adversaries who are, unbeknownst to them, also doves. In this way, confrontations can perpetuate distrust and hostility out of a false fear of exploitation. Consequently, we do not generally anticipate observing recognizably dovish behavior among states with a conflict of interests. Not expecting dovish behavior does not mean that there are no doves but rather that dovelike impulses are masked by the desire of doves (and hawks) to ensure their own security against aggression.

If a clear and significant conflict of interests does not exist between a pair of states or alliances, then dovish, unilateral arms reduction policies are not surprising. We find nothing peculiar about unilateral fluctuations in the military preparedness of our allies, at least insofar as we view such fluctuations in the context of our own security. Changes in British armaments, for instance, do not alarm the U.S. government, whether they go up or down. It simply does not anticipate a conflict of interests of sufficient import to warrant calculating U.S. prospects for gaining an advantage over the British through warfare or exploitation. Unilateral disarmament, as with the Japanese compliance with their war-imposed constitutional restrictions on rearmament, is not problematic among friends.

Arms control agreements are arrangements between nations that harbor suspicions and distrust of one another. If they did not, then either or both could unilaterally elect to alter their military preparedness without fear that the other would misconstrue their intentions. The security dilemma does not arise among those who share common objectives. There may be a security dilemma between some republics of the Soviet Union and the People's Republic of China, between Greece and Turkey, India and Pakistan, or Israel and Syria, but there is not a security dilemma between the United States and Canada, or Holland and Belgium.

Arms reduction agreements can ensure that the probability of success in war (or in other risky interactions) for each signatory is frozen at the pre-agreement level. Such agreements can also foster shifts in that probability toward greater or lesser equality, depending on the precise details of the understanding. If the subjective probability of success decreases for both sides faster than the expected costs of war decrease, then arms control or disarmament reduces the risk of war between the nations. If, however, the costs diminish at a faster rate than the probability of success, and particularly if costs diminish fast enough to reverse the fear of war for one or both sides, then arms control agreements increase the risk of war or exploitation. They do so even when the signatories are sincere in their desire to enhance peaceful relations. As long as the existing conflict of interests—the benefits part of the cost-benefit ratio—remains unaltered, reduced expected costs from violence make the use of force more attractive, holding all else constant. According to the international interaction game, arms control agreements often raise, or at least do not diminish, the risk of war.

Naturally, people in the United States have not recently worried about British military buildups. Because the British are close friends, the U.S. government does not view changes in the military posture as signals of hawkish or dovish intentions toward the United States. Alarm might have been provoked had the British chosen to disarm unilaterally during the Cold War because, at the margin, such an action would have reduced the probability of success of the NATO alliance in a conflict with the Soviet bloc. The United States would not have seen disarmament as an opportunity to impose U.S. goals on the British people or government. Likewise, increases in Canadian armaments are unlikely to provoke concerns about the security of the United States, even on local, limited issues in dispute between the two nations. We must wonder why it is, given the impersonal logic of the international interaction game, that changes in British or Canadian military capabilities are met with no fear in the United States? Why are U.S. citizens free from worries that the British, the Canadians, or other close allies might be contemplating an adventure that could be costly to the United States? The answer, of course, is that the range of disagreements between the United States and its closest allies has been and is very small. And, as we have seen, when the stakes are very small, it is difficult to satisfy the requirements for war. The losses in goodwill among friends and allies are generally expected to outweigh the prospective gains through military conquest. This relative balance is sustained all the better because, as we saw in chapter 5, the United States and most of its allies have democratic governments and so are likely to be constrained not to use force to advance their interests with one another.

Fear of a military confrontation between the United States and allies like Britain must seem so inconceivable that many may find this entire discussion pointless. We think the prospects of such a confrontation are virtually nil but that the discussion can nevertheless be instructive with regard to the emerging world order. This discussion is intended to introduce an assessment of changing relations between the United States and the Soviet Union or its republics and to highlight the applicability of the general principles delineated here to relations between friends and foes alike. Just as the international interaction game provides a logical foundation for our intuition that U.S. policymakers do not worry much about changes in British military postures, so, too, does the game structure provide insights into past, present, and perhaps future evaluations of Soviet military policy.

We would do well to recall that the United States could not always have greeted changes in British military capabilities with just mild interest. In 1776 and in 1812, British ability to project its force across the ocean was of the gravest concern; and that concern was not greatly diminished in 1861–65—barely a century and a quarter ago—when Britain's apparent preference for the Confederate States of America and the British naval presence near U.S. shores was a matter of the utmost importance to the administrations of Abraham Lincoln in the North and Jefferson Davis in the South.

During the Cold War, changes in Soviet military capabilities were closely watched in the United States, for they reflected directly on U.S. calculations about the threat of war. Increased Soviet capabilities were often taken to mean that the Soviet leaders believed their probability of success had risen for certain adventures—not necessarily for nuclear confrontations, perhaps, but for limited objectives in the Middle East, the Caribbean, or elsewhere. Increased Soviet capabilities often implied increased expected costs for the United States in a confrontation with the Soviet Union. Increased defensive capabilities for the Soviets implied reduced expected costs on their part. And all the time, the differences in worldviews suggested that the expected benefits from gaining the upper hand were very large indeed for either side.

Today, a comparable buildup would still attract the wary attention of the U.S. defense and foreign policy establishment. President Gorbachev's hold on power and the stability of the reforms he has implemented within the Soviet Union are not so well ensconced that they are perceived to be irreversible. The failed coup of August 1991 was a harsh reminder of distressing possibilities. But the collapse of the Warsaw Pact and the end of the agreement at Yalta to divide Europe into spheres of influence makes the reassertion of a Soviet empire over Hungary, Czechoslovakia, and Poland extremely difficult. The reunification of Germany makes such a reassertion virtually inconceivable; the costs would be no less than if the Soviets had contemplated an assault on the Federal Republic of Germany during the height of the Cold War. In Bulgaria and Romania the break with the past is not at this writing so certain that a drastic change in leadership and reestablishment of the Soviet Union might not prompt an effort to regain political hegemony over those territories. However, changes in the Soviet Union itself, with its rearrangement into the Russian Republic and into the set of independent states emerging from the Ukraine, Georgia, the Baltic republics, the Central Asian republics, and so forth, make these external dangers unlikely. Within the Soviet Union lies the greatest danger of war in Europe. How willing the leadership of the republics of the Soviet Union will be to accommodate one another's claims for independent borders remains an open and troubling question.

What does this all suggest about arms control, disarmament, or arms races between the United States (or NATO) and the Russian or Soviet Union of the future? It suggests that the shrunken benefits denominator of the cost-benefit ratio has opened the door for significant arms reduction without fear of raising the risks of an East-West confrontation. But the shrunken denominator may also foreshadow new violence elsewhere in the world and even along the eastern frontiers of Europe. The cost-benefit ratio for relations between Hungary and Romania or among the ethnic groups of Yugoslavia, for instance, almost certainly has not diminished. Soviet constraints on these states are reduced—along with the expected costs associated with confrontation—while issues that have lain dormant for decades appear to be reemerging.

The course of events in the past few years has fundamentally altered the political tasks in Europe. The historical desire of the Russian leadership to dominate eastern Europe may or may not have changed; their desire to aggrandize the Soviet empire in Europe may or may not have changed; U.S. antipathy to communism may or may not have changed; U.S. aspirations to contain communism may or may not have changed. All of these matter less than that the Russian/Soviet expectation of achieving any such benefits from a confrontation with the United States and its allies has clearly changed. Economic malaise, the surrender of eastern Europe, and the consolidation of Germany all mean that every feature of a rational calculation for war or peace has moved in the direction of peace between the United States and the new Russian/Soviet republic. The benefits from confrontation have contracted as the Soviets have given up their external empire, moved toward a commonwealth, adopted capitalist modes of exchange, and begun implementing electoral laws that allow genuine competition and that no longer reserve a special status for the Communist Party. Because the benefits have shriveled immensely, we can afford to allow the expected costs from war to shrink as well without altering the risk of violence. Arms control between the United States and the Soviet Union has become much more attractive from the vantage point of promoting peace at the same time that it approaches irrelevance.

The issues that remain conflictual between the United States and the Soviet Union have been so diminished that even unilateral arms control in the form of the so-called peace dividend is entirely conceivable now in the United States or in the Soviet republics (barring the by-no-means trivial risk of a civil war). The nuclear threat that has been a bulwark of the long peace is less consequential in a world in which the stakes of global war are small. To be sure, the nuclear threat is an effective deterrent against the quest for small gains—if it is credible—but it is also an excessive deterrent that encourages economic inefficiency and significant opportunity costs on American and Russian lives. Therefore, for the first time in the postwar period, one can contemplate uncoordinated reductions in nuclear weapons. For the first time, the United States and the Soviet republics can think about reshaping their arsenals to be deterrents against limited adventures for limited gains. Preparedness to respond to limited threats remains important, but the ability to inflict massive punishment is no longer critical to U.S.-Soviet security relations. Domestic political and economic concerns can now dominate U.S. and Soviet armaments policies toward one another, although perhaps not toward other threats around the globe.

The United States has already begun to reap the benefits that accrue from the collapse of the Soviet Union. The contest between socialism and markets has apparently been won in most of the world; the struggle between competitive elections and authoritarian rule has largely been won in Europe; the focus of Soviet policy has been turned inward, away from sentiments supporting the exportation of revolution and the expansion of external influence. The denominator of the cost-benefit ratio has shrunk almost to zero for both the United States and the constituent parts of the Soviet Union, leaving little room for costs that would be tolerable in a military adventure. Even in the hinterlands of the Soviet and U.S. spheres of influence, where the costs of some Cold War confrontations were once tolerable, such encounters seem, at least for the moment, to be extremely unlikely. The Soviets have given up just about everything the United States has sought it to give up over the past forty-five years and has asked for and received little or nothing in return. Whatever the exigencies of the Soviet leadership in the future, important sacrifices already made by the Soviet Union are well enough entrenched that a return to the status quo ante would itself be far too expensive for the Russian or other republics to contemplate seriously.

That is not to say that a domestic backlash that brings more authoritarian rulers to the head of some republics is unlikely. Domestic reform is reversible. However, even if such circumstances arose, they would probably be in weak republics, making a return to the spheres of influence established at Yalta unattainable. It is altogether likely that any threatened eastern European state could count on the support of western European or U.S. forces in a conventional confrontation with an authoritarian challenger. They could not have counted on such support in the past. The prospect of such assistance increases as the days turn to months and the months to years since the Soviets abandoned their control over eastern Europe. As the nations formerly in the Warsaw Pact become more and more integrated into the world economy and the European security system, the benefits to Europe and the United States for maintaining their liberty increase. Integration, in turn, heightens the credibility of deterrent threats from Europe and the United States directed against any hypothetical expansionist leaders in the future.

The United States and NATO can reduce their readiness for a global war because the changed Russian/Soviet republic is less of a threat and more of a friend. The Russian/Soviet republic can contemplate reductions of its own because NATO is less of a threat and more of a helpful, stabilizing influence on the continent. But the rapprochement between eastern Europe and western Europe does not necessarily mean a more peaceful future. Indeed, the international interaction game, viewed from the perspective of other states, looks perilously closer to having violent equilibria.

THE LONG PEACE: IS ALL QUIET ON THE EASTERN FRONT?

Rapprochement between the United States and the constituents of the former Soviet Union assures us that the threat of a war among global powers is vanishingly small. Nuclear weapons, NATO, the Warsaw Pact, the Yalta agreement, and other institutions of the Cold War induced equilibria that avoided such a war. But nuclear deterrence was not the limit of their stabilizing influence. The Cold War institutions diminished the threat of lesser conflicts in ways that the new world is less well equipped to do. The institutions of the Cold War—particularly the institutionalization of containment both by the U.S. and Soviet governments—ensured that most of the world fell within well-understood boundaries. Yalta quite explicitly established those boundaries, the spheres of influence, in Europe. Trial and (costly) error established further boundaries—albeit more fluid ones—elsewhere around the globe.

The Cold War institutions were ambiguous about the interests of the Soviet Union and the United States in Indochina, Korea, the Indian subcontinent, and elsewhere. In some of these regions, vague claims led to expansionist efforts by one or the other great power to test the waters. In this way, the Soviet Union successfully extended its interests into Cuba and tried to in Nicaragua; the United States and its allies, through the Trieste negotiations and settlement, at least neutralized Yugoslavia; and the United States led the way to the reassertion of U.S. and European hegemony over Greece and until 1979 over Iran. In the Middle East, the Cold War framework left competing territorial claims unresolved; spheres of influence were highly fluid, and tensions and threats of war were repeated. In the confrontations between Israel and its Arab neighbors one often saw the not-so-hidden hand of U.S. and Soviet interests at work.

During most of the decades of the Cold War, its institutions raised concern, at least in the minds of U.S. and Soviet leaders, that any conflict in the fluid zone could escalate into a direct confrontation between their countries. Consequently, the two great powers exerted considerable pressure on their respective allies to contain and constrain ambitions. That these efforts did not always succeed is evident from the Arab-Israeli wars of 1967 and 1973, the Korean War, and the several wars in Indochina. They were more successful on other occasions, as in the withdrawal of Israel from Beirut in the early 1980s. But through all of this there was always the specter of global escalation, and that specter damped the frequency of disputes and encouraged putting off efforts to reach a permanent settlement of those disputes that did not appear amenable to negotiated resolution. Thus, the Israelis continue to coexist with the Palestine Liberation Organization (PLO), despite the apparent opportunity in the early 1980s to crush that organization; thus, Anwar Sadat made a separate peace with Israel without insisting on the return of all territories taken from other Arab states.

Although the disputes festered, the quest for ultimate resolution continued to be postponed. The failure to settle these disputes through a decisive victory by one side or the other arose presumably because U.S. and Soviet leaders pressed their allies to act with restraint to avoid a showdown between the superpowers. In the post–Cold War world, the fear of that showdown is diminished. The boundaries of Soviet and U.S. spheres of influence are vaguer than ever—or perhaps they are crystal clear. The Russian/Soviet sphere of influence seems not to exist any longer beyond the borders of the Soviet Union; indeed, the sphere of influence and the zone of security may be even smaller. It may lie just within the borders of the Russian Republic.

In a world in which the Soviet republics no longer have a clear stake in maintaining a sphere of influence outside their own territories, the efficacy of Soviet efforts to restrain its allies is almost nonexistent. When an erstwhile hegemon can neither restrain foreign threats nor control its own friends, it is no longer a hegemon—a leader of a global alliance. The Soviet global alliance has ceased to exist. The Soviet Union has, for now at least, lost as much political influence in its former sphere of influence, including the republics within its borders, as could only have been lost, one imagines, with a catastrophic and complete defeat. The Cold War has given us a third-world-war ending without the attendant death and destruction. And their absence is just what one would anticipate in the rivalry between the United States and the Soviet Union, each manifestly and self-consciously an adherent of the self-defense norm described in chapter 4.

What does the international interaction game imply about a world in which the Soviets no longer play a leadership role in any extensive sphere of influence? With the loss of the Soviet sphere of influence there is a concomitant evaporation of the restraint imposed by the Cold War institutions and Cold War fears in the third world and in much of eastern Europe. The risk that confrontations will engage the superpowers is greatly reduced because they are no longer vying with one another. Under such conditions, the expected costs of expansionist policies by minor states are likely to drop from their previous levels. Diminished costs make adventuresome policies more attractive. This, we believe, is why Saddam Hussein invaded Kuwait in 1990 and not sooner. The end of the Iran-Iraq War left Iraq desperate for increased oil revenues and, therefore, desperate to intimidate Saudi Arabia and others into reducing their production. The benefits of expansion increased relative to their prewar level. Additionally, the Soviets could no longer restrain Saddam Hussein because they no longer feared that his adventure would drag them into a confrontation with the United States. What is more, the removal of the U.S.-Soviet rivalry may also have led Saddam Hussein to conclude that U.S. interests in containing his expansion were diminished. After all, it was reasonable—albeit wrong—for him to believe that such an expansion no longer would be viewed in the United States as an enhancement of the Soviet sphere of influence in the Middle East. Thus, even if Saddam Hussein's subjective probability of success had not risen, circumstances conspired to encourage him to risk war. The anticipated costs of such action decreased at the same time that the anticipated gains, if he were successful, increased. A smaller numerator and a larger denominator for the expected cost-benefit ratio means that war becomes more attractive even if the probability of success is rather low, even lower than it had previously been.

It is apparent from Saddam Hussein's statements in the months leading up to the crisis that he believed the collapse of the Cold War had reduced the risks of adventuresome policies on his part. What previously could have been seen as pushing at the boundaries between U.S. and Soviet interests—with Kuwait leaning in the direction of the U.S. security zone and Iraq clearly in the Soviet camp—now could be seen as just a localized dispute. That it was not so perceived by the United States is another matter. Saddam Hussein may have misjudged the U.S. (and maybe the Soviet and worldwide) response. But the point is that his misjudgment was facilitated and perhaps even encouraged by the collapse of the Cold War institutions. For the first time, Saddam Hussein could believe in advance that his invasion of Kuwait would be viewed as a peripheral dispute not worthy of a U.S. or Russian response.

Where U.S. or Soviet ability to restrain the leaders of a country is diminished or lost, where those leaders derive fewer benefits from associating with the United States or the Soviet Union, and where U.S. or Soviet ability to impose costs on allies for pursuing their narrow interests is decreased, the cost of war has fallen since the Cold War period, yet the potential benefits remain unchanged. Thus, in much of the world not covered by Yalta and in much of eastern Europe, the threat of war has increased, especially the threat of small wars.

In parts of eastern Europe fundamental disputes persist. Borders drawn hastily at the conclusion of World War I or imposed during and after World War II may be fluid. That they have persisted for so long is probably a consequence of the Cold War institutions that made efforts to change them extremely expensive. The Cold War institutions ensured that the cost of confrontation between the two great powers was so high that disputes taking place within a sphere of influence were immune from external intervention. Such internecine confrontations were doomed to be resolved by the sphere's hegemon without outside interference. So it was that the Soviets resolved the Hungarian uprising in 1956 and the Prague Spring of 1968 without any consequential response by the United States and NATO. Alas, for the Hungarians and the Czechs this lesson about war among allied states was learned at a great cost. So it was also that the United States imposed its will in the Dominican Republic in 1965 and in Grenada and Panama in the past few years. Where the spheres were clearly demarcated, the hegemon of the bloc imposed its will without external reprisal.

Once it becomes apparent that a given sphere of influence is no longer central to its hegemon, as became apparent to the nations of eastern Europe during the late 1980s, revolutionary uprisings should be expected to spread like wildflowers in the warm sun. It is no coincidence that all of eastern Europe rose up following the slow, painful, extended, successful struggle of the Poles from 1980 to the end of the 1980s, when the Solidarity movement triumphed. Once the nations of eastern Europe saw that the Soviet army would stand by peacefully and allow the transformation of Poland, they all, one after the other in rapid succession, sought to escape the chains imposed by Yalta. Their efforts remind us that justice is more to be valued than stability. But they also remind us how fragile was the peace within eastern Europe and how dependent it was on the workings of the Cold War institutions.

Thus far, change in eastern Europe has come with minimal bloodshed. Even in Romania—where many feared an orgy of death—the initial violence associated with the ouster of the Ceauşescu regime was modest by revolutionary standards. But many unresolved questions of east European boundaries and nationalities that were in the cauldron of World War I remain: the very existence of Yugoslavia; the border between Hungary and Romania and the existence of significant Hungarian and Romanian minorities across that border; the separation of Soviet Moldavia from Romania; the boundary between Greece and Albania, still contested, although the contest has not been articulated and manifested itself for many years. For the first time in decades, the costs of a struggle over these issues no longer include Soviet and U.S. fears that it will embroil the two superpowers. With that restraint removed, the danger of such conflicts is heightened. The benefits—the settlement of the issues in dispute—remain unaltered. The costs have diminished. The risk of localized war has grown. So, too, has the opportunity for negotiation.

The cost of raising old issues has fallen with the collapse of the Cold War institutions and the old Soviet Union. Negotiation is preferable to war, at least according to the international interaction game. If the dangerous conditions of the prisoner's dilemma can be averted, then negotiation is the likely resolution—not war. How can the risks of the prisoner's dilemma be avoided? One way is for the countries facing such threats to build their own limited military capabilities. Nations with sufficient strength to allay doubts that they can defend themselves are nations that can induce rivals to negotiate. We saw that clearly in the discussion of chapter 4 and in the evidence regarding the frequency of war before and after 1661. Prospects of new institutions will make negotiation even more attractive. The emergence of liberal democratic governments facilitates the articulation of domestic opposition to the use of force. If such opposition is one-sided (as is possible with regard to the differences between Greece and Albania), then there is a grave danger of violence. But if the domestic political costs for using force are high for both principals in a dispute, then negotiation or the status quo are more likely equilibria than violent ones.

The end of the Cold War does not signal the complete collapse of the post–World War II international system. Two states dominated two spheres of influence in the past, with many nations in neither sphere. Today, one nation remains hegemonic over its former sphere of influence and stands as an exemplar for many recently departed from the Soviet sphere. The United States is well positioned to encourage negotiated resolutions of disputes if it can expand its sphere of influence to incorporate more of the zones of confrontation emerging in the new world. The United States might be better able to play this role in any Arab-Israeli disputes of the future.

Key Arab states, including Saudi Arabia, the Gulf states, Syria, and Egypt have seen at first hand in the Iraq-Kuwait war of 1990 the willingness of the United States and other nations in the world to make a genuine commitment in support of their interests. The Israelis, too, have seen this magnitude of U.S. commitment to Arab security for the first time. This commitment may encourage the Israelis to rethink their own strategy for protecting their welfare. It raises the prospect that Israeli access to future U.S. support will be less reliable than it has been in the past.

No longer must the United States rely solely on Israel to promote and protect vital U.S. interests in the region. Now the United States enjoys a special relationship with the most critical Arab states, a relationship forged in the desert sun, one likely, after the Iraq-Kuwait crisis, to provide the United States with a rare chance to make peace between the Arabs and the Israelis.

Five factors have precluded such a peace in the past:

1. When push came to shove, the United States had no alternative but to support Israel. There was no other way to protect U.S. interests in containing terrorism, providing intelligence, and preventing the proliferation of weapon systems of massive destruction to hard-line states in the Middle East.

2. Israel felt free to adopt an uncompromising position toward the Palestinians because of its confidence that the United States would not and could not look elsewhere for support.

3. The critical Arab states did not trust the United States to protect Arab interests beyond the Persian Gulf or to take seriously Arab concern over Palestinian claims.

4. Key Arab states saw the PLO as an essential element of any settlement with Israel.

5. The Soviet Union engaged in superpower competition with the United States for influence over the Arab world.

All of these elements have been challenged. Since the rapprochement between the United States and the former Soviet Union, the post–Cold War world has produced profound realignments in the Middle East. In 1990 the United States began forging a stronger relationship with Saudi Arabia. For the first time, the Saudis accepted the presence of large numbers of foreign troops on their territory and acknowledged that the U.S. presence might have to persist for a long time to guarantee stability in the region. The Saudis saw the consequences of supporting radical Arab action: Hussein had betrayed them.

U.S. access to military bases in Saudi Arabia may break Israel's monopoly as the sole reliable ally for advancing U.S. interests in that part of the world. Surely the Israeli government understands this. The Israelis, therefore, are more likely to respond to U.S. encouragement of a genuine resolution of the Palestinian issues than at any time in the past. As the U.S.-Israeli relationship evolves, Israelis may become the beneficiaries of newfound flexibility on the part of critical Arab leaders and on the part of their own leadership.

When Yassir Arafat embraced Saddam Hussein's aggression, he alienated Arab leaders who had bankrolled him in the past. In doing so, Arafat may have unwittingly opened the way for the Saudis and others to support a Middle East peace conference that excludes him and that accepts alternative representation for the Palestinian people. Excluding Arafat and the PLO provides the Saudis and others with the opportunity to accept a fundamental premise of the Israeli government: legitimate Palestinian representation could shut out radical Palestinian factions.

The Iraqi invasion of Kuwait lay the foundation on which trust between Arab governments and the United States has risen. It made the Israelis realize that the United States no longer needs to depend only on them in the Middle East. It encouraged key Arab leaders to reassess their views of Yassir Arafat and the PLO. It made possible U.S. encouragement of a Middle East peace process that includes the reformed Soviet Union and all other responsible parties. What is more, it gave the United States the flexibility to exert credible pressure on the Arabs and the Israelis. The end of the Soviet sphere of influence has ensured both sides that they must either count on the United States for protection or forge a new order that puts one or the other side at loggerheads with the United States. Such a new order is unlikely to ensure peace without increased reliance on the United States by both sides.

In the Middle East, where Arab states do not provide regular means for their people to articulate domestic political opposition, it is helpful for a third party to foster negotiation. The changed position of the United States places it in a unique position in this regard. Wherever disputes arise in which at least one party faces low political costs for using force, it is imperative that conventional military capabilities be large enough to induce negotiation or that a third party, like the United States, act to induce negotiation. In the future world, the frontiers of violence will shift, and the prospects (and perhaps the responsibilities) of the United States to promote negotiation will greatly increase. If U.S. leaders are prepared to look outward, then the prospect is real that the world will enter a new era of Pax Americana.

Chapter 9

War's Reason and the National Interest

Goya, in his etchings on the Peninsular War, raised two vital questions about international affairs, about war in particular: "Con razón o sin ella?" and "Contra el bien general?" Do national policies follow a course of reason or not, and if so, are the consequences of foreign policy choices contrary to the general welfare, or do they advance that welfare? Now we dare to proffer answers to those inquiries.

We have proposed a theory of the reasoning process that might account for foreign policy choices and have found that theory supported by the record of history. From this, we infer that international interactions follow a path of reasoned judgment. Even war is waged "with reason" rather than without it. But we cannot as readily conclude that the process of strategic calculation necessarily enhances the general welfare of the citizenry embroiled in warfare. Our theory indicates that there are recurring opportunities for states to choose carefully and reasonably paths of action that, nevertheless, lead to undesired results. The selection of such inferior outcomes is motivated by a desire to enhance the national welfare and yet sometimes fails to do so. What knowledge or insights from our exploration might be applied to international affairs?

THE CONFRONTATION BETWEEN DOMESTIC AND INTERNATIONAL IMPERATIVES

Scholars commonly characterize international affairs as divorced from the give and take of domestic politics. In the dominant realist or neorealist view, foreign policy elites interact on a plane of high politics in which matters of national survival, sovereignty, and security prevail over petty thoughts of domestic advantage from this or that course of action. If such a view of the world is correct, then, according to our analysis, the elimination of secrecy and misunderstanding would also mean the perpetuation of peace and harmony.

To be sure, the richest coalitions or best-endowed individual nations would grow richer, and the poorest poorer. They would do so without bloodshed. Only the opportunities fostered by an advantageous surge in technology, by the discovery or development of a valued resource, or by other means of differentially beneficial growth would upset the fundamental progression among states. Those with the greatest leverage would inevitably do better in negotiation, and those without such leverage would pay the price. The realist world might well be a peaceful world, albeit many would have difficulty describing it as a just world.

The historical evidence we have adduced regarding international intercourse over the past two centuries provides no support for the general outlines of the realpolitik perspective. If minimizing the threat of war is what is meant by the general welfare, then a realist world might enhance that welfare. But we probably are not free to choose the design we might wish for the world. Empirically, our study indicates that the world is not as the realists portray it.

In the constrained, domestic version of the international interaction game, domestic imperatives, rather than international considerations alone, play a prominent role in foreign policy choices. The domestic theory does not ensure peace and harmony even in a world devoid of secrecy, misperception, and misjudgment. Even in such a world, reasoned choices tied to a desire to maximize national welfare can nevertheless lead to war and all of its horrors. Whether the possibility is compatible with the general welfare, el bien general, is something to be pondered. That the theory and the empirical record can support the notion of war even under specific conditions of fully informed, reasoned judgment necessitates that we contemplate the merits, if any, of a view that promotes peace for its own sake and the meaning of such a peace in the context of normal notions of justice. A world in which no war is justifiable is a world in which tyrants are free to take everything from well-intentioned pacifists. We are reminded that the domestic theory highlights the prospects of violence and even war initiated by doves.

International affairs have been assessed here from the competing perspectives of realism and domestic politics. The implications for action of alternative foreign policy goals have been evaluated under the assumption that those goals emanate from international or domestic circumstances. This one variation in the origin of interests in our two interpretations of the international interaction game has produced fundamentally different predictions about international affairs. The confrontation of these two theories with the historical record of European relations during the past two centuries points toward the endorsement of the domestic variant and the abandonment of the realpolitik interpretation. This is the broadest significant conclusion to be drawn from our investigation. Realism is difficult to sustain if one believes the structure we have posited is sensible and the evidence we have adduced is meaningful.

Most damaging to the realist point of view is our derivation of an impossibility theorem. With interactions structured as in the realist version of the game we have proposed, an acquiescence by one nation to the demand of another nation is an impossibility. This is true regardless of the beliefs held by the rivals, regardless of the initial demand made by one of the states, and regardless of initial endowments of capabilities, coalitional support, propensities to take risks, or anything else. Whatever one nation seeks of another, in the realist perspective of our game there is always a potential counterdemand that will lead the adversary to believe it is better off making that counterdemand than giving in to the initial request of its rival. After the fact, to be sure, one or another party may learn that it has made a mistaken proposal, but that only is to say that an alternative and superior counterdemand could have been made if better information had been available. That such a counterdemand exists cannot be in question in the realpolitik version of the game. This is true because the actor moving second can always make a proposal that will steer the interaction into a negotiated resolution. Negotiation, in which no side gets everything it seeks, is always better for the state making the second demand than acquiescence, for the party giving in gets nothing and gives up everything asked of it.

Our data include 109 instances of acquiescence. Most of those instances satisfy even our most conservative, most stringent definition of that concept. Yet even one correctly categorized event that is an acquiescence is a critical challenge to the realist viewpoint. If demands are determined solely within the context of the international structure of interactions, not even one mistaken acquiescence is possible. Either realism is wrong, or our proposed structure misrepresents the world. The latter is entirely possible. Realist theories provide little guidance as to the structure of interactions between states. We claim only that we believe the structure we have proposed is a sensible and meaningful framework from which to represent the essential features of international affairs, whether from the realist perspective or not. The evidence seems to encourage us in that view.

The acquiescence impossibility theorem is not the only result we have advanced that leads us to question the realist (or neorealist) perspective. None of the deductions derived from that variant of the game have been supported in the empirical record across the 707 dyadic interactions that constitute our data set. Nor was much encouragement for realism found in our analysis of common systemic realist (or neorealist) hypotheses.

The evidence we have amassed with regard to the domestic/constrained interpretation of the international interaction game stands in sharp contrast to the predictions of realist theory. We have deduced approximately twenty-five propositions from the domestic version of the game. These propositions, which we will review in greater depth, address questions of behavior under full-information and imperfect-information conditions. They focus on conditions that promote negotiation, the status quo, capitulation, acquiescence, or war. They address directions of expected associations and specific functional forms of relationships. In each case, the central tendency of the evidence has been consistent with the deductions. Yet the deduced propositions are often counterintuitive and are always derived completely independently of the evidence used to evaluate their efficacy. Each is the product of axiomatic reasoning from the assumptions set out in chapter 2.

The domestic, constrained perspective, with its emphasis on domestic imperatives in foreign policy making, highlights strategic reasoning coupled with the prospect of inefficient goal selection, at least as evaluated from an internationalist point of view. Under the imperatives of domestic politics, even full information is not sufficient to guarantee negotiation or the status quo as the equilibrium outcome of foreign affairs. As Morgenthau has observed:

> No government that wants to stay in power or simply retain the respect of its people can afford to give up publicly part of what it had declared at the outset to be just and necessary, to retreat from a position initially held, to concede at least the partial justice of the other side's claims. Heroes, not horsetraders, are the idols of public opinion. Public opinion, while dreading war, demands that its diplomats act as heroes who do not yield in the face of the enemy, even at the risk of war, and condemns as weaklings and traitors those who yield, albeit only halfway, for the sake of peace. (1973, 532)

Morgenthau's depiction of the role of public opinion is stated in normative terms and is supported by our analysis as a normative claim. He condemns the tendency, especially among democracies, to drift away from realist precepts. If the world were as described in his realist perspective, then war and all of its evils might be minimized, if not avoided altogether. With full information, violence would never occur. But a central conclusion of our study is that the world operates as in the constrained model, in which domestic imperatives interact with international structural forces to shape foreign policy outcomes.

This positivist statement, however, is not without some support from a normative perspective. Even in a world in which domestic politics shapes foreign policy demands, nevertheless with uniformly distributed preferences and full information, more than 60 percent of international interactions would be expected to culminate in negotiation or the maintenance of the status quo. Under conditions of full information and uniformly distributed preferences, 98.5 percent of all interactions would end without violence, although many such instances would represent acquiescence by one nation to the objectives of another. Cooperation rather than conflict would still remain the predominant relationship between self-interested states. Cooperation apparently prevails, despite anarchy in the international system and possible chaos in the domestic process that creates foreign policy objectives.

In the realist world, imperfect information can only encourage violence. Incorrect beliefs about the intentions of rivals can only steer disputes away from negotiation (or the status quo) and toward the blackmail inherent in a capitulation or the tragedy inherent in a war. Incorrect beliefs, secrecy, misperception, misjudgment, and miscalculation are routine features of human intercourse. In that sense, a realist world could be a dangerous world indeed. The domestically constrained world, however, leads to more sanguine conclusions about an environment in which information is limited and perceptions or judgments are frequently mistaken. To be sure, under conditions of imperfect information, nations may mistakenly stumble into wars and capitulations. But they may also "mistakenly" avoid war and stumble into negotiation or other peaceful solutions to their differences. Thus, when domestic factors play a crucial role in shaping foreign policy demands, the opportunity for uncertainty to ameliorate relations between states is a boon not available in a world controlled by realist imperatives.

CENTRAL PREDICTIONS OF THE INTERNATIONAL INTERACTION GAME

In evaluating the international interaction game, we have only scraped the surface of possible deductions. Although war has been a natural focus of our attention, this is a book about how nations relate to each other generally. We have addressed enduring puzzles, such as why democracies do not appear to fight one another but fight readily with other states; what features are required for a war to reach cataclysmic proportions, defined in terms of death and destruction, and to what extent those features distinguish wars that yield fundamental changes in the international system; and what conditions are necessary and sufficient for nations to cooperate with one another despite self-interests. We have suggested solutions to each of these and many other theoretical or empirical puzzles. In virtually every case the proposed solution has satisfied the following formula: first the solution has been formally deduced and proved in the context of our theory, then the hypothesized solution has been submitted to empirical scrutiny through the analysis of the historical record. We have endeavored to be explicit about the expectations in our empirical tests so that the conditions for falsification are clear. Sometimes we have also tried to illustrate our theoretically deduced solution with an extended historical example.

Our criteria for evaluating evidence have been weaker than we might have hoped, albeit generally higher than is conventional practice in political science. High-quality data do not yet exist for the variables of greatest importance to a theory such as ours. This lack is neither a surprise nor the fault of those who have generously provided us with data. Rather, the tools of measurement in political science have primarily been applied to factors that are not so important in our theory. There are no broad data sets of beliefs, values, and expectations in international affairs.

We think it was more important to test the theory with crude approximations than to leave it stated only in terms of its logical consistency. There was no special reason to believe that the data and indicators we used would yield encouraging results if we were far off the mark. That virtually every empirical evaluation of the domestic version of the international interaction game supports the tested relation in terms of direction, statistical significance, and shape gives us hope that the theory provides a foundation for future theoretical and empirical research, for future refinements in the structure of the game and in the empirical evaluation of its core concepts.

Our investigation has encouraged us to look upon international relations and foreign policy in a new way. Our deductions and empirical assessments have led us to several unexpected conclusions. Before summarizing the distribution of evidence for the theory set out here, we think it is useful to review briefly some of our central conclusions.

Our initial agnosticism about a domestic political perspective has not survived our investigation. We are now firmly convinced that domestic political affairs are a crucial precursor to foreign policy interactions. The optimistic views of foreign policy reflected in notions that domestic rivalry ends at national borders cannot be supported by the evidence we have uncovered. Embedded within this conviction are several detailed expectations about behavior.

A necessary condition for war under imperfect information, for instance, is that at least one party to a dispute must believe strongly that its adversary does not possess a credible retaliatory capability.[1] Yet with full information about international interactions, the initiator of war is necessarily the very state that is not prepared to retaliate if attacked.

Our proposed game structure and assumptions imply the necessary and sufficient conditions for eight different foreign policy outcomes. We found that five of these outcome events—Nego, SQ, Acq$_A$, Acq$_B$, and War$_A$—can arise even under full-information conditions provided the demands originate through some domestic political process rather than through the international interaction game. If the realist view holds and thus demands do emanate from the structure of the situation, then only negotiation or the status quo can occur if there is full information, and acquiescence cannot occur under any circumstances.

The constrained foreign policy viewpoint, with its attentiveness to domestic antecedents of foreign policy choices, encourages an assessment of norms and institutions that help foster cooperation by restricting the possible preferences that can be held over outcomes. With this in mind, we evaluated four prospective norms of action. We found that the conciliatory norm of dovish interaction guarantees peaceful, cooperative, or harmonious relations if there is no uncertainty about the dovish intentions of rivals. Yet we found that even doves are prone to violence if they are uncertain about the intentions of their foes. Indeed, weak doves are apparently more inclined to initiate violence— they have less to lose—than are their stronger counterparts. We also found that if leaders know that their adversaries are prepared to retaliate if attacked, then this knowledge, too, guarantees cooperation or harmony. Like the conciliatory norm, the self-defense or retaliatory norm also begins to break down under uncertainty. We suggested, however, that detecting the readiness of a rival to retaliate is easier than detecting its dovish preferences. This relative availability of knowledge is one possible explanation for the steep decline in the incidence of warfare in Europe following the introduction of peacetime

---

1. Or side A must believe that its adversary believes that A will not retaliate if attacked.

standing armies and other technological innovations in the mid-seventeenth century.

In contrast to the conciliatory and self-defense norms, a norm of reciprocation—do unto others as they have done unto you—is less likely to ensure cooperation. Such a norm can, but need not, lead to cooperative relations between foes engaged in an indefinite sequence of prisoner's dilemmas. The historical record of European interactions does not encourage confidence in the reciprocity norm. Nor does our theory or the evidence encourage a belief that conservative inclinations to preserve the status quo necessarily enhance the prospects of cooperation and the avoidance of violence.

To be sure, we have found two norms that would ensure peace if universally applied, but we have found no norms that guarantee peace if they are observed probabilistically. If everyone knows that everyone is a dovish conciliator or if everyone knows that everyone is a self-defender, then cooperation or harmony will ensue. Yet if everyone knows that everyone is *either* a dovish conciliator *or* a self-defender but cannot tell one from the other, then cooperative or harmonious interactions are not ensured. In such a world even doves may act aggressively and begin wars. Still, some norms, like the self-defense norm, unravel more slowly than other norms in the face of uncertainty. For some, like doves, uncertainty and weakness virtually guarantee violence. For others, violence is only possible in the absence of weakness.

Some political institutions help foster beliefs, albeit not certainty, about the dovish inclinations of certain states. We have given considerable attention to the domestic political constraint term in our theory because it is just such a feature. Doing so has suggested solutions to long-standing puzzles about the behavior of liberal democracies. The theory leads to explanations of why democracies are unlikely to fight with one another but are not unlikely to fight with nondemocratic states. The explanation hinges on beliefs about the magnitude of expected domestic costs for using force. Democratic institutions are visible signs that the state in question is likely to face high political costs for using force in its diplomacy. When both sides are democracies, each actor is likely to be dovish, to see the other as dovish, and to be encouraged to pursue negotiated solutions to differences. However, if one party is not a democracy, then the democratic adversary faces a greater danger of being exploited. To avoid this, the democracy is likely to launch a preemptive strike. These and other deductions about the impact of democratic institutions and high constraints on action are developed theoretically and borne out by empirical assessments.

The investigation has also been attentive to a variety of core concepts from balance-of-power theory and from the theories of hegemonic war and power transition. We have deduced propositions that indicate that both parties to a rivalry must believe their chances for success in war are greater than .5 in order for a high-stakes, high-costs war to ensue. Yet we have also shown that system-transforming consequences can devolve from a low-stakes contest in which there was little or no expectation of overturning the international order. We have found little support for balance-of-power notions but considerable support for a modified version of the theory of power transition. In each case, the conditions that are conducive to wars of various types have been found to be consistent with the expectations of the international interaction game.

We turn now to an evaluation of the general reliability of the theory we have proposed. Our propositions have addressed an unusually broad collection of issues in the areas of international relations and foreign policy. Not every proposition has been tested, but most have. In some instances, when the theory presents an existence proof or the specification of the possibility or impossibility that something can happen, a statistical test is inappropriate or not required. For instance, we have indicated that under the realpolitik variant of the game, acquiescence is impossible. Nations cannot stumble into such an outcome even by mistake. This rare circumstance in which even a single case of acquiescence is a contradiction of the proposition cannot be due to any misspecification of the predictive circumstances. Because the event is held to be impossible, its observation is sufficient to place the realpolitik version of the game in doubt.

Other propositions have not been tested simply because we do not have enough observations to evaluate expectations. We have not, for example, tested the domestic proposition regarding the necessary and sufficient conditions under full information for acquiescence by nation *A* to a demand from *B*, although we have tested the comparable proposition with regard to nation *B*. The reason is that we have only eight cases in which *A* appears to have acquiesced to *B*. These cases are generally consistent with the theoretical expectations of the domestic interpretation of the game, but the number is so small that we are reluctant to attach any significance one way or the other to the pattern of behavior.

For a subset of propositions it was appropriate to undertake a statistical analysis. We review here whether the test was strongly supportive, moderately supportive, or weakly supportive of the theory or at odds with it. Although our data do not represent a random sample of events, we use the strength of statistical significance as a heuristic device for evaluating the confidence one might place in the relation between theory and observation. Strong support is inferred if the theoretically expected relation is observed and the significance level indicates that the relation occurred by chance with no more than a .01 probability. Moderate backing for the proposition is implied by a probability level greater than .01 but less than or equal to .05. Weak support is attached to statistical results with significance greater than .05 but less than .15. Finally, a relation opposite to that predicted by the theory is taken as a contradiction of it. Occasionally a proposition calls for results to be insignificantly different from zero (as in the proposition that the intercept relating stakes to expected costs in war is not different from zero). In such cases, the degree of support is inferred by the confidence we can have that the result is not statistically different from the predicted value of zero.

What have we found? To answer this question we organize the propositions in terms of the degree to which the evidence is supportive of expectations derived from the game. We have been able to test about twenty deductions from the domestic variant of the game and all of the propositions from the realpolitik version. In the case of thirteen propositions, one or more tests offer overall strong support for the domestic variant of the international interaction game. Included among these are predictions of the incidence of BIGWAR given full information, as well as full-information predictions regarding acquiescence by B and negotiated outcomes. Strong backing for the theory is not limited to propositions under conditions of full information. We also find strong support for the domestic version of the theory in terms of several outcomes when information is imperfect. In our assessment of cooperative behavior, for instance, we find strong justification for the claims of the self-defense norm. The evidence also provides a strong foundation for the proposition that democracies do not fight one another because of their unusually high domestic political constraints against using force.

A variety of detailed predictions about wars of varying sizes and consequences and produced under varying circumstances also find strong empirical support. The inconsequential role that values for the status quo play in fostering or avoiding war is also found to be strongly reinforced by the evidence, as are our predictions with regard to the relation between the stakes in war and the associated costs. We have also found strong encouragement in the unusually significant association between our theoretically based estimation of the probability of war and the likelihood of using force. This result reinforces findings from our earlier, decision-theoretic analyses and helps provide a cumulative bridge between those earlier results and the current investigation.

Our definition of strong support greatly exceeds conventional political science standards. That so many results comply with that very demanding standard despite the crudeness of our operational indicators is encouraging. Relaxing our requirements just a bit and accepting instead the more conventional notion of statistical significance ($P \le$ .05) brings further encouragement. How many additional propositions can we say are supported by the evidence if we use the conventional standard?

Because some of our propositions have been subjected to multiple tests, some listed as enjoying strong support might also be categorized as having only moderate support with other tests. For instance, the basic war theorem is strongly consistent with the historical record when the dependent variable is BIGWAR but is moderately associated with the evidence for the broader category of general reciprocated violence, WAR. We mention here, then, just those propositions not already discussed in the context of tests providing strong support for the theory.

The basic status quo theorem, which identifies the necessary and sufficient conditions with full information for the maintenance of the status quo, just fails to meet the threshold for strong support. It is classified as being moderately backed, with a significance level of .016 for both the logit analysis and a cross-tabulation. In a similar vein, our cooperation proposition regarding negotiation among doves with full information finds moderate backing in the historical record, as does the proposition that with imperfect information, pacific doves are increasingly likely to initiate violence the lower their probability of success. As with the basic status quo theorem, this result just fails to satisfy our criterion for strong support, with the attained level of statistical significance being .015. The significance seems noteworthy to us, for the proposition appears counterintuitive and represents a severe test of the theory. The companion proposition that predicts acquiescence or a gamble by dove *B* under imperfect-information conditions is weakly supported by the evidence. Virtually every proposition from the domestic account of international affairs finds at least some overall strong backing or just fails to meet the .01 significance threshold to qualify for our highest standard of evaluation.

None of the evidence for the realpolitik deductions from the theory is consistent with expectations. None of the results for the domestic interpretation of international interactions are inconsistent with the theory. Only a few deductions from that version of the theory are weakly supported empirically; most greatly exceed conventional standards of statistical significance. Several propositions involve severe tests of the theory. Some evaluations are so demanding that specific deduced functional forms are tested and backed by the evidence. Some of these functional forms are so nonobvious that without their revelation through the theoretical structure, we would never have thought to look for them. In all of this we find encouragement.

FUTURE DIRECTIONS

In spite of the encouragement we find in the evidence, we are mindful of many shortcomings in our theory. We hope that future research will build upon and enhance the basic structure of international interactions proposed here. Although we believe that structure captures the essence of such interactions, we recall our own description of the game as a skeletal structure, a mere scaffold. The game has not addressed such questions as timing and dynamics. Nor have we evaluated nation types—doves, hawks, self-defenders, and so forth—on a continuum. Rather, we have viewed them as simple dichotomies. We expect that considerable refinement can be obtained by viewing types and outcomes as continuous.

Another weakness of our theory is its treatment of negotiated outcomes. These have been viewed as having a predictable result: each side expects to get the mean of the competing demands weighted by the coalitional and national support that can be mustered to advance the proposed outcomes. To be sure, such a weighted outcome is not inconsistent with common sense or common experience, but neither is it an immutable solution to a bargaining problem. We have treated negotiation in this way as an analytic convenience. Much excellent research is being done on the problems of bargaining, and many alternative bargaining models have been developed and proposed. None seems to hold a special place as an ideal generalized representation of bargaining. We have been guided here by our desire to derive testable results from our theory. But there is surely much to be gained by developing a more sophisticated view of negotiation than we have proposed, even if such a view is not as readily evaluated empirically.

We hope this volume will encourage the development of more refined tools of measurement. We have confined our modeling technology to the limitations of current tools for assessing the evidence. In the absence of data with which to approximate continuous outcomes, we felt it made more sense to build a theory of discrete outcomes—a theory that could be falsified in practice as well as in principle.

In the end, the most important lesson of any research lies in what it uncovers as work still to be done. For us, many old questions remain unanswered, and many new questions are ready to be posed. We feel some comfort nonetheless in the belief that we have at least elucidated some important puzzles of international affairs.

The course we set for ourselves at the outset was an ambitious one. Whatever the merits or failings of our endeavor, it has brought us many unexpected and unplanned questions and suggested many unexpected and surprising answers. The research has changed the way we look at international affairs and foreign policy. Our changed views recall for us Saint Augustine's dictum on science: "We should not hold rashly an opinion in a Scientific matter, so that we may not come to hate later whatever truth may reveal to us, out of love for our own error."

Appendix 1

Measurement of the Variables

Axiomatic theory, if properly applied, ensures the proof of logically true propositions. Logical proof, however, does not guarantee that the propositions reveal anything of interest about the world in which we live. A logically true but empirically trivial or irrelevant theory is of little interest. Consequently, we are committed to employing empirical tests of the international interaction game when we can. Indeed, we are willing to be risk acceptant in our empirical strategy rather than abandon testing.

Not every proposition from our game requires a full empirical specification of its every term. Some propositions of the theory can be tested without evaluating the actual expected utility components at each terminal node. For instance, we claim that nations that are fond of their mutual status quo can wage war on one another. We can safely assume that nations are satisfied with the status quo when they are closely allied. Yet satisfaction with the status quo does not guarantee its maintenance or even peaceful relations among the satisfied states, as we prove in chapter 3. Therefore, an implication of the theory is that the conditions for war can arise between allies. The proposition requires only that we show that at least one such war has occurred. Many have: this is what makes having a theoretical explanation of the phenomenon interesting. Chapter 7 provides a detailed account of the diplomacy surrounding such an event—the Seven Weeks' War—thereby providing evidence for a deduction of the game without having to measure all of the variables required to derive the logical proof. Similarly, we deduce that in the realpolitik version of the game, acquiescence by one side to the demands of the other is an impossibility under any and all information conditions. To evaluate that proposition, then, we need only observe whether nations ever acquiesce. In chapter 3 we address that question by looking at the incidence of such events. No other variable is required to evaluate the proposition.

Still, many propositions can be evaluated only by appealing directly to observations of relevant variables in the game, and observation requires the development of instruments for approximating some constituents of the theory. The international interaction game implies a variety of testable propositions and clearly defines the theoretical variables of interest in each case. Unfortunately, few high-quality, reliable indicators of key components of the theory currently exist, so all of our empirical tests are necessarily preliminary and tentative. One hope of ours is that the theory will sufficiently interest researchers that appropriate data sets for evaluating beliefs and expectations will be developed. In the meantime, we are prepared to find ourselves out on an empirical limb by using coarse instruments in specifying fundamental variables.

The inadequacy of the available data necessitates focusing in the empirical tests on the extent to which real-world behavior manifests a central tendency to be supportive of our deductions. At this juncture, more stringent tests are simply not possible. Even for evaluating propositions that stipulate necessary and sufficient conditions, our standards are probabilistic. Our empirical concern is, then, with the tendency for the data to point in the direction of the propositions with regard to sign and statistical significance and, when appropriate, with their tendency to support the deduced shape of relations (as in several propositions in chapter 4). This last criterion is, we hasten to add, stringent by normal political science standards, even if the other two are conventional. Should our coarse measures fail to yield results that are statistically supportive of significant central tendencies, then we will consider the theory falsified.

None of the tests do or can fully exploit the potential predictive capabilities of the game, for none of them adequately assess beliefs, uncertainties, utilities for outcomes or costs, or probabilities. But at least the tests use systematic, universal indicators of these concepts, so we avoid any hint of making the data fit the theory by evaluating variables in different ways for different cases.

DOMAIN OF DATA

Most of the empirical evaluations reported in this book draw on data for dyadic relations in Europe between 1815 and 1970, although nothing in the theory suggests a European focus. Indeed, the theory is proposed as a general explanation of international interactions anywhere and at any time. However, practical considerations of resource constraints, availability, and reliability dictate our empirical focus. It will be useful if our tests are replicated on alternative data for Europe, on comparable data for other parts of the world, or on data from other historical periods.

To be eligible for inclusion in the data set, a state had to be sovereign and physically in Europe (according to Small-Singer criteria) or sufficiently active in European diplomatic affairs to influence calculations about European issues. By these criteria, we include Turkey but not, for instance, Iran, its neighbor. The United States is also considered part of the European system from 1916, for it became continually engaged in European affairs and, we believe, influenced European beliefs about foreign policy choices. The year is arbitrary. Our benchmark was the sinking of the *Lusitania,* but one might reasonably argue for 1914 or 1898 or even 1776. Likewise, one might contend that the post–World War I isolationism argues for the exclusion of the United States until its declaration of war against Germany in 1941. Although undoubtedly an important issue for those primarily concerned with U.S. policy, the precise date is a quibble in terms of our broader concerns. Alternative dates are unlikely to affect appreciably any of the empirical findings, nor would they influence at all any of our propositions, which are derived purely from the structure of the game and not from the data.

The data set consists of 469 events in which a nation A and a nation B engaged in a dispute with one another. When, for instance, A engaged B, C, and D in a broad dispute, we include in the list of dyads only cases involving at least one or the other party at the outset of the dispute. We exclude third-party participation. Sometimes only one dyad is listed for a large conflict, sometimes many. We have tried to be responsive to the reasonable criticism that we underrepresented the world wars in earlier analyses. At the same time, we insist on general criteria that reflect ex ante circumstances, not ex post interpretations of history. For the Seven Weeks' War, for instance, we include Prussia's war with each of seven German states as separate dyads because each state made its own explicit choice to defend Austria's position or Prussia's. Most, but not all, of the German Diet members declared that they would join whichever side did not first use force. When push came to shove, most German states sided with Austria, but Mecklenburg-Schwerin sided with Prussia. They had perfectly good and straightforward geopolitical reasons for doing so, but then, that is part of the point of this theory.

Our coding runs into an important statistical issue. Many events consist of multiple dyads in which choices by some dyads are not independent of choices by other dyads. To the extent that the data violate the normal requirement that observations be independent of one another, the data are biased in favor of the realist perspective. The absence of independence between cases is a product of endogenous choices within the international system. Nation C fights B, knowing that *A* has already chosen to fight, thereby inflating *C*'s chances of winning and the value of the demands *C* can hope to attain. *C*'s calculation is precisely part of the realist argument. If we fail to find support for the realist argument, the reader should realize that we have probably overstated the true level of support for that perspective.

The data used here represent the European subset of the militarized dispute data developed by the Correlates of War Project and by Charles Gochman and Zeev Maoz in particular. Daniel Jones of the Correlates of War Project at the University of Michigan is refining the disputes data, adding events as appropriate and eliminating or altering components of some of the events in the data set used here. Conscious that the data are at an early stage of development, we wish to be cautious and tentative in our assessments and ask the reader to bear in mind our view that noisy estimates are better than none at all. Because the errors in the data are unlikely to be systematically biased in favor of our theory, the errors should operate to depress relations.

In addition, our data set includes 238 observations consisting of randomly paired European dyads. To qualify for possible inclusion in this sample, the members of the dyad could not have engaged one another in a dispute during the specified year. These 238 observations serve as a means of estimating decisions to live with the status quo. They constitute a representative random sample of the nonevents so often excluded from empirical analyses of international interactions and yet so important in shaping strategic decisions. We can be confident that the sample reflects the population of events within a 95 percent confidence interval.

Sometimes the data analysis includes all 707 observations or as close to that as data availability permits. At other times, when the proposition in question presumes that a particular node in the game tree has been reached or when some other theory is being imposed on the game through the use of the assumptions of the theory, it is appropriate to pare down the data to the relevant subset of cases. When dealing with the escalation of a dispute, our data reflect the population of events in Europe over the time span investigated. When discussing the propositions, which encompass the full game tree, we include all 707 observations. Including them all creates a potential complication.

The 469 disputatious interactions constitute the population—or nearly so—of such events according to those who assembled the data set on militarized disputes. The 238 nondisputing dyads in our extended data set are but a small—though representative—sample of all such pairs of nations in Europe. How are we to interpret statistical results that seemingly weight actual events much more heavily than the more common nonevents?

Fortunately, the problem we encounter, though unusual in political science, is an everyday occurrence for medical researchers, for whom there is a well-known simple solution. Our mix of sample and population is equivalent to a medical research design that compares the population of patients with a particular diagnosis to a sample of healthy individuals. Clearly, there are too many healthy individuals, or nonconflicting dyads, to study all of them, but there are not too many patients, or disputatious European dyads, to evaluate the population of that category. The danger is that the disproportionate representation of the two subsets may distort the empirical findings. The solution is straightforward.

Christopher Achen addresses this question and shows that "the odds ratio (or its log, the 'logit') is not affected by the irrelevant pairs" (1990, 13). A proof is provided in his footnotes. So long as we utilize logit analysis for evaluating propositions that include the two subsets of data, there is no problem, even though one subset approximates the population of observations and the other is a small random sample of another set of representative cases.

DEPENDENT VARIABLES

The militarized dispute data set is coded on a five-point scale for nation A and for nation B. A sample of the coding that shows the dyads analyzed for the years of the two world wars is found in table A1.1. It is possible and even common for nation A to fall in a different category on the scale from nation B's. Four categories reflect variations in the qualitative characteristics of the disputes, and the fifth is a quantitative variant of the fourth. Although not perfectly matched to our needs, the militarized dispute data set comes very close to providing the information required to evaluate the events in terms of the terminal nodes of the international interaction game.

The first level comprises events in which the nation did nothing. Level 2 includes events in which a nation made a demand but took no subsequent action. For events at level 3 there was a threat (presumably accompanied by a demand that, if satisfied, would vitiate the threat) but no use of force. By level four, there is not only a threat to use force but the actual use of force. Level 5 includes those events in which a nation used sufficient force to satisfy the Small-Singer criteria for an interstate war. Level 5, then, is a quantitatively more stringent version of level 4.

Table A1.1
World War Dyads

1914			1939			1940		
Nation A	Nation B	Level	Nation A	Nation B	Level	Nation A	Nation B	Level
Austria-Hungary	Russia	5 5	Italy	France	2 4	Russia	Romania	4 1
Germany	Russia	5 5	Italy	Britain	2 4	Germany	Romania	4 1
Turkey	Russia	5 5	Russia	Estonia	4 1	Hungary	Romania	3 1
Austria-Hungary	Yugoslavia	5 5	Poland	Germany	5 5	Russia	Lithuania	4 1
Germany	Yugoslavia	5 5	France	Germany	5 5	Britain	Italy	5 5
Turkey	Yugoslavia	5 5	Britain	Germany	5 5	France	Italy	5 5
Austria-Hungary	Britain	5 5	Romania	Hungary	3 1	Switzerland	Germany	3 1
Germany	Britain	5 5	Romania	Germany	3 1	Greece	Italy	5 5
Turkey	Britain	5 5	Germany	Lithuania	3 1	Greece	Germany	5 5
Austria-Hungary	France	5 5	Italy	Yugoslavia	2 1	Russia	Latvia	4 4
Germany	France	5 5	Hungary	Yugoslavia	3 1	Russia	Estonia	4 1
Turkey	France	5 5	Italy	Albania	4 4	Italy	Yugoslavia	4 5
Austria-Hungary	Belgium	5 5	Italy	Germany	3 1	Germany	Yugoslavia	5 5
Germany	Belgium	5 5	Germany	Belgium	5 5	Hungary	Yugoslavia	4 5
Turkey	Belgium	5 5	Germany	Netherlands	5 5	Bulgaria	Yugoslavia	4 5
Germany	Norway	3 3	Switzerland	Germany	3 1	Italy	Britain	4 2
Britain	Netherlands	4 1	Germany	Denmark	5 5	Germany	Britain	5 2
Sweden	Germany	3 1	Germany	Norway	5 5	Hungary	Britain	4 2
Sweden	Russia	3 1	Germany	Sweden	5 1	Bulgaria	Britain	4 2
Sweden	France	3 1	Estonia	Poland	4 4			
Sweden	Britain	3 1	Russia	Latvia	4 1			
Germany	Denmark	4 3	Russia	Poland	4 4			
Portugal	Germany	4 4	Russia	Finland	5 5			

Table A1.2
Distribution of Actions by A and B

	Action by B					
Action by A	0	1	2	3	4	5
0	238	0	0	0	0	0
1	0	1	0	0	2	0
2	0	26	1	8	4	5
3	0	70	5	33	8	7
4	0	53	9	38	90	10
5	0	1	2	7	0	89

The five levels are coded separately for each nation in a dyad, so each falls at a different level. A could fall at level 1 and B into level 4—representing a capitulation by A in the context of the international interaction game—or A could fall at level 3 and B at level 3, representing a dispute settled by negotiation. Table A1.2 displays the distribution of cases by the category of action into which nation A and nation B fell.

Each combination of event levels fits into one and only one empirical specification of a terminal event from the international interaction game. We define our dependent variables in terms of these combinations of levels. The dependent variable BIGWAR is all cases in which A's and B's level of disputatiousness falls into level 5. WAR is all cases in which for both A and B the level is at least as high as 4. That is, BIGWAR is a subset of WAR. As indicated by the international interaction game, then, WAR encompasses all events in which there was the reciprocal use of force.

Negotiation, or Nego, is all cases in which the level for A is less than 4 and the level for B is less than 4, and the level for A and B is greater than zero, and A's level equals B's level. In other words, both sides made demands, and neither side used force. Acquiescence by B is defined as all cases in which A's level is greater than B's, and A's is less than 4. Acquiescence by A is all cases in which B's level is greater than A's, and B's is less than 4. Occasionally, when we wish to be more conservative in our definition of an acquiescence, we will refer only to cases in which A or B was at level 1 while the foe was at a level greater than 1 and less than 4 (and often specifically at level 3). In all cases of acquiescence or negotiation, no deaths occur. Capitulation by A is defined to be all cases in which A's level is less than

4, and B's is greater than 3, and a capitulation by B arises whenever B's level is less than 4 and A's is greater than 3.

The remaining 238 events not drawn from the militarized dispute data set are assigned to level 0: neither A nor B made a demand or threatened the other with punishment and so accepted the status quo. When the theoretical conditions required for the status quo to be the equilibrium outcome are met, we code a dummy variable called SQ as 1.0, coding it as zero otherwise. When the actual conflict category for A and B is zero, we categorize the actual outcome as maintenance of the status quo by coding a dummy variable called STATUS QUO as 1.0.

With these operational specifications in hand, we can codify the terminal event of each observation in our data set. There are 238 instances in which the status quo prevailed, 189 events that satisfy the criteria for WAR, 89 that satisfy the criteria for BIGWAR, 35 that satisfy the criteria for negotiation, 101 that satisfy the criteria for acquiescence by B, and only 8 that satisfy the criteria for acquiescence by A. In the data set, B capitulated 110 times, and A, 26 times.

INDEPENDENT VARIABLES

In chapter 2 we delineate the expected utility associated with each outcome of the game for each player. We begin by identifying the measurement procedure used to estimate each of the variables mentioned in table 2.2.

Utilities

In the theory proposed here, decision makers choose among constrained alternatives. The alternatives are assigned utilities—the value the decision maker attaches to the specified outcome—that are constrained by the probability of their arising. The utility estimates are an attempt to evaluate the intensity of preference for the alternatives. We have defined utilities across three outcomes: gaining one's demand, $U^i(\Delta_i)$; giving the other side its demand, $U^i(\Delta_j)$; and retaining the status quo, $U^i(SQ)$. Each terminal node of the game reflects the value of at least one of these outcomes and often more than one, and each terminal node specifies a particular set of constraints on the expected utility of the outcome: its utility (including associated costs when germane) discounted by the likelihood of reaching the relevant terminal node of the game and realizing the outcome.

At first blush one might conclude that estimating how much a given leader or set of leaders valued a given outcome is readily done for historical events. For instance, it seems reasonable from our contemporary vantage point to suggest that President Johnson must have greatly valued preserving South Vietnam as a noncommunist state or that President Nixon must have greatly valued the information gathered by the Watergate burglars. Each, after all, lost his presidency apparently as a direct consequence of the pursuit of the designated goal. But such a view of estimating utilities is wholly unacceptable. It relies on ex post knowledge of how things turned out. President Nixon may have thought Watergate was too trivial to jeopardize his presidency and realized its impact too late. President Johnson might have thought that preserving the South Vietnamese government was only moderately desirable and may not have anticipated the anguish it would cause in the United States or the eventual threat it would represent to his reelection. Knowing how things turned out can be a misleading basis for inferring back to the value of the outcome.

To estimate utilities for alternative outcomes correctly, we must not take advantage of information that could not have been known to the decision makers when they were choosing (Creasy 1851). Alas, we have yet to uncover a measurement procedure that simultaneously (1) ensures no dependence on hindsight; (2) requires no case by case, ad hoc judgments by researchers; (3) is fully replicable by any researcher; and (4) is truly a measure of utility. However, we have devised measures that satisfy (1) through (3) and that provide information we believe is highly correlated with (4).

In an ideal world, an indicator of utility would encompass all four points. When trying to understand the values or the motives of other people, it is usual to scrutinize their choices. Common sense suggests that doing so is the appropriate way to learn about intentions, perceptions, and expectations. This is, indeed, the foundation of the venerable case study method. But closely scrutinizing the details of each case runs the grave risk of being nonreproducible, highly dependent on the judgments of the individual researcher, and contaminated by post hoc knowledge of how things turned out. It is all too easy for such an approach to violate all four of the strictures we have stated. Consider how Attila's reputation suffers because his history was written by his enemies or how heroic Chinghis Khan is to Mongolians and how barbaric he is considered by many Westerners.

When studying contemporary foreign policy choices in what the policy community calls real time, a case study method is appropriate. In real time, analysts cannot know the outcome and therefore cannot unwittingly bias an assessment of goals through hindsight. What is

more, in real time they can pick the issues over which decisions have
to be made without the further danger of ex post contamination. Using
an ex ante method ensures that choices are made on the basis of what
seems important at the time, rather than what turned out to be important later. To recognize the problem imposed by ex post knowledge,
we have merely to consider the connotation that the agreement
reached at Munich between Britain and Nazi Germany carries today:
unwarranted appeasement of a greedy, grasping dictator, a foolish
policy of capitulation. Then recall that at the time, Neville Chamber-
lain returned to a hero's welcome in Britain. In 1938 people believed
that he had guaranteed "peace in our time." That phrase did not carry
its current unpleasant implications.

One method for estimating utilities for current issues is set out in
Bueno de Mesquita 1984 and delineated in greater detail in Bueno de
Mesquita, Newman, and Rabushka 1985, Beck and Bueno de Mesquita
1985, and elsewhere. That method depends on the exploration of an
individual's preferences with area or subject experts. We use here a
similar methodology for converting data into estimates of utility, but
we do not—because we cannot—use data as reliable as those provided
by experts in studies done in real time.

The utility components of the international interaction game are
estimated using the procedure developed by Bueno de Mesquita (1975,
1978, 1981, 1985, 1990). The similarity in national alliance portfolios
is utilized as a revealed choice measure of national preferences on
questions related to security issues. We assume that the more similar
the patterns of revealed foreign policy choices of two states, the
smaller the utility of any demand that one such state makes on the
other and, concomitantly, the smaller the difference between $U^i(\Delta_i)$
and $U^i(\Delta_j)$. Conversely, the more dissimilar the revealed foreign policy
commitments of two states, the greater the assumed utility for achieving the conditions contained in a demand between them and the greater
the difference between $U^i(\Delta_i)$ and $U^i(\Delta_j)$. We define the stakes in a
dispute as that difference and operationalize a variable called STAKES
as the estimated difference, following the procedures delineated here.

The use of alliance patterns as a basis for estimating the magnitude
of demands between states suffers from several limitations, which have
been discussed at length in Bueno de Mesquita 1981 but which warrant
some repetition, clarification, or elaboration. Large differences in alliance commitments do not guarantee large policy differences or, when
demands are made, large demands. Likewise, great similarities in
alliance commitments do not guarantee small demands. Still, we expect—and have found—that those who are in the same alliance camp

are less likely to have big differences that need redressing than those allied with distinctly different nations.

A further limitation of the indicator we propose is that formal alliance agreements probably change more slowly than the informal relations between states. Still, the pattern of alliances is more responsive to change than is the existence of individual bilateral agreements. The indicator we use depends not just on the presence or absence of a bilateral arrangement between two states but also on the extent to which they have revealed a commonality of interests through the overall portfolio of commitments they have made (or not made) to all other states in the international system, here defined as Europe and states active in European affairs.

Formal military alliances are not adequate to track all the ways in which nations relate to each other, including economic exchange, cultural transactions, defensive military activities, aggressive military postures, and so forth. Still, they do focus on the set of interactions most likely to be relevant for our concerns: the origins and escalation or peaceful resolution of disputes.[1]

Alliance formation may itself be part of an elaborate signaling game. Alliance policies may not be an accurate reflection of preferences precisely because strategic actors realize that alliances may be seen as revelations of true preferences. If so, alliance similarities as indicators of revealed preferences may not move monotonically with actual interests, and our alliance indicator may itself be biased in favor of a realist or neorealist view of alliance formation as a means of augmenting national power or national security. To the extent that such a bias exists, it should imply that the true relation between realism (or neorealism) and behavior is even weaker than that reported here.

The measure of similarity in alliance commitments that we use has several important strengths that are also worth repeating, particularly because many critics have misunderstood the reasoning behind the indicator. The similarity of alliance portfolios is not presented as if the degree of similarity is a leader's utility for this or that outcome. Rather, the pattern of alliance commitments is assumed to be highly correlated with the leader's foreign policy preferences. Although the limitations

1. Recent research on trade and other forms of economic interaction raises serious questions about the time-honored belief that trade enhances cooperation (Gasiorowski and Polachek 1982; Pollins 1988; Sayrs 1990); similarities in alliance portfolios, such as are used here, have proved to be useful tools for assessing the risks of alliances and the behavior of their members (Altfeld and Bueno de Mesquita 1979; Iusi-Scarborough and Bueno de Mesquita 1988; Conybeare 1990).

of alliance patterns are important, that the patterns represent foreign policy orientations hardly seems controversial. Within months of the emerging rapprochement between the United States and the Soviet Union, for instance, both nations codified their new relationship in a treaty of nonaggression. Similarly, the Camp David accords, an alliance of nonaggression, codified the new relationship between Israel, Egypt, and the United States. To be sure, important differences in national policies remain in each case, reflected by a comprehensive view of the patterns of alliance commitments. Thus, the indicator shows the United States and the Soviet Union drawing closer together, likewise Egypt and Israel, but it also reflects enduring differences in interests.

For some purposes, better data than the pattern of alliance commitments are available for approximating the utility leaders attach to alternative foreign policy outcomes. In chapter 7 we use money market discount rates to assess expectations of shifts in the value of the international status quo. However, such data are not available and readily comparable for a long time span across a comprehensive set of nations. Such breadth and scope are essential for evaluating the systematic implications of our theory. The case-by-case construction of indicators of utility on an issue-by-issue basis, as in Bueno de Mesquita, Newman, and Rabushka 1985, is useful when trying to understand this or that issue. But it is not useful when examining broad sweeps of history. There is a great danger of contamination in constructing ex post indicators that are situation specific—the danger of tailoring the indicators to the known results. The danger does not exist with the alliance correlation indicator used here because it is applied in an identical way to each and every case. What is more, it avoids the use of hindsight, relying as it does on information that was readily available to the relevant decision makers at the time. Rather than using ex post knowledge, it uses a tiny fraction of the information presumably available to the decision makers when they made their strategic choices.

The initial building block for our indicator of utilities, then, is the Kendall Tau$_b$ correlation of alliance portfolios. Alliances are ranked according to the implied reduction in the autonomy of a decision maker in choosing policy. Defense pacts are treated as the most costly of alliances because they require one nation to promise to wage war in defense of another nation in the event of an attack. Defense pacts are followed in presumed costliness by nonaggression or neutrality pacts, in which a nation agrees not to aid anyone who attacks the ally.

Ententes require merely that if attacked, the signatories consult with one another before deciding on a course of action. A signatory does not promise to join its attacked ally or not to attack it once it has been attacked. The least commitment of all occurs when no alliance exists, in which case no promise of any sort has been made.

We are not so naive as to believe that just because nations have entered into a mutual alliance, they necessarily honor the agreement in the contingent event. As Alan Sabrosky (1985) has observed, bilateral agreements are not honored all too often. Yet Michael Altfeld and Bueno de Mesquita (1979) and Chae Han Kim (1991) have shown that when commitments are honored or broken is highly predictable if the researcher looks beyond the bilateral agreement to the overall portfolio of commitments with other nations. When the pattern of alliance commitments is weighted by the ally's capability of influencing the outcome of a contingent dispute, then the predictive accuracy is near or above 90 percent (Altfeld and Bueno de Mesquita 1979), depending on the particular set of cases being evaluated. Our application of the correlation of alliance commitments is used, then, to evaluate the similarity in foreign policy commitments under the presumption that a similarity or difference reflects shared preferences among the states in question. The revelation of shared foreign policy preferences embodied in alliance portfolios is further assumed to reflect the magnitude of unresolved issues between the relevant states. As noted earlier, we assume that the larger these unresolved issues are, the larger are the demands between states.

The Kendall Tau$_b$ correlation of the shared pattern of commitments for each pair of states is denoted as K_j^i. The outcome nation i desires is initially reflected by $K_i^i = 1.0$, the correlation of i's portfolio with itself. The utility of i's (or j's) demand is assessed in terms of the worth of marginally changing j's (or i's) goal to be in compliance with i's (or j's) goal. If i and j have identical alliance portfolios, so that the correlation coefficient between their alliance patterns is 1.0, we set K_j^i equal to 0.999 to reflect the possibility that no matter how alike the revealed preferences of two actors, they can always be still more alike.

The correlation of alliance portfolios does not capture important differences across countries that relate to the propensity of this or that leader to take risks. Therefore, the correlations, by themselves, are not our indicator of utility for alternative outcomes, although they are sufficient to provide the implied ordering of preferences across prospective outcomes. The propensity to take risks is an intrinsic part of any utility function as it gives curvature to that function. Risk-aversive

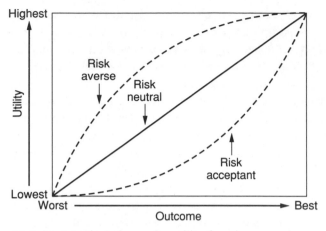

A1.1: Prototypical shapes for utility functions.

decision makers, for instance, have utility functions that are concave from the origin, indicating that the difference in value between, say, a worst-case outcome and an intermediate outcome is greater than the difference between the same intermediate outcome and a better outcome. That is, the utility for outcomes increases at a decreasing rate as outcomes are more and more preferred. For risk takers, in contrast, utility functions bend upward from the origin, with utilities increasing at an increasing rate as outcomes are more and more preferred. Figure A1.1 depicts prototypical utility functions for risk-averse, risk-acceptant, and risk-neutral decision makers.

For our second building block, we take the measure of risk-taking propensities delineated in Bueno de Mesquita 1985 and denoted as r^i here. James Morrow has shown that this measure is generally robust and consistent with conventional economic treatments of risk. He also shows that it suffers from two prospective sources of bias: "Bueno de Mesquita's risk indicator should recover a nation's risk attitude from its alliance decisions . . . except for those cases where the status quo is unusually close to victory or defeat"; the limitations of the measure "point up a higher random error . . . than was originally thought" (1987, 436–37). That random error tends to suppress rather than inflate goodness-of-fit indicators, thereby introducing a conservative bias into our analyses.

The measure is predicated on the assumption that the policies that actors reveal themselves as preferring represent an inherent trade-off between what they really want and what they believe is politically pragmatic. Pragmatism is defined in terms of maximizing a nation's security (or minimizing its vulnerability to attack). In that sense, the measure is a close approximation of the extent to which nations pursue enhanced security as their primary goal. It goes beyond the assumption that security is all that national leaders pursue by treating choices as the reflection of varying degrees of willingness to risk some security in order to seek particular objectives. National leaders establish objectives that combine the quest for security and the search for ways to achieve outcomes that reflect their ideals and values. David Lalman and David Newman (1990) show that alliance formation is frequently motivated by a quest for security, and Altfeld (1984), Bruce Berkowitz (1983), Altfeld and Won Paik (1986), John Conybeare (1990), and Morrow (1991a) provide increasingly sophisticated theories of the trade-offs between the maximization of national security and national autonomy. Each of their results is generally consistent with the logic underlying the measure of risk-taking propensities used here. Risk-averse leaders adopt policies (reflected by patterns of alliances) that minimize their vulnerability, presumably at the expense of some of their autonomous objectives. Risk-acceptant decision makers eschew more security in exchange for more idealistic—perhaps ideological or domestically motivated—preferences.

The indicator of risk-taking propensities that we use is highly correlated with independent indicators of exposure to risk. Risk-averse leaders, for instance, initiate significantly fewer wars that they ultimately lose than do risk-acceptant decision makers, according to the indicator used here (Bueno de Mesquita 1985). Conybeare (1990) has also demonstrated that the risk indicator provides a reliable means of estimating the propensity to engage in risky patterns of behavior in terms of the returns in security of alternative alliances.

With the basic building blocks—K_j^i and r^i—now described, we can begin to assemble them into the relevant variables.[2]

$$U^A(\Delta_A) = 2 - 4 \left[\frac{2 - (1 - K_B^A)}{4} \right] r^A. \tag{A1.1}$$

$$U^A(\Delta_B) = 2 - 4 \left[\frac{2 - (K_B^A - 1)}{4} \right] r^A. \tag{A1.2}$$

2. The 2's and 4's are simply ratchet operators to preserve scale without taking roots of negative values. Negative root values could otherwise arise in those expressions that assess $U^i(\Delta_j)$. If no marginal change in policy positions is expected, then the expected change in $K_i^i - K_j^i$ is zero, so the calculation of the value of the status quo—which is not expected to change—reduces to 0.5^{r^i}.

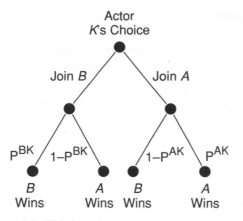

A1.2: Third-party choices to support side A or B.

$$U^A(SQ) = 2 - 4 \left(\frac{2}{4}\right)^{r_A}. \qquad\qquad\qquad (A1.3)$$

$$U^B(\Delta_B) = 2 - 4 \left[\frac{2 - (1 - K_A^B)}{4}\right]^{r_B}. \qquad\qquad (A1.4)$$

$$U^B(\Delta_A) = 2 - 4 \left[\frac{2 - (K_A^B - 1)}{4}\right]^{r_B}. \qquad\qquad (A1.5)$$

$$U^B(SQ) = 2 - 4 \left(\frac{2}{4}\right)^{r_B}. \qquad\qquad\qquad (A1.6)$$

The variable STAKES is derived from these indicators. STAKES is operationalized as (A1.1) − (A1.2) for actor A and as (A1.4) − (A1.5) for state B.

The Probability of Success

We assume that the subjective estimate of the probability of success of actor A is a function of its capabilities and the capabilities of its prospective supporters, discounted by the intensity with which it and each of its prospective supporters prefers success by A to success by B. The precise specification is motivated by a decision-theoretic view of third-party choices to join side A, side B, or remain neutral during an ongoing dispute. Figure A1.2 depicts the decision problem, and expressions (A1.7) and (A1.8) represent it algebraically.

With N as the set of all nations, let A, B, $K \in N$. Let K be any third party to a potential dispute between A and B, so that K is neither A

nor B. In the putative dispute between A and B, there is some probability that A's demand of B will be accomplished and some probability that B will obtain the outcome it desires from A. K attaches some utility to each of these outcomes $[U^K(\Delta_A)$ and $U^K(\Delta_B)]$. If A is successful, then we assume K derives $U^K(\Delta_A)$ from the outcome of A's dispute with B. Likewise, if B succeeds against A, then we assume that K derives a benefit or loss (as the case may be) of $U^K(\Delta_B)$. These utilities apply whether K decides to help A, help B, or remain neutral.

K is capable of influencing the outcome of the dispute between A and B. We assume that in joining A, K cannot decrease A's chances of success and that, likewise, by joining B, K does not diminish B's chances.[3] Let P^{AK} be the probability with which A combined with K defeats B. By combined we mean that K joins the dispute on A's side. Let P^{BK} be the comparable probability of success for B. K's choices, with the associated expected utilities, are

$$P^{AK}[U^K(\Delta_A)] + (1 - P^{AK})[U^K(\Delta_B)] - C_A^K, \qquad (A1.7)$$

and

$$P^{BK}[U^K(\Delta_B)] + (1 - P^{BK})[U^K(\Delta_A)] - C_B^K, \qquad (A1.8)$$

with C_A^K and C_B^K representing the costs K expects in utilities if it joins side A or B, respectively. Each cost term is assumed to be greater than or equal to zero. If $(A1.7) > (A1.8)$, then K anticipates greater value from joining side A than from joining side B and so is expected to do so. If $(A1.7) < (A1.8)$, then K is expected to join side B. If $(A1.7) = (A1.8)$, then K is indifferent, so we assume that K chooses to remain neutral and avoid any of the costs associated with joining in the dispute.

The choice problem for nation K can be rewritten by simply rearranging the terms in $(A1.7)$ and $(A1.8)$:

$$(P^{AK} + P^{BK} - 1)[U^K(\Delta_A) - U^K(\Delta_B)] \gtreqless C_A^K - C_B^K. \qquad (A1.9)$$

Expression $(A1.9)$ helps clarify some important features of $(A1.7)$ and $(A1.8)$. Because we have assumed that P^{AK} and P^{BK} are each at least as large as A's or B's prospects of success without K's assistance, $(P^{AK} + P^{BK} - 1) \geq 0$. As the expected costs for joining one side

3. In this context, A or B can be thought of as an individual state or as the coalition of states on a given side in a dispute, so K can calculate its expected utility from alternative strategies by taking the evolution of the dispute into account. For an interesting treatment of this feature of K's calculations, see C. H. Kim 1991.

approach being equal to the anticipated costs for joining the other side, the side joined, if any, is determined by the sign of $U^K(\Delta_A) - U^K(\Delta_B)$, for K behaves sincerely in choosing sides so long as the cost differential is not large enough to alter its calculations. With the assumption that the differential is not expected to be too large, we apply a modification of Jeffrey Banks's (1990) monotonicity result to (A1.9), as suggested in Bueno de Mesquita and Lalman 1986; Lalman 1985, 1988. We assume that the level of effort made by K is an increasing function of the absolute magnitude of (A1.9). In other words, the greater the intensity of preference or the greater the contribution K makes to the probability of the outcome, the more resources K is prepared to commit to the dispute.

Now we add an operational conceptualization of probability as the gambling odds based on the distribution of capabilities. Let Λ^i equal the resources, or capabilities, of nation i. We estimate Λ^i using the composite capabilities score developed by the Correlates of War Project and widely used in the assessment of national power. We operationalize the two probability terms in (A1.9) as $P^{AK} = (\Lambda^A + \Lambda^K)/(\Lambda^A + \Lambda^B + \Lambda^K)$, and $P^{BK} = (\Lambda^B + \Lambda^K)/(\Lambda^A + \Lambda^B + \Lambda^K)$, so that, with a little algebraic manipulation, it is evident that the probability component of (A1.9) reduces to $\Lambda^K/(\Lambda^A + \Lambda^B + \Lambda^K)$.

As we have stated, we assume that K's level of effort is an increasing function of (A1.9). But we are interested here in estimating P^A or P^B, A's and B's subjective estimates of their respective probabilities of success. If A and B assume that K's level of effort on their behalf or on behalf of their adversary is an increasing function of A1.9, then A and B must make a subjective judgment not only about the capabilities of each third-party K but also about the intensity of preference that K has for A's or B's desired outcome. We denote A's estimate of K's intensity of preference for the outcome A wants compared to the outcome B wants as follows:[4]

$$^AU^K(\Delta_A) - {}^AU^K(\Delta_B) = \frac{(K_A^K - K_B^K)}{2} e^{R^A(K_A^K - K_B^K)}.$$

With the various conditions just stipulated in place, we offer the following operational view of (A1.9):

4. Division by two is to avoid counting capabilities twice. Recall that $-1 \leq$ Kendall's Tau$_b \leq 1$. The term r^A, used in earlier expressions, is a transformed variant of R^A. The details of the transformation and the reasoning behind it are spelled out in Bueno de Mesquita, Newman, and Rabushka 1985.

Let

$$P^A = \frac{\sum\limits_{K \in \psi} \Lambda^K [{}^A U^K(\Delta_A) - {}^A U^K(\Delta_B)]}{\sum\limits_{K=1}^{N} \Lambda^K |({}^A U^K(\Delta_A) - {}^A U^K(\Delta_B)|} , \tag{A1.10}$$

with $\psi \subseteq N$ such that $\forall i \in \psi$, ${}^A U^K(\Delta_A) - {}^A U^K(\Delta_B) > 0$.

Expression (A1.10) has a straightforward interpretation. The numerator, derived as an extension of (A1.9), is the sum of the capabilities of all states that prefer A's objectives to B's, discounted by A's estimate of the intensity of their preferences. The denominator is the discounted sum of all capabilities expected to be available in the dispute, whether on the side of nation A or nation B. Thus, (A1.10) is the proportion of all utilized capabilities that A expects to find supporting its goals. The calculation from B's perspective is analogous.

Costs

The coarsest of our indicators are the approximations of the cost variables. We assume for operational purposes that anticipated domestic costs vary directly as an increasing function of each side's subjective estimate of its probability of success (P^A, P^B) and of the value it attaches to the status quo, so that ϕ_i is presumed to be positively correlated with i's evaluation of the status quo. The rationale is that if the status quo is relatively desirable, then the domestic population is more likely to be agitated by policies that threaten to disrupt it. Consequently, the use of force to alter an already-attractive state of affairs is assumed to prompt greater domestic opposition than the use of force in circumstances in which the status quo is unattractive or irksome. Furthermore, we assume that powerful nations face greater opposition to the use of force than do weaker nations, all else being equal. The rationale behind this assumption is that strong nations are in a better position to get what they want through negotiation and to control relations with other states. If they use force, their foreign policy is perceived as a greater failure exactly because they should have had the leverage to manage their relation with a weak adversary more effectively through peaceful means. After all, peaceful negotiation is generally preferred to using force. The domestic cost term for nation i is operationalized as $U^i(SQ)P^i$.

The costs in terms of lost life and property are assumed to be an inverse function of relative power. The higher the probability of success, the lower the losses in life and property that we assume are expected in the event of violence. Therefore, the loss for the initiator of a war is $\alpha_i(1 - P^i)$, for the target it is $\tau_i(1 - P^i)$, and for a capitulator it is $\gamma_i(1 - P^i)$. Unfortunately, we have not yet devised a way to estimate α, τ, or γ, so we do not distinguish between them. Because we cannot compare the value A (or B) attaches to the outcomes War_A and War_B, we specify only the relevant condition closest to the terminal event of interest if more than one condition must be estimated. If we are estimating the necessary and sufficient conditions for, say, War_A, then any estimate of the expected utility of war is based on War_A and not on War_B. If there is a condition on War_B, then, as we note in the text, that condition remains unestimated.

Clearly, our estimation of expected costs only scrapes the surface of the problem. These very limited approximations may introduce considerable measurement error into our analyses. Assuming that our operational procedures are not systematically biased one way or the other, we expect that, on average, the crudity of our estimation of costs suppresses rather than inflates our results. But we cannot be confident of this claim until better indicators are developed and tested in the future.

Uncertainty

In the game we propose, uncertainty can arise from any number of factors. Leaders may be uncertain about the costs of conflict or the capabilities of their adversaries. They may be uncertain about a foe's preferences for alternative outcomes. They may be uncertain about the beliefs their rivals have about them. We cannot at this time measure each of these and many other prospective sources of uncertainty. We have, however, devised a general indicator that we believe reflects fundamental sources of uncertainty in international relations. How a nation responds to a given circumstance is significantly influenced by its willingness to take risks or its aversion to doing so. We assume that different decision makers respond differently to risks. Furthermore, we assume that a principal source of uncertainty in international politics has to do with how a given nation will respond to risky choices. Therefore, our indicator of uncertainty is the variance in our measure of risk taking on a year-by-year basis.

For each year we calculate the willingness of the leadership of each European nation to take risks. In some years, there is more commonality across leaders in this regard than in other years. When the variance in risk scores is large, we assume that decision makers are not at all certain how any one nation will respond to a risky situation.

When the variance is small, we assume there is less uncertainty about how any given state will respond to a risky situation. Because of these assumptions, the decision makers in our game are more likely to estimate accurately the utilities that their rivals (or third parties) attach to alternative outcomes in years of low risk variance than they are in years of high risk variance, meaning that in years when risk variance is low, A's estimate of B's ordering, say, and B's actual ordering (in each case, estimated by our methods) are less likely to be reversed.

COMMENTS

With the operational indicators in place, we are able to estimate most of the terms of our theory and to provide empirical assessments for almost all the propositions we deduce from the international interaction game. We again caution the reader, however, to expect no more than the central tendency to be reflected in the empirical results. More than that is extremely difficult to attain with the set of indicators we use. At the same time, we also caution the reader to be wary of measurement approaches that seemingly circumvent such coarseness by using ex post information about how events turned out or by using assessments that are particular to each case. Such approaches run grave risks of nonreproducibility, dependence on the knowledge of outcomes, and selection or interpretation biases. General indicators weaken the overall goodness of fit, but they avoid many other pitfalls that would make the empirical results all but uninterpretable.

Appendix 2

Domestic Constraints and the Prospects of Bluffing

DOMESTIC CONSTRAINT PROPOSITION 5.4. *If type II A nations hold the preferences delineated in the basic war theorem and if type I A nations prefer War$_B$ to Cap$_A$, then there is no value of δ ($0 < \delta < 1$) such that expression (5.13) can be satisfied. In other words, type II A nations cannot engage successfully in strategic deception to induce negotiations when war would otherwise have occurred.*

Proof. We show that there is no value for δ ($0 < \delta < 1$) consistent with the preferences stipulated for either type I or type II nations.

Substituting the values for ρ from expressions (5.12) and (5.13), we find that the mixed-strategy equilibrium requires that

$$\frac{(\tau_A - \alpha_A)(1 - P^A)}{\tau_A(1 - P^A) + \delta\phi_A P^A}$$

$$\leq \frac{P^A[U^A(\Delta_A) - U^A(\Delta_B)] + (\gamma_A - \alpha_A)(1 - P^A) - \phi_A P^A}{P^A[U^A(\Delta_A) - U^A(\Delta_B)] + \gamma_A(1 - P^A)}. \quad (A2.1)$$

We begin by identifying all the possible conditions under which the inequality in expression (A2.1) can hold.

1. Suppose the numerator on the left side of (A2.1) is less than or equal to the numerator on the right side of (A2.1). Then

$$(\tau_A - \gamma_A)(1 - P^A) + \phi_A P^A \leq P^A[U^A(\Delta_A) - U^A(\Delta_B)]. \quad (A2.2)$$

The assumption that type II A prefers Cap$_A$ to War$_B$ means that

$$(\tau_A - \gamma_A)(1 - P^A) + \phi_A P^A > P^A[U^A(\Delta_A) - U^A(\Delta_B)]. \quad (A2.3)$$

Therefore condition (A2.2) cannot be true. The numerator on the left *must* be bigger than the numerator on the right side of (A2.1).

2. Suppose the numerator and denominator on the left side of the inequality in (A2.1) are greater than the numerator and denominator on the right side of the inequality. Then

$$(\tau_A - \gamma_A)(1 - P^A) + \delta\phi_A P^A > P^A[U^A(\Delta_A) - U^A(\Delta_B)]. \qquad (A2.4)$$

Proposition 5.4 specifies that type I A nations prefer War$_B$ to Cap$_A$. This preference is equivalent to

$$(\tau_A - \gamma_A)(1 - P^A) + \delta\phi_A P^A < P^A[U^A(\Delta_A) - U^A(\Delta_B)]. \qquad (A2.5)$$

Expression (A2.5) contradicts the inequality in expression (A2.4). No admissible value of δ can support the equilibrium in this case.

3. The remaining possible mixes of numerator and denominator inequalities all contradict the inequality in expression (A2.1). If the left denominator equals the right denominator, the left numerator cannot simultaneously be larger than the right numerator and maintain the inequality in (A2.1). Likewise, if the left denominator is smaller than the right denominator in (A2.1), then the left numerator cannot be greater than the right numerator. Otherwise, the direction of the inequality in (A2.1) would be reversed. QED

DOMESTIC CONSTRAINT PROPOSITION 5.5. *If a type II B nation bears* $\delta\phi_B$ *and a type I B nation incurs* ϕ_B, *with* $0 < \delta < 1$, *and if for both types of B,* $U^B(War_A) > U^B(Cap_B)$, *then there is no level of strategic deception that can sufficiently revise A's belief about B's type to induce negotiations when war or acquiescence by B to A would otherwise occur.*

Proof. The proof of this proposition is an examination of all cases consistent with our initial assumptions and the restriction that $0 < \delta < 1$. We note that it is not possible for type I B nations to prefer war to acquiescence to A if type II B nations prefer to acquiesce rather than retaliate against an attack by A. Given the payoffs we have stipulated, such an ordering would require that $\delta\phi > \phi$ for B, which violates the restriction that $\delta < 1$.

Case 1. Let $U^B(\Delta_B) - \phi_B$ and $U^B(\Delta_B) - \delta\phi_B > U^B(Nego)$, so that for B, $U^B(Cap_A) > U^B(Nego)$ for all B. Then, $D^B \to War_A$ and $\tilde{D}^B \to$ Acq$_B$. Then the equilibrium depends only on whether B prefers a war initiated by A to acquiescence. If type II prefers war and type I prefers to acquiesce, then the only possible equilibrium is

$$\tilde{D}^B, D^B, F^A, F^B, F^B; \theta^* = 0. \qquad (A2.6)$$

The equilibrium described by (A2.6) provides no opportunity to reach a negotiated settlement of the dispute even though all uncertainty about B's type is removed by the time A reaches its information set.

Case 2. If $U^B(\text{Nego}) > U^B(\Delta_B) - \delta\phi_B P^B$, and therefore $U^B(\text{Nego})$
$> U^B(\Delta_B) - \phi_B P^B$, then uncertainties about domestic costs do not
influence the equilibrium of the game. In this case, $D^B \to \tilde{F}^A$ (by A2.4)
and $\tilde{F}^A \to$ Nego. Then $D^B \to U^B(\text{Nego})$ and $\tilde{D}^B \to U^B(\Delta_A)$, $U^B(\text{Nego})$
$> U^B(\Delta_A)$. Therefore, regardless of the difference between $\delta\phi_B$ and
ϕ_B, the equilibrium is

$$D^B, D^B, \tilde{F}^A, \tilde{F}^B, \tilde{F}^B; \theta^* \geq 0. \qquad (A2.7)$$

Case 3. Let

$$[U^B(\Delta_B) - \delta\phi_B P^B] > [P^B U^B(\Delta_B)$$
$$+ (1 - P^B)U^B(\Delta_A)] > [U^B(\Delta_B) - \phi_B P^B],$$

and let

$$[P^B U^B(\Delta_B) + (1 - P^B)U^B(\Delta_A) - \phi_B P^B - \tau^B(1 - P^B)] > U^B(\Delta_A).$$

Then $D^B > \tilde{D}^B$ for all B regardless of A's decision to use force or A's
offer to negotiate. Thus, A cannot update its belief about B's type at
its information set. The equilibria under these conditions are

$$D^B, D^B, \tilde{F}^A, \tilde{F}^B, F^B; \theta^* > (d - e)/(b - e), \qquad (A2.8)$$

and

$$D^B, D^B, F^A, F^B, F^B; \theta^* < (d - e)/(b - e). \qquad (A2.9)$$

The action A takes is dependent on its prior belief (θ) about B's type
but not on the action B takes. B can neither increase the probability
of negotiations nor decrease the risk of war by exploiting A's uncertainty about the magnitude of its domestic opposition to the use of
force.

Case 4. Assume the same conditions as in case 3, except let
$U^B(\text{Acq}_B) > U^B(\text{War}_A)$ for all B. If $\theta > (d - e)/(b - e)$, $D^B \to \tilde{F}^A$, and
if $\theta < (d - e)/(b - e)$, $D^B \to F^A$. Because $U^B(\text{Acq}_B) > U^B(\text{War}_A)$ for
all B in this case, if $\theta < (d - e)/(b - e)$, then $\tilde{D}^B > D^B$ for both type
I and type II Bs. A learns nothing at the information set, and the
posterior probability remains unaltered. The subgame perfect equilibria in this case are

$$D^B, D^B, \tilde{F}^A, \tilde{F}^B, F^B; \theta^* > (d - e)/(b - e), \qquad (A2.10)$$

and

$$\tilde{D}^B,\ \tilde{D}^B,\ F^A,\ F^B,\ F^B;\ \theta^* < (d - e)/(b - e). \qquad (A2.11)$$

As with case 3, there are no strategies available to player B by which it can manipulate A's beliefs about domestic reactions in B to B's use of force.

Case 5. Let

$$[U^B(\Delta_B) - \delta\phi_B P^B] > [P^B U^B(\Delta_B)$$
$$+ (1 - P^B)U^B(\Delta_A)] > [U^B(\Delta_B) - \phi_B P^B],$$

and let

$$P^B U^B(\Delta_B) + (1 - P^B)U^B(\Delta_A) - \delta\phi_B P^B - \tau^B(1 - P^B) > U^B(\Delta_A)$$
$$> P^B U^B(\Delta_B) + (1 - P^B)U^B(\Delta_A) - \phi_B P^B - \tau^B(1 - P^B).$$

A will choose $\tilde{F}^A$ if $\theta^* > (d - e)/(b - e)$, and it will select F^A if $\theta^* < (d - e)/(b - e)$. If $\theta^* > (d - e)/(b - e)$, type I B will negotiate with A because it prefers negotiating to forcing A to capitulate. Type II B will exploit A, leading to a capitulation by A to B's enforced demand. Only at the end of the game will A learn whether B is type I or type II. At its information set A will not obtain new information (beyond its prior belief) about B's type.[1] The equilibrium is

$$D^B,\ D^B,\ \tilde{F}^A,\ \tilde{F}^B,\ F^B;\ \theta^* > (d - e)/(b - e). \qquad (A2.12)$$

In the event that the initial belief θ is less than $(d - e)/(b - e)$, type I B and type II B will behave differently prior to A's choice at its information set. Type I B nations are better off acquiescing to A's demands than they are fighting a war with A, whereas type II B nations, with their lower domestic costs for resorting to force, are better off fighting than they are giving in at the outset. Type I B will choose $\tilde{D}^B$, and type II B will choose D^B if the prior belief θ is less than $(d - e)/(b - e)$. Given such a prior belief, the equilibrium is

$$\tilde{D}^B,\ D^B,\ F^A,\ F^B,\ F^B;\ \theta^* = 0. \qquad (A2.13)$$

1. If the game is repeated, A's end-of-game knowledge might lead to different behavior on its part or on B's part. However, in conflictual international interactions, a likely outcome of a single round of play is that the expected payoffs in future interactions are altered by the results of the first interaction. Consequently, even though the set of available strategies may be repeated, the payoffs are unlikely to be repeated.

Can type I B improve its prospects by pursuing a mixed strategy, sometimes making a demand and sometimes not making a demand when $\theta < (d - e)/(b - e)$? The answer is no. To do at least as well as in (A2.13), type I B might try a mixed strategy designed to raise $\theta^* = 0$ to $\theta^* = (d - e)/(b - e)$.

Let ρ be the probability with which type I B makes a demand when $\theta < (d - e)/(b - e)$. Let λ be the probability with which A offers to negotiate. A selects λ such that it is indifferent to either of two outcomes: F^A (in which case A fights a war for sure) and $\tilde{F}^A$ (in which case A will negotiate if B is type I and A will be forced to capitulate if B is type II), given that B selects D^B with probability ρ. This condition is satisfied when

$$\lambda = \frac{\tau_B(1 - P^B) + \phi_B P^B - P^B[U^B(\Delta_B) - U^B(\Delta_A)]}{\tau_B(1 - P^B) + \phi_B P^B}. \tag{A2.14}$$

For λ to satisfy (A2.14), A must update θ at the information set so that $\theta^* = (d - e)/(b - e)$. Following Bayes's theorem,

$$\rho = [(1 - \theta)(d - e)]/[\theta(b - d)]. \tag{A2.15}$$

If equation (A2.15) could be satisfied, the equilibrium would be

$$[\rho D^B, (1 - \rho)\tilde{D}^B], D^B, [\lambda \tilde{F}^A, (1 - \lambda)F^A]; \theta^* = (d - e)/(b - e),$$

so that type I B, rather than acquiescing to A, would with probability $\rho \lambda$ end up negotiating a resolution of the dispute that is better for itself but at the price of waging a costly war with probability $\rho(1 - \lambda)$. The possibility of inducing such negotiated solutions through the strategy of picking D^B with probability ρ would contradict the theorem. However, because $0 < \rho < 1$, equation (A2.15) implies that $\theta(b - d) > (1 - \theta)(d - e)$. This can only be true if $\theta > (d - e)/(b - e)$. But type I B would not select $\tilde{D}^B$ when $\theta > (d - e)/(b - e)$, for the equilibrium in (A2.12) is superior for type I B to the proposed mixed-strategy equilibrium. Therefore, a mixed-strategy equilibrium is not supportable as a means to increase the prospects of attaining a negotiated settlement.

We have exhausted the feasible cases. In no case can B alter A's initial belief about B's type to induce negotiations and avoid war. QED

Bibliography

Achen, C. 1992. "After Democracy: Basic Research and Its Implications for American Policy toward Eastern Europe." In D. Snidal, ed., *Economics, Peace and Security*. Boulder, Colo.: Westview Press.

Albrecht-Carrié, R. 1973. *A Diplomatic History of Europe since the Congress of Vienna*. Rev. ed. New York: Harper and Row.

Allison, G. 1971. *The Essence of Decision*. Boston: Little, Brown.

Altfeld, M. 1984. "The Decision to Ally: A Theory and Test." *Western Political Quarterly* 37:523–44.

Altfeld, M., and B. Bueno de Mesquita. 1979. "Choosing Sides in Wars." *International Studies Quarterly* 23:87–112.

Altfeld, M., and W. Paik. 1986. "Realignment in ITOs: A Closer Look." *International Studies Quarterly* 30:107–14.

Arrow, K. 1951. *Social Choice and Individual Values*. New York: John Wiley.

Axelrod, R. 1984. *The Evolution of Cooperation*. New York: Basic Books.

Banks, J. 1990. "Equilibrium Behavior in Crisis Bargaining Games." *American Journal of Political Science* 34:599–614.

Banks, J., and R. Sundaram. 1990. "Repeated Games, Finite Automata, and Complexity." *Games and Economic Behavior* 2:97–117.

Beck, D., and B. Bueno de Mesquita. 1985. "Forecasting Policy Decisions: An Expected Utility Approach." In S. Andriole, ed., *Corporate Crisis Management*. New York: Petrocelli Books.

Bendor, J., and D. Mookherjee. 1987. "Institutional Structure and the Logic of Ongoing Collective Action." *American Political Science Review* 81:129–54.

Berkowitz, B. 1983. "Realignment in International Treaty Organizations." *International Studies Quarterly* 27:77–96.

Bianco, W. 1988. "The Limits of Cooperation: Sanctioning Problems in Dilemma Games." Paper presented at the annual meetings of the Midwest Political Science Association, Chicago, April 14–16.

Bismarck, Otto von. 1924–35. *Bismarck: Die Gesammelten Werke*. 15 vols. Berlin: O. Stollberg.

Blainey, G. 1973. *The Causes of War*. New York: Free Press.

Brams, S. 1975. *Game Theory and Politics*. New York: Free Press.

Brams, S., and D. Wittman. 1981. "Nonmyopic Equilibria in 2 × 2 Games." *Conflict Management and Peace Science* 6:39–62.

Brecher, M., and J. Wilkenfeld. 1989. *Crisis, Conflict, and Instability*. Oxford: Pergamon Press.

Brito, D., and M. Intriligator. 1980. "A Game Theoretic Approach to Bureaucratic Behavior." In P. T. Liu, ed., *Dynamic Optimization and Mathematical Economics*. New York: Plenum Press.

Buchanan, J., and G. Tullock. 1962. *The Calculus of Consent*. Ann Arbor: University of Michigan Press.

Bueno de Mesquita, B. 1975. "Measuring Systemic Polarity." *Journal of Conflict Resolution* 19:187–215.

———. 1978. "Systemic Polarization and the Occurrence and Duration of War." *Journal of Conflict Resolution* 22:241–66.

———. 1980. "Theories of International Conflict: An Analysis and an Appraisal." In T. R. Gurr, ed., *The Handbook of Political Conflict*. New York: Free Press.

———. 1981. *The War Trap*. New Haven: Yale University Press.

———. 1984. "Forecasting Policy Decisions: An Expected Utility Approach to Post-Khomeini Iran." *PS* 17:226–36.

———. 1985. "The War Trap Revisited." *American Political Science Review* 79:157–76.

———. 1990. "Multilateral Negotiations: A Spatial Analysis of the Arab-Israeli Dispute." *International Organization* 44:317–40.

Bueno de Mesquita, B., and D. Lalman. 1986. "Reason and War." *American Political Science Review* 80:1113–31.

———. 1988. "Systemic and Dyadic Explanations of War." *World Politics* 41:1–20.

Bueno de Mesquita, B., D. Newman, and R. Rabushka. 1985. *Forecasting Political Events: Hong Kong's Future*. New Haven: Yale University Press.

Bueno de Mesquita, B., R. Siverson, and G. Woller. 1991. "War and the Fate of Regimes." Hoover Institution. Photocopy.

Carr, E. H. 1951. *The Twenty Years' Crisis*. London: Macmillan.

Cho, I., and D. Kreps. 1987. "Signaling Games and Stable Equilibria." *Quarterly Journal of Economics* 102:179–222.

Claude, I. 1962. *Power and International Relations*. New York: Random House.

Conybeare, J. 1990. "A Portfolio Diversification Model of Alliances: The Triple Alliance and the Triple Entente, 1879–1914." University of Iowa. Mimeo.

Craig, G. 1964. *The Battle of Königgrätz: Prussia's Victory over Austria, 1866*. Philadelphia: J. B. Lippincott.

Crankshaw, E. 1981. *Bismarck*. London: Macmillan.

Crawshaw, N. 1978. *The Cyprus Revolt: An Account of the Struggle for Union with Greece*. London: George Allen and Unwin.

Creasy, E. 1851. *The Fifteen Decisive Battles of the World: From Marathon to Waterloo*. New York: Harper.

Davis, O., M. DeGroot, and M. Hinich. 1974. "Social Preference Orderings and Majority Rule." *Econometrica* 40:147–57.

Denzau, A., W. Riker, and K. Shepsle. 1985. "Farquharson and Fenno: Sophisticated Voting and Home Style." *American Political Science Review* 79:1117–34.

Department of Military History of the Prussian Staff. 1872. *The Campaign of 1866 in Germany*. Trans. V. Wright and H. Hozier. London: Topographical and Statistical Department of the War Office.

Domke, W. 1988. *War and the Changing Global System*. New Haven: Yale University Press.

Doran, C. 1989. "Power Cycle Theory of Systems Structure and Stability: Commonalities and Complementarities." In M. Midlarsky, ed., *Handbook of War Studies*. Boston: Unwin Hyman.

Doran, C., and W. Parsons. 1980. "War and the Cycle of Relative Power." *American Political Science Review* 74:947–65.

Downs, G., and D. Rocke. 1990. *Tacit Bargaining, Arms Races, and Arms Control*. Ann Arbor: University of Michigan Press.

Doyle, M. 1986. "Liberalism and World Politics." *American Political Science Review* 80:1151–71.

Foley, C., and W. I. Scobie. 1975. *The Struggle for Cyprus*. Stanford, Calif.: Hoover Institution Press.

Garnham, D. 1976. "Power Parity and Lethal International Violence." *Journal of Conflict Resolution* 20:379–94.

Gasiorowski, M., and S. Polachek. 1982. "Conflict and Interdependence: East-West Trade and Linkages in the Era of Detente." *Journal of Conflict Resolution* 26:709–29.

Gaubatz, K. 1991a. "Election Cycles and War." *Journal of Conflict Resolution* 35:212–44.

———. 1991b. "Elections and War." Ph.D. diss., Department of Political Science, Stanford University.

Gilpin, R. 1981. *War and Change in World Politics*. Cambridge: Cambridge University Press.

———. 1989. "The Theory of Hegemonic War." In R. Rotberg and T. Rabb, eds., *The Origin and Prevention of Major Wars*. Cambridge: Cambridge University Press.

Goldstein, J., and J. Freeman. 1990. *Three-Way Street*. Chicago: University of Chicago Press.

Gowa, J. 1986. "Cooperation and International Regimes." *International Organization* 40:167–86.

Greenstein, F. 1982. *The Hidden-Hand Presidency*. New York: Basic Books.

Grenville, J. A. S. 1964. *Lord Salisbury and Foreign Policy: The Close of the Nineteenth Century*. London: Athlone Press.

Grützner, F. 1986. *Die Politik Bismarcks, 1862 bis 1871 in der deutschen Geschichtsschreibung*. Frankfurt am Main: Peter Lang.

Gulick, E. 1955. *Europe's Classical Balance of Power*. Ithaca: Cornell University Press.

Gurr, T. R. 1978. *Polity Data Handbook*. Ann Arbor: ICPSR.

Hacking, I. 1975. *The Emergence of Probability*. Cambridge: Cambridge University Press.

Hamerow, T., ed. 1973. *The Age of Bismarck: Documents and Interpretations*. New York: Harper and Row.

Hart, P. T. 1990. *Two NATO Allies at the Threshold of War: Cyprus—A Firsthand Account of Crisis Management, 1965–1968*. Durham, N.C.: Duke University Press.

Hartmann, F. 1978. The Relations of Nations. 5th ed. New York: Macmillan.

Hermann, C. 1972. "Some Issues in the Study of International Crises." In Hermann, ed., *International Crises: Insights from Behavioral Research*. New York: Free Press.

Herodotus. 1954. *Histories of Herodotus*. Trans. A. De Selincourt. London: Penguin Books.

Hobbes, T. 1962. *Leviathan*. New York: Collier Books.

Holborn, H. 1960. "Bismarck's Realpolitik." *Journal of the History of Ideas* 21:84–98.

Houweling, H., and J. Siccama. 1988. "Power Transitions as a Cause of War." *Journal of Conflict Resolution* 32:87–102.

Iusi-Scarborough, G., and B. Bueno de Mesquita. 1988. "Threat and Alignment Behavior." *International Interactions* 14:85–93.

James, P. 1988. *Crisis and War*. Montreal: McGill-Queens University Press.

James, P., and J. Oneal. 1991. "The Influence of Domestic and International

Politics on the President's Use of Force." *Journal of Conflict Resolution* 35:307–32.

Jervis, J. 1976. *Perception and Misperception in International Politics.* Princeton: Princeton University Press.

Kahn, P. 1984. *The Secret History of the Mongols: The Origin of Chinghis Khan.* Berkeley, Calif.: North Point Press.

Kant, I. 1977. *The Philosophy of Kant: Immanuel Kant's Moral and Political Writings.* Trans. C. Friedrich. New York: Modern Library.

Kaplan, M. 1957. *System and Process in International Politics.* New York: John Wiley.

Kegley, C., and G. Raymond. 1990. *When Trust Breaks Down: Alliance Norms and World Politics.* Columbia: University of South Carolina Press.

Kennedy, P. 1987. *The Rise and Fall of the Great Powers.* New York: Random House.

Keohane, R. 1984. *After Hegemony.* Princeton: Princeton University Press.

————. 1986. "The Study of International Regimes and the Classical Tradition in International Relations." Paper presented at the annual meetings of the American Political Science Association.

Keohane, R., and J. Nye. 1977. *Power and Interdependence: World Politics in Transition.* Boston: Little, Brown.

Kim, C. H. 1991. "Third-Party Participation in Wars." *Journal of Conflict Resolution* 35:659–77.

Kim, W. 1989. "Power, Alliance, and Major Wars, 1816–1975." *Journal of Conflict Resolution* 33:255–73.

Kim, W., and J. D. Morrow. 1991. "When Do Power Transitions Lead to War?" Hoover Working Paper in International Studies. Hoover Institution.

Kissinger, H. 1982. *Years of Upheaval.* Boston: Little, Brown.

Kramer, G. 1972. "Sophisticated Voting over Multidimensional Choice Spaces." *Journal of Mathematical Sociology* 2:165–80.

Krasner, S. 1978. *Defending the National Interest: Raw Materials, Investments and U.S. Foreign Policy.* Princeton: Princeton University Press.

Kreps, D., and R. Wilson. 1982. "Sequential Equilibria." *Econometrica* 50:863–94.

Kugler, J., and A. F. K. Organski. 1989. "The End of Hegemony?" *International Interactions* 15:113–28.

Kugler, J., and F. Zagare. 1990. "The Long-Term Stability of Deterrence." *International Interactions* 15:255–78.

Lalman, D. 1988. "Conflict Resolution and Peace." *American Journal of Political Science* 32:590–615.

Lalman, D., and D. Newman. 1991. "Security and Alliances." *International Interactions* 16:239–53.

Lamborn, A. 1990. *The Price of Power: Risk and Foreign Policy in Britain, France, and Germany.* Boston: Unwin Hyman.

Lamborn, A., and S. Mumme. 1988. *Statecraft, Domestic Politics, and Foreign Policy Making.* Boulder, Colo.: Westview Press.

Langlois, J. P. 1990. "A Theory of Rational Expectations in Recurrent International Disputes." Department of Mathematics, San Francisco State University. Mimeo.

Lebow, R. N. 1981. *Between Peace and War: The Nature of International Crisis.* Baltimore: Johns Hopkins University Press.

Levy, J. 1983. *War in the Modern Great Power System, 1495–1975.* Lexington: University Press of Kentucky.

Locke, J. 1937. *Treatise of Civil Government and a Letter Concerning Tolera-tion.* New York: Appleton-Century-Crofts.

Luce, R. D., and H. Raiffa. 1957. *Games and Decisions.* New York: John Wiley.

McGinnis, M. 1986. "Issue Linkage and the Evolution of International Coopera-tion." *Journal of Conflict Resolution* 30:141–70.

Machiavelli, N. 1950. *The Prince and the Discourses.* Trans C. Detmold. New York: Random House.

MacKinder, H. 1962. "The Geographical Pivot of History." In A. Pearce, ed., *Democratic Ideals and Reality.* New York: W. W. Norton.

McNeill, W. 1976. *Plagues and Peoples.* New York: Doubleday.

———. 1982. *The Pursuit of Power: Technology, Armed Force, and Society since A.D. 1000.* Chicago: University of Chicago Press.

Malet, A. 1870. *The Overthrow of the Germanic Confederation by Prussia in 1866.* London: Longmans, Green.

Maoz, Z., and N. Abdolali. 1989. "Regime Type and International Conflict: 1816–1976." *Journal of Conflict Resolution* 33:3–35.

Marcet, A., and T. Sargent. 1987a. "Convergence of Least Squares Learning in Environments with Hidden State Variables and Private Information." Hoover Institution. December. Photocopy.

———. 1987b. "The Fate of Systems with 'Adaptive Expectations.'" Hoover Institution. November. Photocopy.

Markides, K. C. 1977. *The Rise and Fall of the Cyprus Republic.* New Haven: Yale University Press.

Maxwell, N. 1970. *India's China War.* London: Jonathan Cape.

Michaelis, H. 1968. "Königgrätz, 1866: Defeat of Liberalism and Universalism." In Pflanze 1968.

Midlarsky, M. 1988. The Onset of World War. Boston: Unwin Hyman.

Mill, J. S. 1937. *Essay on Government.* Ed. E. Baker. Cambridge: Cambridge University Press.

Modelski, G. 1987. *Long Cycles in World Politics.* Seattle: University of Wash-ington Press.

Morgan, T. C., and S. Campbell. 1991. "Domestic Structure, Decisional Con-straints and War: So Why Kant Democracies Fight?" *Journal of Conflict Reso-lution* 35:187–212.

Morgenthau, H. 1973. *Politics among Nations.* 5th ed. New York: Alfred A. Knopf.

Morrow, J. D. 1985. "A Continuous Outcome Expected Utility Theory of War." *Journal of Conflict Resolution* 29:473–502.

———. 1987. "On the Theoretical Basis of a Measure of National Risk Atti-tudes." *International Studies Quarterly* 31:423–38.

———. 1991a. "Alliances and Asymmetry." *American Journal of Political Sci-ence* 35:904–33.

———. 1991b. "Electoral and Congressional Incentives and Arms Control." *Journal of Conflict Resolution* 35:245–65.

Mowat, R. 1932. *The States of Europe: 1815–1871.* London: Edward Arnold.

Niemi, R., and H. Weisberg. 1968. "A Mathematical Solution for the Probability of the Paradox of Voting." *Behavioral Science* 13:317–23.

Niou, E., P. Ordeshook, and G. Rose. 1989. *The Balance of Power.* Cambridge: Cambridge University Press.

O'Neill, B. 1989. "A Survey of Game Theory Models on Peace and War." York University, Toronto. Mimeo.

Ordeshook, P. 1986. *Game Theory and Political Theory*. Cambridge: Cambridge University Press.

Organski, A. F. K. 1958. *World Politics*. New York: Alfred A. Knopf.

Organski, A. F. K., and J. Kugler. 1980. *The War Ledger*. Chicago: University of Chicago Press.

Ostrom, C., and B. Job. 1986. "The President and the Political Use of Force." *American Political Science Review* 80:541–66.

Palmer, A. 1976. *Bismarck*. London: Weidenfeld and Nicolson.

Pflanze, O. 1963. *Bismarck and the Development of Germany: The Period of Unification, 1815–1871*. Princeton: Princeton University Press.

———, ed. 1968. *The Unification of Germany, 1848–1871*. New York: Holt, Rinehart and Winston.

Plato. 1937. *The Dialogues of Plato*. Trans. B. Jowett. New York: Random House.

Pollins, B. 1988. "Does Trade Still Follow the Flag: A Model of International Diplomacy and Commerce." Paper presented at the annual meetings of the Midwest Political Science Association.

Popper, K. 1963. *Conjectures and Refutations: The Growth of Scientific Knowledge*. New York: Basic Books.

Posen, B. 1984. *The Sources of Military Doctrine: France, Britain, and Germany between the World Wars*. Ithaca: Cornell University Press.

Powell, R. 1987. "Crisis Bargaining, Escalation, and MAD." *American Political Science Review* 81:717–35.

Prange, G. 1981. *At Dawn We Slept: The Untold Story of Pearl Harbor*. New York: Penguin Books.

Putnam, R. 1988. "Diplomacy and Domestic Politics: The Logic of Two-Level Games." *International Organization* 42:427–60.

Ramm, A. 1967. *Germany, 1789–1919: A Political History*. London: Methuen.

Rapoport, A., and A. Chammah. 1965. *Prisoners' Dilemma*. Ann Arbor: University of Michigan Press.

Rapoport, A., and M. Guyer. 1966. "A Taxonomy of 2 × 2 Games." *General Systems* 11:203–14.

Ray, J., and J. D. Singer. 1973. "Measuring the Concentration of Power in the International System." *Sociological Methods and Research* 1:403–36.

Richardson, L. F. 1960. *Arms and Insecurity*. Chicago: Quadrangle.

Riker, W. 1963. *The Theory of Political Coalitions*. New Haven: Yale University Press.

———. 1982. *Liberalism against Populism*. San Francisco: W. H. Freeman.

———. 1986. *The Art of Political Manipulation*. New Haven: Yale University Press.

Rosenau, J. 1971. *The Scientific Study of Foreign Policy*. New York: Free Press.

Rubinstein, A. 1982. "Perfect Equilibrium in a Bargaining Model." *Econometrica* 50:97–109.

Rummel, R. 1963. "Dimensions of Conflict Behavior within and between Nations." *General Systems Yearbook* 8:1–50.

———. 1979. *Understanding Conflict and War: War, Power and Peace*. Vol. 4. Beverly Hills, Calif.: Sage Publications.

———. 1981. *Understanding Conflict and War: The Just Peace*. 5 vols. Beverly Hills, Calif.: Sage Publications.

———. 1983. "Libertarianism and International Violence." *Journal of Conflict Resolution* 27:27–71.

Russett, B. 1972. *No Clear and Present Danger*. New York: Harper and Row.

————. 1985. "The Mysterious Case of Vanishing Hegemony; or, Is Mark Twain Really Dead?" *International Organization* 39:207–31.

————. 1989. "Economic Decline, Electoral Pressure, and the Initiation of Interstate Conflict." In C. Gochman and A. Sabrosky, eds., *Prisoners of War? Nation-States in the Modern Era.* Lexington, Mass.: D. C. Heath.

————. 1990. *Controlling the Sword: The Democratic Governance of National Security.* Cambridge: Harvard University Press.

Sabrosky, A. 1985. "Alliance Aggregation, Capability Distribution, and the Expansion of Interstate War." In Sabrosky, ed., *Polarity and War.* Boulder, Colo.: Westview Press.

Sayrs, L. 1990. "Expected Utility and Peace Science: An Assessment of Trade and Conflict." *Conflict Management and Peace Science* 11:17–44.

Schelling, T. 1960. *The Strategy of Conflict.* Cambridge: Harvard University Press.

Schumpeter, J. 1955. "The Sociology of Imperialism." In Schumpeter, *Imperialism and Social Classes.* Cleveland, Ohio: World Publishing.

Selten, R. 1975. "Reexamination of the Perfectness Concept for Equilibrium Points in Extensive Games." *International Journal of Game Theory* 4:25–55.

Shepsle, K. 1979. "Institutional Arrangements and Equilibrium in Multidimensional Voting Models." *American Journal of Political Science* 23:27–59.

Shepsle, K., and B. Weingast. 1981. "Structure-Induced Equilibrium and Legislative Choice." *Public Choice* 37:503–19.

————. 1987. "The Institutional Foundations of Committee Power." *American Political Science Review* 81:85–104.

Showalter, D. 1975. *Railroads and Rifles: Soldiers, Technology and the Unification of Germany.* Hamden, Conn.: Archon Books.

Simon, W. M. 1968. *Germany in the Age of Bismarck.* London: George Allen and Unwin.

Singer, J. D., and M. Small. 1972. *The Wages of War, 1816–1965: A Statistical Handbook.* New York: John Wiley.

Siverson, R., and J. Emmons. 1991. "Birds of a Feather: Democratic Political Systems and Alliance Choices." *Journal of Conflict Resolution* 35:285–306.

Siverson, R., and H. Starr. 1990. "Opportunity, Willingness, and the Diffusion of War." *American Political Science Review* 84:47–68.

Small, M., and J. D. Singer. 1976. "The War-Proneness of Democratic Regimes, 1816–1965." *Jerusalem Journal of International Relations* 1:50–69.

————. 1982. *Resort to Arms: International and Civil Wars, 1816–1980.* Beverly Hills, Calif.: Sage Publications.

Smith, A. 1937. *The Wealth of Nations.* New York: Random House.

Snyder, G., and P. Diesing. 1977. *Conflict among Nations: Bargaining, Decision Making, and System Structure in International Crises.* Princeton: Princeton University Press.

Starr, H., and B. Most. 1976. "The Substance and Study of Borders in International Relations Research." *International Studies Quarterly* 20:581–620.

————. 1978. "A Return Journey: Richardson, 'Frontiers,' and Wars in the 1946–1965 Era." *Journal of Conflict Resolution* 22:441–67.

Stoessinger, J. 1974. *Why Nations Go to War.* New York: Random House.

Tanter, R. 1966. "Dimensions of Conflict Behavior within and between Nations, 1958–1960." *Journal of Conflict Resolution* 10:41–64.

Taylor, A. J. P. 1976. *The Habsburg Monarchy, 1809–1918.* Chicago: University of Chicago Press.

Taylor, M. 1976. *Anarchy and Cooperation.* London: John Wiley.

————. 1987. *The Possibility of Cooperation*. Cambridge: Cambridge University Press.

Thompson, W. 1988. *On Global War*. Columbia: University of South Carolina Press.

Thucydides. 1954. *History of the Peloponnesian War*. Trans. R. Warner. New York: Penguin Books.

————. 1959. *History of the Peloponnesian War*. Trans. T. Hobbes. Vol. 3. Ann Arbor: University of Michigan Press.

Vertzberger, Y. 1984. *Misperceptions in Foreign Policymaking: The Sino-Indian Conflict, 1959–1962*. Boulder, Colo.: Westview Press.

Waltz, K. 1959. *Man, the State and War*. New York: Columbia University Press.

————. 1979. *Theory of International Politics*. Reading, Mass.: Addison-Wesley.

Wang, K., and J. L. Ray. 1991. "Beginners and Winners: The Fate of Initiators of Interstate Wars Involving Great Powers since 1495." Paper presented at the annual meeting of the International Studies Association, Washington, D.C., April 10–14, 1990.

Weede, E. 1976. "Overwhelming Preponderance as a Pacifying Condition among Contiguous Asian Dyads." *Journal of Conflict Resolution* 20:395–412.

Weiner, A., and H. Kahn. 1962. *Crisis and Arms Control*. Harmon-on-Hudson, N.Y.: Hudson Institute.

Whiting, A. 1975. *The Chinese Calculus of Deterrence: India and Indochina*. Ann Arbor: University of Michigan Press.

Wilkenfeld, J. 1972. "Models for the Analysis of Foreign Conflict Behavior of States." In B. Russett, ed., *Peace, War and Numbers*. Beverly Hills, Calif.: Sage Publications.

Young, O. 1968. *The Politics of Force: Bargaining during International Crises*. Princeton: Princeton University Press.

Zagare, F. 1987. *The Dynamics of Deterrence*. Chicago: University of Chicago Press.

————. 1990. "Rationality and Deterrence." *World Politics* 62:238–60.

Zinnes, D. 1968. "The Expression and Perception of Hostility in a Prewar Crisis, 1914." In J. D. Singer, ed., *Quantitative International Politics*. New York: Free Press.

Index

Abdolali, Nassin, 145, 152

Achen, Christopher, 107, 283

Acquiescence, 33, 59–65 *passim,* 79–91 *passim,* 117, 118, 136, 176, 241, 269, 286; defined, 32, 65, 285; in domestic variant, 80–82, 273–75, 302; in Fashoda crisis, 82–85, 200; and prisoner's dilemma, 138; preference for, 47–49; propositions, 80–82; in realpolitik variant, 67–68, 267–68, 271, 279; in Sino-Indian War (*1962*), 200–202; as tacit coercion, 102–3; and uncertainty, 108–11, 121, 275; and war, 73–75, 189

Albania, 260, 261

Albrecht-Carrié, René, 83

Alliance, 100, 151, 236, 237, 251, 252, 258; Austro-Prussian, 229, 231, 235; in measurement of utility, 288–94; power, 182–85, 222; as signaling game, 289; types, 290–91

Allies, 206, 250–54, 257–59, 279; democratic, 147, 151, 166–67; reliability of, 166; at war, 147, 151, 166–67, 226

Allison, Graham, 13, 28, 29

Altfeld, Michael, 289, 291, 293

Amherst, Lord Jeffrey, 5

Anarchy, 23, 36, 51, 95, 100, 101, 142, 269. *See also* Game theory: noncooperative

Arab states, 75, 261–63

Arafat, Yassir, 262, 263

Arms control, 250–55

Arms race, 20, 250, 254

Army in peacetime, 131, 133

Arrow, Kenneth, 30

Assumptions, 36–46 *passim,* 193, 206, 266, 297, 301; *A1* (subgame perfection), 40–50 *passim,* 171, 173, 203, 284, 285, 292–298, 301; *A2* (negotiation and war are probabilistic), 40–43, 49, 73, 78–81, 85, 86, 105, 301–5; *A3* (capitulation and acquiescence as certainties), 8, 10, 16–18, 26–54 *passim,* 71–86 *passim,* 104, 105, 124, 139–141, 151, 155, 193, 206, 208, 242, 266, 275, 292–301

passim; A4 (preference for negotiation) 8, 10, 16–18, 26–54 *passim,* 62, 71–86 *passim,* 104, 105, 124, 139, 140, 141, 151, 155, 168, 193, 206, 208, 242, 266, 275, 292–303 *passim; A5* (utility of demands), 8, 10, 16–18, 26–54 *passim,* 71–87 *passim,* 104, 105, 124, 139–141, 151, 155, 193, 206, 208, 242, 266, 275, 292–301 *passim; A6* (costs), 40, 43–46, 68, 79–87 *passim,* 206, 224, 242, 297; *A7a* (realpolitik variant), 17, 27, 30, 41, 46, 51, 71, 72, 74, 266; *A7b* (domestic variant), 17, 27, 41, 46, 51, 72–86 *passim,* 266; anarchy as, 36; about balance of power, 182–84; about democratic puzzles, 149–51, 155; in domestic variant, *see* Assumptions: *A7b;* and information, 8, 26, 51, 54, 74, 271, 299, 301–2; of monotonicity, 208, 275, 296; about norms, 96, 104, 105, 124, 143; about power transition (hegemonic) war, 224, 225, 228, 243; about prisoner's dilemma, 138–41; of rationality, 16, 18; in realpolitik variant, *see* Assumptions: *A7a;* about security and risk taking, 292–93; of uniform preference distribution, 51; of unitary actor, 10, 11, 13, 15–18, 26–30

Augustine, Saint, 277

Austria, 115, 117, 119, 207, 220, 224–242 *passim,* 281

Axelrod, Robert, 137, 139, 140

Backward induction, 59, 62, 136, 158, 170

Balance of power, 9, 11, 20, 29, 54, 69, 127, 181–217 *passim,* 239, 247, 273; assumptions about, 182–84; proposition, 211

Banks, Jeffrey, 38, 42, 208, 209, 211, 214, 296

Bargaining, 28, 33, 111, 201, 276

Basic status quo theorem, 85, 88, 275

Basic war theorem, 72, 167, 169, 194

Bavaria, 115–19